ASP.NET Core 2 and Angular 5

Full-stack web development with .NET Core and Angular

Valerio De Sanctis

BIRMINGHAM - MUMBAI

ASP.NET Core 2 and Angular 5

First published: November 2017

Production reference: 1221117

Published by Packt Publishing Ltd.
Livery Place
35 Livery Street
Birmingham
B3 2PB, UK.

ISBN 978-1-78829-360-0

· www.packtpub.com

Credits

Author
Valerio De Sanctis

Reviewers
Ramchandra Vellanki
Juergen Gutsch

Commissioning Editor
Ashwin Nair

Acquisition Editor
Reshma Raman

Content Development Editor
Onkar Wani

Technical Editor
Akhil Nair

Copy Editor
Shaila Kusanale

Project Coordinator
Devanshi Doshi

Proofreader
Safis Editing

Indexer
Rekha Nair

Graphics
Jason Monteiro

Production Coordinator
Aparna Bhagat

About the Author

Valerio De Sanctis is a skilled IT professional with over 12 years of experience in lead programming, web-based development, and project management using ASP.NET, PHP, and Java. He previously held senior positions at a range of financial and insurance companies, most recently serving as Chief Technology Officer and Chief Operating Officer at a leading after-sales and IT service provider for many top-tier life and non-life insurance groups.

In the course of his career, Valerio De Sanctis helped many private organizations to implement and maintain .NET-based solutions, working side-by-side with many IT industry experts and leading several frontend, backend, and UX development teams. He designed the architecture and actively oversaw the development of a wide number of corporate-level web application projects for high-profile clients, customers, and partners, including London Stock Exchange Group, Zurich Insurance Group, Allianz, Generali, Harmonie Mutuelle, AIG, QBE, Marsh & McLennan, Lloyd's, Honda Motor, FCA Group, Luxottica, ANSA, Saipem, ENI, Enel, Terna, Banzai Media, Virgilio.it, Repubblica.it, and Corriere.it.

He is an active member of the Stack Exchange Network, providing advice and tips for .NET, JavaScript, HTML5, and other web-related topics on the StackOverflow, ServerFault, and SuperUser communities. Most of his projects and code samples are available under open source licenses on GitHub, BitBucket, NPM, CocoaPods, JQuery Plugin Registry, and WordPress Plugin Repository.

Starting from 2015, he also runs an IT-oriented, web-focused blog at www.ryadel.com featuring news, reviews, code samples and guides to help developers and enthusiasts worldwide. Between 2016 and 2017, he wrote two books on web development: *ASP.NET Core and Angular 2*, and *ASP.NET Core: Cloud-ready, Enterprise Web Application Development*, with over 5,000 copies sold worldwide.

I would like to thank those who supported me in writing this book: my beloved and beautiful wife, Carla, for her awesome encouragement and invaluable support; my children, Viola and Daniele; my parents and my sister for always being there in times of need; and my IT friends, colleagues, and partners working at Ryadel.com, Kapusons, Teleborsa and Assirecre Group for their enduring friendship. A special thanks to Onkar, Reshma, and all Packt Publishing folks who worked hard to bring this book to life. Last but not least, I would like to thank you, the reader, for picking up this book. I really hope you will enjoy it!

About the Reviewers

Ramchandra Vellanki is a passionate programmer. He has 13 years of programming experience, has worked in different roles, and has experience in building and maintaining large-scale products/applications. He started his career with IBM iSeries, and then worked on C++, MFC, .NET, and JavaScript. Currently, he is working on .NET and JavaScript technologies. He enjoys exploring and learning new technologies.

> *I would like to thank my parents (Saroja and Ramaiah), wife (Sirisha) and kids (Abhi and Ani) for their love, understanding, and constant support. I also would like to thank all my friends and relatives for their continuous encouragement and support throughout my career and life.*

Juergen Gutsch is a .NET-addicted web developer. He has been working with .NET and ASP.NET since the early versions in 2002. Before that, he wrote server-side web applications using classic ASP. Juergen is also an active person in the German speaking .NET developer community. He is leading the .NET user group in Basel (Switzerland) and the INETA Germany Association. Due to that, Microsoft awarded him to be a Microsoft Most Valuable Professional in the Visual Studio and Development Technologies category several times.

Jurgen writes for the dotnetpro magazine, one of the most popular German-speaking developer magazines, and he also publishes articles in English on his blog at `https://asp.net-hacker.rocks`. The best way to contact him and to stay in touch with him is using Twitter--`https://twitter.com/sharpcms`.

He is working as a developer, consultant, and trainer for the digital agency YooApplications Inc. (`http://yooapps.com`), located in Basel, Switzerland. YooApplications serves national as well as international clients and specializes in creating custom digital solution for distinct business needs.

www.PacktPub.com

For support files and downloads related to your book, please visit www.PacktPub.com. Did you know that Packt offers eBook versions of every book published, with PDF and ePub files available? You can upgrade to the eBook version at www.PacktPub.com and as a print book customer, you are entitled to a discount on the eBook copy. Get in touch with us at service@packtpub.com for more details.

At www.PacktPub.com, you can also read a collection of free technical articles, sign up for a range of free newsletters and receive exclusive discounts and offers on Packt books and eBooks.

https://www.packtpub.com/mapt

Get the most in-demand software skills with Mapt. Mapt gives you full access to all Packt books and video courses, as well as industry-leading tools to help you plan your personal development and advance your career.

Why subscribe?

- Fully searchable across every book published by Packt
- Copy and paste, print, and bookmark content
- On demand and accessible via a web browser

Customer Feedback

Thanks for purchasing this Packt book. At Packt, quality is at the heart of our editorial process. To help us improve, please leave us an honest review on this book's Amazon page at https://www.amazon.com/dp/1788293606.

If you'd like to join our team of regular reviewers, you can e-mail us at customerreviews@packtpub.com. We award our regular reviewers with free eBooks and videos in exchange for their valuable feedback. Help us be relentless in improving our products!

Table of Contents

Preface

It's only been a year since I wrote *ASP.NET Core and Angular 2*, but it definitely feels a lot more, at least from a web developer's perspective. Modern web technologies are still improving at lightning-fast speed, with an increasing, perceptible, and measurable interest being in the client-side aspects of the game. Angular, React, and VueJS collected no less than 150,000 StackOverflow questions in the latest 18 months, which is more than 250 per day--and the trend is still growing.

That's to be expected, since most of the major conceptual changes that occurred between 2015 and 2017 have been hitting the clients way more than the servers; we switched from a *reactive* approach of *doing* stuff--that led us to build responsive, resilient, elastic, and message-driven **Single-Page Apps (SPAs)**--to a progressive way of seeing things--which materialized into **Progressive Web Apps (PWAs)**. The change of perspective is slight, yet prominent; far from being a different paradigm, what we've seen was nothing less than the natural and inevitable evolution of the same original concepts.

Compared to the SPA revolution that took place in 2015-2016, the rise of *Progressive Web Apps* is not a game-breaking event; we can say that PWAs inherit all the major concepts that were already part of the Reactive Manifesto and bring them further on with brand new features--such as Service Workers--that would not have been possible without some relevant client-side accomplishments such as HTML5, modern browsers, and ECMAScript 6. PWAs are a much expected improvement in the present that also emphasizes its increasing distance from the past. At the same time, PWAs are not meant to be the future, not because they won't become a standard--they definitely will--but because they will also improve and, eventually, collapse into something else. This is how *the client side of the moon* always worked and--hopefully--always will.

What happened to the other side, then? We can't possibly say that 2017 wasn't an intense year for server-side technologies; Node.js is still dominating the scene, with more than 8 million confirmed instances online at the moment and trustable surveys telling us that three developers out of four will deal with it even more than they did. As well as the raw and naked usage, there is also a crowded galaxy of modern web frameworks based on Node, boosting its popularity even more, such as Hapi, Express, Restify, Koa, Sails, and Adonis, just to mention some of them. *Django* continues to focus on stability, with the 1.11 LTS bringing a lot of minor and major fixes; the next major release, expected for December, will also bring some neat improvements such as simplified URL routing syntax, window expressions, and improved Phyton 3.x support. The whole *PHP* ecosystem, which seemed to be slowly but steadily doomed to lose ground, regained some breath thanks to the great performance achievements reached by PHP 7.1 (in late 2016) and the huge number of available frameworks--Symfony, Laravel, Zend, Yii, Expressive, Silex, Slim, and more--each of which is best suited for a distinctive set of patterns, use cases, and scenarios. Last but definitely not least, comes *ASP.NET*; the .NET Core 2.0 release features some major improvements that make it easier to use and also more capable as a platform: major performance boosts in both framework and runtime, six new supported platforms-- including Debian, SUSE, and macOS--and even ARM32-native builds for running apps on Raspberry Pi.

If we try to connect all these dots, we can easily see how most of the innovative, experimental, and rule-changing aspects of web development are nowadays skewed toward the *client side*, while the *server-side* race is more focused on performance and stability. Nonetheless, both sides of the coin share a strong common ground built upon the concepts of readability, maintainability, and overall simplicity of the source code.

Back in 2016, among all those different and yet kindred environments, we chose to focus on two of them: ASP.NET Core to cover the *server-side* aspects, and Angular to deal with the *client side*. Apart from the technical reasons, we also did this because these two frameworks had something in common that we did like: both of them were a reboot of a massively popular previous installment that played a leading role in their respective field. That was a bold, revolutionary move that we liked a lot. Should we do the same in 2017 as well? Are ASP.NET Core 2 and Angular 5 still a viable choices to deal with *Progressive Web Apps*, lightning-speed performance, and code simplicity?

In short, the answer is yes, and the book you're about to read will do its very best to prove it.

What this book covers

Chapter 1, *Getting Ready*, introduces the ASP.NET Core and Angular frameworks, explaining how they can effectively be used to build a feature-rich, modern web application. It then enumerates the core aspects of a common SPA project, which will be addressed throughout the following chapters. The last part covers the required steps for setting up a .NET Core web application project, along with its required packages and components, up to a buildable and running app skeleton.

Chapter 2, *Backend with .NET Core*, explains how we can build our very own set of APIs to exchange JSON data between a *server-side* ASP.NET Core Controller and a *client-side* Angular Component. The reader will learn how to handle the HTTP request-response cycle and also how to configure the improved routing logic built upon the .NET Core pipeline.

Chapter 3, *Frontend with Angular*, focuses on the *client-side* aspects; the reader will learn how to fetch JSON objects with Angular and show the retrieved data onscreen using the Angular Template Syntax. They will also understand how to deal with *client-side* routing in Angular and how to implement a viable routing pattern using the PathLocationStrategy approach.

Chapter 4, *Data Model with Entity Framework Core*, guides the reader through implementing a proper, DBMS-based Data Model using Entity Framework (EF) Core. They will learn how to install and properly configure the required EF Core packages, then use them to build a lightweight set of *entities* and persist them into a database structure using the *Code-First* approach.

Chapter 5, *Client-Server Interactions*, shows how the existing code can be upgraded to make full use of the EF Core *Entities* defined in the last chapter. The reader will learn how to fetch and persist the application data using the database instead of the sample objects mocked by the previous data-retrieval methods.

Chapter 6, *Style Sheets and UI Layout*, introduces LESS, a powerful dynamic style sheet language that can be compiled into CSS. After a brief overview of the LESS language syntax, the reader will learn how to add, implement, and compile LESS scripts within the application project to greatly improve the frontend UI.

Chapter 7, *Forms and Data Validation*, is mostly dedicated to passing data from the client to the server, from account-related features--such as user registration--to more complex interactions with the whole range of existing *Entities*. The reader will learn how to send PUT- and POST-based requests using the versatile Angular *Model-Driven* approach, and how to properly respond to them by extending the existing .NET Core Controllers accordingly.

Chapter 8, *Authentication and Authorization*, starts as a recap of the most relevant auth-related concepts for building a web application and then shows how to turn these concepts into practice. The reader will learn how to implement a sample token-based auth provider and also how to properly add and configure it throughout the existing Entity Framework entities, .NET core services, and HTTP middleware list.

Chapter 9, *Advanced Topics*, shows how to implement a specific set of features required to finalize a production-ready web application, such as token expiration, refresh tokens, new user registration, and third-party authentication.

Chapter 10, *Finalization and Deployment*, describes the most common tasks to publish a potentially shippable web application onto a production server. The reader will learn how to replace the localDb instance with an external SQL Server, create FTP and FileSystem publishing profiles, upload their compiled application to an external server, and configure it to run under IIS using the .NET Core Windows Server Hosting bundle; they will also learn how to deal with the most common issues with the help of some .NET Core-specific troubleshooting techniques.

What you need for this book

- Windows 7 SP1 or newer, up to and including Windows 10
- Visual Studio 2017 15.4.2 (or newer): any version will work, including the freely available Community Edition
- Microsoft SQL Server 2017 (o newer) for Chapter 10, *Finalization and Deployment* only: any version will work, including the freely available Express Edition
- Windows Server 2008 R2 (or newer) for Chapter 10, *Finalization and Deployment* only
- Microsoft .NET Core SDK 2.0.1, freely available as an official Microsoft download
- TypeScript 2.1.5.0 (or newer), freely available
- NodeJS 6.11.2 (or newer), freely available
- Angular 5.0.0 final release (or newer), freely available

All ASP.NET, Angular, JavaScript, and CSS packages used throughout the book are also *open source* and freely available for download using Visual Studio package managers such as NuGet and npm.

Who this book is for

This book is for seasoned ASP.NET developers who already know about ASP.NET Core and Angular in general, but want to know more about them and/or understand how to blend them together to craft a production-ready SPA.

Conventions

In this book, you will find a number of text styles that distinguish between different kinds of information. Here are some examples of these styles and an explanation of their meaning. Code words in text, database table names, folder names, filenames, file extensions, pathnames, dummy URLs, user input, and Twitter handles are shown as follows:

"Fill it with its corresponding `pagenotfound.component.html` template file."

A block of code is set as follows:

```
import { Component } from "@angular/core";

@Component({
    selector: "pagenotfound",
    templateUrl: "./pagenotfound.component.html"
})

export class PageNotFoundComponent {
    title = "Page not Found";
}
```

When we wish to draw your attention to a particular part of a code block, the relevant lines or items are set in bold:

```
<h1>Welcome to TestMakerFree</h1>
<p>A sample SPA project made with .NET Core and Angular.</p>
<quiz-list class="latest"></quiz-list>
<quiz-list class="byTitle"></quiz-list>
<quiz-list class="random"></quiz-list>
```

Any command-line input or output is written as follows:

```
dotnet ef database update
```

New terms and **important words** are shown in bold. Words that you see on the screen, for example, in menus or dialog boxes, appear in the text like this:

"Open a **PowerShell** Command Prompt and navigate through the project's root folder."

Warnings or important notes appear like this.

Tips and tricks appear like this.

Reader feedback

Feedback from our readers is always welcome. Let us know what you think about this book-what you liked or disliked. Reader feedback is important for us as it helps us develop titles that you will really get the most out of. To send us general feedback, simply email feedback@packtpub.com, and mention the book's title in the subject of your message. If there is a topic that you have expertise in and you are interested in either writing or contributing to a book, see our author guide at www.packtpub.com/authors.

Customer support

Now that you are the proud owner of a Packt book, we have a number of things to help you to get the most from your purchase.

Downloading the example code

You can download the example code files for this book from your account at http://www.packtpub.com. If you purchased this book elsewhere, you can visit http://www.packtpub.com/support and register to have the files emailed directly to you. You can download the code files by following these steps:

1. Log in or register to our website using your email address and password.
2. Hover the mouse pointer on the **SUPPORT** tab at the top.
3. Click on **Code Downloads & Errata**.

4. Enter the name of the book in the **Search** box.
5. Select the book for which you're looking to download the code files.
6. Choose from the drop-down menu where you purchased this book from.
7. Click on **Code Download**.

Once the file is downloaded, please make sure that you unzip or extract the folder using the latest version of:

- WinRAR / 7-Zip for Windows
- Zipeg / iZip / UnRarX for Mac
- 7-Zip / PeaZip for Linux

The code bundle for the book is also hosted on GitHub at `https://github.com/PacktPublishing/ASP.NET-Core-2-and-Angular-5`. We also have other code bundles from our rich catalog of books and videos available at `https://github.com/PacktPublishing/`. Check them out!

Errata

Although we have taken every care to ensure the accuracy of our content, mistakes do happen. If you find a mistake in one of our books-maybe a mistake in the text or the code-we would be grateful if you could report this to us. By doing so, you can save other readers from frustration and help us improve subsequent versions of this book. If you find any errata, please report them by visiting `http://www.packtpub.com/submit-errata`, selecting your book, clicking on the **Errata Submission Form** link, and entering the details of your errata. Once your errata are verified, your submission will be accepted and the errata will be uploaded to our website or added to any list of existing errata under the Errata section of that title. To view the previously submitted errata, go to `https://www.packtpub.com/books/content/support` and enter the name of the book in the search field. The required information will appear under the **Errata** section.

Piracy

Piracy of copyrighted material on the internet is an ongoing problem across all media. At Packt, we take the protection of our copyright and licenses very seriously. If you come across any illegal copies of our works in any form on the internet, please provide us with the location address or website name immediately so that we can pursue a remedy. Please contact us at copyright@packtpub.com with a link to the suspected pirated material. We appreciate your help in protecting our authors and our ability to bring you valuable content.

Questions

If you have a problem with any aspect of this book, you can contact us at questions@packtpub.com, and we will do our best to address the problem.

1

Getting Ready

ASP.NET Core MVC is a framework that runs on top of the full .NET framework (Windows) or .NET Core (cross-platform), specifically made for building efficient HTTP services that will be able to be reached by a massive range of clients, including web browsers, mobile devices, smart TVs, web-based home automation tools, and more.

Angular is the successor of AngularJS, a world-renowned development framework born with the idea of providing the coder with the toolbox needed to build reactive and cross-platform web-based apps optimized for desktop and mobile. It features a structure-rich template approach based upon a natural, easy-to-write, and readable syntax.

Technically, these two frameworks have little or nothing in common: ASP.NET Core is mostly focused on the **server-side** part of the web development stack, while Angular is dedicated to cover all the **client-side** aspects of web applications such as UI and UX. However, they were put together here because they share a common vision--the HTTP protocol is not limited to serving web pages; it can also be used as a viable platform to build web-based APIs to effectively send and receive data. A thought that slowly made its way through the first 20 years of the World Wide Web and is now an undeniable, widely acknowledged statement and also a fundamental pillar of almost every modern web development approach.

As for the reasons behind this perspective switch, there are plenty of good reasons for that, the most important of them being related to the intrinsic characteristics of the HTTP protocol: rather simple to use, and flexible enough to match most development needs of the always-changing environment that the World Wide Web happens to be in. Not to mention how universal it has become nowadays--almost any platform that we can think of has an HTTP library, so HTTP services can reach a broad range of clients, including browsers, mobile devices, and traditional desktop applications.

Two players, one goal

From the perspective of a fully-functional web-based application, we can say that the web API interface provided with the ASP.NET Core framework is a programmatic set of server-side handlers used by the server to expose a number of hooks and/or endpoints to a defined request-response message system, typically expressed in structured markup languages, such as JSON or XML. As we already said, this is achieved by making good use of the HTTP protocol handled by a publicly-available web server (typically IIS). Similarly, Angular can be described as a modern, feature-rich client-side library that pushes the HTML5 features--along with the modern browser's capabilities--to their full extent by binding the input and/or output parts of an HTML web page into a flexible, reusable, and easily testable JavaScript model.

These assumptions allow us to answer to a simple, yet inevitable question "can we combine the backend strengths of ASP.NET Core's web API with the frontend capabilities of the Angular framework in order to build a modern, feature-rich, and highly versatile web application?

The answer, in short terms, is yes. In the following chapters, we'll see how we can do that by analyzing all the fundamental aspects of a well-written, properly designed web-based product, and how ASP.NET Core and/or Angular can be used to handle each one of them.

The ASP.NET core revolution

To summarize what happened in the ASP.NET world within the last two years is not an easy task; in short words, we can say that we're undoubtedly facing the most important series of changes in the .NET Framework since the year it came to life. ASP.NET Core 1.0, which came out in Q3 2016, was a complete re-implementation of the ASP.NET we knew; the brand new framework unites all the previous web application technologies, such as MVC, Web API, and web pages, into a single programming module, formerly known as **MVC6**. The new framework introduces a fully-featured cross-platform component, also known as **.NET Core**, shipped with a brand new open source .NET Compiler Platform (currently known as **Roslyn**), a cross-platform runtime (known as **CoreCLR**), and an improved x64 Just-In-Time compiler (**RyuJIT**).

The 1.0 final release was shortly followed by ASP.NET Core 1.1 (Q4 2016), which brought some new features and performance enhancements, and also addressed many bugs and compatibility issues affecting the former one.

The third and, at the time of writing, the latest step was taken with ASP.NET Core 2.0, which came out in Q2 2017 as a preview and then in Q3 2017 for the final release; the newer version features among a number of significant improvements with a huge effort to standardize the shared APIs among the .NET Framework, .NET Core, and Xamarin, making it easy for developers to share and reuse code across the whole .NET ecosystem.

Someone might be wondering about what happened to ASP.NET 5 and Web API 2, as these used to be quite popular names until mid-2016. ASP.NET 5 was no less than the original name of ASP.NET Core, before the developers chose to rename it to emphasize the fact that it is a complete rewrite. The reasons for that, along with the Microsoft vision about the new product, are further explained in the following *Scott Hanselman's* blog post that anticipated the changes on Jan 16, 2016:
`http://www.hanselman.com/blog/ASPNET5IsDeadIntroducingASPNETCore 10AndNETCore10.aspx`

For those who don't know, *Scott Hanselman* is the outreach and community manager for .NET/ASP.NET/IIS/Azure and Visual Studio since 2007. Additional information regarding the perspective switch is also available in the following article by *Jeffrey T. Fritz*, Program Manager for Microsoft and NuGet team leader:
`https://blogs.msdn.microsoft.com/webdev/2016/02/01/an-update-on-asp-net-core-and-net-core/`

As for Web API 2, it was a dedicated framework for building HTTP services returning pure JSON or XML data instead of web pages. Initially born as an alternative to the MVC platform, it has been merged with the latter into the new, general-purpose web application framework known as MVC6, which is now shipped as a separate module of ASP.NET Core.

What's new in Angular?

The new release of AngularJS, simply known as **Angular**, is a complete rewrite of the previous one, entirely based upon TypeScript and ECMAScript 6 specifications.

If you're a seasoned web developer, most likely, you already know what TypeScript is. In case you don't, no worries, we'll get to that later on.

The choice of not making Angular backward compatible with AngularJS clearly demonstrates the intention of the author's team to adopt a completely new approach--any developer who already knows AngularJS will undoubtedly face a huge number of breaking changes, not only in the code syntax, but also in the way of thinking and designing the client app. Angular is highly modular, component-based, comes with a new and improved dependency injection model and a whole lot of programming patterns its older cousin never heard of.

However, the most important reason we're picking Angular over other excellent JS libraries such as ReactJS and EmberJS is the fact that it already comes out with a huge pack of features out of the box, making it most suited, although maybe not as simple to use than the aforementioned competitors; if we combine that with the consistency given by the TypeScript language, we can say that despite being the youngster, Angular embraced the framework approach more convincingly than the others. This has been confirmed over the course of the past 9 to 12 months, where the project hit two major versions (Angular 2 in Q3 2016 and Angular 4 in Q1 2017), gaining a lot in terms of stability, performances, and features, without losing much in terms of backward compatibility, best practices, and overall approach. All these reasons are solid enough to invest in it, hoping it will continue to keep up with these compelling premises.

A full-stack approach

Learning to use ASP.NET Core and Angular together would mean being able to work to both the **frontend** (client side) and **backend** (server side) of a web application; to put it in other words, it means being able to design, assemble, and deliver a complete product.

Eventually, in order to do that, we'll need to dig through the following:

- Backend programming
- Frontend programming
- UI styling and UX design
- Database design, modeling, configuration, and administration
- Web server configuration and administration
- Web application deployment

At first glance, it can seem that this kind of approach goes against common sense; a single developer should not be allowed to do everything by himself. Every developer knows well that the backend and the frontend require entirely different skills and experiences, so why in the world should we do that?

Before answering the question, we should understand what we really meant when we said "being able to". We don't have to become experts on every single layer of the stack; no one expects us to do so. When we choose to embrace the full-stack approach, what we really need to do is **to raise our awareness level** throughout the whole stack we're working on; it means that we need to know how the backend works and how it can and will be connected to the frontend. We need to know how the data will be stored, retrieved, and then served through the client; we need to acknowledge the interactions we will need to layer out between the various components that our web application is made of, and we need to be aware of security concerns, authentication mechanisms, optimization strategies, load-balancing techniques, and so on.

This doesn't necessarily mean that we have to have strong skills in all these areas; as a matter of fact, we hardly ever will. Nonetheless, if we want to pursue a full-stack approach, we need to understand the meaning, role, and scope of any of them, and possibly, be able to work there whenever we need to.

Single-Page Application

In order to demonstrate how ASP.NET Core and Angular can work together to their full extent, we couldn't think of anything better than building a **Single-Page Application (SPA)** project. The reason for that is quite obvious--there is no better approach to show some of the best features they have to offer nowadays. We'll have the chance to work with modern interfaces and patterns such as HTML5 pushState API, webhooks, data transport-based requests, dynamic web components, UI data bindings, and a stateless, AJAX-driven architecture capable to flawlessly encompass all of these.

Common features of a competitive SPA

To put it briefly, a SPA is a web-based application that struggles to provide the same user experience as a desktop application. If we consider the fact that all SPAs are still served through a web server and thus accessed by web browsers just like any other standard website, we can easily understand how that desired outcome can only be achieved by changing some of the default patterns commonly used in web development, such as resource loading, DOM management, and UI navigation. In a good SPA, both contents and resources--HTML, JavaScript, CSS, and such—are either retrieved within a single page load or dynamically fetched when needed; this also means that the page doesn't reload or refresh, it just changes and adapts in response to user actions, performing the required server-side calls behind the scenes.

These are some of the key features provided by a competitive SPA nowadays:

- **No server-side roundtrips**: A competitive SPA is able to redraw any part of the client UI without requiring a full server-side round trip to retrieve a full HTML page. This is mostly achieved by implementing a **Separation of Concerns** design principle, which means that the data will be separated from the presentation of data using a model layer that will handle the former, and a view layer that reads from the latter.

- **Efficient routing**: A competitive SPA is able to keep track of the user current state and location during its whole navigation experience using organized, JavaScript-based routers. This is usually accomplished in one of two ways: the **Hashbang** technique, or the HTML5 **History API** usage. We'll talk about either one of them in `Chapter 2`, *Backend with .NET Core*.

- **Performance and flexibility**: A competitive SPA usually transfers all of its UI to the client, thanks to its JavaScript SDK of choice (Angular, JQuery, Bootstrap, or any such). This is often good for network performance, as increasing client-side rendering and offline processing reduces the UI impact over the network. However, the real deal brought by this approach is the flexibility granted to the UI, as the developer will be able to completely rewrite the application frontend with little-to-no impact on the server, aside from a few of the static resource files.

The list can easily grow, as these are only some of the major advantages of a properly-designed, competitive SPA. These aspects play a major role nowadays, as many business websites and services are switching from their traditional **Multi-Page Application** mindset (**MPA**) to full-committed or hybrid SPA-based approaches. The latter ones, which have been increasingly popular since 2015, are commonly called **Native Web Applications** (**NWA**), because they tend to implement a number of small-scale, single-page modules bound together upon a multipage skeleton rather than building a single, monolithic SPA.

Not to mention the fact that there are also a lot of enterprise-level SPAs and Native Web Applications flawlessly serving thousands of users every day, want to name a few? WhatsApp Web and Teleport Web, Flickr, plus a wide amount of Google web services, including Gmail, Contacts, Spreadsheet, Maps, and more. These services, along with their huge user base, are the ultimate proof that we're not talking about a silly trend that will fade away with time; conversely, we're witnessing the completion of a consolidated pattern that's definitely meant to stay.

Product Owner expectations

One of the most interesting, yet underrated concepts brought out by many modern agile software development frameworks, such as SCRUM, is the importance given to the meanings and definitions of roles; among these, there's nothing as important as the Product Owner, also known as **the customer** in **Extreme Programming** methodology or customer representative elsewhere. They're the one who brings to the development table the expectations we'll struggle to satisfy. They will tell us what's most important to deliver and when they will prioritize our work based on its manifest business value rather than its underlying architectural value; they'll be entitled by the management to take decisions and make tough calls, which is sometimes great, sometimes not; this will often have a great impact on our development schedule. To cut it short, they're the one in charge of the project; that's why, in order to deliver a web application matching their expectancy, we'll need to understand their vision and feel it as if it were ours.

This is always true, even if the project's Product Owner is our dad, wife, or best friend: that's how it works.

Now that we made it clear, let's take a look at some of the most common Product Owner's expectations for a typical web-based SPA project. We ought to see if the choice of using ASP.NET Core and Angular will be good enough to fulfill each one of them.

- **Early release(s)**: No matter if we're selling a bunch of salad or web-based services, the customer will always want to see what he's buying. If we're using **SCRUM**, we'll have to release a potentially-shippable product at the end of each sprint; we'll have Milestones in a Waterfall-based approach, and so on. One thing is for sure--the best thing we can do in order to efficiently organize our development efforts will be to adopt an iterative and/or modular-oriented approach. ASP.NET Core and Angular, along with the strong Separation of Concerns granted by their underlying **MVC** or **MVVM** based patterns, will gracefully push us into the mindset needed to do just that.

- **GUI over backend**: We'll often be asked to work to the GUI and frontend functionalities, because that will be the only real viewable and measurable thing for the customer. This basically means that we'll have to mock the data model and start working on the frontend as soon as possible, delaying everything that relies under the hood, even if that means leaving it empty; we can say that the hood is what we need the most. Note that this kind of approach is not necessarily bad; by all means, we're not tying up the donkey where the (product) owner wants. On the contrary, the choice of using ASP.NET Core along with Angular will grant us the chance to easily decouple the presentation layer and the data layer, implementing the first and mocking the latter, which is a great thing to do. We'll be able to see where we're going before wasting valuable time or being forced to make potentially wrong decisions. ASP.NET Core's Web API interface will provide the proper tools to do that by allowing us to create a sample web application skeleton in a matter of seconds using **Visual Studio** Controller templates and in-memory data contexts powered by **Entity Framework 6**, which we'll be able to access using entity models and code-first. As soon as we do that, we'll be able to switch to GUI design using the Angular presentation layer toolbox as much as we want until we reach the desired results; once we're satisfied, we'll just need to properly implement the Web API controller interfaces and hook up the actual data.

- **Fast completion**: None of the preceding will work unless we also manage to get everything done in a reasonable time span. This is one of the key reasons to choose to adopt a server-side framework and a client-side framework working together with ease. ASP.NET Core and Angular are the tools of choice not only because they're both built on solid, consistent ground, but also because they're meant to do precisely that--get the job done on their respective side and provide a usable interface to the other partner.

- **Adaptability**: As stated by the Agile manifesto, being able to respond to change requests is more important than following a plan. This is especially true in software development, where we can even claim that anything that cannot handle changes is a failed project. That's another great reason to embrace the Separation of Concerns enforced by our two frameworks of choice, as this grants the developer ability to manage--and even welcome, to some extent--most of the layout or structural changes that will be expected during the development phase.

 A few lines ago, we mentioned **SCRUM**, which is one of the most popular agile software development frameworks out there. Those who don't know it yet should definitely take a look at what it can offer to any result-driven Team Leader and/or Project Manager. Here's a good place to start--https://en.wikipedia.org/wiki/Scrum_(software_development).

That's about it. Note that we didn't cover everything here, as it will be impossible without knowing an actual assignment. We just tried to give an extensive answer to the following general questions: if we were to build a SPA, would ASP.NET Core and Angular be an appropriate choice? The answer is undoubtedly yes, especially when used together.

Does it mean that we're done already? Not a chance, as we have no intention of taking this assumption for granted. Conversely, it's time for us to demonstrate it by ceasing to speak in general terms and starting to put things in motion.

A sample Single-Page Application project

What we need now is to conceive a suitable test case scenario similar to the ones we will eventually have to deal with--a fully-featured, production-ready Single-Page Application project, complete with all the core aspects we would expect from a potentially shippable product.

In order to do this, the first thing we need to do is to become our own customer for a minute and come up with an idea, a vision to share with our own other self. We'll then be able to put our developer shoes back on and split our abstract plan into a list of items we'll need to implement; these will be the core requirements of our own project. Finally, we'll set up our workstation by getting the required packages, adding the resource files, and configuring both the ASP.NET Core and Angular frameworks into the Visual Studio IDE.

The vision

If we're going to demonstrate the key features of ASP.NET Core and Angular in a practical way such as committing ourselves into a full-stack SPA project and bringing it to life, we definitely need to go for a project where they can shine the most.

That's why we can't really take into consideration most presentation-oriented websites such as demos, product galleries, corporate or marketing showcases, photo/video/media reels, blogs, and the likes; we need something that can make better use of the asynchronous and parallel request processing capabilities of both frameworks, bringing them both toward their full extent; in order to fulfill these expectations, we would rather think about something similar to a CMS engine, a community-driven wiki, or even better, an interactive web application featuring some strong client-server interactions such as auth tokens, RESTful data transfer, and push notifications.

The latter seems to be the most appropriate, as it will mean going through a number of not-so-trivial implementation challenges while keeping the expected amount of source code small enough to fit into this book.

Not your usual "Hello World!"

The application we will build won't be just a shallow demonstration, we won't throw some working code here and there and expect the reader to connect the dots. Our objective is to create a solid, realistic web application using the frameworks we've chosen while following the current development best practices.

Each chapter will be dedicated to a single core aspect; if you feel like you already know your way there, feel free to skip to the next one. Conversely, if you're willing to follow us through the whole loop, you'll have a great journey through the most useful aspects of ASP.NET Core and Angular and how they can work together to deliver the most common and useful web-development tasks, from the most trivial one to the more complex beasts. It's an investment that will pay dividends, as it will leave you with a maintainable, extensible, and well-structured project, plus the knowledge needed to build your own.

To avoid making things too boring, we'll try to pick an enjoyable theme that will also have some usefulness in the real world; do you know anything about personality tests? They are questionnaires designed to reveal aspects of an individual's nature, trace a psychological makeup, or identify similarities with other notable real or fictional characters. The web is nothing less than full of them, featuring the most popular themes from the movie and entertainment industry--*which Game of Thrones character are you? Are you a Jedi or a Sith?* and so on.

Introducing TestMakerFree

I hope you like these kinds of questionnaires because we will build a web application that will allow users from anywhere in the world to build their own test(s). In order to do so, we'll put together a wizard-like tool that can be used to add questions and answers, upload images, choose a scoring method, assign a score to each answer, and define the possible outcomes/results. At the end of the wizard, the user will receive a unique URL that can be used to take the test and/or share it via email, blog/forum posts, IMs, social networks, and so on.

Ultimately, they will have a small yet useful web application featuring a server-side engine powered by ASP.NET Core and a web client mostly built using Angular.

The chosen name? **TestMakerFree**, also known as www.testmakerfree.com; needless to say, the *free* word means that our application will be free of charge. Luckily enough, the domain was still available at the time of writing this book. If you go there now, you'll be able to see the final outcome of what we will build from scratch during the course of this book; don't do that if you don't like spoilers, as it can ruin some of your fun.

Core features and requirements

Let's try to visualize how our application should work.

Our users will definitely need to register, so we'll be able to grant them the ownership of their own tests; once done, they will be able to create a new **test**. Each test will have a name, a description, a list of questions, and a series of possible results; each **question** will have a descriptive text, a list of answers, and an optional image; each **answer** will have a descriptive text, an optional image, and a list of score points; and each **result** will have a descriptive text and a score value.

The score points and the score value will be extensively discussed later on. For now, we'll just state the obvious--whenever a user completes the test, the sum of score points among all the given answers will be matched with the score value given to each possible result in order to determine the final outcome. The numbers will be shown or hidden to the user as per the test owner's choice.

 If you ever heard about the **Myers-Briggs Type Indicator (MBTI)** and/or the **Five Factor Model (FFM)**, you most likely already know how we'll make use of *score points* and *score values*. In case you want to know more about these testing models, we strongly suggest you take a look at the en.wikipedia.org/wiki/Myers-Briggs_Type_Indicator and en.wikipedia.org/wiki/Big_Five_personality_traits Wikipedia pages.

That's about it. It might sound easy or not, depending on our programming experience, but one thing is certain--we got a plan.

Now that we have identified the key features, let's break them down into a list of development topics:

- **Routing**: The application will have to properly respond to client requests, that is, routing them according to what they're up to.
- **Data model**: We'll definitely adopt a database engine to store our tests, questions, answers, and so on; hence, we'll also need to develop the proper tools to access it in a modern, fashionable way. In order do so, we need to define our data architecture by setting up data repositories and domain entities that will be handled by the server and hooked to Angular through the most suited ASP.NET Core interface to handle HTTP communications--the **Controller** class.
- **Controllers**: From an MVC-based architectural perspective, one of the main differences between multi-page and single-page applications is that the former's **Controllers** are designed to return views, while the latter ones, also known as **API Controllers**, mostly return serialized data. These are what we will need to implement to put Angular components in charge of the presentation layer.
- **Angular components**: Switching to the client side, we will need to define a set of components to handle UI elements and state changes. As we probably already know, components are the most fundamental elements in Angular, replacing the AngularJS controllers and scopes. We'll get to know more about them soon enough.
- **Authentication**: Soon enough, we'll have to deal with user login and registration. We'll take care of that by adding a membership context, so we'll be able to limit **CRUD** operations to authenticated users only, keeping track of each user action, requiring registration to access some pages/views, and so on.
- **UI styling**: We will take our time to come to that, as we will stick to the core topics first, but we'll definitely get there eventually; the initial ugliness of our web client will flourish into a responsive, good-looking, and mobile-friendly user interface.

These will be our main development challenges. As we said earlier, we definitely have to understand how to properly handle each one of them, or we won't be able to succeed. Hence, let's get to work without further ado!

The following chapters will guide us through the journey; we'll also cover other important aspects such as **SEO**, **Security**, **Performance Issues**, **Best Coding Practices**, and **Deployment**, as they will be very important later on.

Preparing the workspace

The first thing we have to do is to set up our workstation; it won't be difficult, because we only need a small set of essential tools. These include Visual Studio 2017, the web platform installer, the Node.JS runtime, a web server such as **IIS** or **IIS Express**, and a decent source code control system such as Git, Mercurial, or Team Foundation. We will take the latter for granted, as we most likely already have it up and running.

 In the unlikely case we don't, we should really make amends before moving on! Stop reading, go to www.github.com or www.bitbucket.com, create a free account, and spend some time to learn how to effectively use these tools; we won't regret it, that's for sure.

Disclaimer-Do (not) try this at home

There's something very important that we need to understand before proceeding. If we're a seasoned web developer we will most likely know about it already, however, since this book is for (almost) everyone, I feel like it's very important to deal with this matter as soon as possible.

This book will make an extensive use of a number of different programming tools, external components, third-party libraries and so on. Most of them, such as TypeScript, NuGet, NPM, Gulp, .NET Core Frameworks/runtimes, and so on are shipped together with Visual Studio 2017, while others such as Angular and its required JS dependencies will be fetched from their official repositories. These things are meant to work together in a 100% compatible fashion, however they are all subject to changes and updates during the inevitable course of time: as time passes by, the chance that these updates might affect the way they interact with each other and the project health will increase.

The broken code myth

In an attempt to minimize the chances that this can occur, this book will always work with fixed versions/builds of any *third-party* component that can be handled using the configuration files. However, some of them, such as Visual Studio and/or .NET framework updates, might be out of that scope and might bring havoc to the project. The source code might cease to work, or Visual Studio can suddenly be unable to properly compile it.

When something like that happens, the less experienced reader will always be tempted to put the blame on the book itself. Some of them may even start thinking something like this:

There are a lot of compile errors, hence the source code must be broken!

Alternatively, they may think like this:

The code sample doesn't work: the author must have rushed things here and there and forgot to test what he was writing.

There can be many other things like these.

It goes without saying that such hypotheses are hardly true, especially considering the amount of time that the authors, editors, and technical reviewers of these books spent in writing, testing, and refining the source code before building it up, making it available on GitHub and even publishing a working instance of the resulting application to a worldwide-available public website.

Any non-amateur developer will easily understand that most of these things couldn't even be done if there was some "broken code" somewhere; there's no way this book can even attempt to hit the shelves unless it comes with a 100% working source code, except for few possible minor typos that will quickly be reported to the publisher and thus fixed within the GitHub repository in a short while. In the unlikely case that it looks like it doesn't, such as raising unexpected compile errors, the non-novice reader should spend a reasonable amount of time trying to understand the root cause. Here's a list of questions they should try to answer before anything else:

- Am I using the same development framework, third-party libraries, versions, and builds adopted by the book?
- If I updated something because I felt like I needed to, am I aware of the changes that might affect the source code? Did I read the relevant change logs? Have I spent a reasonable amount of time looking around for breaking changes and/or known issues that could have had an impact on the source code?
- Is the book's GitHub repository also affected by this issue? Did I try to compare it with my own code, possibly replacing mine?

Stay hungry, stay foolish, yet be responsible as well

Don't get it wrong: whenever you want to use a newer version of Visual Studio, update your Typescript compiler or upgrade any *third-party* library; you are free and also very encouraged to do that. This is nothing less than the main scope of this book--making the readers fully aware of what they're doing and capable of going on their path, way beyond the given code samples.

However, if you feel you're ready to do that, you will also have to adapt the code accordingly; most of the time, we're talking about trivial stuff, especially these days when you can Google out the issue and/or get the solution on StackOverflow. They changed the *typings*? Then you need to load the new *typings*; they moved the class somewhere else? Then you need to find the new namespace and change it accordingly; and so on.

That's about it, nothing more, nothing less. The code reflects the passage of time; the developer just needs to keep up with the flow, performing minimum changes to it when required. You can't possibly get lost and blame someone other than you if you update your environment and fail to acknowledge that you have to change a bunch of code lines to make it work again.

Am I implying that the author is not responsible for the source code of the book? It's the exact opposite, the author is always responsible. They're supposed to do their best to fix all the reported compatibility issues while keeping the GitHub repository updated. However, the reader should also take his very own level of responsibility; more specifically, he should understand how things work for *any* development book and the inevitable impact of the passage of time on *any* given source code. No matter how hard the author can work to maintain it, the patches will never be fast or comprehensive enough to make these lines of code always work on any given scenario. That's why the most important thing the reader needs to understand--even before the book topics--is the most valuable concept in modern software development: being able to efficiently deal with the inevitable changes that *will* always occur.

Whoever refuses to understand that is doomed; there's no way around it.

Versions and builds

These are the releases we will use:

- Visual Studio 2017 version 15.4.4
- Microsoft .NET Core SDK 2.0.3
- TypeScript 2.4.2

- NuGet Package Manager 4.1.0
- NodeJS 6.9.0
- Angular 5.0.2 final release

We strongly suggest using the same version used within this book, or newer, at your own risk! Jokes aside, if you prefer to use a different version, that's perfectly fine, as long as you will take responsibility if something doesn't work, just like we said a paragraph ago.

Setting up the project

The first thing we need to do is to download the .NET Core SDK, unless the release we want to use is already shipped with Visual Studio 2017. We can download the latest version from either the official Microsoft URL, that is, `https://www.microsoft.com/net/core`, or from the official GitHub project page, at `https://github.com/dotnet/cli/tree/v2.0.3#installers-and-binaries`.

The installation is very straightforward, just follow the wizard until the end to get the job done:

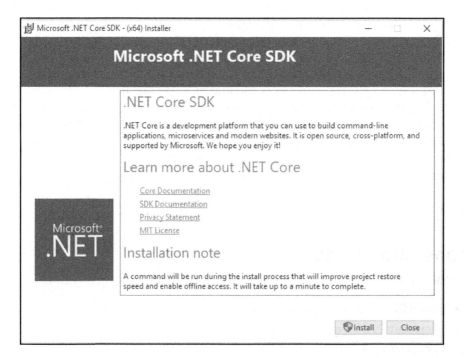

Once installed, launch Visual Studio 2017 and create a new **ASP.NET Core Web Application project**. Let's do that by following the mentioned steps:

1. Fire up Visual Studio 2017 and, from the **File** menu, expand **New** and select **Project** to open a **New Project** modal window.
2. From the **Templates** tree, expand the **Visual C#** node and select the **Web** subfolder; the right section of the modal window will be populated by a number of available project templates. Among these, there are two choices for creating an **ASP.NET Core Web Application project**: **.NET Core and .NET Framework**, as we can see in the following diagram:

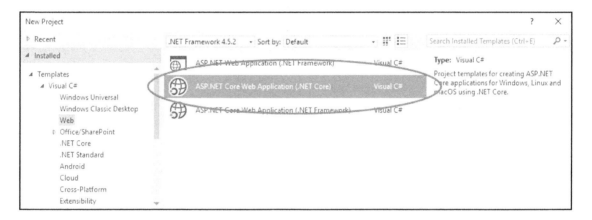

3. The first one, optimized for cross-platform deployment, entirely relies upon the new .NET Core framework; the latter, ideal for a Windows environment, is based upon the latest .NET Framework version (4.6.2 at the time of writing) instead.

The good thing here is that, thanks to the ASP.NET Core versatility, we are free to choose the approach we like the most, as both frameworks are mature enough to support almost everything we will use within this book. That said, in order to have better compatibility with most NuGet packages we might choose to add, we'll be choosing the template based on **.NET Core**.

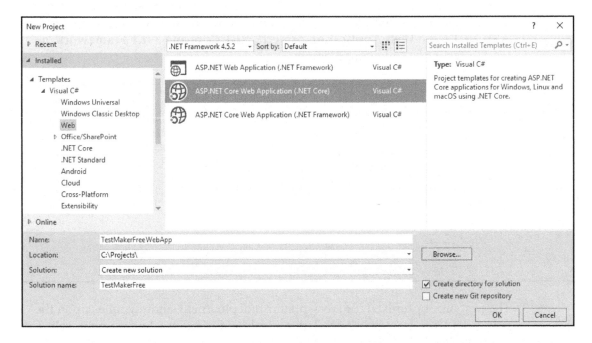

4. Select the **ASP.NET Core Web Application (.NET Core)** template and fill the relevant **Name**, **Location**, and **Solution** name fields; set `TestMakerFreeWebApp` as Project Name and `TestMakerFree` as **Solution name**, just to not confuse them, and then click on **OK** to continue.

5. In the next modal window, we can further customize our template by choosing the default contents to include in our project (**Empty**, **Web API**, or **Web Application**) and the authentication mechanism, should we want to use one. Select **.NET Core** and **ASP.NET Core 2.0** from the drop-down list, and then select the **Angular** template icon with **No Authentication**; the **Enable Docker Support** checkbox, if present, should be disabled by default. Eventually, click on the **OK** button to create the project:

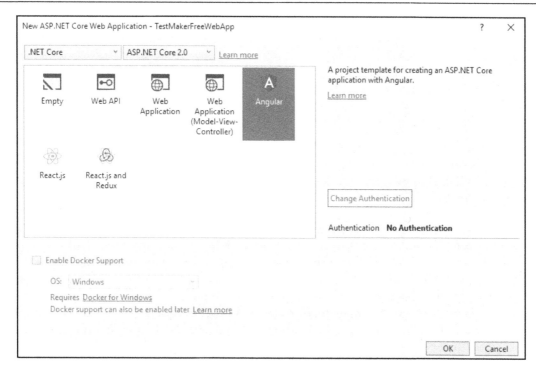

Those who're used to the Visual Studio Web Application Project templates for the previous ASP.NET versions will be tempted to choose **Empty** instead, thus avoiding the insane amount of sample classes, folders, and components, including a number of potentially outdated versions of various client-side frameworks such as **Bootstrap**, **KnockoutJS**, **JQuery**, and more. Luckily enough, these new ASP.NET Core project templates are quite lightweight and just ship the required files, resources, and dependencies to the project to Bootstrap a sample template based on the chosen *client-side* technology:

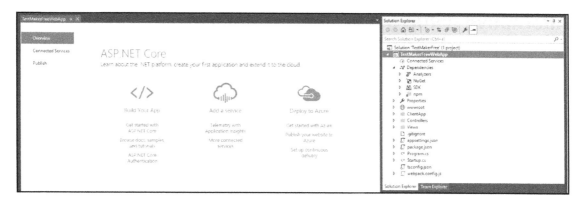

In our specific case, our template will set up a rather clean working environment containing the following:

- The default ASP.NET MVC `/Controllers/` and `/Views/` folders, with some sample controllers and views
- The `/ClientApp/` folder, with some **TypeScript** files containing the source code of a sample Angular app
- The `/wwwroot/` folder, which will be used by VS2017 to build an optimized version of the client-side code whenever we need to execute it locally or have it published anywhere; that folder is initially empty, but it will be populated upon *first-run*

If we spend some time to browse through this folder and take a look at the content, we can see how the .NET Core developers did a tremendous job in easing the MVC-with-Angular setup and kickstart process. This template already supports **SEO optimization** and **Server-Side Rendering** (SSR), and also features a bunch of useful optimizations; those who fought with *task runners* and *client-side* building strategies in the recent past will most likely appreciate the fact that this template features a build process completely handled by **NPM**, **Webpack**, and **.NET Core** with specific loading strategies for development and production.

More details on this approach, including a summary of the main reasons behind it, are well explained by the following .NET WebDev blog, which explains the great work done by *Steve Sanderson* to properly support Single-Page Applications in .NET Core:

`https://blogs.msdn.microsoft.com/webdev/2017/02/14/building-single-page-applications-on-asp-net-core-with-javascriptservices/`

Alternative setup using the command line

If we take a look at the article mentioned in the information box at the end of the previous paragraph, we can see how the SPA templates are fetched and installed using the *command line*. Although we did that using the VS2017 GUI, we can also do that using the *command line* in the following way:

```
dotnet new angular
```

When using this command, the Angular project will be created within the folder where the command is executed.

The command line can also come in handy whenever we want to get the latest versions of the SPA templates, which is currently not supported within the GUI:

```
dotnet new --install Microsoft.AspNetCore.SpaTemplates::*
```

Test run

Before moving further, we should definitely attempt a quick test run to ensure that everything is working properly. Doing that should be just as easy as hitting the **Run** button or the *F5* key:

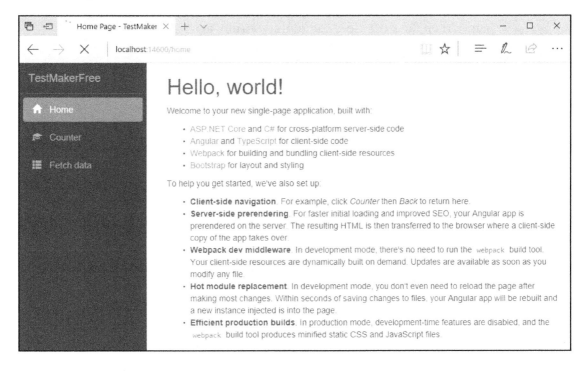

This is an excellent consistency check to ensure that our development system is properly configured. If we see the sample Angular SPA up and running, as shown in the preceding screenshot, it means that we're good to go; if we don't, it probably means that we're either missing something or that we've got some conflicting software preventing VS2017 and its external web tools (NPM/NODE) from properly compiling the project.

In order to fix that, we can try to do the following:

- **Uninstall/reinstall Node.JS**, as we can possibly have an outdated version installed.
- **Uninstall/reinstall Visual Studio 2017**, as our current installation might be broken or corrupt. The.NET Core SDK should come shipped with it already; however, we can also try reinstalling it.
- **Update the SPA templates** using the command-line interface by following the instructions we gave in the previous paragraph.
- Install **VS2017** on a clean environment (be it either a physical system or a VM) to overcome any possible issue related to our current operating system configuration.

If none of these works, the best thing we can do is to ask for specific support on the .NET Core community forum, at `https://forums.asp.net/1255.aspx/1?ASP+NET+Core`.

Looking around

Now that our project has been created, it's time to take a quick look around and try to understand some of the hard work that the .NET Core SPA Template has done to make it work. Hey, wait a minute! Shouldn't we skip all these setup technicalities and just jump into coding? As a matter of fact, yes, we'll definitely be doing that in a little while. However, before doing that, it can be wise to highlight a couple of aspects of the code that has been put in place already so that we'll know how to properly move within our project in advance: where to find the *server-side* and *client-side* code, where to put some new content, how to change our initialization parameters, and so on. It will also be a good chance to review our base knowledge about the Visual Studio environment and the required packages we will need.

IMPORTANT! The sample code we're reviewing here is the one that's being shipped with the Angular SPA Visual Studio Template at the time of writing--*MVC ASP.NET Core with Angular*. In the (likely) event that this sample code will get updated in future releases, ensure to get the former source code from the web using this book's official NuGet repository and use it to replace the contents of your `/TestMakerFreeWebApp/` folder. If we avoid doing that, our sample code might differ from the one featured in this book.

The first thing that meets the eye is that, as we already mentioned, the layout of a standard ASP.NET Core solution is quite different from what it used to be in ASP.NET 4 and earlier versions. The main difference is the brand new `/wwwroot/` folder, which will contain the compiled, *ready-to-publish* contents of our application: HTML, JS, and CSS files, along with fonts, images, and everything else we want our users to have access to in terms of **static files**.

Other things worth noting are as listed:

- The good old `/Controllers/` and `/Views/`, which come shipped with any MVC-based ASP.NET application since the former release of the MVC framework
- The `/ClientApp/` folder, which already hosts a bunch of Angular source code files; we can see that they all have a `.ts` extension, which means we'll be using the **TypeScript** programming language (we'll say more about this in a bit)
- The `Dependencies` virtual folder, which is basically the replacement of the old `Resources` folder and contains all the internal, external, and *third-party* references required to build and run our project
- A bunch of root-level `.cs`, `.json`, and `.js` files that will determine our web application's configuration, the available *client-side* and *server-side* modules and also their setup, compilation, and publishing rules; we'll address them in a while

Just by observing these folders, provided that we already got a glimpse of ASP.NET MVC experience, we are already able to figure out how things will be handled:

- Each request will be received by the **MvcApplication**, which will handle them at the *server-side* level and route those related to the GUI through the appropriate **Controller**
- The **Controller** will do the required *server-side* tasks and then, depending on the given request, either serve raw JSON data or return the response content using a **View**
- The **View** will serve the required *client-side* content (HTML, JS, and CSS), including the required JS modules that will be served in a highly-optimized fashion using a dedicated dynamic loader (**Webpack**)

Let's quickly review the whole process, starting with the root configuration files.

The configuration files

Let's start with the main .NET Core startup files: `Program.cs` and `Startup.cs`.

Program.cs

The `Program.cs` file will most likely raise the curiosity of most seasoned ASP.NET programmers, as it's not something we usually see in a web application project. First introduced in ASP.NET Core 1.0, the `Program.cs` file's main purpose is to set up and build the `IWebHost`.

That's great to know, but what is a **Web Host**? In a very few words, a *host* is the execution context of any ASP.NET Core app. In a web-based application, the host must implement the `IWebHost` interface, which exposes a collection of web-related features and services and also a Start method. The Web Host references the server that will handle requests.

The preceeding statement can lead to thinking that the web host and the web server are the same thing; however, it's very important to understand that they're not, as they serve very different purposes. The following excerpt from the .NET Core GitHub project does a great job explaining the key difference between them:

The host is responsible for application startup and lifetime management. The server is responsible for accepting HTTP requests. Part of the host's responsibility includes ensuring that the application's services and the server are available and properly configured. We could think of the host as being a wrapper around the server. The host is configured to use a particular server; the server is unaware of its host.

Source: `http://aspnetcore.readthedocs.io/en/stable/fundamentals/hosting.html`

If we open the `Program.cs` file, we can easily see that the web host is built in an extremely easy way:

```
public class Program
{
    public static void Main(string[] args)
    {
        BuildWebHost(args).Run();
    }
```

```
    public static IWebHost BuildWebHost(string[] args) =>
        WebHost.CreateDefaultBuilder(args)
            .UseStartup<Startup>()
            .Build();
}
```

The `WebHost.CreateDefaultBuilder()` method is one of the many improvements of ASP.NET Core 2.0 over its 1.x counterpart as it simplifies the amount of source code required to set up basic use cases, thus making it easier to get started with a new project.

To understand this better, let's take a look at the sample `Program.cs` equivalent, like it was in ASP.NET Core 1.x:

```
public class Program
{
    public static void Main(string[] args)
    {
        var host = new WebHostBuilder()
            .UseKestrel()
            .UseContentRoot(Directory.GetCurrentDirectory())
            .UseIISIntegration()
            .UseStartup<Startup>()
            .UseApplicationInsights()
            .Build();

        host.Run();
    }
}
```

This used to perform the following steps:

- Setting up the **Kestrel** web server
- Setting the Content root folder, that is, where to look for the `appsettings.json` file and other configuration files
- Setting up the IIS Integration
- Defining the `Startup` class to use (usually defined in the `Startup.cs` file)
- Finally, **Build** and **Run** the now configured `IWebHost`

In .NET Core 1.x, all these steps must be called explicitly here and also manually configured within the `Startup.cs` file; in .NET Core 2.0, we can still do this, yet using the `WebHost.CreateDefaultBuilder()` method will generally be better as it will take care of most of the job, also letting us change the defaults whenever we want.

If you're curious about this method, you can even take a peek at the source code on GitHub at `https://github.com/aspnet/MetaPackages/blob/rel/2.0.0/src/Microsoft.AspNetCore/WebHost.cs`.

At the time of writing, the `WebHost.CreateDefaultBuilder()` method implementation starts at line #152.

Startup.cs

Let's move to the `Startup.cs` file. If you're a seasoned .NET developer, you might be already familiar with it, since it was first introduced in OWIN-based applications to replace most of the tasks previously handled by the good old `Global.asax` file.

OWIN (for Open Web Interface for .NET) and comes as part of **Project Katana**, a flexible set of components released by Microsoft back in 2013 for building and hosting OWIN-based web applications. For additional info, refer to `https://www.asp.net/aspnet/overview/owin-and-katana`.

However, the similarities end here; the class has been completely rewritten to be as pluggable and lightweight as possible, which means that it will include and load only what's strictly necessary to fulfill our application's tasks. More specifically, in .NET Core, the `Startup.cs` file is the place where we can do the following:

- Add and configure **Services** and **Dependency Injection**, in the `ConfigureServices` method
- Configure **HTTP request pipeline** by adding the required `Middleware` packages, in the `Configure` method

To better understand this, let's take a look at the following lines taken from the `Startup.cs` source code shipped with the project template we chose:

```
// This method gets called by the runtime. Use this method to configure the
HTTP request pipeline.
public void Configure(IApplicationBuilder app, IHostingEnvironment env)
{
    if (env.IsDevelopment())
    {
        app.UseDeveloperExceptionPage();
        app.UseWebpackDevMiddleware(new WebpackDevMiddlewareOptions
        {
            HotModuleReplacement = true
        });
    }
```

```
    else
    {
        app.UseExceptionHandler("/Home/Error");
    }

    app.UseStaticFiles();

    app.UseMvc(routes =>
    {
        routes.MapRoute(
            name: "default",
            template: "{controller=Home}/{action=Index}/{id?}");

        routes.MapSpaFallbackRoute(
            name: "spa-fallback",
            defaults: new { controller = "Home", action = "Index" });
    });
}
```

This is the `Configure` method implementation, where--as we just said--we can set up and configure the HTTP request pipeline.

The code is very readable, so we can easily understand what happens here:

- The first bunch of lines features an `if-then-else` statement that implements two different behaviors to handle runtime exceptions in development and production, throwing the exception in the former case or showing an opaque error page to the end user in the latter; that's a neat way to handle runtime exceptions in a very few lines of code.
- The `app.UseStaticFiles()` call adds the `Microsoft.AspNetCore.StaticFiles` middleware to the HTTP pipeline, which will allow our web server to serve the static files within the web root. Without this line, we won't be able to serve locally hosted assets such as JS, CSS, and images; hence, having it there is a good thing. Also, note how the method is called with no parameters; the `StaticFiles` middleware default settings are more than enough for us, so there's nothing to configure or override here.
- We can't say the same for the subsequent `app.UseMvc()` call, which comes with some interesting configuration parameters. We'll extensively talk about that in `Chapter 2`, *Backend with .NET Core*; for now, let's just understand that these lines serve the purpose of adding the MVC Middleware within the HTTP pipeline and also setting up a couple of HTTP routing rules pointing to the `HomeController` `Index` action method, which will be the web application main entry point.

Let's perform a quick test to ensure that we properly understand how these *Middlewares* work. From Visual Studio's **Solution Explorer**, go to the /wwwroot/ folder and add a new test.html page to our project. Once done, fill it with the following contents:

```
<!DOCTYPE html>
<html>
<head>
    <meta charset="utf-8" />
    <title>Time for a test!</title>
</head>
<body>
    Hello there!
    <br /><br />
    This is a test to see if the StaticFiles middleware is working
properly.
</body>
</html>
```

Now, let's launch the application in *debug* mode--using the **Run** button or the *F5* keyboard key--and point the address bar to http://localhost:<port>/test.html.

We should be able to see our test.html file in all its glory:

Now, let's go back to our Startup.cs file and comment out the app.UseStaticFiles() call to prevent the StaticFiles middleware from being loaded:

```
// app.UseStaticFiles();
```

Once done, run the application again and go back to the previous URL:

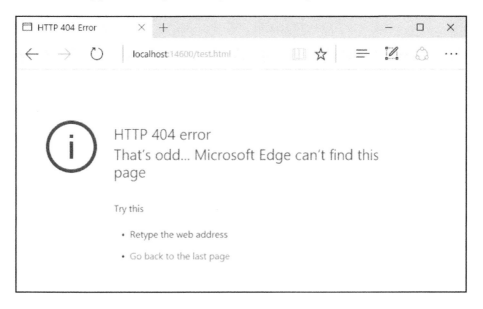

As expected, static files aren't being served anymore. If we point our address bar to /home, we can see how this new behavior is also preventing the sample SPA provided by the Angular template from even loading, which means that we just broke our web app, yay!

Now that we proved our point, let's bring the StaticFiles middleware back in place by removing the comments and go ahead.

For additional information regarding the StaticFiles middleware and static files handling in .NET Core, visit and read https://docs.asp.net/ en/latest/fundamentals/static-files.html.

All in all, we can honestly say that the Startup.cs file shipped with the Angular SPA template already has everything we need, so we can leave it as it is for now. However, before going ahead, let's take another look at the if-then-else statement contained within this code snippet; we can easily see that there are other things planned when the application is in development mode. We're talking about the UseWebpackDevMiddleware() method with the HotModuleReplacement option set to true. This is one of the great features shipped with the Microsoft.AspNetCore.SpaServices package for those who use **Webpack**, which includes us; we'll get there later on, when talking about the Webpack configuration file.

Now, it's time to take a quick look at the three `.json` files also lying in the root folder. Each one of them is a configuration file for something; let's look at a bunch of words for each one of them.

The appsettings.json file

The `appsettings.json` file is nothing less than the replacement of the good old `Web.config` file; the XML syntax has been replaced by a more readable (and less verbose) JSON format. Moreover, the new configuration model is based upon key/value settings that can be retrieved from a wide variety of sources, including--yet not limited to--Json files, using a centralized interface.

Once retrieved, they can be easily accessed within our code using **Dependency Injection** via literal strings (using the vanilla `IConfiguration` class):

```
public SampleController(IConfiguration configuration)
{
    var myValue = configuration["Logging:IncludeScopes"];
}
```

Alternatively, even in a *strongly-typed* fashion using a custom `POCO` class (we'll get there later on).

It's worth noting that there's also an `appsettings.Development.json` file nested below the former one. Such file serves the same purpose of the old `Web.Debug.config` file since ASP.NET 4.x; everything is written there will override the `appsettings.json` values as long as the application runs in the *development* mode.

Back in .NET Core 1.x, this overriding behavior had to be specified manually within the `Startup.cs` file; in .NET Core 2, the `WebHost.CreateDefaultBuilder()` method within the `Program.cs` file takes care of that automatically, assuming that you don't need to add another custom `.json` configuration file.

Assuming that we understood everything here, it's time to move on to the next configuration file.

The package.json file

The `package.json` file is the **NPM Configuration File**; it basically contains a list of **NPM packages** that the developer want to be restored before the project starts. Those who already know what NPM is and how it works can skip to the next paragraph, while the others should definitely keep reading.

NPM (shortcode for **Node Package Manager**) started its life as the default package manager for the JavaScript runtime environment known as **Node.js**. During the latest years, though, it was also being used to host a number of independent JS projects, libraries, and frameworks of any kind, including *Angular*; eventually, it became the de facto package manager for JavaScript frameworks and tooling. If you never used it, you may easily think of it as the *Nuget* for the JavaScript world.

Although *NPM* is mostly a *command-line* tool, the easiest way to use it from Visual Studio is to properly configure a `package.json` file containing all the NPM packages we want to get, restore, and keep up to date later on. These packages get downloaded in the `/node_modules/` folder within our project directory, which is hidden by default within Visual Studio; however, all the retrieved packages can be seen from the `/Dependencies/npm/` virtual folder. As soon as we add, delete, or update the `package.json` file, Visual Studio will automatically update that folder accordingly.

In the Angular SPA template we've been using, the shipped `package.json` contains a huge amount of packages--all **Angular** packages plus a good bunch of dependencies, tools, and third-party utilities such as **Karma** (a great Test Runner for JavaScript/TypeScript).

Before moving ahead, let's take an additional look at our `package.json` file and try to get the most out of it. We can see how all the packages are listed within a standard JSON object entirely made of *key-value* pairs; the package name is the *key*, while the *value* is used to specify the version number. We can either input precise build numbers or use the standard **npmJS** syntax to specify *auto-update rules* bound to custom version ranges using the supported prefixes, such as the following:

- **The Tilde (~)**: A value of `"~1.1.4"` will match all 1.1.x versions, excluding 1.2.0, 1.0.x, and so on

- **The Caret (^)**: A value of `"^1.1.4"` will match everything above 1.1.4, excluding 2.0.0 and above

This is another scenario where *Intellisense* will come inhandy, as it will also suggest how to do that.

> For an extensive list of available **npmJS** commands and prefixes, it's advisable to check out the official **npmJS** documentation at
> `https://docs.npmjs.com/files/package.json`.

Upgrading (or downgrading) Angular

As we can see, the Angular SPA Template uses fixed version numbers for all the Angular-related packages; this is definitely a wise choice since we have no guarantees that newer versions will seamlessly integrate with our existing code without raising some potentially breaking issues and/or compiler errors. Needless to say, the version number will naturally increase with the passage of time, because the template developers will definitely try to keep their good work up to date.

That said, these are the Angular packages and releases that will be used within this book:

```
"@angular/animations": "5.0.2",
"@angular/common": "5.0.2",
"@angular/compiler": "5.0.2",
"@angular/compiler-cli": "5.0.2",
"@angular/core": "5.0.2",
"@angular/forms": "5.0.2",
"@angular/http": "5.0.2",
"@angular/platform-browser": "5.0.2",
"@angular/platform-browser-dynamic": "5.0.2",
"@angular/platform-server": "5.0.2",
"@angular/router": "5.0.2"
```

As we can see, the version number is the same for all packages and corresponds to the Angular release currently installed.

> The final version of **Angular 5**, codename *Pentagonal Donut*, has been released on November 1, 2017--just days before this book will hit the shelves: we did our best to use the latest possible final (non-*beta*, non-*rc*) version to give the reader the best possible experience with the most recent technology available. That said, that "freshness" will eventually decrease over time and this book's code will start to become obsolete: when it will happen, don't blame us for that!

If we want to ensure the highest possible level of compatibility between our project and this book's source code, we should definitely adopt that same release, which, at the time of writing, also corresponds to the latest stable one. We can easily perform the upgrade--or downgrade--by changing the version numbers; as soon as we save the file, Visual Studio will automatically fetch the new versions through NPM. In the unlikely case it won't, manually deleting the old packages and issuing a full rebuild should be enough to fix the issue.

As always, we're free to overwrite such behavior and get newer (or older) versions of these packages, assuming that we properly understood the consequences and according to this chapter's **Disclaimer**.

If you encounter problems while updating your package.json file, such as conflicting packages or "broken" code, ensure that you download the full source code from the official GitHub repository of this book, which includes the same package.json file that has been used to write, review, and test this book; it will definitely ensure a great level of compatibility with the source code you'll find here.

Upgrading (or downgrading) the other packages

As we can easily expect, if we upgrade (or downgrade) Angular to 5.0.0 final, we also need to take care of a series of other NPM packages that might require to be updated (or downgraded) as well. Here's the full package list we'll be using in our package.json file throughout the book: the important packages are highlighted--be sure to triple-check them!

```
{
  "name": "TestMakerFree",
  "private": true,
  "version": "0.0.0",
  "scripts": {
    "test": "karma start ClientApp/test/karma.conf.js"
  },
  "dependencies": {
    "@angular/animations": "5.0.2",
    "@angular/common": "5.0.2",
    "@angular/compiler": "5.0.2",
    "@angular/compiler-cli": "5.0.2",
    "@angular/core": "5.0.2",
    "@angular/forms": "5.0.2",
    "@angular/http": "5.0.2",
    "@angular/platform-browser": "5.0.2",
    "@angular/platform-browser-dynamic": "5.0.2",
```

```
    "@angular/platform-server": "5.0.2",
    "@angular/router": "5.0.2",
    "@ngtools/webpack": "1.8.2",
    "@types/webpack-env": "1.13.2",
    "angular2-template-loader": "0.6.2",
    "aspnet-prerendering": "3.0.1",
    "aspnet-webpack": "2.0.1",
    "awesome-typescript-loader": "3.4.0",
    "bootstrap": "3.3.7",
    "css": "2.2.1",
    "css-loader": "0.28.7",
    "es6-shim": "0.35.3",
    "event-source-polyfill": "0.0.9",
    "expose-loader": "0.7.3",
    "extract-text-webpack-plugin": "2.1.2",
    "file-loader": "1.1.5",
    "html-loader": "0.5.1",
    "isomorphic-fetch": "2.2.1",
    "jquery": "3.2.1",
    "json-loader": "0.5.7",
    "preboot": "5.1.7",
    "raw-loader": "0.5.1",
    "reflect-metadata": "0.1.10",
    "rxjs": "5.5.2",
    "style-loader": "0.19.0",
    "to-string-loader": "1.1.5",
    "es6-shim": "0.35.3",
    "typescript": "2.4.2",
    "url-loader": "0.6.2",
    "webpack": "2.6.1",
    "webpack-hot-middleware": "2.20.0",
    "webpack-merge": "4.1.1",
    "zone.js": "0.8.12"
  },
  "devDependencies": {
    "@types/chai": "4.0.1",
    "@types/jasmine": "2.5.53",
    "chai": "4.0.2",
    "jasmine-core": "2.6.4",
    "karma": "1.7.0",
    "karma-chai": "0.1.0",
    "karma-chrome-launcher": "2.2.0",
    "karma-cli": "1.0.1",
    "karma-jasmine": "1.1.0",
    "karma-webpack": "2.0.3"
  }
}
```

It's advisable to perform a manual *command-line* `npm update` from the project's root folder right after applying these changes to the `package.json` file, in order to trigger a batch update of all the project's NPM packages: sometimes Visual Studio doesn't update the packages automatically and doing that using the GUI can be tricky.

For this very reason, a convenient `update-npm.bat` batch file has been added to this book's source code repository on GitHub to handle that-- without manually having to type the above command.

For further reference and/or future updates, please also check the updated source code within this book's official GitHub repository, which will always contain the latest improvements, bug fixes, compatibility fixes and so on.

The tsconfig.json file

The `tsconfig.json` file is the **TypeScript** configuration file. Again, those who already know what TypeScript is won't need to read all this, although the others should most likely stay.

In less than 100 words, TypeScript is a free, open source programming language developed and maintained by Microsoft that acts as a JavaScript superset; this means that any JavaScript program is also a valid TypeScript program. TypeScript also compiles to JavaScript, so it can seamlessly work on any JS-compatible browser without external components. The main reason to use it is to overcome the syntax limitations and overall shortcomings of JavaScript when developing large-scale applications or complex projects: in very short terms, to ease the developer's life when he's forced to deal with non-trivial JavaScript code.

In this project, we will definitely use **TypeScript** for a number of good reasons; the most important ones of them are as follows:

- TypeScript has a number of features over JavaScript, such as static typing, classes, and interfaces. Using it in Visual Studio also gives us the chance to benefit from the *built-in* IntelliSense, which is a great benefit and often leads to a remarkable productivity burst.
- For a large *client-side* project, TypeScript will allow us to produce a more robust code, which will also be fully deployable anywhere a plain JavaScript file would run.

Not to mention the fact that the Angular SPA template we chose is using it, hence we can say that we got a leg in that boat already!

Jokes aside, we're not the only ones praising TypeScript; it's something acknowledged by the Angular team itself, considering the fact that *the Angular source code has been written using TypeScript since Angular 2,* as proudly announced by Microsoft in the following MDSN blog post in March 2015:

```
https://blogs.msdn.microsoft.com/typescript/2015/03/05/angular-2-built-on-types
cript/
```

It was further emphasized by this great post by *Victor Savkin* (co-founder of Narwhal Technologies and acknowledged Angular consultant) on his personal blog in October 2016:

```
https://vsavkin.com/writing-angular-2-in-typescript-1fa77c78d8e8
```

Getting back to the `tsconfig.json` file, there's not much to say; the option values used by the Angular SPA Template are more or less what we need to configure both Visual Studio and **TSC** (the TypeScript compiler) to properly transpile the TS code files included in the `/ClientApp/` folder: however, while we're here, we can take the chance to tweak them a little more:

```json
{
  "compilerOptions": {
    "module": "es2015",
    "moduleResolution": "node",
    "target": "es5",
    "sourceMap": true,
    "experimentalDecorators": true,
    "emitDecoratorMetadata": true,
    "skipDefaultLibCheck": true,
    "skipLibCheck": true,
    "strict": true,
    "lib": [ "es6", "dom" ],
    "types": [ "webpack-env" ]
  },
  "exclude": [ "bin", "node_modules" ],
  "atom": { "rewriteTsconfig": false },
  "angularCompilerOptions": {
    "strictMetadataEmit": true
  }
}
```

The interesting stuff here is the `angularCompilerOptions` object, which can be used to configure the behavior of the Angular AoT compiler: the **strictMetadataEmit** setting which we added will tell the compiler to report syntax errors immediately rather than produce an error log file.

For more info regarding the new Angular AoT compiler, read the following URL: `https://angular.io/guide/aot-compiler`

The webpack configuration files

Last but not least we must spend some words on the `webpack.config.js` and `webpack.config.vendor.js` files, which play the most important role for the *client-side* components of our project because of the insane amount of tasks they take care of. Let's start with the usual question: what is **Webpack** to begin with? Those who know can move forward; as for the others, keep reading.

In short, **Webpack** is the most used--and arguably the most powerful nowadays--module bundler for modern JavaScript applications. Its main job is to recursively build a *dependency graph* of all the NPM modules needed by the *client-side* application *before* starting it, package them all into a small number of bundles--often only one--and then feed them (or it) to the browser.

The benefits brought to the developer by this revolutionary approach are simply too many and too great to be summarized in a short paragraph like this, as they will require too much space to be properly explained. We'll just scratch the surface by mentioning the most important ones:

- **Dramatically reduces the HTTP requests** to load the *client-side* assets in normal scenarios, that is, when no package managers, task runners, or concatenation strategies are being used
- **Dramatically reduces the chance of variable conflicts** when using standard concatenation strategies such as the `.concat().uglify().writeTo()` chains featured by **Gulp**, **Grunt**, and the likes
- **Dramatically increases the control over static files**, as it can be configured to skip all the "dead" JS/CSS and even image (!) assets, reduce/optimize the size of CSS files even before minifying them, easily switch between CDNs URLs and locally hosted files, and so on

All these good things are real, as long as the tool is properly configured, which brings us to the only real bad thing about Webpack; it's not easy to set it up properly, especially for a newcomer, for a number of good reasons--the documentation has been greatly improved within the past 2 years, yet it's still not as good as other projects; the configuration file is quite hard to read and the syntax might be quite confusing at times.

Luckily enough, despite the steep learning curve, there's a gigantic amount of established examples, boilerplate projects, and code snippets available through the web that can be easily adapted to be used within most projects. The Angular SPA Template we've chosen is no exception, as it comes with two great configuration files - `webpack.config.js` and `webpack.config.vendor.js` - that already do all we need: the former one will be used to construct the bundle containing the application code, while the latter will bundle all the required vendor dependencies.

If we open them, we can see how they're both set up to build three main configuration objects:

- The `sharedConfig` object for the assets that will be used within either the *client-side* and *server-side* bundles
- The `clientBundleConfig` object used to bundle together the *client-side* assets for running-in browsers
- The `serverBundleConfig` object used to bundle together the *server-side* (prerendering) assets

The former section acts as a prerequisite bundle that gets merged with the other two before they are deployed within the `/wwwroot/` folder.

> If you want to know more about Webpack, we strongly suggest you to take a look at the official documentation, available at `https://webpack.js.org/`.

> Also, it's worth noting that Webpack v2.x introduced a built-in validator for the config files that will greatly help the developer to track most coding errors; this new feature is extremely handy for those who want to update/improve the existing configuration files.

> For specific instruction on how to properly set up Webpack for Angular, it's also advisable to read the `https://angular.io/docs/ts/latest/guide/webpack.html` article from the official Angular documentation.

Do you remember the `UseWebpackDevMiddleware()` method we found in the `Startup.cs` file a short while ago? Now that we shed some light on **Webpack**, we can bring back the topic and easily explain what it was.

That middleware, only available when the web application is running in *development* mode, will intercept any request that will match files built by Webpack, dynamically build those files on demand and serve them to the browser without writing them to disk. Basically, it will act as an *in-memory* webhook.

Needless to say, such behavior will bring some benefits during development, such as these:

- **No need to run Webpack manually or set up file watchers**: If you've been using task runners, you know how difficult it can be to have these always up in terms of resources
- **The browser will always receive up-to-date built output**: No more outdated code due to caching issues or watchers not being up
- **Overall speed increase** (at least arguably): The built artifacts *should* be served extremely quickly since the active Webpack instance should keep their partial compilation states already cached in memory

 For further information regarding the **Webpack Dev Middleware**, we suggest you to read the official documentation on the `Microsoft.AspNetCore.SpaServices` GitHub repository, available at `https://github.com/aspnet/JavaScriptServices/tree/dev/src/Microsoft.AspNetCore.SpaServices#webpack-dev-middleware`.

Updating the webpack.config.js file

Switching from Angular 4 to Angular 5 requires to perform a manual update to the `webpack.config.js` file to replace the previous `AotPlugin` to the new `AngularCompilerPlugin`: both of them are Webpack plugins that perform an AoT compilation of Angular components and modules. The former has been used since Angular 2 and up to Angular 4, while the latter has been released to work with Angular 5.

Open the `webpack.config.js` file with the Visual Studio editor and update line 4 in the following way (updated code highlighted):

```
const AotPlugin = require('@ngtools/webpack').AngularCompilerPlugin;
```

Right after that, scroll down to the `sharedConfig : module : rules` section and replace the simple `test: /\.ts$/` rule with the following one:

```
[...]

module: {
    rules: [
        { test: /(?:\.ngfactory\.js|\.ngstyle\.js|\.ts)$/, [...]

[...]
```

At the time of writing these steps are required because the template package still built around Angular 4 and `AotPlugin`. However, this will most likely change in the near future: if the `AngularCompilerPlugin` is already present in the `webpack.config.js` file we can skip this paragraph and go ahead.

Patching the webpack.config.vendor.js file

Before going further, the `webpack.config.vendor.js` file needs to be updated as well in order to fix a nasty bug that would prevent it from working as expected with Angular 5. Open that file and add the following line to the already existing `sharedConfig.plugin` array in the following way (new line highlighted):

```
[...]

plugins: [
    new webpack.ProvidePlugin({ $: 'jquery', jQuery: 'jquery' }), // Maps
these identifiers to the jQuery package (because Bootstrap expects it to be
a global variable)
    new webpack.ContextReplacementPlugin(/\@angular\b.*\b(bundles|linker)/,
path.join(__dirname, './ClientApp')), // Workaround for
https://github.com/angular/angular/issues/11580
    new
webpack.ContextReplacementPlugin(/angular(\\|\/)core(\\|\/)@angular/,
path.join(__dirname, './ClientApp')), // Workaround for
https://github.com/angular/angular/issues/14898
    new webpack.ContextReplacementPlugin(/\@angular(\\|\/)core(\\|\/)esm5/,
path.join(__dirname, './ClientApp')), // Workaround for
https://github.com/angular/angular/issues/20357
    new webpack.IgnorePlugin(/^vertx$/) // Workaround for
https://github.com/stefanpenner/es6-promise/issues/100
]

[...]
```

For further info regarding this fix, you can refer to the relevant GitHub issue at the following URL: https://github.com/angular/angular/issues/20357

At the time of writing, this patch has to be done manually; however, it's more than likely that it will be included in a future release of the template package, together with the other GitHub issues already present. Needless to say, if that's the case we can skip this paragraph and go ahead.

Why use a dynamic module bundler?

Before moving ahead, it can be useful to explain why we just did so much hard work with a dynamic module packer/bundler such as **Webpack** instead of dropping a bunch of links pointing to all the relevant JS files--either hosted locally or, even better, through a high-performance CDN--right from the beginning.

To keep it simple, we did that because it's the only way to efficiently handle any modern JavaScript modular system such as `Angular`, `RxJS`, and also all applications based upon them, including the one we're working on right now.

What's a modular system exactly? It's nothing more than a package, library, or application split into a series of smaller files depending on each other using reference statements such as `import` and `require`. ASP.NET, Java, Python, and most compilation-based languages have it; that's not the case of script-based languages such as PHP and JavaScript, which are doomed to preload everything in memory before being able to determine whenever they'll be using it or not. All these change with the introduction of **ECMAScript 6** (also known as **ES6**), which brings a full-featured module and dependency management solution for JavaScript.

Module bundlers such as **Webpack** pack a number of relevant JS/CSS resources at build time, including most ES6-polyfills for browsers that don't support it already, allowing us to get that module system working in modern browsers. Since both Angular and `RxJS` leverage such an approach, implementing it within our project will result in a huge performance gain.

We chose **Webpack** over other module packers, bundlers, and/or loaders (such as **SystemJS**) because of its great flexibility, as it provides a great way to properly package our application (concat, uglify, and the likes) with the additional knowledge given by its *dependency graph*. Additionally, **Webpack** received a great level of support in .NET Core 2, thanks to the introduction of the **Microsoft ASP.NET Core JavaScript Services** project and the **Webpack Middleware**, as we've already seen in this paragraph, making it the most logical choice when developing with .NET Core and Angular.

Refreshing the Webpack-generated files

To force Webpack to re-compile the vendor configuration file taking into account the fix we applied early on, we need to run the following command-line instruction from the project's root folder:

```
> node node_modules/webpack/bin/webpack.js --config
webpack.config.vendor.js
```

A convenient `update-webpack.bat` batch file has been added to this book's source code repository on GitHub to handle that--without manually having to type the above command.

Alternatively, we can also delete the `/wwwroot/dist/` folder to force a full re-compilation upon the first project build.

It's generally wise to recompile the vendor configuration file everytime whenever we perform a task that could impact the generated bundles, such as: update the `package.json` file, perform a manual `npm update` from the command-line, alter the `webpack.config.js` configuration file, and so on.

The server-side code

Now that we've understood the meaning of the root configuration files, we can take a look at the *Server-Side* code shipped with the Angular SPA Template. As we already saw, we're talking about the contents of the `/Controllers/` and `/Views/` folders; let's start with the former.

Controllers/HomeController.cs

If we remember what we've seen within the `Startup.cs` file, we already know that it is the controller that all the requests not pointing to static files will be routed to. In other words, **HomeController** will handle all the requests that point (or get redirected to) our *Single-Page Application* first landing page, which we'll call **Home View** from now on.

More specifically, these requests will be handled by the `Index` action method. If we open the `HomeController.cs` file, we can see that the method does indeed exist, although being extremely lightweight--a single line of code that just returns the default **Index** View. That's more than enough; there's nothing to add there, as this is precisely what we need for a *Single-Page Application* entry page--just serve the **Home View** and let the *client-side* framework, Angular via Webpack, in our scenario, handle the rest.

The only exception for such behavior will be when we need to route the user away from the SPA, for example, when he's hitting an unrecoverable error. For these kinds of scenarios, an `Error()` action method was also implemented within the **HomeController**, which returns a dedicated **Error** View; however, before doing that, it will add some basic debug information to the **ViewData** collection (the current request unique identifier). This level of error handling is far from ideal, but we can live with it for the time being.

Controllers/SampleDataController.cs

The **HomeController** is a perfect example of a standard MVC Controller returning **Views**; conversely, the SampleDataController.cs is only returning structured JSON data, thus making it conceptually closer to the **APIControllers** featured by the ASP.NET Web API framework. Luckily enough, the new MVC 6 merged the best of both worlds into one, which means that there's no difference between these two kinds of controllers anymore; we're free to return any content we want from within the same controller class.

That said, there's no need to dig much into this controller's code for now; we'll do that soon enough, starting from Chapter 2, *Backend with .NET Core*. Let's just take a look at the resulting JSON data by issuing a couple of requests.

Start the application in *debug* mode by clicking on the **Run** button or pressing the *F5* keyboard key; then, replace the /home part of the address bar URL with /api/SampleData/WeatherForecasts. The full URL should be just like the following:

http://localhost:<port>/api/SampleData/WeatherForecasts

We should be able to see something like this:

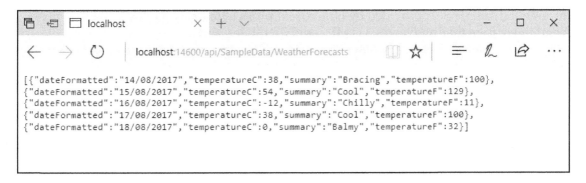

These are the raw (sample) data elements coming out from the server. Now, point the URL back to /home, which will bring us back to the **Home View**. From there, click on the **Fetch data** link from the left menu to get the following:

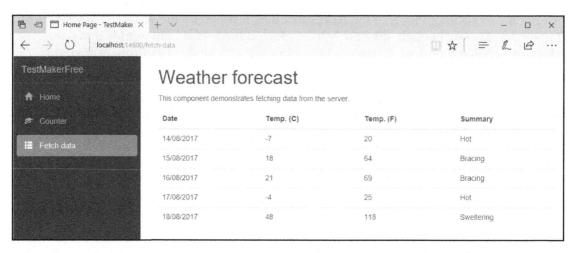

These are the same data elements mentioned earlier, fetched and served by Angular through the sample SPA provided by our current project template. All the GUI elements-- menu links, page title, and labels, HTML code, CSS styles, and so on--are inside the /ClientApp/ folder; the *server-side* code only provides the raw data, just like it's meant to be.

The /Views/ folder

A quick look at the /Views/ folder is more than enough, as the view files merely contain the least possible amount of required code:

- A minimalistic HTML5 skeleton to host the <head> and <body> elements, along with some child elements, such as the <title> page
- Some <script> and <link> elements pointing to the local paths where the **Webpack** bundles will be built
- The <app> element, which is the DOM placeholder used by Angular to inject the SPA into

Those who are used to the ASP.NET MVC and Razor convention can easily see how the template did a good job in putting all the common HTML structure in the **Layout** view (the _Layout.cshtml file), leaving the **Index** and **Error** views as lightweight as possible. The result is stunning and also very easy to read--the whole HTML base structure is comprised within a few lines of Razor and HTML code.

The client-side code

Last but not least, let's pay a visit to the sample Angular app and see how it works. Rest assured, we won't stay for long; we just want to take a glimpse of what's under the hood.

By expanding the /ClientApp/ directory, we can see that there are three subfolders and two files. However, the only thing that we should take into consideration, for the time being, is the /ClientApp/app/ folder, along with all its subfolders; this is the place containing all the Angular TypeScript files. In other words, the whole source code of our *client-side* application is meant to be put here.

Before going there, let's spend a couple words on its siblings:

- The /ClientApp/dist/ folder and the boot.server.ts file are both used by **Webpack** to build the server bundles that will be used to enable the **Angular Universal**'s *Server-Side Rendering* (SSR), which has been adopted and implemented by .NET Core 2.0 within the **Microsoft ASP.NET Core JavaScript Services** package. We'll get back to it later on; however, we can safely ignore them both for now.
- The /Client/test/ folder is where we'll put our unit tests; we can entirely skip it for now and get back once we're ready.
- The boot.browser.ts file contains the first code that will be executed by the browser, thus acting as the *client-side* bootstrapper of our Angular application; if we open it and take a look at the code, we can see how it imports the required packages to perform the bootstrap--including the AppModule from the /ClientApp/app/ folder--and then perform the app initialization within the <app> HTML element, also using different behaviors for *development* and *production*. Although it plays a very important role, we won't need to change its contents for a while; hence it's better to leave it as it is for now and focus on the application source code instead.

If you're curious about **Angular Universal** and **Server-Side Rendering** and want to know more about them, we strongly suggest you to start with reading this good article by *Burak Tasci*:

```
https://medium.com/burak-tasci/angular-4-with-server-side-
rendering-aka-angular-universal-f6c228ded8b0
```

Although not diving deep into these concepts, it does a good job of explaining the core concept of this innovative approach. As soon as you get the basics, you can take a look at the real deal here:

```
https://universal.angular.io/
https://github.com/aspnet/JavaScriptServices
```

The /ClientApp/app/ folder

The `/ClientApp/app/` folder loosely follows the Angular folder structure best practices, thus containing the following:

- A `/component/` folder, containing all the Angular components. We will talk more about them in Chapter 3, *Frontend with Angular*; for now, we'll just say that these are the building UI blocks of any Angular application, to the point that we can say that it is basically a tree of **components** working together. Each component has its very own namespace, which is represented with a subfolder, and comes with the following:
    - A *required* TypeScript file, which follows the `<componentName>.component.ts` naming conventions
    - An *optional* HTML file containing the component template, or (in other words) its UI layout structure
    - An *optional* CSS file to handle the UI styling
    - Other *optional* files, such as the `counter.component.spec.ts` in the `/components/counter/` folder, which can be used whenever we need to split the component code into multiple files for readability or code reuse purposes
- Three TypeScript files: `app.module.browser.ts`, `app.module.server.ts`, and `app.module.shared.ts` containing the Angular root module class, also known as the `AppModule`.

If you already have some Angular experience, you most likely know what the `AppModule` is and how it works. If you don't, the only thing you need to understand is that it serves as the main application entry point, the one that gets bootstrapped by the boot file(s) we talked about earlier.

Here's a schema of the standard **Angular Initialization Cycle** that will help us better visualize how it works:

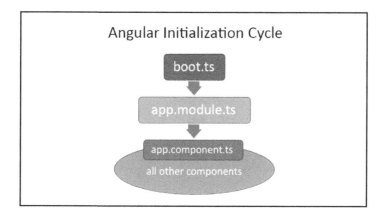

As we can see, the `boot.ts` file bootstraps the `app.module.ts` (**AppModule**), which then loads the `app.component.ts` file (**AppComponent**); the latter will then load all the other components whenever the application needs them.

We can find such structure in any Angular application, it being the default initialization behavior enforced by the `Angular.io` project developers. However, the Angular SPA template we've chosen features a slightly more complex scenario because, as we said earlier, it also supports **Server-Side Rendering**; for this very reason, it needs to take care of the *server-side* part as well. This is why we got two very different boot files --`boot.browser.ts` and `boot.server.ts`, respectively--to load our app into the browser and to support **Server-Side Rendering**, and also two different `AppModule` classes to boot: the `app.module.browser.ts` and `app.module.server.ts`, both of them including the common `app.module.shared.ts` file.

Here's the improved schema when using **SSR**:

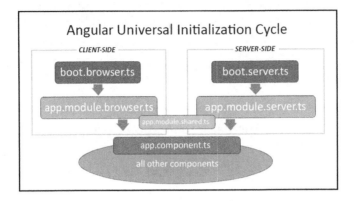

All these files will then be processed by **Webpack** and built in the /wwwroot/dist/main-client.js and /ClientApp/dist/main-server.js files, which will contain the "bundled" version of our Angular app, respectively, for *Client-Side* and *Server-Side* rendering.

That's about it, at least for now. If you feel like you're still missing something here, don't worry, we'll be back there soon enough to understand all of this better.

Getting to work

Now that we've got a general picture of our new project, it's time to do something. Let's start with two simple exercises that will also come handy in the future: the first one of them will involve the *server-side* aspects of our application, while the latter will be performed on the *client-side*. Both will help us acknowledge whether we really understood everything there is to know before proceeding to the subsequent chapters.

Static file caching

Let's start with the *server-side* task. Do you remember the /wwwroot/test.html file we added when we wanted to check how the StaticFiles middleware works? We will use it to do a quick demonstration of how our application will internally cache static files.

The first thing we have to do is to run the application in debug mode (by clicking on the **Run** button or pressing the *F5* key) and put the following URL in the address line, so we can have another good look at it.

Right after that, without stopping the application, open the `test.html` file and add the following lines to its existing content (new lines are highlighted):

```
<!DOCTYPE html>
<html>
<head>
    <meta charset="utf-8" />
    <title>Time for a test!</title>
</head>
<body>
    Hello there!
    <br /><br />
    This is a test to see if the StaticFiles middleware is working
properly.
    <br /><br />
    IT DOES, BUT THE FILES ARE CACHED ON CLIENTS BY DEFAULT!
</body>
</html>
```

Save the file, then go back to the browser address bar and press *Enter* again to issue another HTTP request to the `test.html` file. Ensure that you don't use *F5* or the refresh button, as it will force a page refresh from the server, which is not what we want; you will see that the preceding changes won't be reflected by your browser, which means that you hit a *client-cached* version of that page.

Caching static files on the clients can be a good thing in production servers, but is definitely annoying during development. Luckily enough, as we said earlier, the **Webpack** middleware will automatically fix this issue for all the TypeScript files, and also for all the static assets we'll serve through Webpack itself. However, what about the other ones? We'll most likely have some static HTML files, favicons, image files, audio files, or anything else that we would like to be directly served by the web server.

Is there a way to *fine-tune* the caching behavior for static files? If so, can we also set up different behaviors for the debug/development and release/production scenarios?

The answer is yes for both questions; let's see how we can do that.

A blast from the past

Back in ASP.NET 4, we could easily disable static files caching by adding some lines to our main application's `Web.config` file, such as the following:

```
<caching enabled="false" />
<staticContent>
  <clientCache cacheControlMode="DisableCache" />
```

```
  </staticContent>
  <httpProtocol>
    <customHeaders>
      <add name="Cache-Control" value="no-cache, no-store" />
      <add name="Pragma" value="no-cache" />
      <add name="Expires" value="-1" />
    </customHeaders>
  </httpProtocol>
```

That would be it; we can even restrict such behavior to the *debug* environment by adding these lines to the Web.debug.config file.

We can't use the same approach in .NET Core, as the configuration system has been redesigned from scratch and is now quite different from the previous versions; as we said earlier, the Web.config and Web.debug.config files have been replaced by the appsettings.json and appsettings.Development.json files, which also work in a completely different way. Now that we understood the basics, let's see whether we can solve that caching issue by taking advantage of the new configuration model.

Back to the future

The first thing to do is to understand how we can modify the default HTTP headers for static files; as a matter of fact, we can do that by adding a custom set of options to the app.UseDefaultFiles() method call in the Startup.cs file that adds the StaticFiles middleware to the HTTP request pipeline.

In order to do that, open Startup.cs, scroll down to the Configure method, and replace that single line with the following code (new/modified lines are highlighted):

```
app.UseStaticFiles(new StaticFileOptions()
{
    OnPrepareResponse = (context) =>
    {
        // Disable caching for all static files.
        context.Context.Response.Headers["Cache-Control"] = "no-cache,
         no-store";
        context.Context.Response.Headers["Pragma"] = "no-cache";
        context.Context.Response.Headers["Expires"] = "-1";
    }
});
```

That wasn't hard at all; we just added some additional configuration values to the method call, wrapping them all within a dedicated `StaticFileOptions` object instance.

However, we're not done yet; now that we learned how to change the default behavior, we just need to change these static values with some convenient references pointing to the `appsettings.Development.json` file. To do that, we can add the following *key/value* section to the `appsettings.Development.json` file in the following way (new lines highlighted):

```
{
  "Logging": {
    "IncludeScopes": false,
    "Debug": {
      "LogLevel": {
        "Default": "Debug",
        "System": "Information",
        "Microsoft": "Information"
      }
    },
    "Console": {
      "LogLevel": {
        "Default": "Debug",
        "System": "Information",
        "Microsoft": "Information"
      }
    }
  },
  "StaticFiles": {
    "Headers": {
      "Cache-Control": "no-cache, no-store",
      "Pragma": "no-cache",
      "Expires": "-1"
    }
  }
}
```

Then, change the preceding `Startup.cs` code accordingly (modified lines highlighted):

```
app.UseStaticFiles(new StaticFileOptions()
{
    OnPrepareResponse = (context) =>
    {
        // Disable caching for all static files.
        context.Context.Response.Headers["Cache-Control"] =
            Configuration["StaticFiles:Headers:Cache-Control"];
        context.Context.Response.Headers["Pragma"] =
            Configuration["StaticFiles:Headers:Pragma"];
```

```
            context.Context.Response.Headers["Expires"] =
                Configuration["StaticFiles:Headers:Expires"];
        }
    });
```

Ensure that you add these values to the non-development version of the `appsettings.json` file as well, otherwise the application won't find them (when executed outside a development environment) and throw an error.

Since this will most likely happen in a production environment, we can take the chance to relax these caching policies a bit:

```
{
  "Logging": {
    "IncludeScopes": false,
    "Debug": {
      "LogLevel": {
        "Default": "Warning"
      }
    },
    "Console": {
      "LogLevel": {
        "Default": "Warning"
      }
    }
  },
  "StaticFiles": {
    "Headers": {
      "Cache-Control": "max-age=3600",
      "Pragma": "cache",
      "Expires": null
    }
  }
}
```

That's about it. Learning how to use this pattern is strongly advisable, as it's a great and effective way to properly configure our application's settings.

Testing it up

Let's see whether our new caching strategy is working as expected. Run the application in *debug* mode, and then issue a request to the `test.html` page by typing the following URL in the browser address bar:

```
http://localhost:<port>/test.html
```

We should be able to see the updated contents with the phrase we wrote earlier; if not, press *F5* from the browser to force a page retrieval from the server:

Now, without stopping the application, edit the `test.html` page and update its contents in the following way (updated lines are highlighted):

```html
<!DOCTYPE html>
<html>
<head>
    <meta charset="utf-8" />
    <title>Time for a test!</title>
</head>
<body>
    Hello there!
    <br /><br />
    This is a test to see if the StaticFiles middleware is working
     properly.
    <br /><br />
    It seems like it works, and now it doesn't even cache those files!
</body>
</html>
```

Right after that, go back to the browser, select the address bar, and press *Enter*; again, ensure that you did not press the refresh button or the *F5* key, or you'll have to start over. If everything worked properly, we will immediately see the updated contents on screen:

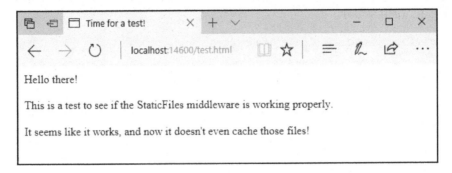

We did it! Our *server-side* task was successfully completed.

The strongly-typed approach(es)

The approach that we chose to retrieve the `appsettings.json` configuration values makes use of the generic **IConfiguration** object, which can be queried using the preceding string-based syntax. This approach is rather practical; however, if we want to retrieve this data in a more robust way, for example, in a *strongly-typed* fashion, we can--and *should*--implement something better. Although we won't dive deeper into that within this book, we can suggest reading the following great articles showing three different approaches to achieve this result:

The first one, written by *Rick Strahl*, explains how to do that using the `IOptions<T>` provider interface:

`https://weblog.west-wind.com/posts/2016/may/23/strongly-typed-configuration-settings-in-aspnet-core`

The second, by *Filip W*, explains how to do that with a simple `POCO` class, thus avoiding the `IOptions<T>` interface and the extra dependencies required by the preceding approach:

`https://www.strathweb.com/2016/09/strongly-typed-configuration-in-asp-net-core-without-ioptionst/`

The third, by *Khalid Abuhakmeh*, shows an alternative way to use a standard POCO class and directly register it as a `Singleton` with the `ServicesCollection`, while also (optionally) shielding it from unwanted modifications due to development mistakes:

```
https://rimdev.io/strongly-typed-configuration-settings-in-asp-net-core-part-ii/
```

All of these approaches were meant to work with .NET Core 1.x; however, they can still be very usable in .NET Core 2. That said, if we were to choose, we would probably go with the latter, as we found it to be the most clean and clever one.

Client app cleanup

Now that our *server-side* journey has come to an end, it's time to challenge ourselves with a quick *client-side* exercise. Don't worry, it will be just a rather trivial demonstration of how we can update the Angular source code that lies within the `/ClientApp/` folder to better suit our needs. More specifically, we will remove all the stuff we don't need from the sample Angular app shipped with our chosen Angular SPA Template and replace them with our own content.

 We'll never say it enough, so it's worth repeating it again. The sample source code explained in the following paragraphs is taken from the **MVC ASP.NET Core with Angular** project template originally shipped with Visual Studio 2017 v15.3; since it might be updated in the future, it's important to check it against the code published in this book's GitHub repo. If you find relevant differences between the book code and yours, feel free to get the one from the repository and use that instead.

Trimming down the component list

If we navigate through the `/ClientApp/app/components/` folder, we can take another close look at the components that are currently in place:

- The `/app/` folder contains the files related to the `AppComponent`, which is the main application component file; it's the one in charge to dynamically load all the other components, hence we definitely want to keep it.
- The `/home/` folder contains the files related to `HomeComponent`, which hosts the *Home View* contents. Do you remember the introductory text shown on the browser when we run the project? This is where we can find (and update) it. Our SPA will most likely need a home as well, so it's better to keep it too.

- The /navmenu/ folder contains the files related to NavMenuComponent, which handles the layout and the functionalities of the navigation menu to the left. Even if we will make a lot of changes to this menu, keeping it as a working base would be a good idea.

The /counter/ and /fetchdata/ folders contain two sample components, which demonstrate how to implement two very common Angular features: respectively, affect the DOM in real time and fetch data from the web server. Although they can still use them as valuable code samples, keeping them within our client code will eventually confuse us, hence it's better to move these two folders outside the project - or just entirely delete them - to prevent the Visual Studio TypeScript compiler from messing with the .ts files contained there.

However, as soon as we do that, the Visual Studio **Error List** view will immediately raise two blocking TypeScript-based issues:

```
Error TS2307 (TS) Cannot find module
'./components/fetchdata/fetchdata.component'.
Error TS2307 (TS) Cannot find module
'./components/counter/counter.component'.
```

Both errors will point to the app.module.shared.ts file, which, as we already know, contains the references of all the TypeScript files used by our Angular application and required by either the client (for browser rendering) and the server (to enable server-side rendering). If we open the file, we can clearly see where the problem is:

```
app.module.shared.ts

TestMakerFreeWebApp_Chapter_01 (tsconfig project)          {} "app.module.shared"

1   import { NgModule } from '@angular/core';
2   import { CommonModule } from '@angular/common';
3   import { FormsModule } from '@angular/forms';
4   import { HttpModule } from '@angular/http';
5   import { RouterModule } from '@angular/router';
6
7   import { AppComponent } from './components/app/app.component';
8   import { NavMenuComponent } from './components/navmenu/navmenu.component';
9   import { HomeComponent } from './components/home/home.component';
10  import { FetchDataComponent } from './components/fetchdata/fetchdata.component';
11  import { CounterComponent } from './components/counter/counter.component';
12
```

To fix it, we need to remove the offending references. However, when we do that, the following **TypeScript** errors will be raised:

```
Error TS2304 (TS) Cannot find name 'CounterComponent'.
Error TS2304 (TS) Cannot find name 'FetchDataComponent'.
Error TS2304 (TS) Cannot find name 'CounterComponent'.
Error TS2304 (TS) Cannot find name 'FetchDataComponent'.
```

All these issues will also point to the `app.module.shared.ts` file, which now has four names without a valid reference:

Remove all the four lines containing the errors to fix them.

Once done, our updated `AppModuleShared` file should look like this:

```
import { NgModule } from '@angular/core';
import { CommonModule } from '@angular/common';
import { FormsModule } from '@angular/forms';
import { HttpModule } from '@angular/http';
import { RouterModule } from '@angular/router';
```

```
import { AppComponent } from './components/app/app.component';
import { NavMenuComponent } from './components/navmenu/navmenu.component';
import { HomeComponent } from './components/home/home.component';

@NgModule({
    declarations: [
        AppComponent,
        NavMenuComponent,
        HomeComponent
    ],
    imports: [
        CommonModule,
        HttpModule,
        FormsModule,
        RouterModule.forRoot([
            { path: '', redirectTo: 'home', pathMatch: 'full' },
            { path: 'home', component: HomeComponent },
            { path: '**', redirectTo: 'home' }
        ])
    ]
})
export class AppModuleShared {
}
```

Since we're here, those who don't know how Angular works should spend a couple of minutes to understand how an `AppModule` class actually works. We already know why we got three files instead of one--to allow **SSR**--but we never talked about the source code.

The AppModule class(es)

Angular **Modules**, also known as **NgModules**, have been introduced in Angular 2 RC5 and are a great and powerful way to organize and bootstrap any Angular application; they help developers consolidate their own set of **components**, **directives**, and **pipes** into *reusable* blocks.

Every Angular application since v2 RC5 must have at least one module, which is conventionally called *root module* and thus given the `AppModule` class name.

`AppModule` is usually split into two main code blocks:

- A list of **import** statements, pointing to all the references (in the form of TS files) required by the application.

- The root `NgModule` declaration, which--as we can see--is basically an array of named arrays, each one containing a set of Angular objects that serves a common purpose: **directives**, **components**, **pipes**, **modules**, **providers**, and so on. The last one of them contains the component we want to bootstrap, which in most scenarios--including ours--is the main application component, the `AppComponent`.

Updating the NavMenu

If we run our project in *debug* mode, we can see that our code changes don't prevent the client app from booting properly. We didn't break it this time, yay! However, if we try to use the navigation menu to go to the **Counter** and/or **Fetch data**, nothing will happen; this is hardly a surprise, since we just moved these components out of the way. To avoid confusion, let's remove these links from the menu as well.

Open the `/ClientApp/app/components/navmenu/navmenu.component.html` file and delete the offending lines. Once done, the updated source code should look as follows:

```
<div class='main-nav'>
    <div class='navbar navbar-inverse'>
        <div class='navbar-header'>
            <button type='button' class='navbar-toggle' data-
              toggle='collapse' data-target='.navbar-collapse'>
                <span class='sr-only'>Toggle navigation</span>
                <span class='icon-bar'></span>
                <span class='icon-bar'></span>
                <span class='icon-bar'></span>
            </button>
            <a class='navbar-brand' [routerLink]="
            ['/home']">TestMakerFree</a>
        </div>
        <div class='clearfix'></div>
        <div class='navbar-collapse collapse'>
            <ul class='nav navbar-nav'>
                <li [routerLinkActive]="['link-active']">
                    <a [routerLink]="['/home']">
                        <span class='glyphicon glyphicon-home'></span>
                            Home
                    </a>
                </li>
            </ul>
        </div>
    </div>
</div>
```

While we're here, let's take the chance to get rid of something else. Do you remember the *Hello, World!* introductory text shown by the browser when we firstly ran the project? Let's change it with our own content.

Open the `/ClientApp/app/components/home/home.component.html` file and replace its whole content with the following:

```
<h1>Greetings, stranger!</h1>
<p>This is what you get for messing up with .NET Core and Angular.</p>
```

Save, run the project in *debug* mode and get ready to see the following:

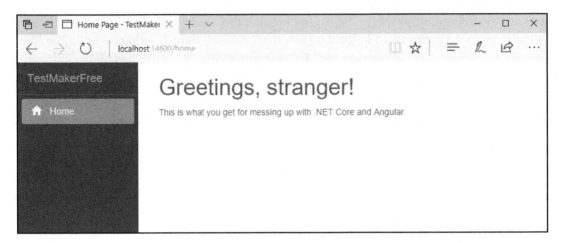

The **Counter** and **Fetch data** menu links are gone, and our **Home View** welcome text couldn't be sleeker.

That's about it for now. Rest assured, we can easily do the same with other components and completely rewrite their text, including the navigation menu; we'll do that in the following chapters, where we'll also update the UI layout, add new components, and so on. For the time being, understanding how easy it is to change the content--and also how fast **Webpack** will handle our modifications--is good enough.

References

- *Native Web Apps, Henrik Joreteg, 2015*
- *Manifesto for Agile Software Development, Kent Beck, Mike Beedle & many others, 2001*

Suggested topics

SCRUM, Extreme Programming, MVC and MVVM architectural patterns, ASP.NET Core, .NET Core, Roslyn, CoreCLR, RyuJIT, Single-Page Application (SPA), NuGet, NPM, ECMAScript 6, Bower, Webpack, SystemJS, RxJS, Cache-Control, HTTP Headers, .NET Middleware, Angular Universal, Server-Side Rendering (SSR).

Summary

So far so good; we just set up a working skeleton of what's about to come. Before moving further, let's do a quick recap of what we just did in this chapter.

We briefly described our platforms of choice--ASP.NET Core and Angular--and acknowledged their combined potential in the process of building a modern web application. Then, we chose a Native Web Application with a Single-Page Application approach as the ideal field of choice for testing what our frameworks are able to do (and how to do it).

In an attempt to reproduce a realistic production-case scenario, we also went through the most common SPA features, first from a technical point of view, and then putting ourselves in the shoes of a typical Product Owner and trying to enumerate their expectations. We also made a quick list of everything we need to put together a potentially shippable product featuring all the expected goodies.

Eventually, we did our best to properly set up our development environment; we chose to do that using the default Angular SPA Template shipped with Visual Studio, thus adopting the standard ASP.NET Core approach. Right after that, we also spent some valuable time to look up and understand its core components, how they're working together, and their distinctive roles: the root configuration files, the *server-side* code, and the *client-side* code.

Finally, we performed some quick tests to see whether we're ready to hold our ground against what's coming next: setting up an improved request-response cycle, building our own Controllers, defining additional routing strategies, and more.

2
Backend with .NET Core

Now that we have our skeleton up and running, it's time to explore the *client-server* interaction capabilities of our frameworks; to put it in other words, we need to understand how Angular will be able to fetch data from .NET Core using its brand new MVC and web API all-in-one structure.

We won't be worrying about how will .NET Core retrieve this data, be it from session objects, data stores, DBMS, or any possible data source; we will come to that later on. For now, we'll just put together some sample, static data in order to understand how to pass them back and forth using a well-structured, highly-configurable, and viable interface, following the same approach used by the **SampleDataController** shipped with the Angular SPA Template that we chose in Chapter 1, *Getting Ready*.

The data flow

As you might already know, a Native Web App following the Single-Page Application approach will roughly handle the client-server communication in the following way:

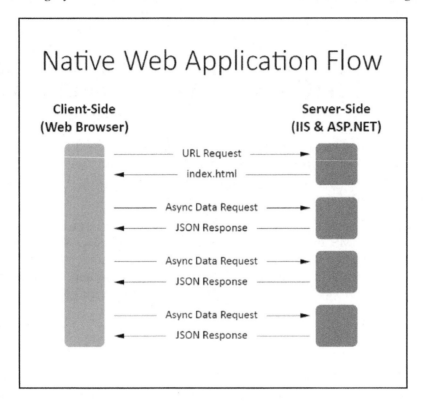

In our specific scenario, the index.html role is covered by the /Views/Index.cshtml view file that is returned by the Index action method within the HomeController; however, the base concept is still the same.

In case you're wondering about what these **Async Data Requests** actually are, the answer is simple--everything, as long as it needs to retrieve data from the server, which is something that most of the common user interactions will normally do, including (yet not limited to) pressing a button to show more data or to edit/delete something, following a link to another action view, submitting a form, and so on. That is, unless the task is so trivial--or it involves a minimal amount of data--that the client can entirely handle it, which means that it already has everything it needs. Examples of such tasks are show/hide element toggles, in-page navigation elements (such as internal anchors), and any temporary job requiring to click on a *confirmation* or *save* button to be pressed before being actually processed.

The preceding picture shows, in a nutshell, what we will do; define and implement a pattern to serve these JSON-based, server-side responses our application will need to handle the upcoming requests. Since we've chosen to develop an application featuring a strongly data-driven application pattern, we'll surely need to put together a bunch of common **CRUD**-based requests revolving around a defined set of objects that will represent our various entries.

 For those who never heard of it, *CRUD* is an acronym for *create*, *read*, *update*, and *delete*, the four basic functions of persistent storage. The term became popular, thanks to James Martin, who mentioned it in his 1983 book *Managing the Database Environment*, and it's commonly used in computer programming contexts since then.

If we consider the master plan we put down in Chapter 1, *Getting Ready*, we can already define most of the entries we will need. We'll definitely have **Quizzes**, which will be the main entities of our application; they will contain one or more **Questions**, each one with a list of **Answers**, and a number of possible **Results**. Eventually, we'll most likely add **Users** to the loop, so we'll be able to implement an authentication/authorization mechanism that will be used by our application to determine who can view/edit/delete what.

For each one of them, we'll develop a set of requests that will address some common tasks such as display a list of entries of the same type, view/edit an entry's data, and delete an entry.

Before moving ahead, let's take a more detailed look at what happens between any of these **Data Requests** issued by the client and **JSON Responses** sent out by the server, that is, what's usually called the **Request/Response flow**:

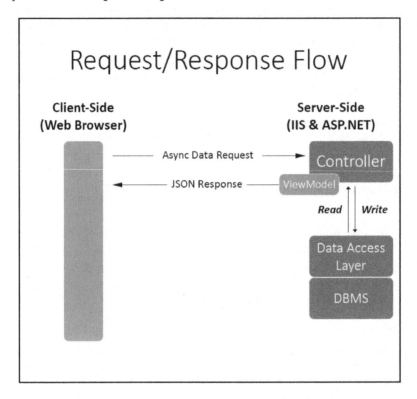

As we can see, in order to respond to any client-issued **Data Request**, we need to set up a *server-side* **Controller** featuring the following capabilities:

- **Read and/or write data** using the *Data Access Layer*
- **Organize these data** in a suitable, JSON-serializable *ViewModel*
- **Serialize the *ViewModel* and send it to the client** as a *Response*

Based on these points, we can easily conclude that the *ViewModel* is the key item here. That's not always correct, it could or couldn't be the case, depending on the project we're building. To better clarify that, before going ahead, we should definitely spend a couple of words on the **ViewModel** object itself.

The role of ViewModel

We all know that a **ViewModel** is a container-type class that represents only the data we want to display on our web page. In any standard MVC-based ASP.NET application, the *ViewModel* is instantiated by the **Controller** in response to a GET request using the data fetched from the **Model**; once built, the *ViewModel* is passed to the **View**, where it's used to populate the page contents/input fields.

The main reason for building a *ViewModel* instead of directly passing the Model entities is that it only represents the data that we want to use, and nothing else; all the unnecessary properties that are in the model domain object will be left out, keeping the data transfer as lightweight as possible. Another advantage is the additional security it gives, since we can protect any field from being serialized and passed through the HTTP channel.

In a standard Web API context, where the data is passed using conventions via serialized formats such as JSON or XML, the *ViewModel* can be easily replaced by a JSON-serializable dynamic object created on the fly, such as this:

```
var response = new {
    Id = "1",
    Title = "The title",
    Description = "The description"
};
```

This approach is often viable for small or sample projects, where creating one (or many) *ViewModel* classes can be a waste of time. That's not our case, though conversely, our project will greatly benefit from having a well-defined, strongly-typed *ViewModel* structure, even if they will all be eventually converted into JSON strings.

Our first ViewModel

Now that we have a clear vision of the request/response flow and its main actors, we can start building something. Our client doesn't even exist yet, but we can easily guess what we need to build it up--a set of CRUD methods for each one of the entries we identified early.

If we already used ASP.NET MVC at least once, we already know that the most straightforward way to do that is to create a dedicated **Controller** for each entry type. However, before adding each one of them, it can be wise to create the corresponding **ViewModel** so that it can handle the entry data in a *strongly-typed* fashion.

QuizViewModel

We might as well start with the flagship entry of our application, which will also be the most relevant and complex one.

Wait a minute, why are we starting with the ViewModel if we don't have a data model in place? Where will we get the data from?

Such questions are anything but trivial and deserve a concise explanation before going further. One of the biggest advantages of building a web application using ASP.NET and Angular is that we can start writing our code without worrying too much about data sources; that will come later, and only after we're sure about what we really need. This is not a requirement either; we're also free to start with our data source for a number of good reasons, such as the following:

- We already have a clear idea of what we'll need
- We already have our entity set(s) and/or a defined/populated data structure to work with
- We're used to starting with the data, then moving to the GUI

All the preceding reasons are perfectly fine; we won't ever get fired for doing that. Yet, the chance to start with the frontend might help us a lot if we're still unsure about how your application will look, either in terms of GUI and/or data. In building this application, we'll take advantage of that; hence, why we will start playing with our **QuizViewModel** even if we don't have its *Data Source* and *Entity* class yet.

From **Solution Explorer**, *right-click* on the **TestMakerFreeWebApp** node (the project's root node) and create a new /ViewModels/ folder; once done, right-click on that newly-added folder and issue the usual **Add** | **New Item** command.

From the **ASP.NET Core** | **Code** treeview node, select a **Class** file, call it QuizViewModel.cs, and click on **OK** to have it added under the /ViewModels/ folder.

Once done, replace the new file's sample contents with the following:

```
using Newtonsoft.Json;
using System;
using System.Collections.Generic;
using System.ComponentModel;
using System.Linq;
using System.Threading.Tasks;

namespace TestMakerFreeWebApp.ViewModels
{
```

```
[JsonObject(MemberSerialization.OptOut)]
public class QuizViewModel
{
    #region Constructor
    public QuizViewModel()
    {

    }
    #endregion

    #region Properties
    public int Id { get; set; }
    public string Title { get; set; }
    public string Description { get; set; }
    public string Text { get; set; }
    public string Notes { get; set; }
    [DefaultValue(0)]
    public int Type { get; set; }
    [DefaultValue(0)]
    public int Flags { get; set; }
    public string UserId { get; set; }
    [JsonIgnore]
    public int ViewCount { get; set; }
    public DateTime CreatedDate { get; set; }
    public DateTime LastModifiedDate { get; set; }
    #endregion

}
}
```

As we can see, this is basically a POCO object with a rather common set of general-purpose properties; our **Quiz** will have a *Title*, a *Description*, and so on. There are still some missing things, such as the aforementioned *Questions*, *Answers*, and *Results*, but these will come later on.

QuizController

Let's move on to **QuizController**:

1. From **Solution Explorer**, open the /Controllers/ folder.
2. Right-click on the folder and select the usual **Add** | **New Item** command.

 Ensure **not** to use the **Add** | **Controller** option available there, as it will activate a wizard-like feature that will also add some dependencies to our project, which is something we definitely don't need (yet).

3. From the **ASP.NET Core** | **Web** treeview node, select **Web API Controller Class**; call the new file `QuizController.cs` and click on **OK** to have it added under the `/Controllers/` folder, along with the already existing `HomeController.cs` and `SampleDataController.cs`, which we reviewed in Chapter 1, *Getting Ready*.

The controller will be created with a bunch of sample methods, which we'll not use. Delete the entire file content and replace it with the following code:

```
using System;
using Microsoft.AspNetCore.Mvc;
using Newtonsoft.Json;
using TestMakerFreeWebApp.ViewModels;
using System.Collections.Generic;

namespace TestMakerFreeWebApp.Controllers
{
    [Route("api/[controller]")]
    public class QuizController : Controller
    {
        // GET api/quiz/latest
        [HttpGet("Latest/{num}")]
        public IActionResult Latest(int num = 10)
        {
            var sampleQuizzes = new List<QuizViewModel>();

            // add a first sample quiz
            sampleQuizzes.Add(new QuizViewModel()
            {
                Id = 1,
                Title = "Which Shingeki No Kyojin character are you?",
                Description = "Anime-related personality test",
                CreatedDate = DateTime.Now,
                LastModifiedDate = DateTime.Now
            });

            // add a bunch of other sample quizzes
            for (int i = 2; i <= num; i++)
            {
                sampleQuizzes.Add(new QuizViewModel()
                {
                    Id = i,
                    Title = String.Format("Sample Quiz {0}", i),
                    Description = "This is a sample quiz",
                    CreatedDate = DateTime.Now,
                    LastModifiedDate = DateTime.Now
                });
```

```
        }

        // output the result in JSON format
        return new JsonResult(
            sampleQuizzes,
            new JsonSerializerSettings()
            {
                Formatting = Formatting.Indented
            });
    }
  }
}
```

Let's take a quick look at the code to see what we've done.

As we can see, we started defining the Latest method accepting a single (optional) *integer* parameter value called num, which defaults to 10. The method accepts any GET request using the custom routing rules configured via the HttpGet attribute. This approach is called **Attribute routing**, and we'll be digging into it further later in this chapter. For now, let's stick to the code inside the method itself.

The behavior is really simple, since we don't (yet) have a *Data Source*; we're basically returning a couple of sample QuizViewModel objects. Note that, although it's just a fake response, we're doing it in a structured and credible way, respecting the number of items issued by the request and also providing different content for each one of them. As a matter of fact, we're basically following the same approach used by the SampleDataController.cs provided by our Visual Studio Angular SPA Template, which we looked up back in Chapter 1, *Getting Ready*.

It's also worth noting that we're using a JsonResult return type, which is the best thing we can do as long as we're working with ViewModel classes featuring the JsonObject attribute provided by the Newtonsoft.Json framework, that's definitely better than returning plain string or IEnumerable<string> types, as it will automatically take care of serializing the outcome and setting the appropriate response headers (*Content-Type, charset*, and so on).

Adding more action methods

Before going further, let's take the chance to implement two more action methods to the QuizController to emulate a couple of different retrieval strategies: getting the quizzes in alphabetical order and in a completely random fashion.

ByTitle()

Go right after the `Latest()` method and add the following code:

```
/// <summary>
/// GET: api/quiz/ByTitle
/// Retrieves the {num} Quizzes sorted by Title (A to Z)
/// </summary>
/// <param name="num">the number of quizzes to retrieve</param>
/// <returns>{num} Quizzes sorted by Title</returns>
[HttpGet("ByTitle/{num:int?}")]
public IActionResult ByTitle(int num = 10)
{
    var sampleQuizzes = ((JsonResult)Latest(num)).Value
        as List<QuizViewModel>;

    return new JsonResult(
        sampleQuizzes.OrderBy(t => t.Title),
        new JsonSerializerSettings()
        {
            Formatting = Formatting.Indented
        });
}
```

As we can see, this internally calls the `Latest()` method itself--which actually just returns some sample quizzes created *on-the-fly*--and outputs them in alphabetical order.

Random()

The same technique can be used to implement the `Random()` method as well:

```
/// <summary>
/// GET: api/quiz/mostViewed
/// Retrieves the {num} random Quizzes
/// </summary>
/// <param name="num">the number of quizzes to retrieve</param>
/// <returns>{num} random Quizzes</returns>
[HttpGet("Random/{num:int?}")]
public IActionResult Random(int num = 10)
{
    var sampleQuizzes = ((JsonResult)Latest(num)).Value
        as List<QuizViewModel>;

    return new JsonResult(
        sampleQuizzes.OrderBy(t => Guid.NewGuid()),
        new JsonSerializerSettings()
        {
            Formatting = Formatting.Indented
```

```
        });
    }
```

Testing it up

Let's try our Controller by running our app in **Debug Mode**; in order to test it, we need to manually type the following URL in the browser's address bar:

```
http://localhost:<port>/api/quiz/latest/3
```

If we did everything correctly, it will show something like this:

Note how the `ViewCount` property is not present in the JSON-serialized output; that's by design, since it has been flagged with the `JsonIgnore` attribute, meaning that we're explicitly opting it out.

Our first **Controller** is up and running. Do not underestimate it! Eventually, it will be in charge of all quiz-related operations within our web application.

Adding other controllers

Now that we know the trick, we can add a bunch of other ViewMode and Controller pairs, one for each entry type we came up with earlier. In order to avoid repetition we'll skip the create file part and jump directly to the source code for each one of them, while also adding some useful hints where we need to.

QuestionViewModel

What will a quiz be without some questions? Here's how we can deal with the `QuestionViewModel.cs` file that we need to add within the `/ViewModels/` folder:

```
using Newtonsoft.Json;
using System;
using System.Collections.Generic;
using System.ComponentModel;
using System.Linq;
using System.Threading.Tasks;

namespace TestMakerFreeWebApp.ViewModels
{
    [JsonObject(MemberSerialization.OptOut)]
    public class QuestionViewModel
    {
        #region Constructor
        public QuestionViewModel()
        {

        }
        #endregion

        #region Properties
        public int Id { get; set; }
        public int QuizId { get; set; }
        public string Text { get; set; }
```

```
    public string Notes { get; set; }
    [DefaultValue(0)]
    public int Type { get; set; }
    [DefaultValue(0)]
    public int Flags { get; set; }
    [JsonIgnore]
    public DateTime CreatedDate { get; set; }
    public DateTime LastModifiedDate { get; set; }
    #endregion
  }
}
```

As we can see, this is quite similar to the QuizViewModel, except that it has slightly different properties; one of these is the QuizId, which is rather obvious since each question will be related to its Quiz in a classic *one-to-many* relationship; each single Quiz will have multiple Questions.

QuestionController

Here's the QuestionController, which we also need to create in the /Controllers/ folder as a .cs file, just like we did with the QuizController:

```
using System;
using Microsoft.AspNetCore.Mvc;
using Newtonsoft.Json;
using TestMakerFreeWebApp.ViewModels;
using System.Collections.Generic;

namespace TestMakerFreeWebApp.Controllers
{
    [Route("api/[controller]")]
    public class QuestionController : Controller
    {
        // GET api/question/all
        [HttpGet("All/{quizId}")]
        public IActionResult All(int quizId)
        {
            var sampleQuestions = new List<QuestionViewModel>();

            // add a first sample question
            sampleQuestions.Add(new QuestionViewModel()
            {
                Id = 1,
                QuizId = quizId,
```

```
                    Text = "What do you value most in your life?",
                    CreatedDate = DateTime.Now,
                    LastModifiedDate = DateTime.Now
            });

            // add a bunch of other sample questions
            for (int i = 2; i <= 5; i++)
            {
                sampleQuestions.Add(new QuestionViewModel()
                {
                    Id = i,
                    QuizId = quizId,
                    Text = String.Format("Sample Question {0}", i),
                    CreatedDate = DateTime.Now,
                    LastModifiedDate = DateTime.Now
                });
            }

            // output the result in JSON format
            return new JsonResult(
                sampleQuestions,
                new JsonSerializerSettings()
                {
                    Formatting = Formatting.Indented
                });
        }
    }
}
```

As we can see, we ditched the `Latest` method we defined in the `QuizController` and replaced it with an `All` method that will give us the chance to retrieve all the questions related to a specific `Quiz`, given its `Id`.

Implementing a `Latest` method will have little sense here, as **Questions** won't have a distinctive meaning on their own. They are only meant to be retrieved--and presented to the user--along with the **Quiz** they're related to; that's why the `All` method makes much more sense.

AnswerViewModel

The `Answers` have with their `Question` the same *one-to-many* relationship that `Questions` have with their `Quiz`, hence the `AnswerViewModel` that we need to add will be quite similar to the `QuestionViewModel`:

```
using Newtonsoft.Json;
using System;
using System.Collections.Generic;
using System.ComponentModel;
using System.Linq;

namespace TestMakerFreeWebApp.ViewModels
{
    [JsonObject(MemberSerialization.OptOut)]
    public class AnswerViewModel
    {
        #region Constructor
        public AnswerViewModel()
        {

        }
        #endregion

        #region Properties
        public int Id { get; set; }
        public int QuizId { get; set; }
        public int QuestionId { get; set; }
        public string Text { get; set; }
        public string Notes { get; set; }
        [DefaultValue(0)]
        public int Type { get; set; }
        [DefaultValue(0)]
        public int Flags { get; set; }
        [DefaultValue(0)]
        public int Value{ get; set; }
        [JsonIgnore]
        public DateTime CreatedDate { get; set; }
        public DateTime LastModifiedDate { get; set; }
        #endregion
    }
}
```

As we can see, there are only two significant differences:

- We added a property, that references the `QuestionId` that represents the `Question` the `Answer` is related to
- We added a `Value` property, that we'll use later to give a *score value* to each answer

AnswerController

Let's go ahead with adding the `AnswerController`:

```
using System;
using Microsoft.AspNetCore.Mvc;
using Newtonsoft.Json;
using TestMakerFreeWebApp.ViewModels;
using System.Collections.Generic;

namespace TestMakerFreeWebApp.Controllers
{
    [Route("api/[controller]")]
    public class AnswerController : Controller
    {
        // GET api/answer/all
        [HttpGet("All/{questionId}")]
        public IActionResult All(int questionId)
        {
            var sampleAnswers = new List<AnswerViewModel>();

            // add a first sample answer
            sampleAnswers.Add(new AnswerViewModel()
            {
                Id = 1,
                QuestionId = questionId,
                Text = "Friends and family",
                CreatedDate = DateTime.Now,
                LastModifiedDate = DateTime.Now
            });

            // add a bunch of other sample answers
            for (int i = 2; i <= 5; i++)
            {
                sampleAnswers.Add(new AnswerViewModel()
                {
                    Id = i,
                    QuestionId = questionId,
```

```
                    Text = String.Format("Sample Answer {0}", i),
                    CreatedDate = DateTime.Now,
                    LastModifiedDate = DateTime.Now
                });
        }

        // output the result in JSON format
        return new JsonResult(
            sampleAnswers,
            new JsonSerializerSettings()
            {
                Formatting = Formatting.Indented
            });
        }
    }
}
```

As we can see, the code is almost identical to that of `QuestionController`, although it will most likely change later on.

ResultViewModel

So far, so good. Let's proceed with the `ResultViewModel`:

```
using Newtonsoft.Json;
using System;
using System.Collections.Generic;
using System.ComponentModel;
using System.Linq;

namespace TestMakerFreeWebApp.ViewModels
{
    [JsonObject(MemberSerialization.OptOut)]
    public class ResultViewModel
    {
        #region Constructor
        public ResultViewModel()
        {

        }
        #endregion

        #region Properties
        public int Id { get; set; }
        public int QuizId { get; set; }
```

```
            public string Text { get; set; }
            public string Notes { get; set; }
            [DefaultValue(0)]
            public int Type { get; set; }
            [DefaultValue(0)]
            public int Flags { get; set; }
            [JsonIgnore]
            public DateTime CreatedDate { get; set; }
            public DateTime LastModifiedDate { get; set; }
            #endregion
        }
    }
```

We're using the same code here as well; these controllers aren't much more than placeholders for now; however, we'll greatly improve them later on.

ResultController

Its corresponding ResultController is as follows:

```
using System;
using Microsoft.AspNetCore.Mvc;
using Newtonsoft.Json;
using TestMakerFreeWebApp.ViewModels;
using System.Collections.Generic;

namespace TestMakerFreeWebApp.Controllers
{
    [Route("api/[controller]")]
    public class ResultController : Controller
    {
        // GET api/question/all
        [HttpGet("All/{quizId}")]
        public IActionResult All(int quizId)
        {
            var sampleResults = new List<ResultViewModel>();

            // add a first sample result
            sampleResults.Add(new ResultViewModel()
            {
                Id = 1,
                QuizId = quizId,
                Text = "What do you value most in your life?",
                CreatedDate = DateTime.Now,
                LastModifiedDate = DateTime.Now
            });
```

```
// add a bunch of other sample results
for (int i = 2; i <= 5; i++)
{
    sampleResults.Add(new ResultViewModel()
    {
        Id = i,
        QuizId = quizId,
        Text = String.Format("Sample Question {0}", i),
        CreatedDate = DateTime.Now,
        LastModifiedDate = DateTime.Now
    });
}

// output the result in JSON format
return new JsonResult(
    sampleResults,
    new JsonSerializerSettings()
    {
        Formatting = Formatting.Indented
    });
```

It's worth noting that the `ResultViewModel` and `ResultController` source code is much similar to `QuestionViewModel` and `QuestionController`. The reason for that is rather obvious--both `Questions` and `Results` are related to their `Quiz` without any intermediate relationship, such as the `Answers` have with the `Questions`.

Now that our .NET Core **Controllers** and **ViewModels** have been set in place, we can safely get rid of the `SampleDataController.cs` file, as we don't need it anymore. From **Solution Explorer**, navigate to the `/Controllers/` folder, right-click on it and delete it. Doing this won't cause issues, as we already removed all the relevant *client-side* code back in Chapter 1, *Getting Ready*.

 If we want to keep the `SampleDataController.cs` for further reference, we can also create a `/Controllers/_deleted/` subfolder and move it there instead, just like we did with the **counter** and **fetchdata** Angular components back in Chapter 1, *Getting Ready*.

After the cleanup, let's take a clear look at the **routing** aspect of what we just did; since it is a major topic, it's well worth some of our time.

Understanding routes

In Chapter 1, *Getting Ready*, we acknowledged the fact that the ASP.NET Core pipeline has been completely rewritten in order to merge the MVC and WebAPI modules into a single, lightweight framework to handle both worlds. Although this is certainly a good thing, it comes with the usual downside that we need to learn a lot of new stuff. Handling **routes** is a perfect example of this, as the new approach defines some major breaking changes from the past.

Defining routing

The first thing we should do is to give out a proper definition of what **routing** actually is.

To cut it simple, we can say that URL routing is the server-side feature that allows a web developer to handle HTTP requests pointing to URIs not mapping to physical files. Such a technique can be used for a number of different reasons, including these:

- Giving dynamic pages semantic, meaningful, and *human-readable* names in order to advantage readability and/or **Search Engine Optimization** (**SEO**)
- Renaming or moving one or more physical files within your project's folder tree without being forced to change their URLs
- Set up alias and redirects

Routing through the ages

In earlier times, when ASP.NET was just **Web Forms**, URL routing was strictly bound to physical files. In order to implement viable URL convention patterns, the developers were forced to install/configure a dedicated URL rewriting tool using either an external ISAPI filter such as **Helicontech's SAPI Rewrite** or, starting with IIS7, the **IIS URL Rewrite Module**.

When **ASP.NET MVC** was released, the **routing** pattern was completely rewritten, and developers could set up their own convention-based routes in a dedicated file (RouteConfig.cs or Global.asax, depending on template) using the Routes.MapRoute method. If you've played along with MVC 1 through 5 or WebAPI 1 and/or 2, snippets like this should be quite familiar to you:

```
Routes.MapRoute(
name: "Default",
url: "{controller}/{action}/{id}",
defaults: new { controller = "Home", action = "Index", id =
```

```
        UrlParameter.Optional }
    );
```

This method of defining routes, strictly based on pattern matching techniques used to relate any given URL requests to a specific Controller's Actions, went by the name of **Convention-based routing**.

ASP.NET MVC5 brought something new, as it was the first version supporting the so-called **Attribute-based routing**. This approach was designed as an effort to give a more versatile approach to developers. If you used it at least once, you'll probably agree that it was a great addition to the framework, as it allowed developers to define routes within the Controller file. Even those who chose to keep the convention-based approach could find it useful for one-time overrides, such as the following, without having to sort it out using some regular expressions:

```
    [RoutePrefix("v2Products")]
    public class ProductsController : Controller
    {
        [Route("v2Index")]
        public ActionResult Index()
        {
            return View();
        }
    }
```

In **ASP.NET Core MVC (aka MVC 6)**, with the routing pipeline being completely rewritten, *attribute-based* routing is quickly becoming a *de-facto* standard, replacing the *convention-based* approach in most boilerplates and code samples. However, setting routing conventions using the `Routes.MapRoute()` method is still a viable way to define a limited amount of high-level, default routing rules, as our `Startup.cs` file clearly shows (relevant lines are highlighted):

```
    app.UseMvc(routes =>
    {
        routes.MapRoute(
            name: "default",
            template: "{controller=Home}/{action=Index}/{id?}");
        routes.MapSpaFallbackRoute(
            name: "spa-fallback",
            defaults: new { controller = "Home", action = "Index" });
    });
```

This code snippet, taken from the `Configure` method, demonstrates that *convention-based* routing is still a viable approach when developing an SPA. The only difference between ASP.NET 4.x and earlier releases is the fact that the routes are directly sent to the MVC middleware when we add it to the `HTTP` request pipeline as part of its configuration parameters, thus resulting in a more streamlined approach.

Handling routes in .NET Core

As we just saw, the new routing implementation is basically handled by the two `services.AddMvc()` and `app.UseMvc()` methods called within the `Startup.cs` file, which perform the following tasks respectively:

- Registering MVC using the **Dependency Injection** framework built into ASP.NET Core
- Adding the required middleware to the `HTTP` request pipeline, while also (optionally) setting a pack of default routes

We can take a look at what happens under the hood by looking at the current implementation of the `app.UseMvc()` method in the framework code (relevant lines are highlighted):

```
public static IApplicationBuilder UseMvc(
    [NotNull] this IApplicationBuilder app,
    [NotNull] Action<IRouteBuilder> configureRoutes)
{
    // Verify if AddMvc was done before calling UseMvc
    // We use the MvcMarkerService to make sure if all the services
      were added.
    MvcServicesHelper.ThrowIfMvcNotRegistered(app.ApplicationServices);

    var routes = new RouteBuilder
    {
        DefaultHandler = new MvcRouteHandler(),
        ServiceProvider = app.ApplicationServices
    };

    configureRoutes(routes);

    // Adding the attribute route comes after running the user-code
      because
    // we want to respect any changes to the DefaultHandler.
    routes.Routes.Insert(0, AttributeRouting.CreateAttributeMegaRoute(
        routes.DefaultHandler,
        app.ApplicationServices));
```

```
        return app.UseRouter(routes.Build());
    }
```

The good thing about this is the fact that the framework now handles all the hard work, iterating through all the Controller's **Actions** and setting up their default routes, thus saving us some work. It's worth noting that the default ruleset follows the standard *RESTFUL* conventions, which means that it will be restricted to the `Get`, `Post`, `Put`, `Delete` action names. Here, we can say that ASP.NET Core is enforcing a strict *WebAPI-oriented* approach, which is much to be expected since it incorporates the whole ASP.NET Core framework.

Following the RESTful convention is generally a great thing to do, especially if we aim to create a set of pragmatic, RESTful-based public APIs to be used by other developers. Conversely, if we're developing our own app and we want to keep our API accessible to our eyes only, going for custom routing standards is just as viable. As a matter of fact, it can even be a better choice to shield our Controllers against some of the most trivial forms of request floods and/or DDoS-based attacks. Luckily enough, both the **Convention-based Routing** and the **Attribute-based Routing** are still alive and well, allowing us to set up our own standards. If we want to enforce the former approach, we can extend the code already present in the `Startup.cs` file; conversely, we can keep doing what we previously did within our Controllers source code, where **Attribute-Based Routing** is widely present either at **Controller** level:

```
    [Route("api/[controller]")]
    public class ItemsController : Controller
```

Alternatively, it can be present at the **action method** level:

```
    [HttpGet("GetLatest")]
    public JsonResult GetLatest()
```

Three choices to route them all

Long story short, ASP.NET Core is giving us three different choices for handling routes: enforcing the standard **RESTful conventions**, reverting back to the good old **Convention-based Routing**, or decorating the Controller files with the **Attribute-based Routing**. That said, we will definitely keep using a mix all of these approaches in our application to better learn when, where, and how to properly make use of either of them.

 It's worth noting that *Attribute-based* routes, if/when defined, will override any matching *Convention-based* pattern: both of them, if/when defined, will override the default *RESTful conventions* created by the built-in `app.UseMvc()` method.

Adding more routes

Let's get back to our `QuizController`. Now that we're aware of the various routing patterns available, we can use them to implement the API calls we're still missing.

Open the `QuizController.cs` file and add the following code (new lines are highlighted):

```
using System;
using Microsoft.AspNetCore.Mvc;
using Newtonsoft.Json;
using TestMakerFreeWebApp.ViewModels;
using System.Collections.Generic;

namespace TestMakerFreeWebApp.Controllers
{
    [Route("api/[controller]")]
    public class QuizController : Controller
    {
        #region RESTful conventions methods
        /// <summary>
        /// GET: api/quiz/{}id
        /// Retrieves the Quiz with the given {id}
        /// </summary>
        /// <param name="id">The ID of an existing Quiz</param>
        /// <returns>the Quiz with the given {id}</returns>
        [HttpGet("{id}")]
        public IActionResult Get(int id)
        {
            // create a sample quiz to match the given request
            var v = new QuizViewModel()
            {
                Id = id,
                Title = String.Format("Sample quiz with id {0}", id),
                Description = "Not a real quiz: it's just a sample!",
                CreatedDate = DateTime.Now,
                LastModifiedDate = DateTime.Now
            };

            // output the result in JSON format
            return new JsonResult(
                v,
                new JsonSerializerSettings()
                {
                    Formatting = Formatting.Indented
                });
        }
```

```
#endregion

#region Attribute-based routing methods
/// <summary>
/// GET: api/quiz/latest
/// Retrieves the {num} latest Quizzes
/// </summary>
/// <param name="num">the number of quizzes to retrieve</param>
/// <returns>the {num} latest Quizzes</returns>
[HttpGet("Latest/{num}")]
public IActionResult Latest(int num = 10)
{
    var sampleTests = new List<QuizViewModel>();

    // add a first sample quiz
    sampleQuizzes.Add(new QuizViewModel()
    {
        Id = 1,
        Title = "Which Shingeki No Kyojin character are you?",
        Description = "Anime-related personality test",
        CreatedDate = DateTime.Now,
        LastModifiedDate = DateTime.Now
    });

    // add a bunch of other sample quizzes
    for (int i = 2; i <= num; i++)
    {
        sampleQuizzes.Add(new QuizViewModel()
        {
            Id = i,
            Title = String.Format("Sample Quiz {0}", i),
            Description = "This is a sample quiz",
            CreatedDate = DateTime.Now,
            LastModifiedDate = DateTime.Now
        });
    }

    // output the result in JSON format
    return new JsonResult(
        sampleQuizzes,
        new JsonSerializerSettings()
        {
            Formatting = Formatting.Indented
        });
}
#endregion
    }
}
```

As we can see, we did a bunch of significant improvements here:

- We added a `Get` method that follows the *RESTful conventions* we explained earlier; we will definitely need it each time we'll have to retrieve a specific `Quiz`, given its `Id`.
- We also decorated each class member with a dedicated `<summary>` *documentation tag* explaining what it does and its return value. These tags will be used by *IntelliSense* to show real-time information about the type within the Visual Studio GUI. They will also come inhandy when we'll want to generate an autogenerated *XML Documentation* for our project using industry-standard documentation tools, such as *Sandcastle*.
- Finally, we added some `#region` / `#endregion` *pre-processor directives* to separate our code into blocks. We'll do this a lot from now on, as this will greatly increase the readability and usability of our source code, allowing us to expand or collapse different sections/parts when we don't need them, thus focusing more on what we're working with.

For more information regarding **documentation tags**, take a look at the MSDN official documentation page, at `https://msdn.microsoft.com/library/2d6dt3kf.aspx`.

If you want know more about C# pre-processor directives, check out `https://msdn.microsoft.com/library/9a1ybwek.aspx` instead.

The Dummy Data Provider

As we can easily see, we're *emulating* the role of a *Data Provider* returning one or more sample **Quizzes** in a credible fashion. The reason for this can't be more obvious; we don't have any *Data Provider* in place for the time being (and we won't until we reach `Chapter 4`, *Data Model with Entity Framework Core*); hence, this is the only way we have to output some stuff and see some decent results on screen.

It's also worth noting that we built it in a way that it will always return identical items, as long as the `num` parameter value remains the same:

- The generated items `Id` will follow a linear sequence, from 1 to `num`.
- Any generated item will have incremental `CreatedDate` and `LastModifiedDate` values; the higher the `Id` is, the most recent these dates will be. This follows the assumption that most recent items will have a higher `Id`, as it normally is for DBMS records featuring numeric, auto incremental keys.

While it obviously lacks any insert/update/delete feature, this trivial technique is viable enough to serve our purposes until we'll replace it with an actual, persistence-based **Data Source**.

Technically speaking, we can do something better than we did using one of the many Mocking Frameworks available through **NuGet**: *Moq*, *NMock3*, *NSubstitute*, or *Rhino*, just to name a few.
These frameworks are the ideal choice when using a **Test-Driven Development (TDD)** approach, which is not the case in this book. In this specific scenario, our *Dummy Data Provider* is still a viable way to get what we need, while keeping the focus on our main topic--ASP.NET Core and Angular interaction.

Dealing with single entries

Our updated `QuizController` class gives us a way to retrieve a single **Quiz** entry; it will definitely be very useful when our users will select one of them within the **Latest** list, as we'll be able to point them to something similar to a detail page. It will also be very useful when we'll have to deal with **CRUD** operations such as `Delete` and `Update`.

We're not dealing with the client-side code yet, so we don't know *how* we'll present such a scenario to the user. However, we already know *what* we'll eventually need, a `Get`, `Put`, `Post`, and `Delete` method for each one of our entries--**Quizzes**, **Questions**, **Answers**, and **Results**--as we'll definitely have to perform these operations for all of them.

Luckily enough, we don't need to implement them now. However, since we're working with these *Controllers*, it can be a good time to set up a basic interface:

```
   #region RESTful conventions methods
/// <summary>
/// Retrieves the Answer with the given {id}
/// </summary>
/// &lt;param name="id">The ID of an existing Answer</param>
/// <returns>the Answer with the given {id}</returns>
[HttpGet("{id}")]
public IActionResult Get(int id)
{
    return Content("Not implemented (yet)!");
}

/// <summary>
    /// Adds a new Answer to the Database
/// </summary>
```

```
/// <param name="m">The AnswerViewModel containing the data to
insert</param>
[HttpPut]
public IActionResult Put(AnswerViewModel m)
{
    throw new NotImplementedException();
}

/// <summary>
/// Edit the Answer with the given {id}
/// </summary>
/// <param name="m">The AnswerViewModel containing the data to
update</param>
[HttpPost]
public IActionResult Post(AnswerViewModel m)
{
    throw new NotImplementedException();
}

/// <summary>
/// Deletes the Answer with the given {id} from the Database
/// </summary>
/// <param name="id">The ID of an existing Answer</param>
[HttpDelete("{id}")]
public IActionResult Delete(int id)
{
    throw new NotImplementedException();
}
#endregion
```

This is the code that we have to add to `AnswerController`. As soon as we do that, we also need to perform the same operation with the other controllers: `QuestionController`, `ResultController`, and also `QuizController` (except for the `Get` method we added earlier). Ensure that you change the comments and the ViewModel reference accordingly (each **Controller** must reference the **ViewModel** related to their specific entry).

 Our brand new `RESTful` methods won't do anything other than returning a not-implemented text message (or a **NotImplementedException**) to the client/browser issuing the request; this is by design, as we'll implement them later on.

To test our new methods, select **Debug** | **Start Debugging** from the main menu (or press *F5*) and type the following URLs in the browser's address bar:

- For quizzes, type `/api/quiz/1`:

```
{
    "Id": 1,
    "Title": "Sample quiz with id 1",
    "Description": "Not a real quiz: it's just a sample!",
    "Text": null,
    "Notes": null,
    "Type": 0,
    "Flags": 0,
    "UserId": null,
    "CreatedDate": "2017-10-14T04:14:16.8482708+02:00",
    "LastModifiedDate": "2017-10-14T04:14:16.8482761+02:00"
}
```

- For question, type `/api/question/1`:

```
Not implemented (yet)!
```

- For answer, type `/api/answer/1`:

- For result, type `/api/result/1`:

Everything works as it should be. As we already said, the exception brought on screen by the *Response* is perfectly fine; we did it on purpose, to demonstrate how we can handle these kinds of errors. This is also a good practice when dealing with ASP.NET Core API interfaces: if we don't have it implemented yet, throw a `NotImplementedException` until we're done to prevent any unwanted *Request* from having nasty effects on our still unfinished web application.

So far, so good, we got ourselves a number of *server-side* APIs to retrieve JSON arrays filled by a client-defined (or default) number of latest items, and an additional one to retrieve a single item from its unique ID. All these calls will be very handy in the next chapter, where we'll start developing *client-side* components using Angular.

Suggested topics

HTTP Request, HTTP Response, Convention-based Routing, Attribute-based Routing, RESTful Conventions, Mock Objects, Test-Driven Development, XML Documentation Tags, and C# Pre-Processor Directives

Summary

We spent some time putting the standard application data flow under our lens--a two-way communication pattern between the server and their clients, built upon the HTTP protocol. We acknowledged the fact that we'll mostly be dealing with JSON-serializable object such as **Quizzes**, so we chose to equip ourselves with a `QuizViewModel` *server-side* class, along with a `QuizController` that will actively use it to expose the data to the client.

We started building our MVC6-based Web API interface by implementing a number of methods required to create the *client-side* UI; we routed the requests to them using a custom set of *Attribute-based* routing rules, which seemed to be the best choice for our specific scenario.

While we were there, we also took the chance to add dedicated methods to get, insert, update, and delete single entries from our controllers. We did that following the *RESTful conventions* enforced by the `Get`, `Put`, `Post`, `Delete` methods.

In the next chapter, we will see how we can consume the ASP.NET Core Web API using Angular in order to build an interactive user interface for our application.

3

Frontend with Angular

Our ASP.NET Core Web API is working fine, but the *server-side* controllers we built in `Chapter 2`, *Backend with .NET Core*--`QuizController`, `QuestionController`, `AnswerController`, and `ResultController`--are still missing something we will eventually need, some POST-based methods to insert, update, and delete their records. There's no sense in adding them now, since we're still dealing with sample data objects that are created *on-the-fly*; however, we'll definitely add these methods in due course, when we'll switch to a real **Data Model**.

As for the time being, let's see how we can make good use of what we just did by implementing all the new stuff in the Angular source code shipped along with the Visual Studio Angular SPA template we chose to use. Needless to say, this means that we will perform a series of structural changes on the existing sample in terms of UI, layout, navigation, and data retrieval strategies.

Let's summarize what we will do in this chapter:

- Greet our users with a brand new *Home View* that will show three different lists of **Quizzes**--*Latest, By Title (A-Z), Random*. We'll populate these by fetching the relevant data using the **QuizController** API methods built in `Chapter 2`, *Backend with .NET Core*.
- Let our users navigate to a *Test Detail View* upon clicking any given Test, where they'll be able to read some basic information about the chosen test.
- Allow our users to go back from the *Test Detail View* to the *Home View* upon clicking a standard **Back** link.
- Update the side menu and all the text labels according to these changes.

Navigation pattern

If we try to visualize all this, we can easily see that we're talking about a standard, straightforward *Master/Detail* navigation pattern; the same approach, with minor differences, can also be found on countless websites. When we're done, users will be able to perform a basic navigation loop, as follows:

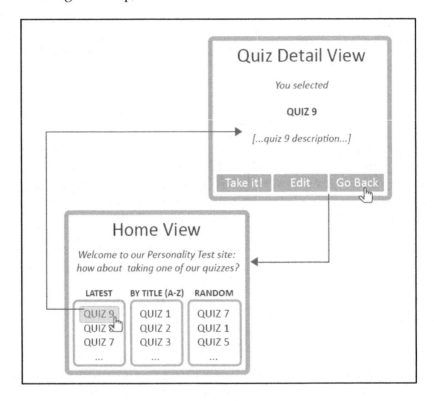

Note that we will also give the user two additional choices, other than going back:

- Actually try the quiz by clicking on the **Take It!** button
- Change the quiz details and settings by clicking on the **Edit** button

We'll dedicate this chapter to creating the main navigation interface and implementing the **Go Back** button, which is by far the easiest one; the other buttons will require additional effort and will be addressed later on.

Any experienced developer will hardly miss the fact that the **Edit** button will most likely require the greatest amount of effort, as it will force us to deal with the underlying **Data Model** on both the *client-side* and *server-side* levels. Doing that in Angular is a rather seamless task, thanks to the framework's built-in **two-way data binding** features. Persisting these changes to the application's Data Source will be a whole different story, though, as it will require us to implement a couple more features, such as the following:

- A dedicated *server-side* API that will receive the updated data from the client Model and sync it to the server Model
- A *client-side* update command pattern--such as a button, a focus event, or something like that--that will trigger the aforementioned update API call

This is something we'll do in the next chapter, when we'll implement a persistent **Data Source** and replace our *Dummy Data Provider* sample with a working one; we won't be able to properly handle any persisting update command until then.

Master/detail binding

Our main focus now is to implement a standard *master/detail* navigation pattern. We'll do that in two consecutive steps to demonstrate all the relevant Angular features better, as follows:

1. Put together a temporary, component-based *master/detail* relationship **within the same view** using the Angular data-binding capabilities.
2. Improve that temporary code, replacing the *single-view* display with an actual *view-based* navigation pattern with full client-side routing support.

Truth be told, the former step isn't needed at all; we could just implement the latter and get the task over with. However, by choosing that quick and straight path, we would skip some really important concepts regarding Angular and its interactions with the web API structure we just built. We're talking about something that will come in handy later on, so it's highly recommended that we restrain ourselves from rushing things.

The Quiz client-side interface

The first thing we need to do is to add the **Quiz** interface to our Angular-enabled client. Wait a minute, should we really do that? Can't we just use the raw JSON data sent by the QuizController's Get and GetLatest methods defined earlier, consuming them as anonymous JavaScript objects?

Theoretically speaking, we can, just as much as we can output raw JSON from the Controllers instead of creating all the ViewModel classes, like we did instead. In a well-written app, though, we should always resist the temptation to handle raw JSON data and/or to use anonymous objects for a number of good reasons:

- We have chosen TypeScript over JavaScript because we want to work with type definitions. Anonymous objects and properties are the exact opposite; they lead to the JavaScript way of doing things, which is something we wanted to avoid in the first place.
- Anonymous objects (and their properties) are not easy to validate: we don't want our data items to be error prone or forced to deal with missing properties or anything like that.
- Anonymous objects are hardly reusable, and won't benefit from many Angular handy features--such as the *object mapping*--that will require our objects to be actual instances of an interface and/or a type.

The first two arguments are very important, especially if we're aiming for a production-ready application; no matter how easy our development task might seem at first, we should never think that we can afford losing that level of control over our application's source code.

The third reason is also crucial as long as we want to use Angular to its full extent. If that's the case, using an undefined array of properties such as raw JSON data is basically out of the question; we will use a TypeScript interface, as it is the most lightweight way to work with structured JSON data in a strongly-typed fashion. More specifically, we'll add a dedicated **Quiz** interface to properly map our JSON-serialized QuizViewModel *server-side* class.

From **Solution Explorer**, right-click on the /ClientApp/app/ folder and create a new /interfaces/ subfolder, and then right-click on it and add a new TypeScript file in there; call it quiz.ts and fill its content with this source code:

```
interface Quiz {
    Id: number;
    Title: string;
    Description: string;
```

```
        Text: string;
    }
```

Note that we're not (yet) mapping all the properties present in the `QuizViewModel` class; as a general rule of thumb, we'll be keeping these classes as lightweight as possible, defining only what we know we will use for the time being. We can always add more properties later, as soon as we need them.

The QuizList component

What we will do here is to create a dedicated component that will show a list of items task on screen. It's important to understand that we can also do that in our already-present `AppComponent` class; however, it won't be the ideal thing to do. We're working on a rather complex app that is expected to grow fast, thus it's advisable to embrace a modular approach right from the start and split our planned features into separate, reusable assets.

To be more specific, what we need now is a flexible and pluggable `QuizListComponent` that we can use--once or even multiple times as separate instances--within our existing `AppComponent`; we plan to use this pattern throughout all our *client-side* development experience.

Again, from **Solution Explorer**, add a new `TypeScript` file in the `/ClientApp/app/components/quiz/` folder, call it `quiz-list.component.ts`, and fill it with the following content:

```typescript
import { Component, Inject } from "@angular/core";
import { HttpClient } from "@angular/common/http";

@Component({
    selector: "quiz-list",
    templateUrl: './quiz-list.component.html',
    styleUrls: ['./quiz-list.component.css']
})

export class QuizListComponent {
    title: string;
    selectedQuiz: Quiz;
    quizzes: Quiz[];

    constructor(http: HttpClient,
        @Inject('BASE_URL') baseUrl: string) {
        this.title = "Latest Quizzes";
        var url = baseUrl + "api/quiz/Latest/";
```

```
        this.http.get<Quiz[]>(url).subscribe(result => {
            this.quizzes = result;
        }, error => console.error(error));
    }

    onSelect(quiz: Quiz) {
        this.selectedQuiz = quiz;
        console.log("quiz with Id "
            + this.selectedQuiz.Id
            + " has been selected.");
    }
}
```

That's a good amount of non-trivial source code. Let's see what we just did in detail:

- In **lines 1-2**, we import the Angular references that we need from the `@angular/core` and `@angular/common/http` packages; since we're creating a *Component*, we need the `Component` base class. Other than that, we also need to import the `Inject` decorator, which we're using within the class constructor to make the `baseUrl` parameter available through **Dependency Injection (DI)**, and the `HttpClient` class to perform `HTTP` requests, also being instantiated using **DI**.
- In **lines 4-8**, we set up the component UI layout and following settings:
    - The **selector**, which gives a name to the HTML pseudo-element we'll have to use to include the component within another component's template; in this case, with the given value, it will be `<quiz-list></quiz-list>`
    - The `templateUrl`, pointing to a single HTML file containing the component template
    - The `styleUrls`, pointing to the CSS files that will contain the component styles; the expected value is an array, meaning that we can split the component styling into multiple CSS files
- Starting from **line 10**, we can find the `QuizListComponent` class declaration, along with all its properties, its constructor, and methods.

Before adding the template and style files, there are still a couple of things in the preceding source code that we need to look at; let's try to shed some light on them.

The new Angular HttpClient

Being able to efficiently send and receive JSON data from our .NET Core Controllers is probably the most important requirement for our SPA. We chose to do that using the *brand new* Angular `HttpClient`, first introduced in Angular 4.3.0-RC.0, which is among the best answers the framework can give to get the job done. For this very reason, we will use it a lot throughout the whole book; however, before doing that, it might be advisable to properly understand what it is, why is it better than the former implementation, and how to properly implement it.

A match against the old standard

The new `HttpClient` was introduced in *July 2017* as an improved version of the former Angular HTTP client API, also known as `@angular/http`, or simply HTTP. Instead of replacing the old version in the `@angular/http` package, the Angular development team has put the new classes in a separate package--`@angular/common/http`. They chose to do that to preserve the *backward-compatibility* with the existing code bases and also to ensure a slow, yet steady migration to the new API.

Those who used the old Angular **HTTP** service class at least once will most likely remember its main limitations:

- JSON was not enabled by default, forcing the developers to explicitly set it within the request *Headers*--and JSON.parse/stringify the data--when working with RESTful APIs.
- There was no easy way to access the HTTP request/response pipeline, thus preventing the developer from intercepting or altering the *request* and/or *response* calls after they were issued or received, by using some ugly and pattern-breaking hacks. As a matter of fact, extensions and wrapper classes were basically the only way to customize the service, at least on a global scope.
- There was no native *strong-typing* for request and response objects (although we can cast *JSON-as-interfaces* as a workaround).

The great news is that the new `HttpClient` does all of this and much more; other features include testability support and better error handling via APIs entirely based on *Observables*.

How to install it

In the *ASP.NET Core MVC with Angular* template we've been using, the new `HttpClient` class is not enabled by default. In order to use that, we need to add its references to the Angular's `AppModule` class. We already know from Chapter 1, *Getting Ready*, that we have three files to properly configure it: `app.module.browser.ts`, `app.module.server.ts`, and `app.module.shared.ts`. Since we definitely want the `QuizListComponent` to be available for both *client-side* and *server-side* rendering, we will add it to the `app.module.shared.ts` file.

Go to the `/ClientApp/app/` folder, open the `app.module.shared.ts` file, and replace the references to the former **HTTP** service with the new one in the following way (changed lines are highlighted):

```
import { NgModule } from '@angular/core';
import { CommonModule } from '@angular/common';
import { FormsModule } from '@angular/forms';
import { HttpClientModule } from '@angular/common/http';
import { RouterModule } from '@angular/router';

import { AppComponent } from './components/app/app.component';
import { NavMenuComponent } from './components/navmenu/navmenu.component';
import { HomeComponent } from './components/home/home.component';
import { QuizListComponent } from './components/quiz/quiz-list.component';
import { QuizComponent } from './components/quiz/quiz.component';

@NgModule({
    declarations: [
        AppComponent,
        NavMenuComponent,
        HomeComponent,
        QuizListComponent,
        QuizComponent
    ],
    imports: [
        CommonModule,
        HttpClientModule,
        FormsModule,
        RouterModule.forRoot([
            { path: '', redirectTo: 'home', pathMatch: 'full' },
            { path: 'home', component: HomeComponent },
            { path: '**', redirectTo: 'home' }
        ])
    ]
})
export class AppModuleShared {
}
```

How to use it

The first thing that catches our eye is that we're using the `HttpClient` class within the constructor; we only got the `quizzes` property to store its results. As a matter of fact, we don't even instantiate it within our code, we just have an `HTTP` parameter to the constructor and take it for granted, as if there was some guy who would instantiate it for us.

As a matter of fact, it is just like that, but the guy is Angular itself, or--to better say it--its very own **Dependency Injection** framework.

Dependency Injection

If we're used to work with modern languages such as .NET Core, ReactJS, AngularJS, or Angular, we most likely already know what **Dependency Injection** (**DI** from now on), as well as the huge amount of benefits it brings in terms of code reusability, testability, readability, simplicity, and so on. In the unlikely case you don't, we'll make fun of ourselves trying to shrink one of the most important code design patterns in the last 20 years in less than 20 words using a coding technique where a class receives its dependencies from external sources rather than directly instantiating them.

 For the sake of simplicity, we will stop here; however, those who want to know more about this topic can take an extensive look at this great guide from the official Angular documentation, which explains how DI works both in general terms and within the Angular framework:

`https://angular.io/guide/dependency-injection`

Get and subscribe

When you return to the code, we can see that we use the `HttpClient` class by calling two consecutive methods: `.get<Quiz[]>()` and `.subscribe()`. The former, as the name suggests, issues a standard HTTP request to our .NET Core `QuizController` to fetch an array of quizzes; we use a local string variable to assemble the controller's endpoint URL and then toss it as a parameter. The latter instantiates an **Observable** object that will execute two very different actions right after a *result* and/or in case of an *error*. Needless to say, all this will be done *asynchronously*, meaning that it will run in a separate thread (or scheduled for later execution), while the rest of the code continues to execute.

It's very important to understand that we're only scratching the surface of what an **Observable** can do. However, this is all we need for now: we'll have the chance to talk more about them later on.

Observables are a powerful feature for managing async data; they are the backbone of the *ReactiveX JavaScript Library* (**RxJS**), which is one of the Angular required dependencies, and are planned to be included in the final release of **EcmaScript 7**. If you're familiar with ES6 **Promises**, you can think of them as an improved version of that approach.

Angular makes extensive use of both **Observables** when dealing with data. Those who want to get additional information can take a look at the following URL, taken from the **RxJS** official documentation:

```
http://reactivex.io/rxjs/class/es6/Observable.js~Observable.html
```

The onSelect() method

For the time being, our `QuizListComponent` features a single method, which is meant to be executed whenever the user selects one of the quizzes. The implementation is quite straightforward; we accept the selected quiz as a parameter, store it into a local variable, and use the standard `console.log` JS command to output what happened to the client console.

However, we're still unable to see the code that will actually render the list of quizzes and allow the user to perform the selection. We can, however, easily guess that both of these tasks will be handled by the component's template file.

The template file

From **Solution Explorer**, right-click on the `/ClientApp/app/components/quiz/` folder and add a new HTML file; call it `quiz-list.component.html`, and replace the sample code with the following:

```html
<h2>{{title}}</h2>
<ul class="quizzes">
    <li *ngFor="let quiz of quizzes"
        [class.selected]="quiz === selectedQuiz"
        (click)="onSelect(quiz)">
        <span>{{quiz.Title}}</span>
    </li>
</ul>
```

It's important to understand that we're free to use any filename we want for the template file, as long as it reflects the value we used in the `templateUrl` property within the `quiz-list.component.ts` file. We can even share the same template among two (or more) different components. However, the Angular best practices suggest that we use the same name of the component, as it will lead to a cleaner, more readable code structure.

Among these few lines, we can see the two things we were looking for:

- The HTML code to render the quiz list, handled with a `ngFor` cycle that will iterate through the `quizzes` array and create a number of `<li>` elements as soon as it is filled by the `.subscribe()` method of `HttpClient` in the component class source code
- The `(click)` event handler that will raise a call to the `onSelect()` method, where the currently iterated `quiz` is passed as a parameter

There are also a couple of other things worth noting:

- In **line 4**, we added a simple logic that will decorate the `<li>` element hosting the selected quiz with the **selected** CSS class so that we can style it in a different way.
- In **line 1** and **line 6**, we make use of the *double-curly braces of interpolation*, an important Angular feature that allows us to insert calculated strings into the text between HTML element tags and within attribute assignments. The text between the braces is almost always the name of a component property; the whole block will be replaced with the string value of the corresponding component property. This means that, in our specific scenario, we can expect to see the component title between the `<h2>` element in line 1 and the quiz title between the `<span>` element in line 6.

The *double-curly braces of interpolation* are part of the **Angular Template Syntax**, a collection of expressions, shortcuts, and keywords that can be used in templates--along with HTML--to grant them additional features. We'll introduce more of them later on, as soon as we need to use them. Nonetheless, if you just can't wait to see what else is in store, you can take a look at the official documentation, which is available on the Angular website at the following address:

`https://angular.io/guide/template-syntax`

The Stylesheet file

Last but not least, we need to add the CSS asset that we declared in the `styleUrls` array within the `quiz-list.component.ts` file.

From **Solution Explorer**, right-click on the `/ClientApp/app/components/quiz/` folder and create a new CSS file; call it `quiz-list.component.css` and replace the sample code with the following:

```
ul.quizzes li {
    color: #000acb;
    cursor: pointer;
}

    ul.quizzes li.selected {
        background-color: #cccccc;
    }
```

There's nothing fancy here, just some minimal styling to make things look less ugly.

Adding the component

We just created our very first Angular component! However, before we can test it, we need to properly add it into our Angular application. This basically means that we'll have to reference its path(s), class(es), and pseudo-element(s) to one or more already existing files, depending on the component role. This is something that we'll always need to do whenever we create a component, so it's really important to pay close attention to all the required steps.

In most cases, such as this one, the affected files won't be more than two: the `AppModule` and the template file of the parent component that will contain the one that we just made. In our specific scenario, we want the `QuizListComponent` to be shown as part of the `HomeComponent`, so we'll put it into the `home.component.html` template file.

The AppModule file(s)

The first thing we need to do is to add the component references within the application module files; once again, we want to put them in the shared file.

Open the `app.module.shared.ts` file and update its contents in the following way (new lines are highlighted):

```
import { NgModule } from '@angular/core';
import { CommonModule } from '@angular/common';
import { FormsModule } from '@angular/forms';
import { HttpClientModule } from '@angular/common/http';
import { RouterModule } from '@angular/router';

import { AppComponent } from './components/app/app.component';
import { NavMenuComponent } from './components/navmenu/navmenu.component';
import { HomeComponent } from './components/home/home.component';
import { QuizListComponent } from './components/quiz/quiz-list.component';

@NgModule({
    declarations: [
        AppComponent,
        NavMenuComponent,
        HomeComponent,
        QuizListComponent
    ],
    imports: [
        CommonModule,
        HttpClientModule,
        FormsModule,
        RouterModule.forRoot([
            { path: '', redirectTo: 'home', pathMatch: 'full' },
            { path: 'home', component: HomeComponent },
            { path: '**', redirectTo: 'home' }
        ])
    ]
})
export class AppModuleShared {
}
```

We only added two lines:

- The `imports` statement, with a reference to the `TypeScript` file hosting the `QuizListComponent` class
- An actual reference to the `QuizListComponent` class in the `declarations` array

The HomeComponent template

Now that our `QuizListComponent` is properly referenced in the `AppModule`, we can add it to the `HomeComponent` template file.

Open the `/ClientApp/app/components/home/home.component.html` file and add the single highlighted line:

```
<h1>Greetings, stranger!</h1>
<p>This is what you get for messing up with .NET Core and Angular.</p>
<quiz-list></quiz-list>
```

That's all we need to do here; **Angular** and **WebPack** will handle the rest.

Testing it up

Let's perform a quick test to see whether our brand new Angular component is working as expected. Run the application in *debug* mode and cross your fingers, hoping to see something like this:

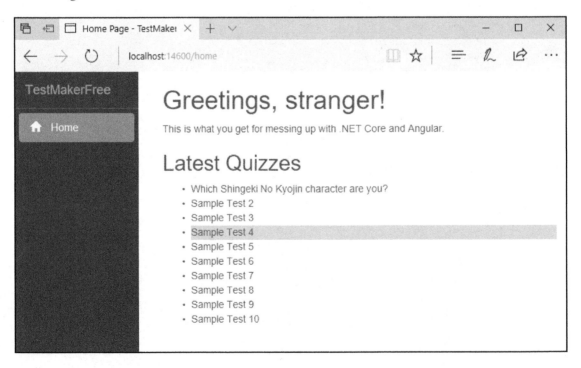

It's not bad at all! If we take some time playing with the new content, we can confirm that the CSS styles are also working properly, with the mouse cursor becoming a pointer when clicking on the `<li>` elements and the items being highlighted in grey when they're selected with a click.

This is more than enough to tell us that everything is going well; now we can go back to work and add the component that will allow our users to view the details of the selected quiz.

The QuizComponent class

Now that we know how to add a component, along with its template and style files, we can avoid explaining the most trivial steps and focus more on the code.

Adding the Component files

Let's start with adding a new `/ClientApp/app/components/quiz/quiz.component.ts` file with the following content:

```
import { Component, Input } from "@angular/core";

@Component({
    selector: "quiz",
    templateUrl: './quiz.component.html',
    styleUrls: ['./quiz.component.css']
})

export class QuizComponent {
    @Input() quiz: Quiz;
}
```

Once done, follow up with the `/ClientApp/app/components/quiz/quiz.component.html` template file:

```
<div *ngIf="quiz" class="quiz">
    <h2>{{quiz.Title}}</h2>
    <ul>
        <li>
            <label>Title:</label>
            <input [(ngModel)]="quiz.Title" placeholder="Insert the
            title..." />
        </li>
        <li>
            <label>Description:</label>
```

```
            <textarea [(ngModel)]=" quiz.Description"
            placeholder="Insert a suitable description..."></textarea>
        </li>
    </ul>
</div>
```

Right after that add, the `/ClientApp/app/components/quiz/quiz.component.css` stylesheet file:

```css
.quiz {
    margin: 5px;
    padding: 5px 10px;
    border: 1px solid black;
    background-color: #dddddd;
    width: 300px;
}

    .quiz * {
        vertical-align: middle;
    }

    .quiz ul li {
        padding: 5px 0;
    }
```

The only new thing in this component is the `@Input` decorator, which is required in Angular to define a target property. Target properties, as the name suggests, are expected to be the target of a data binding. A data binding takes place whenever a component property (or a DOM element) takes its value from an external source instead of having its own value; the external source is usually another property from the same component or from a parent component.

In our scenario, we used the `@Input` decorator with the `quiz` local property, because we want to make it available for binding; more specifically, we plan to *bind* it to the `selectedQuiz` of `QuizListController`.

 It's important to understand what the `@Input` decorator does under the hood and why we need to use it. In a few words, it appends metadata to the class hosting the affected property; thanks to the metadata, Angular will know that the given property is available for binding and will seamlessly allow it. Without the metadata, the binding will be rejected by Angular for security reasons.

Adding the component

Our second Angular component is ready; let's add it to our Angular app and test it.

Open the `app.module.shared.ts` file and add the required references (new lines are highlighted):

```
[...]

import { HomeComponent } from './components/home/home.component';
import { QuizListComponent } from './components/quiz/quiz-list.component';
import { QuizComponent } from './components/quiz/quiz.component';

@NgModule({
    declarations: [
        AppComponent,
        NavMenuComponent,
        HomeComponent,
        QuizListComponent,
        QuizComponent
    ],

[...]
```

Then, open the `quiz-list.component.html` file and append the `<quiz>` pseudo-element in the following way (new lines highlighted):

```
<h2>{{title}}</h2>
<ul class="quizzes">
    <li *ngFor="let quiz of quizzes"
        [class.selected]="quiz === selectedQuiz"
        (click)="onSelect(quiz)">
        <span>{{quiz.Title}}</span>
    </li>
</ul>
<quiz *ngIf="selectedQuiz" [quiz]="selectedQuiz"></quiz>
```

In the preceding code, we added a `<quiz>` pseudo-element with a couple of Angular-specific attributes that deserve some explanation:

- The `*ngIf` is a condition that will hide the whole `<quiz>` element if the `selectedQuiz` value resolves to `false`, meaning that it's null or empty. This is a good thing because we want to render the `QuizComponent` only when the user selects a quiz from the list.

- The [quiz] attribute clearly references the @Input() quiz local property of the QuizComponent class that we just talked about. The *Angular Template Syntax* requires that the targets of a property binding must be wrapped into square brackets so that they won't be mistaken for standard HTML attributes.

Testing it up

It's time for another test. Run the project in *debug* mode, wait for the *home view* to load, and then select a quiz from the list and see what happens:

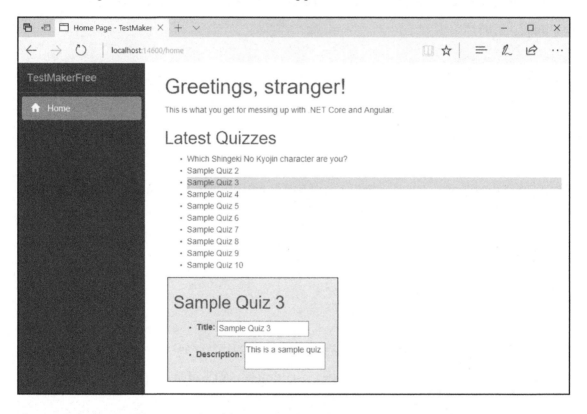

If everything is working as it should, as we change the selectedQuiz, the bottom panel should be updated as well, showing the details of that newly-selected test.

Adding additional lists

Our *Home View* isn't done yet; two out of three item lists are yet to be done, at least on the *client-side*. We're talking about the most viewed items and the randomly picked ones; let's add them to the loop. Basically, we have two ways to do this:

- Adding two more Angular components very similar to the `QuizListComponent` one
- Extending our `QuizListComponent` and make it configurable, thus making it able to handle all the three item listings

Adding two more components will be rather easy; we can clone the `quiz-list.component.ts` file a couple of times, and change the inner method of the two new files to make it fetch the relevant data from the `/quiz/ByTitle` and `/quiz/Random` server-side APIs already available through our `QuizController`. Once done, we can define a different selector for each one of them, add the required stuff in the `AppModule` and `HomeComponent` templates, and we will be done.

However, this is also a horrible approach. We will restrain ourselves from cloning any part of our code unless there's really no other way to get the things done; we're using Angular because we want to build *versatile* and *reusable* components, and we will stick to this path as much as we can. We also don't want to spawn unnecessary components, as it will be a pain to keep them in sync each and every time we have to apply a definition update, a member rename, an interface change, or any other source code modification that will affect either of them.

For these reasons, we'll definitely choose the second option. It's worth mentioning it's also will be just as easy, once we know how to properly do it.

Regarding that choice, it can be easily noted that we already started with the right foot; we called it `QuizListComponent` instead of `LatestQuizzesComponent`, because we never really wanted to restrict it to a single API call.

We can say that we already knew that we would be choosing the second option right from the start; that's hardly a surprise. Though, since we're fully committed to building *reusable* components.

Multiple components instances

The first thing we need to do is to configure the AppComponent HTML template to make it render a couple more <quiz-list> component tags; while doing that, we also need to find a way to uniquely identify them in order to issue a different behavior for each instance, including latest items, most viewed items, and random items.

Open the /ClientApp/app/components/home/home.component.html file and update our preceding code in the following way (added/modified lines are highlighted):

```
<h1>Greetings, stranger!</h1>
<p>This is what you get for messing up with .NET Core and Angular.</p>
<quiz-list class="latest"></quiz-list>
<quiz-list class="byTitle"></quiz-list>
<quiz-list class="random"></quiz-list>
```

Then, add a home.component.css style sheet file in that same folder and fill it with the following:

```
quiz-list {
    width: 400px;
    display: block;
    padding: 2px 20px;
    margin: 0px 5px;
    float: left;
}

    quiz-list.latest {
        background-color: #f0f0f0;
    }

    quiz-list.byTitle {
        background-color: #e0e0e0;
    }

    quiz-list.random {
        background-color: #d0d0d0;
    }
```

Needless to say, all these CSS rules won't work unless we add a reference to their file in the home.component.css file. Let's do that (new lines are highlighted):

```
import { Component } from '@angular/core';

@Component({
    selector: 'home',
    templateUrl: './home.component.html',
```

```
      styleUrls: ['./home.component.css']
})
export class HomeComponent {
}
```

Let's take a closer look at what we did here:

- We added two more `<quiz-list>` elements.
- We defined a standard `class` attribute with a different value for each instance; this is what we will use to uniquely identify each one of them. Note that we could've used the `id` attribute or any other standard or custom attribute; using `class` seems to be a rather elegant choice, as it can also be used to apply different styles.
- We took the chance to implement some minimalistic CSS styles to arrange the three elements horizontally and add some space between them; since they have different `class` attribute values , we also gave a unique *background-color* to each element.

Now is a good time to perform a quick debug **run** to see whether everything is working as expected:

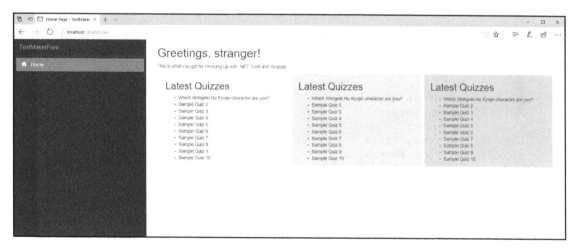

We successfully managed to get three identical `QuizListComponent` instances within the `HomeComponent`. Despite the different UI styling determined by the distinctive `class` attribute value we gave them in the `HomeComponent` template, they all work in the same way. What we need to do now is to change their behavior according to their `class` so that each one of them will fetch different quizzes by consuming its own API.

Open the `quiz-list.component.ts` file and perform the following changes to the existing code (new and updated lines are highlighted):

```typescript
import { Component, Inject, Input } from "@angular/core";
import { HttpClient } from '@angular/common/http';

@Component({
    selector: "quiz-list",
    templateUrl: './quiz-list.component.html',
    styleUrls: ['./quiz-list.component.css']
})

export class QuizListComponent {
    @Input() class: string;
    title: string;
    selectedQuiz: Quiz;
    quizzes: Quiz[];

    constructor(http: HttpClient,
            @Inject('BASE_URL') baseUrl: string) {
        var url = baseUrl + "api/quiz/";

        switch (this.class) {
            case "latest":
            default:
                this.title = "Latest Quizzes";
                url += "Latest/";
                break;
            case "byTitle":
                this.title = "Quizzes by Title";
                url += "ByTitle/";
                break;
            case "random":
                this.title = "Random Quizzes";
                url += "Random/";
                break;
        }

        this.http.get<Quiz[]>(url).subscribe(result => {
            this.quizzes = result;
        }, error => console.error(error));
```

```
        }

    onSelect(quiz: Quiz) {
        this.selectedQuiz = quiz;
        console.log("quiz with Id "
            + this.selectedQuiz.Id
            + " has been selected.");
    }
}
```

We've got a fair amount of changes here. Let's see what we did:

- In **line 1**, we added a reference to the `Input` decorator from `@angular/core`; we need it here so that our class will be able to issue a *data-binding* between the `class` input property (see **line 11**) and the **class** attribute defined in the `HomeComponent` template file. In other words, we plan to get the `<quiz-list>` class value so that we can use it programmatically (read further).
- In **line 11**, we added a local `@Input class` property that we'll use to get the class value at runtime.
- In **lines 16-33**, we re-implement the `HTTP` request logic by adding a *switch-case* statement that will configure some of the component settings--specifically, the title and the Controller API URL--depending on the `@Input class` property value, which is *bound* to the component CSS class.

Testing and debugging

We might think that these changes will be enough to do what we want; however, if we hit the run command and take a look at the browser's `HomeView`, we can see that nothing has changed. We still get three identical `QuizListComponent` instances with the same title and quizzes.

What's going on there? The best thing we can do to understand it will be to debug our client app, inspect our `class` property, and see why the *switch-case* statement is not working as expected.

We can do that by taking advantage of the TypeScript runtime debugging capabilities provided by Visual Studio:

```
16   constructor(http: Http, @Inject('BASE_URL') baseUrl: string) {
17       var url = baseUrl + "api/quiz/";
18
19   switch (this.class) {
20       case "latest":
21       default:
22           this.title = "Latest Quizzes";
23           url += "Latest/";
24           break;
25       case "byTitle":
26           this.title = "Quizzes by Title";
27           url += "ByTitle/";
28           break;
29       case "random":
30           this.title = "Random Quizzes";
31           url += "Random/";
32           break;
33   }
```

Alternatively, we can do that using the JavaScript console log in the following way (the `quiz-list.component.ts` file, new lines are highlighted):

```
[...]

    constructor(http: HttpClient,
            @Inject('BASE_URL') baseUrl: string) {
        console.log("QuizListComponent " +
            " instantiated with the following class: "
            + this.class);

[...]
```

Regardless of how we do that, the result won't change; the `class` local property will have a *undefined* value, meaning that the *binding* isn't working. This makes the *switch-case* fallback to its default condition, hence we get three identical *Latest Quizzes* component instances regardless of their `class` attribute value.

Now that we've found the issue, we just have to understand the reasons behind it; to do that, we have to take a closer look at the Angular components life cycle.

The OnInit interface and lifecycle hooks

In software engineering, the term *life cycle* is often used to symbolize a list of sequential steps marking the various phases of any given *item*, starting from the first relevant one and ending up with the last. Depending on the given context, the *item* can either be a project, an application, a thread, and so on. Different kinds of items can also have different relevant phases worth measuring. For example, in *Object-Oriented Programming* languages, the *item* is often an object, and the *lifecycle* marks the steps from its *creation* phase (usually issued by constructors, initializers, or builders) up to its *destruction* phase (usually handled by destructors, dispose statements, garbage collections, and so on).

Most modern frameworks, including .NET Core and Angular, manage their objects through a known and measurable life cycle; on top of that, they also provide a number of *lifecycle hooks* bound to the most relevant steps that can be used by developers to perform actions whenever they occur.

In Angular, each component is subject to a life cycle; the framework creates it, renders it, creates and renders its children, checks it when its *data-bound* properties change, and eventually, destroys and removes it from the DOM; most of these steps are bound to a dedicated *lifecycle hook*, as we can see in the following overview:

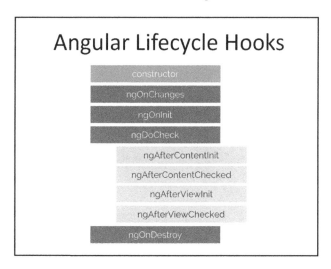

It's important to understand that each *lifecycle hook*, in addition to being exposed to the developers, is also used in the Angular framework to perform required internal tasks.

With regard to the preceding diagram, the non-indented hooks are available for *component* and *directive* instances, while the indented ones are for *component* instances only. The reason is fairly obvious--*directives* don't have contents and views that can trigger them.

This is good to know, but what about our binding problem? What does this have to do with it? We can easily answer that by taking a look at the Angular official documentation and reading what happens during the ngOnInit *lifecycle hook*:

ngOnInit(): Initializes the directive/component after Angular first displays the data-bound properties and sets the directive/component's input properties. These are called once, after the first ngOnChanges(). Here lies our answer--we are expecting to get our @Input class value within the **constructor**, but the framework will only set it during the ngOnInit() lifecycle hook, which comes later on. This means that our code is fine, except that *we chose the wrong hook.*

For a detailed description of all the available Angular *lifecycle hooks*, you can check out the following URL from the official docs:

https://angular.io/guide/lifecycle-hooks

Implementing ngOnInit

Now that we know what we did wrong, we can fix our issue by properly implementing a ngOnInit hook within our QuizListComponent class.

Open the quiz-list.component.ts file and add the following code (new/updated lines are highlighted):

```
import { Component, Inject, Input, OnInit } from "@angular/core";
import { HttpClient } from "@angular/common/http";

@Component({
    selector: "quiz-list",
    templateUrl: './quiz-list.component.html',
    styleUrls: ['./quiz-list.component.css']
})

export class QuizListComponent implements OnInit {
    @Input() class: string;
    title: string;
    selectedQuiz: Quiz;
    quizzes: Quiz[];
    http: HttpClient;
    baseUrl: string;
```

```
constructor(http: HttpClient,
    @Inject('BASE_URL') baseUrl: string) {
    this.http = http;
    this.baseUrl = baseUrl;
}

ngOnInit() {
    console.log("QuizListComponent " +
        " instantiated with the following class: "
        + this.class);

    var url = this.baseUrl + "api/quiz/";

    switch (this.class) {
        case "latest":
        default:
            this.title = "Latest Quizzes";
            url += "Latest/";
            break;
        case "byTitle":
            this.title = "Quizzes by Title";
            url += "ByTitle/";
            break;
        case "random":
            this.title = "Random Quizzes";
            url += "Random/";
            break;
    }

    this.http.get<Quiz[]>(url).subscribe(result => {
        this.quizzes = result;
    }, error => console.error(error));
}

onSelect(quiz: Quiz) {
    this.selectedQuiz = quiz;
    console.log("quiz with Id "
        + this.selectedQuiz.Id
        + " has been selected.");
}
}
```

Here's an explanation of what we just did:

- In **line 1**, we added a reference to the `OnInit` interface, which is required to implement the `ngOnInit()` hook.
- In **lines 15-16**, we added two new local properties that will store the constructor variables; we need to do that because we will use them within the `ngOnInit()` method, so we need to have them referenced somewhere. Since they are instantiated through DI, this won't have performance or memory impact.
- In **lines 19-20**, we assigned the DI instances to our new properties. Note how all the class logic has been removed from the constructor, which is now very shallow.
- Starting from **line 23**, we implemented the `ngOnInit()` method, which now handles the tasks that were previously done within the constructor.

The only downside of this new implementation is the amount of code bloat required to declare and assign these new properties; we can definitely use some syntactic sugar to shrink it out. Luckily enough, Angular support a neat constructor syntax that will allow us to skip these properties, declaration, and assignment. Consider writing the following:

```
http: HttpClient;
baseUrl: string;

constructor(http: HttpClient,
    @Inject('BASE_URL') baseUrl: string) {
    this.http = http;
    this.baseUrl = baseUrl;
}
```

We can write this instead:

```
constructor(private http: HttpClient,
    @Inject('BASE_URL') private baseUrl: string) {
}
```

We will achieve the following result--as soon as we give them an explicit access modifier, these parameters will be exposed accordingly. In our specific scenario, the **private** modifier is more than enough, as it makes them available throughout the whole class; let's change our code to use this new syntax and go ahead.

Testing it up

Now it's time to run the project and see whether our improvements fixed our lifecycle issue for good:

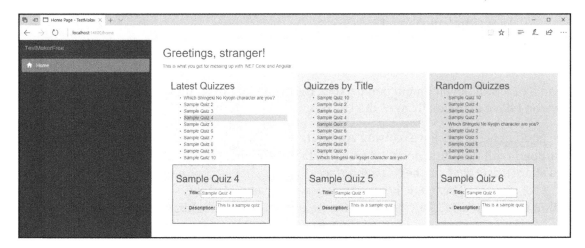

It definitely looks like we did it. While we're here, we can also take the chance to check whether the `QuizComponent` instances lying within each `QuizListComponent` instance are still working properly; they seem to be in good shape as well.

Our application is growing fast; we already got a decent *server-side* API set, and we're beginning to make good use of it by putting together a small yet versatile set of working Angular Components able to fetch and display our sample data. However, we're still missing an important Angular feature that will help us a lot later on; let's do what it takes to close the gap.

Two-way data binding

We already mentioned it a number of times as one of the most convenient and widely-known features of Angular, as well as in many other reactive frameworks out there. Nonetheless, before going further, let's ensure that we know what we're talking about.

Two-way data binding, also known as **two-way binding,** means that whenever the *Data Model* changes, the *UI* changes accordingly and vice versa. To be more specific, consider the following:

- Whenever the *model* is updated, the changes are immediately reflected to the *views* implementing it
- Whenever a *view* is updated, the changes are immediately reflected in the underlying *model*

From a practical development perspective, **two-way data binding** will help us a lot, because we won't have to manually sync the UI components with the Data Model.

The good news is, since we're using Angular, we're already set; our application is already equipped with fully-functional **two-way data binding** between two Angular components that share a *data bind* via the Quiz interface: the QuizListComponent and the QuizComponent. The magic lies in the way we implemented the [(ngModel)] directive within the QuizComponent template file (relevant lines are highlighted):

```
<div *ngIf="quiz" class="quiz">
    <h2>{{quiz.Title}}</h2>
    <ul>
        <li>
            <label>Title:</label>
            <input [(ngModel)]="quiz.Title" placeholder="Insert the
            title..." />
        </li>
        <li>
            <label>Description:</label>
            <textarea [(ngModel)]=" quiz.Description"
             placeholder="Insert a suitable description..."></textarea>
        </li>
    </ul>
</div>
```

We can easily check this out by running the application in *Debug* mode, then selecting a quiz and changing its Title property using the input textbox provided by the QuizComponent. We can easily note how any change will be immediately reflected in the QuizListComponent accordingly:

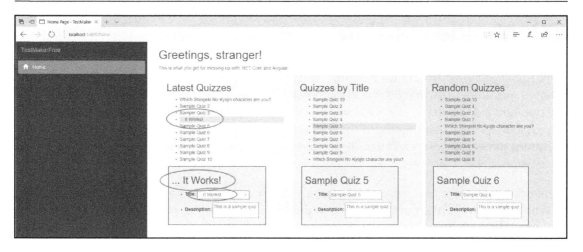

As we already said, all of these things are happening on the *client-side* only, so order to persist them through the server Model, we will need to implement a fully-featured **Data Source**, which is something we will do in the next chapter.

Disabling two-way data binding

In case we don't like having a *two-way binding* relationship, we can easily turn it off by removing the parentheses around the ngModel directive within the quiz.component.html file, leaving only the square brackets:

```
<input [ngModel]="test.Title" placeholder="Insert the title..."/>
```

The *parentheses within brackets* that enable two-way binding [()] are widely known as *banana brackets*. This funny name has its roots in the **Adventure in Angular** podcast episode 078, featuring *Brad Green*, *Misko Hevery*, and *Igor Minar*, in which they referred to that syntax by calling it a "box of bananas". Other than being an impressive visualization, the *banana-box* concept helps us to avoid common mistakes such as placing the brackets inside the parentheses.

Client-side routing

Our Master/Detail relationship is indeed working, yet it has some major flaws. The current *in-page navigation* approach, for example, is completely different from the original plan. We wanted our users to switch back and forth between the `HomeView` containing the list of quizzes and a dedicated `QuizView` whenever he selects one of them, but the app doesn't do that; it just opens something like a "quiz detail panel" under each list. Not just one but **three different panels**, one for each item lists--that doesn't make any sense! We need to fix that as soon as possible.

While doing that, we also have another issue to solve. You may have noted that, regardless of what we do within our app, the URL in the browser's address bar is always the same. It will mean that we won't be able to share, say, a URL that will directly lead to a specific quiz; we'll be forced to share the starting URL because it is the only supported one.

Wait a minute, isn't this our Native Web application's most expected behavior? This is what the *Single-Page* approach is all about after all, isn't it? The answer is no. The *Single-Page application* approach has nothing to do with keeping an immutable URL in the browser's address Bar. URLs are not pages, as the name suggests; they are unique identifiers for accessing resources.

Standard Web applications are usually built upon a rather small number of pages that answer to multiple URLs and serve specific contents based upon query string parameter values and/or URL rewriting techniques. *Single-Page applications* make no exceptions, as they can adapt their inner state according to the request URL and also track the user navigation by updating the browser's address bar accordingly. This technique is called **client-side routing**, which has the same meaning as navigation; luckily enough, the sample SPA shipped with our Angular template already implements all we need to set everything up. Remember the `counter` and `fetchdata` components that we removed back in `Chapter 1`, *Getting Ready*? They also had their own *client-side* routes registered in the `AppModule` and implemented in the `NavMenuComponent`, which we also removed because we didn't need them anymore. Now that we need something similar, all we have to do is go back there and get the job done.

Before doing that, we need to understand how the router can help us achieve what we want, changing the browser's location and history whenever the user navigates within the app, without triggering a new page request to the server.

PathLocationStrategy versus HashLocationStrategy

The Angular router can be configured to follow one of two different patterns: `PathLocationStrategy` or `HashLocationStrategy`. The former is based upon the HTML5 `history.pushState` technique, which is by far the prefered one. It is worth noting, however, that such techniques won't work well on older browsers, because they will automatically send a page request every time the current `location.href` value changes, ruining the whole SPA approach, unless the change is limited to the part of the URL that is after a hash character (#).

`HashLocationStrategy` is mostly a workaround that exploits such behavior, as it will instruct the router to compose all the navigation URLs prepending them with a hash character (#) in the following way:

```
http://localhost:14600/app/#/quiz-detail/2
```

The Angular **Router Module** uses `PathLocationStrategy` by default, hence our app will do the same. Should we prefer to take the other route, we can switch to `HashLocationStrategy` with an override during the bootstrap phase; we will see how to do that in a short while.

Refactoring our app

If we want to transform our current approach into an effective Master/Detail navigation pattern, implementing the routes isn't the only thing we need to do--we also need to change our existing component structure to make it *routing-friendly*. Actually, it can be wise to get this done first, since it will involve some minor refactoring.

Let's try to get a visual picture of what we need to do before proceeding. It's time to get rid of this working, yet rather inconsistent, cascading structure:

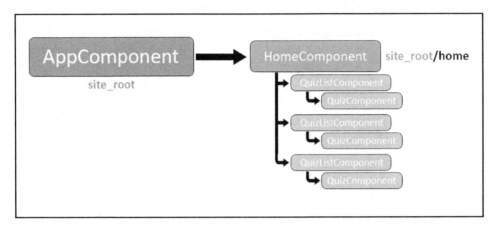

We'll switch to this navigable one:

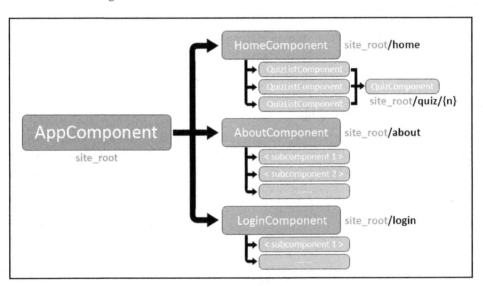

While we were there, we took the chance to enrich our app with a couple more components (AboutComponent and LoginComponents) that we will implement later on.

In order to achieve all of this, we need to take care of the following tasks:

- Register and implement a new route that will make our `QuizComponent` load in *stand-alone* mode instead of being a mere element of the `QuizListComponent` template.
  - Change the `QuizComponent` loading behavior so that it can work independently; more specifically, it should fetch the selected quiz details with a *server-side* API call using a single parameter (such as the quiz `ID`), instead of receiving the whole object from its parent using the *data-bind* feature.
- Add more sample Components to test the routing behavior with a number of different requests and configure them into the `AppRouting` scheme as well.

Let's do this.

Registering a new Route

Open the `app.module.shared.ts` file and add the following highlighted line to the existing code:

```
[...]

@NgModule({
    declarations: [
        AppComponent,
        NavMenuComponent,
        HomeComponent,
        QuizListComponent,
        QuizComponent
    ],
    imports: [
        CommonModule,
        HttpClientModule,
        FormsModule,
        RouterModule.forRoot([
            { path: '', redirectTo: 'home', pathMatch: 'full' },
            { path: 'home', component: HomeComponent },
            { path: 'quiz/:id', component: QuizComponent },
            { path: '**', redirectTo: 'home' }
        ])
    ]
})

[...]
```

The meaning of this is quite straightforward; each time the app receives an HTTP request pointing to /quiz/<id>, it will load the QuizComponent, passing the <id> value as a GET parameter corresponding to the ID key.

Angular will iterate through these rules starting with the first one until it finds a match; ensure to add the new routing rules *before* the ** global fallback that redirects everything to home, or they will never be executed!

Upgrading the QuizComponent

Now we need to perform some important changes to the quiz.component.ts file to ensure that our QuizComponent will properly receive and handle it.

Since we're removing the parent property binding, we can safely remove the reference to the Input interface module, as well as the @Input decorator, from our local quiz variable, as we're not using them here anymore.

It's important to understand that as soon as we do this, the *binding* relationship between the QuizListComponent and QuizComponent will cease to work. However, this is hardly an issue; although it has been being very useful to demonstrate how *two-way binding* works, the time has come to replace it with a more reasonable, route-based navigation mechanism.

```
[...]

export class QuizComponent {
    quiz: Quiz;
}

[...]
```

We still need to retrieve the quiz data through the *server-side* API, however to do that, we will need the quiz ID that is expected to come as a GET parameter through the routed HTTP request.

Getting the ID parameter

Here's how we can retrieve it:

```
import { Component } from "@angular/core";
import { ActivatedRoute, Router } from "@angular/router";
```

```
@Component({
    selector: "quiz",
    templateUrl: './quiz.component.html',
    styleUrls: ['./quiz.component.css']
})

export class QuizComponent {
    quiz: Quiz;

    constructor(private activatedRoute: ActivatedRoute,
        private router: Router) {

        // create an empty object from the Quiz interface
        this.quiz = <Quiz>{};

        var id = +this.activatedRoute.snapshot.params["id"];
        console.log(id);
        if (id) {
            // TO-DO: load the quiz using server- side API
        }
        else {
            console.log("Invalid id: routing back to home...");
            this.router.navigate(["home"]);
        }
    }
}
```

What we did here is quite simple to explain:

- In **line 2**, we added a reference to the `ActivatedRoute` interface and to the `Router` class, so we can use both of them later on; the former will give us information about the currently active route, which will contain the GET parameter that we need to retrieve; the latter will allow us to redirect the user to the `HomeView` in case of an error.
- In **lines 13-28**, we implemented the `constructor` class, where we get the ID GET parameter from the active route using the `ActivateRoute` interface. If the ID is not null or empty, we load the quiz using server-side API (this is yet to be done, hence the *to-do* comment), otherwise we route the user back to the `HomeView`.

 Note that we're already using the `private` access modifier for the constructor parameters, as we will most likely need to have them available through the whole class later on.

The usage of the injected `ActivatedRoute` object instance is somewhat cryptic, hence it deserves a brief explanation. As you may know, this is the place where we can find information about route parameters, query parameters, and URL fragments for the currently active route. In order to access the `ID` query parameter, we need to look into the `params` property, which happens to be an `Observable` object. This basically means that we will normally need to *subscribe* to it in the following way, just like we did with the `get()` method result of `HttpClient`:

```
this.activatedRoute.params.subscribe(
    params => {
        let id = +params['id'];
        // do something with id
    });
```

This will indeed work; however, we were able to retrieve the `ID` parameter using a smaller amount of code and avoiding `Observable` entirely thanks to the `snapshot` property, which returns a flatten representation of the currently active route. As a general rule of thumb, we can--and should--use the `snapshot` whenever we don't need to actively monitor the `Observable` changes.

 As we already mentioned once, *Observables* are one of the most interesting features introduced by Angular; we'll definitely talk more about them later on.

Adding the HttpClient

So far, so good; now we need to replace that *to-do* with a working code that will get the quiz from the .NET Core `QuizController`. We can easily do that with the `HttpClient` service, just like we did to get the quiz array in the `QuizListController` a while ago. In order to use it, we need to add the required import reference to the top of the `quiz.controller.ts` file:

```
import { Component, Inject } from "@angular/core";
import { ActivatedRoute, Router } from "@angular/router";
import { HttpClient } from "@angular/common/http";

[...]
```

While we were there, we also added the `Inject` decorator in line 1, as we will use it in a few.

The next step is to have the `HttpClient` available somewhere. As usual, we can achieve that through **Dependency Injection**, by adding an attribute variable to the constructor:

```
[...]

constructor(private activatedRoute: ActivatedRoute,
    private router: Router,
    private http: HttpClient) {
}

[...]
```

Fetching the data

Finally, we need to replace our *TO-DO* comment with the code that will allow our component to fetch the quiz JSON data from the .NET Core `QuizController` from the ID `GET` parameter provided by the current route and store it into a local property. Here it is (new/updated lines are highlighted):

```
constructor(private activatedRoute: ActivatedRoute,
    private router: Router,
    private http: HttpClient,
    @Inject('BASE_URL') private baseUrl: string) {

    var id = +this.activatedRoute.snapshot.params["id"];
    console.log(id);
    if (id) {
        var url = this.baseUrl + "api/quiz/" + id;

        this.http.get<Quiz>(url).subscribe(result => {
            this.quiz = result;
        }, error => console.error(error));
    }
    else {
        console.log("Invalid id: routing back to home...");
        this.router.navigate(["home"]);
    }
}
```

It's worth noting that we also had to inject the `baseUrl` reference in the constructor, which is required to properly build the Web API endpoint address.

Updating the QuizListComponent

We're done with the `QuizComponent`, but now we need to make it work by changing the way the `QuizListComponent` makes use of it. The first thing that we need to do is to remove its element tag from the `quiz-list.component.html` template file:

```html
<h2>{{title}}</h2>
<ul class="quizzes">
    <li *ngFor="let quiz of quizzes"
        [class.selected]="quiz === selectedQuiz"
        (click)="onSelect(quiz)">
        <span>{{quiz.Title}}</span>
    </li>
</ul>
<!-- <quiz *ngIf="selectedQuiz" [quiz]="selectedQuiz"></quiz> -->
```

We commented it out, but we can delete it as well. Now, open the `quiz-list.component.ts` file and add something to the implementation of the `onSelected()` method so that it will route the user to the `QuizComponent` instead of relying on a *data-bind* that is long gone:

```
[...]

onSelect(quiz: Quiz) {
    this.selectedQuiz = quiz;
    console.log("quiz with Id "
        + this.selectedQuiz.Id
        + " has been selected.");
    this.router.navigate(["quiz", this.selectedQuiz.Id]);
}

[...]
```

Wait a minute, this line will never compile, as there is no `this.router` in the `QuizListComponent` file! Let's fix that in the **constructor**, with the help of the Angular syntatic sugar we learned of earlier (new lines are highlighted):

```
import { Component, Inject, Input, OnInit } from "@angular/core";
import { Router } from "@angular/router";
import { HttpClient } from "@angular/common/http";

@Component({
    selector: "quiz-list",
    templateUrl: './quiz-list.component.html',
    styleUrls: ['./quiz-list.component.css']
})
```

```
export class QuizListComponent implements OnInit {
    @Input() class: string;
    title: string;
    selectedQuiz: Quiz;
    quizzes: Quiz[];

    constructor(private http: HttpClient,
        @Inject('BASE_URL') private baseUrl: string,
        private router: Router) {
    }

[...]
```

Needless to say, we had to **import** the **Router** class as well.

Master/Detail Routing test

It's time to test our improved Master/Detail approach. Run the application in *debug* mode and wait for the *Home* view to load, then select a quiz element and see what happens:

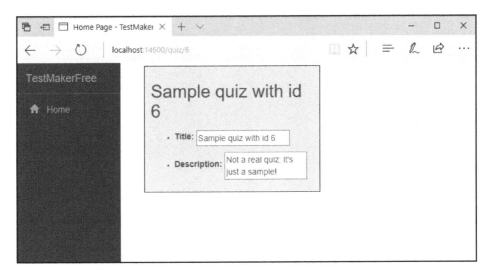

We did it, it works! The page is as ugly as hell, but there's no reason to worry about that now; we'll save the styling for another chapter. For now, we'll just stick to the plan and add the additional components we talked about earlier.

Adding new components

If we remember correctly, these were the names we chose for them:

- AboutComponent
- LoginComponent
- PageNotFoundComponent

Considering what we just did, we should be able to add them in the blink of an eye. They won't be much more than a placeholder for the time being. We will properly implement each one of them as soon as we need to.

AboutComponent

From **Solution Explorer**, create a new /ClientApp/app/components/about/ folder, and then add a new about.component.ts file with the following content:

```
import { Component } from "@angular/core";

@Component({
    selector: "about",
    templateUrl: "./about.component.html"
})

export class AboutComponent {
    title = "About";
}
```

Once done, add the about.component.html template file:

```
<h2>{{title}}</h2>
<div>
    TestMakerFree: a production-ready, fully-featured SPA sample
    powered by ASP.NET Core and Angular.
</div>
```

To be honest, we ought to say that we're neither production-ready nor fully-featured yet, but that's what we're aiming for, so a little encouragement won't hurt. It won't be a lie forever, after all!

LoginComponent

Back to **Solution Explorer**, create a new `/ClientApp/app/components/login/` folder and fill it out with the following `login.component.ts` file:

```
import { Component } from "@angular/core";

@Component({
    selector: "login",
    templateUrl: "./login.component.html"
})

export class LoginComponent {
    title = "Login";
}
```

Also, put in the `login.component.html` template file:

```
<h2>{{title}}</h2>
<div>
    TO-DO: Not implemented yet.
</div>
```

As we already said, this is just a placeholder; there's no way we can implement a proper *login view* or any authentication mechanism now, as we're still missing a real, persistent **Data Source**. If we have the urge to mock it out, we can arrange something similar to what we did in `Chapter 2`, *Backend with .NET Core*. There's no need to do that yet, however, since we'll start implementing the real deal in the following chapter.

PageNotFoundComponent

Last but not least, create a new `/ClientApp/app/components/pagenotfound/` folder and fill it out with the following `pagenotfound.component.ts` file:

```
import { Component } from "@angular/core";

@Component({
    selector: "pagenotfound",
    templateUrl: "./pagenotfound.component.html"
})

export class PageNotFoundComponent {
    title = "Page not Found";
}
```

Also fill it with its corresponding `pagenotfound.component.html` template file:

```
<h2>{{title}}</h2>
<div>
    Oops... This page does not exist (yet!).
</div>
```

Wait a minute, aren't we forgetting something that we're require to do each and every time we add a new component? As a matter of fact, we do; we still need to add them all to the `AppModule` class.

Updating the AppModule

Open the `/ClientApp/app/app.module.shared.ts` file and add the new references accordingly (new lines highlighted):

```
import { NgModule } from '@angular/core';
import { CommonModule } from '@angular/common';
import { FormsModule } from '@angular/forms';
import { HttpClientModule } from '@angular/common/http';
import { RouterModule } from '@angular/router';

import { AppComponent } from './components/app/app.component';
import { NavMenuComponent } from './components/navmenu/navmenu.component';
import { HomeComponent } from './components/home/home.component';
import { QuizListComponent } from './components/quiz/quiz-list.component';
import { QuizComponent } from './components/quiz/quiz.component';
import { AboutComponent } from './components/about/about.component';
import { LoginComponent } from './components/login/login.component';
import { PageNotFoundComponent } from
'./components/pagenotfound/pagenotfound.component';

@NgModule({
    declarations: [
        AppComponent,
        NavMenuComponent,
        HomeComponent,
        QuizListComponent,
        QuizComponent,
        AboutComponent,
        LoginComponent,
        PageNotFoundComponent
    ],
    imports: [
        CommonModule,
        HttpClientModule,
```

```
        FormsModule,
        RouterModule.forRoot([
            { path: '', redirectTo: 'home', pathMatch: 'full' },
            { path: 'home', component: HomeComponent },
            { path: 'quiz/:id', component: QuizComponent },
            { path: 'about', component: AboutComponent },
            { path: 'login', component: LoginComponent },
            { path: '**', component: PageNotFoundComponent }
        ])
    ]
})
export class AppModuleShared {
}
```

As we can see, we also added the proper routing rules to ensure that these components will actually be reached whenever the user clicks on the related link within the NavMenuComponent. At the moment, though, there are no links in the NavMenuComponent pointing to these components! We almost forgot that, didn't we? Let's fix that.

Open the /ClientApp/app/components/navmenu/navmenu.component.html file and add the following content to the existing template code (new lines are highlighted):

```
<div class='main-nav'>
    <div class='navbar navbar-inverse'>
        <div class='navbar-header'>
            <button type='button' class='navbar-toggle' data-
                toggle='collapse' data-target='.navbar-collapse'>
                <span class='sr-only'>Toggle navigation</span>
                <span class='icon-bar'></span>
                <span class='icon-bar'></span>
                <span class='icon-bar'></span>
            </button>
            <a class='navbar-brand' [routerLink]="
                ['/home']">TestMakerFree</a>
        </div>
        <div class='clearfix'></div>
        <div class='navbar-collapse collapse'>
            <ul class='nav navbar-nav'>
                <li [routerLinkActive]="['link-active']">
                    <a [routerLink]="['/home']">
                        <span class='glyphicon glyphicon-home'></span>
                                        Home
                    </a>
                </li>
                <li [routerLinkActive]="['link-active']">
                    <a [routerLink]="['/about']">
                        <span class='glyphicon glyphicon-info-sign'>
```

```
                            </span> About
                    </a>
                </li>
                <li [routerLinkActive]="['link-active']">
                    <a [routerLink]="['/login']">
                        <span class='glyphicon glyphicon-log-in'>
                        </span> Login
                    </a>
                </li>
            </ul>
        </div>
    </div>
</div>
```

That will do. We also took the opportunity to add some neat icons from the **Glyphicon Halflings** set, which is freely available for the **Bootstrap** framework, which is the *frontend* library shipped with the .NET Core MVC with Angular template we've been using. We'll talk more about it in Chapter 6, *Style Sheets and UI Layout*.

Before moving ahead, let's spend a moment explaining how we handled the PageNotFoundComponent. For obvious reasons, it can't have a direct link on the NavMenuComponent along with the other existing routes; that won't make any sense, as it's intended to kick in whenever the user ends up with a *non-existing* route. To properly implement this, we changed the behavior of the global fallback routing rule so that it will load the PageNotFoundComponent instead of redirecting to **Home**.

Full-Scale test

It's almost time to hit *F5* and see whether our revised Angular app is still holding its ground. Before we do that, let's quickly open the

/ClientApp/app/components/home/home.component.html file and replace our witty welcome text with something that can define our application better:

```html
<h1>Welcome to TestMakerFree</h1>
<p>A sample SPA project made with .NET Core and Angular.</p>
<quiz-list class="latest"></quiz-list>
<quiz-list class="byTitle"></quiz-list>
<quiz-list class="random"></quiz-list>
```

If we did everything correctly, we should be greeted with something like this:

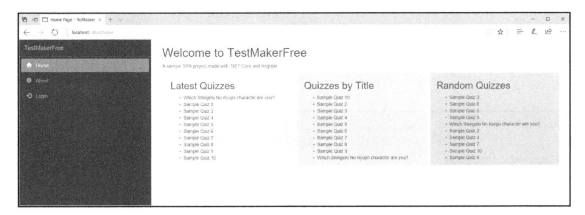

This definitely looks like the `HomeView` we wanted. Let's check whether the improved *Master-Detail* navigation pattern is still working by clicking on one of the available quizzes. The `HomeView` should be replaced by the `QuizView`, displaying the test detail data:

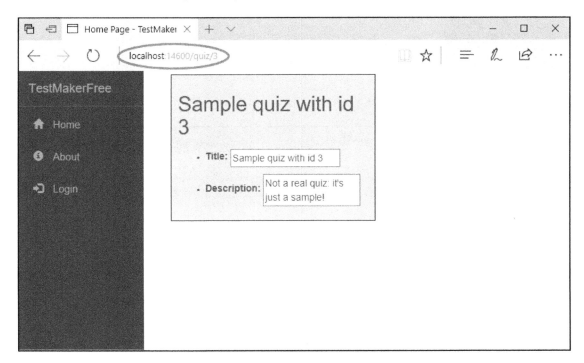

Still ugly, yet still up and running. Note how the **URL** in the *address bar* properly switches from `localhost/home` to `localhost/quiz/{n}`, thus reflecting the user navigation up to this point.

Since the *Master/Detail* route seems to be working, let's test the changes we made to the `NavMenuComponent`. Clicking on the **About** link element should update our page in the following way:

The **Login** link should be working as well:

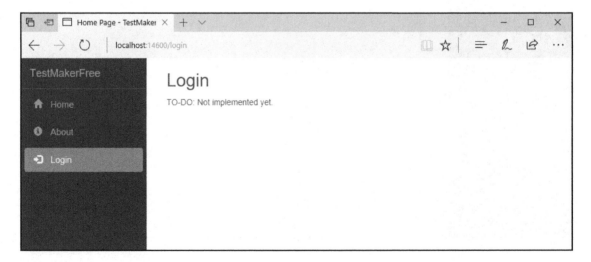

Finally, we can go back to the `HomeView` and take another look at the initial layout:

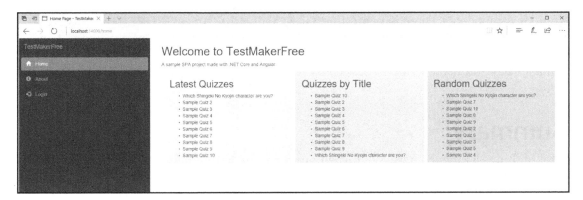

If we compare the preceding screenshot with the previous one, we should be able to see some small differences, such as the **Random Quizzes** listing showing different entries. Mind you, this is hardly a surprise, since we want our app to always refresh that content by issuing a new API call each time. Neither Angular nor .NET Core will serve cached content unless we tell them to do so.

 Conversely, the web server and/or the browser can definitely do that due to their default behavior for static files; that's why we explicitly disabled file caching back in `Chapter 1`, *Getting Ready*.

Did we forget about our `PageNotFoundComponent`? We didn't put it in the `NavMenuComponent` for obvious reasons, but it will be a shame not to test it as well. To do that, just write a non-existing route in the browser's address bar and see what happens:

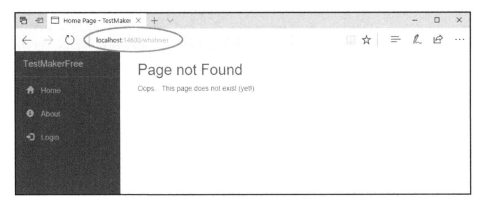

That's it.

Suggested topics

Angular components, Directives and Interfaces, XMLHttpRequest (XHR), Two-Way Data Binding, Master-Detail navigation patterns, PathLocationStrategy, HashLocationStrategy, location.pushState, URL Rewrite Module, URL Rewriting, Promise, Observable, EcmaScript6, and EcmaScript7.

Summary

A lot of things happened here. We turned our attention to the *client-side* components of our app, switching the focus from Web API to Angular. We chose to implement a *Home View* featuring multiple listings of clickable tests, giving our users the chance to navigate to their detail page through a classic *Master-Detail* relationship.

To achieve such results, we created a bunch of Angular-related items: the Quiz interface for the model, the `QuizListComponent` class to retrieve the required data from the .NET Core Controller and show them to the user, and the `QuizComponent` to access the detail of each selected quiz. We connected them all with the Angular native *data-binding* strategies and updated the `HomeComponent` accordingly; right after that, we improved the `QuizListComponent` by turning it into a versatile and reusable class so that we were able to add multiple instances of it into the `HomeComponent` template.

Everything we did was indeed working, but it didn't reach our expectations in terms of seamless navigation between views. We chose to address this issue by refactoring our app and improving the implementation of the **Angular Routing Module**, thus improving our previous *Master/Detail* approach.

As soon as we built our improved, *navigation-based* pattern, we performed a final test to see whether everything was working as expected; since it did, we added other components, including a `PageNotFoundComponent` that will be shown to our users whenever they try to visit a non-existing route.

In the last section, we implemented a minimalistic, *dummy-based*, yet functional Web API using .NET Core MVC. In this chapter, we built an unpolished--yet working--Angular *client-side* App. In the subsequent chapters, we'll address these flaws by adding a **Data Model**, further improving our controllers and also working on the *frontend* for a better UI.

4

Data Model with Entity Framework Core

Our *Single-Page Application* is growing fine, yet it's also starting to show its limits:

- There's no way we can add, update, or delete our sample records
- We cannot properly implement our **Login** view, since it will require handling some sort of user authentication in terms of credential storage and session persistence, to say the least
- Truth be told, we can't even say we're actually showing something close to our original plan; our quizzes are still shallow items with titles and descriptions put together by a sample method providing some *autogenerated* data

It's time to get rid of that provisional demo and start working on the real thing. We won't use Angular for the time being, as what we need to implement has little or nothing to do with the *client-side* portion of our app. Nonetheless, we're fully aware of the fact that most entities of the **Data Model** we're about to build will have their correspondence in an Angular model class, just like we did in Chapter 3, *Frontend with Angular*, with the C# QuizViewModel and the TypeScript Quiz interface. As long as we don't forget that we're doing this for feeding Angular, we'll be good.

Getting ready

We need to do a lot of things here, so it's better to avoid wasting time by introducing the whole **Data Model** concept as well as the various meanings of these two words. The experienced reader, as well as the seasoned developer, will be most likely aware of all the relevant stuff. We'll just say that when we are talking about a **Data Model**, we don't mean anything more or anything less than a lightweight, *definitely-typed* set of entity classes representing *persistent*, *code-driven* **Data Structures** that we can use as resources within our Web API code.

The word *persistent* has been used for a reason; we want our data structure to be stored in a **Database**. That's rather obvious for any application based on data. Our `TestMakerFree` app won't be an exception, since we want it to act as a *collection*--or a *repository*--of user made quizzes. More than requiring a Database, our *Single-Page Application* aims to be a web-brows able Database by itself.

Installing Entity Framework Core

We will create our Database with the help of the **Entity Framework Core** (also known as **EF Core**), the well-known open source **Object Relational Mapper** (ORM) for **ADO.NET** developed by Microsoft. The reasons for such a choice are many:

- Seamless integration with the Visual Studio IDE
- A conceptual model based upon entity classes (*Entity Data Model* or *EDM*) that will enable us to work with data using *domain-specific* objects without the need to write data-access code, which is precisely what we're looking for
- Easy to deploy, use, and maintain in development and production phases
- Compatible with all the major *open source* and commercial SQL-based engines, including **MSSql**, **MySql**, **PostgreSql**, **Oracle**, and more, thanks to the official and/or third-party EF-compatible *Connectors* available via NuGet

 It's worth mentioning that **Entity Framework Core** was previously known as **Entity Framework 7** until its latest RC release. The name change follows the ASP.NET 5 / ASP.NET Core perspective switch we already talked about, as it also emphasizes the EF Core major rewrite/redesign if we compare it to the previous installments.

You might be wondering why we're choosing to adopt a SQL-based approach instead of going for a NoSQL alternative; there are many good NoSQL products such as *MongoDB*, *RavenDB*, and *CouchDB* that happen to have a C# connector library. What about using one of them instead?

The answer is rather simple; they are not yet supported by **Entity Framework Core 2.0**, which--at the time of writing--happens to be the latest stable release. If we look at the EF Core team backlog, we can see that non-relational Database providers such as Azure Table Storage, Redis, and others are indeed mentioned for upcoming support, yet it's unlikely that we'll be able to see any of them implemented within the EF Core's next releases as well.

If you want to know more about the upcoming release, and/or if you feel bold enough to use it anyway--maybe with a NoSQL DB as well--we suggest you read more about the EF Core project status by visiting the following links:

Project Roadmap:

https://github.com/aspnet/EntityFramework/wiki/Roadmap

Source Code on GitHub:

https://github.com/aspnet/EntityFramework

Official documentation:

https://docs.efproject.net/en/latest/

In order to install **Entity Framework Core**, we need to add the relevant packages to the dependencies section of our project file. We can easily do that using the visual GUI in the following way:

1. *Right-click* on the **TestMakerFreeWebApp** project.
2. Select **Manage NuGet Packages**.
3. Ensure that the Package source drop-down list is set to **All**.

4. Go to the **Browse** tab and search for the packages containing the `Microsoft.EntityFrameworkCore` keyword:

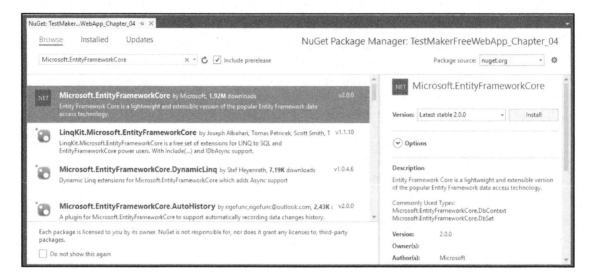

Install the following packages (latest at the time of writing):

- `Microsoft.EntityFrameworkCore` version 2.0.1
- `Microsoft.EntityFrameworkCore.SqlServer` version 2.0.1
- `Microsoft.EntityFrameworkCore.SqlServer.Design` version 2.0.0-preview1-final
- `Microsoft.EntityFrameworkCore.Tools` version 2.0.1
- `Microsoft.EntityFrameworkCore.Tools.DotNet` version 2.0.0

If we prefer to do that using the NuGet package manager command line, we can input the following:

```
PM> Install-Package Microsoft.EntityFrameworkCore -Version 2.0.1
PM> Install-Package Microsoft.EntityFrameworkCore.SqlServer -Version 2.0.1
PM> Install-Package Microsoft.EntityFrameworkCore.SqlServer.Design -Version
2.0.0-preview1-final
PM> Install-Package Microsoft.EntityFrameworkCore.Tools -Version 2.0.1
PM> Install-Package Microsoft.EntityFrameworkCore.Tools.DotNet -Version
2.0.0
```

Among the installed namespaces, we can easily note the presence of
`Microsoft.EntityFrameworkCore.SqlServer`, which is the Microsoft SQL Database
Provider for Entity Framework Core. This highly versatile connector provides an interface
with the whole Microsoft SQL Server Database family, including SQL Server 2008 to 2016,
as well as the Express and Compact editions for personal and development usage.
We're free to choose between using one of them and picking another DBMS engine such as
MySQL, PostgreSQL, or any other EF-compatible product. Should we take this decision
now? It entirely depends on the data modeling approach we want to adopt; for the time
being, and for the sake of simplicity, we choose to stick to the MS family.

Data Modeling approaches

Now that we have Entity Framework installed, we have to choose between one of the three
available approaches to model the data structure: **Model-First**, **Database-First**, or **Code-
First**. Each one of them comes with its fair amount of advantages and disadvantages, as the
experienced readers and seasoned .NET developers will most certainly know. While we
won't dig too much into these, it could be useful to briefly summarize each one of them
before taking the choice.

Model-First

If we're not familiar with the Visual Studio IDE design tools such as the **XML-based
DataSet Schema (XSD)** and the **Entity Designer Model XML visual interface (EDMX)**, the
Model-First approach can be rather confusing. The key to understanding it is to
acknowledge the fact that the word *Model* here is meant to define a *visual diagram* built with
the design tools. That diagram will then be used by the Framework to autogenerate the
Database SQL script and the Data Model source code files.

To summarize, we can say that going *Model-First* will mean "working on a visual EDMX diagram and letting **Entity Framework** create/update the rest accordingly":

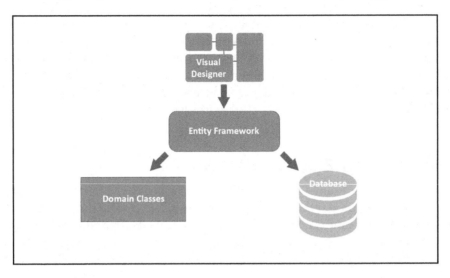

Such an approach has the following benefits:

- We will be able to create the Database schema and the class diagram as a whole using a visual design tool, which can be great when the data structure is quite big
- Whenever the Database changes, the model can be updated accordingly without data loss

Yet there are some downsides, as follows:

- The *diagram-driven*, autogenerated SQL scripts can lead to data loss in case of updates. An easy workaround for that will be generating the scripts on disk and manually modifying them, which will require decent SQL knowledge.
- Dealing with the diagram can be tricky, especially if we want to have precise control over our Model classes; we won't always be able to get what we want, as the actual source code will be autogenerated by a tool.

Database-First

Given the disadvantages of *Model-First*, we can think that *Database-First* might be the way to go. This can be true if we either have a Database already or don't mind building it beforehand. That being the case, the *Database-First* approach is similar to the *Model-First* one, except that it goes the other way around; instead of designing the EDMX manually and generating the SQL script to create the Database, we build the latter and then generate the former using the Entity Framework Designer tool.

We can summarize it by saying that going *Database-First* will mean "building the Database and letting **Entity Framework** create/update the rest accordingly":

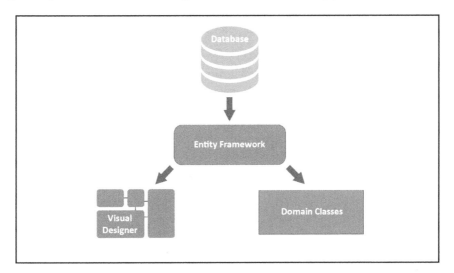

Here are the pros of this alternative approach:

- If we have an already-existing Database in place, this will most likely be the way to go as it will spare us the need to recreate it
- Risk of data loss will be kept to a minimum, because any change or update will be always performed on the Database

And here are the cons:

- Manually updating the Database can be tricky if we're dealing with clusters, multiple instances, or a number of development/testing/production environments, as we will have to manually keep them in sync instead of relying on code-driven updates/migrations or autogenerated SQL scripts

- We will have even less control over the autogenerated Model classes (and their source code) than when using *Model-First* approach; it will require an extensive knowledge over EF conventions and standards, otherwise we'll often struggle to get what we want

Code-First

Last but not least comes the Entity Framework flagship approach since EF4, which enables an elegant, highly-efficient Data Model development workflow. The appeal of this approach can be easily found in its premise; the *Code-First* approach allows the developer to define model objects using only standard classes, without the need of any design tool, XML mapping files, or cumbersome piles of autogenerated code.

To summarize, we can say that going *Code-First* means writing the Data Model entity classes we'll be using within our project and letting Entity Framework generate the Database accordingly:

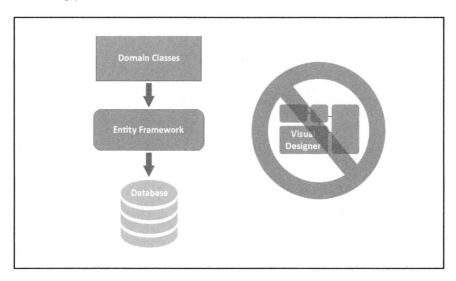

Pros

- There is no need for diagrams and visual tools whatsoever, which can be great for small-to-medium size projects as it will save a lot of time
- A fluent code API that allows the developer to follow a *Convention over Configuration* approach, to handle the most common scenarios, while also giving them the chance to switch to custom, *attribute-based* implementation overrides the need to customize the Database mapping

Cons

- A good knowledge of C# and updated EF conventions is required
- Maintaining the Database can often be tricky, as well as handling updates without suffering data loss; the *migrations* support, which was added in 4.3 to overcome the issue and has been continuously updated since then, greatly mitigates the problem, although it also affected the learning curve in a negative way

Taking a choice

As we can see by reading the advantages and disadvantages of these three options, there is no such thing as an overall *better* or *best* approach; conversely, we can say that each project scenario will likely have a best suited approach.

Regarding our project, considering the fact that we don't have a Database yet and we're aiming for a flexible, mutable small-scale data structure, adopting the *Code-First* approach will probably be a good choice. That's what we will do, starting from the following paragraph.

Creating Entities

We'll definitely make use of one of the big advantages of the *Code-First* approach and start writing our **Entity** classes immediately, without worrying too much about what Database Engine we'll use.

Truth be told, we already know something about what we'll eventually use. We won't be adopting a NoSQL solution, as they are not supported by EF yet; we also don't want to commit ourselves into purchasing expensive license plans, so Oracle and the commercial editions of SQL Server are most likely out of the picture as well.

This leaves us with relatively few choices: SQL Server Compact Edition, SQL Server Express, MySql, or other less-known solutions such as PostgreSql. That being said, adopting *Code-First* will give us the chance to postpone the call until our Data Model is ready.

ApplicationUser

Let's start with the entity that will be used to store all the user-related info. We'll use it for a number of useful tasks, such as keeping record of who created each quiz, tracking those who will take the quizzes, handling the login and authentication phase, and more.

Switch to **Solution Explorer**, then do the following:

1. Create a new `/Data/` folder at the root level of the `TestMakerFreeWebApp` project; this will be where all our EntityFramework-related classes will reside.
2. Create a `/Data/Models/` folder.
3. Add a new **ASP.NET Core | Code | Class** file, name it `ApplicationUser.cs`, and replace the sample code with the following:

```
using System;
using System.Collections.Generic;
using System.ComponentModel;
using System.ComponentModel.DataAnnotations;
using System.ComponentModel.DataAnnotations.Schema;

namespace TestMakerFreeWebApp.Data
{
    public class ApplicationUser
    {
        #region Constructor
        public ApplicationUser()
        {

        }
        #endregion
```

```
#region Properties
[Key]
[Required]
public string Id { get; set; }

[Required]
[MaxLength(128)]
public string UserName { get; set; }

[Required]
public string Email { get; set; }

public string DisplayName { get; set; }

public string Notes { get; set; }

[Required]
public int Type { get; set; }

[Required]
public int Flags { get; set; }

[Required]
public DateTime CreatedDate { get; set; }

[Required]
public DateTime LastModifiedDate { get; set; }
#endregion
    }
}
```

Note how there are no foreign keys pointing at quizzes, questions, and so on here; there's nothing strange about that, as these are all *one-to-many* relationships that will be handled from the other side.

 We can ask ourselves why we used the `ApplicationUser` class name instead of **User**. The answer is pretty simple--`ApplicationUser` is the conventional name given to the custom implementation of the `IdentityUser` base class used by the **ASP.NET Identity** module. We're using that in compliance with that convention, as we plan to implement this module later on.

Quiz

The next entity will be the one identifying the quizzes, which will allow us to rewrite most of the `QuizController` sample code. Right-click on the `/Data/Models/` folder, add a `Quiz.cs` class file, and fill it with the following code:

```
using System;
using System.Collections.Generic;
using System.ComponentModel;
using System.ComponentModel.DataAnnotations;
using System.ComponentModel.DataAnnotations.Schema;

namespace TestMakerFreeWebApp.Data
{
    public class Quiz
    {
        #region Constructor
        public Quiz()
        {

        }
        #endregion

        #region Properties
        [Key]
        [Required]
        public int Id { get; set; }

        [Required]
        public string Title { get; set; }

        public string Description { get; set; }

        public string Text { get; set; }

        public string Notes { get; set; }

        [DefaultValue(0)]
        public int Type { get; set; }

        [DefaultValue(0)]
        public int Flags { get; set; }

        [Required]
        public string UserId { get; set; }

        [Required]
```

```
public int ViewCount { get; set; }

[Required]
public DateTime CreatedDate { get; set; }

[Required]
public DateTime LastModifiedDate { get; set; }
#endregion
    }
}
```

Note the presence of the `UserId` foreign key, which will point to the user who created the quiz.

It's also worth noting that we used a lot of **Data Annotations** attributes, as they are the most convenient way to override the default *Code-First* conventions.

If you want to know more about Data Annotations in EF Core, we strongly suggest reading the official documentation at the following URL:

`https://docs.efproject.net/en/latest/modeling/index.html`

As we can see, this `Quiz` entity class is very similar to the `QuizViewModel` class we created in `Chapter 2`, *Backend with .NET Core*. That's perfectly fine, because that class was originally meant to resemble the public properties of the Data Source underlying model, which is precisely what we're defining now.

The following diagram can help us better understand this:

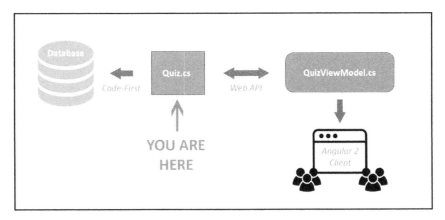

As we can see, we're creating the `Quiz` entity that will be used by EF to generate the Database (using *code-first*) and also translated (using *property mapping*) into the `QuizViewModel` we'll use to serve our content to our Angular client.

As we might guess, the `ApplicationUser` and `Quiz` entities alone will hardly be enough to achieve what we want. In order to complete our initial requirements, we need to define some more entity classes, such as the following:

- `Question`, which will be used to store the questions related to each quiz
- `Answer`, which will be used to store the answers related to each question
- `Result`, which will be used to store the results related to each quiz

Other than that, sooner or later we'll also need the entities to store the user response, but we can postpone them for the time being.

Question

Right-click on the `/Data/Models/` folder and add a `Question.cs` class file with the following code:

```
using System;
using System.Collections.Generic;
using System.ComponentModel;
using System.ComponentModel.DataAnnotations;
using System.ComponentModel.DataAnnotations.Schema;

namespace TestMakerFreeWebApp.Data
{
    public class Question
    {
        #region Constructor
        public Question()
        {

        }
        #endregion

        #region Properties
        [Key]
        [Required]
        public int Id { get; set; }

        [Required]
        public int QuizId { get; set; }
```

```
        [Required]
        public string Text { get; set; }

        public string Notes { get; set; }

        [DefaultValue(0)]
        public int Type { get; set; }

        [DefaultValue(0)]
        public int Flags { get; set; }

        [Required]
        public DateTime CreatedDate { get; set; }

        [Required]
        public DateTime LastModifiedDate { get; set; }
        #endregion
    }
}
```

That's it. Note the `QuizId` foreign key we have here instead of the `UserId`; this is because each question is a child element of the quiz, so we don't need an `UserId` property, we'll just fetch the value from the parent.

> It's important to understand that the preceding assumption is true only if we can take for granted that the quiz author will be the only user allowed to add/manage questions to each quiz; this is precisely what we're about to do, hence, the `UserId` property can be omitted.

Answer

A question will most likely require some answers. Right-click on the `/Data/Models/` folder and add the following `Answer.cs` class file:

```
using System;
using System.Collections.Generic;
using System.ComponentModel;
using System.ComponentModel.DataAnnotations;
using System.ComponentModel.DataAnnotations.Schema;

namespace TestMakerFreeWebApp.Data
{
    public class Answer
    {
        #region Constructor
```

```
            public Answer()
            {

            }
            #endregion

            #region Properties
            [Key]
            [Required]
            public int Id { get; set; }

            [Required]
            public int QuestionId { get; set; }

            [Required]
            public string Text { get; set; }

            [Required]
            public int Value { get; set; }

            public string Notes { get; set; }

            [DefaultValue(0)]
            public int Type { get; set; }

            [DefaultValue(0)]
            public int Flags { get; set; }

            [Required]
            public DateTime CreatedDate { get; set; }

            [Required]
            public DateTime LastModifiedDate { get; set; }
            #endregion
        }
    }
```

Again, we only have the foreign key that we need to traverse up the *one-to-many* dependency tree that we're slowly building. There's also a new Value property that we can use to give a variable weight to different answers. That value can be a positive or even a negative number, depending on how we want to implement our quiz *backend* mechanics. There will be chances to talk more about this soon.

It seems that we're only missing the results here; let's add them.

Result

Here's the content of the /Data/Models/Result.cs class file:

```
using System;
using System.Collections.Generic;
using System.ComponentModel;
using System.ComponentModel.DataAnnotations;
using System.ComponentModel.DataAnnotations.Schema;

namespace TestMakerFreeWebApp.Data
{
    public class Result
    {
        #region Constructor
        public Result()
        {

        }
        #endregion

        #region Properties
        [Key]
        [Required]
        public int Id { get; set; }

        [Required]
        public int QuizId { get; set; }

        [Required]
        public string Text { get; set; }

        public int? MinValue { get; set; }

        public int? MaxValue { get; set; }

        public string Notes { get; set; }

        [DefaultValue(0)]
        public int Type { get; set; }

        [DefaultValue(0)]
        public int Flags { get; set; }

        [Required]
        public DateTime CreatedDate { get; set; }

        [Required]
```

```
        public DateTime LastModifiedDate { get; set; }
        #endregion
    }
}
```

Here we go. The `QuizId` foreign key property is back as the results are bound to the quiz itself, not to questions or answers. Other than that, we can also note the `MinValue` and `MaxValue` properties; these will be the boundaries that will be used--along with the total score points earned by the user by picking the various answers--to determine the proper result(s) after the quiz is over. If multiple results are available for that given score, a random one will be picked.

Note how `MinValue` and `MaxValue` are initialized using a C# `int?` type, which defines a *nullable* `int` type. We did that to give the quiz author the chance to create results without boundaries so that they can act as a catch-all. For example, a result with a *null* `MinValue` will be picked for all score values up to its `MaxValue`; similarly, a result with a null `MaxValue` will be picked for all score values equal or greater than its `MinValue`. Needless to say, this also means that a result with both these values set to *null* will always be picked, unless we keep the author from doing that.

Defining relationships

Now that we have built our main entity skeleton, we need to create some relationships between them. We want to be able to do stuff like retrieve a **Quiz**, then browse to their related **Questions** and get the available **Answers**. We'll also need to fetch the **Result**(s) for any given score, find out the `ApplicationUser` who made the quiz, and so on. To do this, we have to implement a set of entity-related properties that Entity Framework will load on demand using its default *Lazy-Load* retrieval feature.

The first thing we'll do is add a new region to our `Quiz` class containing these three new properties:

```
#region Lazy-Load Properties
/// <summary>
/// The quiz author: it will be loaded
/// on first use thanks to the EF Lazy-Loading feature.
/// </summary>
[ForeignKey("UserId")]
public virtual ApplicationUser User { get; set; }

/// <summary>
```

```
/// A list containing all the questions related to this quiz.
/// It will be populaed on first use thanks to the EF Lazy-Loading feature.
/// </summary>
public virtual List<Question> Questions { get; set; }

/// <summary>
/// A list containing all the results related to this quiz.
/// It will be populaed on first use thanks to the EF Lazy-Loading feature.
/// </summary>
public virtual List<Result> Results { get; set; }
#endregion
```

Whoever has some experience with *Entity Framework* won't miss the `ForeignKey` *Data Annotation*; this is one of the many *Code-First* configuration overrides we'll need to use to have our Data Model properly built. There's nothing complex here, we're just telling EF that this property should be loaded using the `UserId` property defined earlier; this will also create a *one-to-many* binding relationship (also known as *constraint*), as long as our chosen Database will support the feature.

In order to use the `ForeignKey` attribute (and all other EF Data Annotation), you need to add a reference to the `System.ComponentModel.DataAnnotations.Schema` namespace in the `using` section of the `Quiz` class. You shouldn't need to do that, as the most recent Visual Studio releases should automatically add it for you.

Let's do the same with the other entities, starting with the **Question**:

```
#region Lazy-Load Properties
/// <summary>
/// The parent quiz.
/// </summary>
[ForeignKey("QuizId")]
public virtual Quiz Quiz { get; set; }

/// <summary>
/// A list containing all the answer related to this question.
/// </summary>
public virtual List<Answer> Answers { get; set; }
#endregion
```

Then, move on to the **Answer**:

```
#region Lazy-Load Properties
/// <summary>
/// The parent question.
/// </summary>
[ForeignKey("QuestionId")]
public virtual Question Question { get; set; }
#endregion
```

Continue with the **Result**:

```
#region Lazy-Load Properties
/// <summary>
/// The parent quiz.
/// </summary>
[ForeignKey("QuizId")]
public virtual Quiz Quiz { get; set; }
#endregion
```

Now, conclude with the `ApplicationUser`:

```
#region Lazy-Load Properties
/// <summary>
/// A list of all the quiz created by this users.
/// </summary>
public virtual List<Quiz> Quizzes { get; set; }
#endregion
```

That's it. As we can see, for each **Quiz**, we want to retrieve the owner *user* and all the *questions* and *results*; for each **Question**, we want the parent *quiz* and all the *answers*; for each **Answer**, the parent *question*; for each **Result**, the parent *quiz*; last but not least, for each `ApplicationUser`, the list of *quizzes* that they created.

The one-to-many EF Lazy-Load pattern

If we take a wider look at the amount of source code we have written, we can easily note how each *Foreign Key* spawned:

- A **single-object entity** *property* with the same type of the entity we're referring to in the class containing the Foreign Key
- A **type-defined listing** *property* in the related class

This pattern won't change as long as we're defining *one-to-many* relationships only; an object to the left, leading to a list of related objects to the right.

Are we done with our entities? Yes. Are we ready to deploy our *code-first* Database? Hardly. Before doing that, we need to take care of two more things:

1. Set up an appropriate **Database Context**.
2. Enable the **Code-First Migrations** support within our project.

Let's do that right now.

Setting up the DbContext

To interact with data as objects/entity classes, Entity Framework Core uses the `Microsoft.EntityFrameworkCore.DbContext` class, also called `DbContext` or simply **Context**. This class is in charge of all the entity objects during runtime, including populating them with data from the Database, keeping track of changes, and persisting them to the Database during CRUD operations.

We can easily create our very own `DbContext` class for our project--which we will call `ApplicationDbContext`--by doing the following:

1. From **Solution Explorer**, right-click on the `/Data/` folder we created a while ago and add a new `ApplicationDbContext.cs` class file.
2. Fill it up with the following code:

```
using Microsoft.AspNetCore.Identity.EntityFrameworkCore;
using Microsoft.EntityFrameworkCore;
using Microsoft.EntityFrameworkCore.Metadata;

namespace TestMakerFreeWebApp.Data
{
    public class ApplicationDbContext : DbContext
    {
        #region Constructor
        public ApplicationDbContext(DbContextOptions options) :
          base(options)
        {
        }
        #endregion Constructor

        #region Methods
        protected override void OnModelCreating(ModelBuilder
```

```
        modelBuilder)
    {
        base.OnModelCreating(modelBuilder);

        modelBuilder.Entity<ApplicationUser>().ToTable("Users");
        modelBuilder.Entity<ApplicationUser>().HasMany(u =>
         u.Quizzes).WithOne(i => i.User);

        modelBuilder.Entity<Quiz>().ToTable("Quizzes");
        modelBuilder.Entity<Quiz>().Property(i =>
            i.Id).ValueGeneratedOnAdd();
        modelBuilder.Entity<Quiz>().HasOne(i => i.User).WithMany(u
            => u.Quizzes);
        modelBuilder.Entity<Quiz>().HasMany(i =>
            i.Questions).WithOne(c => c.Quiz);

        modelBuilder.Entity<Question>().ToTable("Questions");
        modelBuilder.Entity<Question>().Property(i =>
            i.Id).ValueGeneratedOnAdd();
        modelBuilder.Entity<Question>().HasOne(i =>
            i.Quiz).WithMany(u =>    u.Questions);
        modelBuilder.Entity<Question>().HasMany(i =>
            i.Answers).WithOne(c => c.Question);

        modelBuilder.Entity<Answer>().ToTable("Answers");
        modelBuilder.Entity<Answer>().Property(i =>
            i.Id).ValueGeneratedOnAdd();
        modelBuilder.Entity<Answer>().HasOne(i =>
            i.Question).WithMany(u => u.Answers);

        modelBuilder.Entity<Result>().ToTable("Results");
        modelBuilder.Entity<Result>().Property(i =>
            i.Id).ValueGeneratedOnAdd();
        modelBuilder.Entity<Result>().HasOne(i =>
            i.Quiz).WithMany(u => u.Results);
    }
    #endregion Methods

    #region Properties
    public DbSet<ApplicationUser> Users { get; set; }
    public DbSet<Quiz> Quizzes { get; set; }
    public DbSet<Question> Questions { get; set; }
    public DbSet<Answer> Answers { get; set; }
    public DbSet<Result> Results { get; set; }
    #endregion Properties
    }
}
```

There are a couple of important things we did here:

- We overrode the `OnModelCreating` method to manually define our Data Model relationships for our entity classes. Note that we manually configured the table names for each entity using the `modelBuilder.Entity<TEntityType>().ToTable` method; we did that with the sole purpose of showing how easy it is to customize the *Code-First* generated Database.
- We added a `DbSet<T>` property for each of our entities, so we can easily access them later on.

Database initialization strategies

Creating the Database for the first time isn't the only thing we need to worry about; for example, how can we keep track of the changes that will definitely occur to our Data Model?

In previous versions of EF (up to 6.x), we could choose between one of the Database management patterns (known as *Database Initializers* or *DbInitializers*) offered by the *Code-First* approach, that is, by picking the appropriate Database initialization strategy for our specific needs: `CreateDatabaseIfNotExists`, `DropCreateDatabaseIfModelChanges`, `DropCreateDatabaseAlways`, and `MigrateDatabaseToLatestVersion`. Additionally, should we need to address specific requirements, we can also set up our own custom initializer by extending one of the preceding and overriding their core methods.

The major flaw of **DbInitializers** was them not being immediate and streamlined enough for the average developer. They were viable, yet difficult to handle without an extensive knowledge of the whole Entity Framework logic.

In EF Core, the pattern has been greatly simplified; there are no *DbInitializers*, and automatic migrations have also been removed. The Database initialization aspect is now entirely handled through *PowerShell* commands, with the sole exception of a small set of commands that can be placed directly on the `DbContext` implementation constructor to partially automatize the process; they are as follows:

- `Database.EnsureCreated()`
- `Database.EnsureDeleted()`
- `Database.Migrate()`

There's currently no way to create migrations programmatically; they must be added via *PowerShell*, as we will see shortly.

Choosing the Database Engine

Before doing that, though, we need to choose which Database engine we would like to use. We'll take this as an opportunity to demonstrate the versatility of the *Code-First* approach.

From the main Menu, select **View** | **SQL Server Object Explorer** and look through the available *development-ready* Databases; you should have at least one **MSSQLLocalDB** Database instance under the **SQL Server** node:

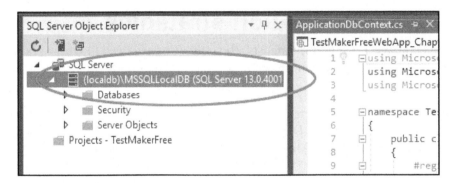

If you have one or more instances of *SQL Server* and/or *SQL Express* installed, you will also find a reference for each one of them.

If you have no entries (no SQL Server node), you are most likely missing the **SQL Server Data Tools** component from your Visual Studio installation; in order to fix that, you need to open the **Visual Studio Installer** and add the **SQL Server Data Tools** components. Once you're done, restart Visual Studio; the default **MSSQLLocalDB** instance should be ready and available.

For now, we'll use the **(localdb)\MSSQLLocalDB** instance; we need to keep track of that name, as we'll need to use it in the `appsettings.json` file in a short while.

The default **(localdb)\MSSQLLocalDB** instance we have just choosen might be viable enough for development, but it won't work on production. Don't worry, though, we will choose a whole different Database engine when we get to the deployment phase. As we said before, we're doing that on purpose in order to demonstrate the versatility of the *Code-First* approach.

Updating the appsettings.json file

From **Solution Explorer**, open the `appsettings.json` file and add the following (new lines highlighted):

```
{
  "ConnectionStrings": {
    "DefaultConnection": "Data Source=(localdb)\\MSSQLLocalDB;Initial
    Catalog=TestMakerFree;Integrated Security=True;
    MultipleActiveResultSets=True"
  },
  "Logging": {
    "IncludeScopes": false,
    "Debug": {
      "LogLevel": {
        "Default": "Warning"
      }
    },

  [...]
```

This is the connection string we'll be referencing in our project's `Startup.cs` file later on.

Creating the Database

Now that we have our own `DbContext` and a valid *Connection String*, we can easily add the Initial *Migration* and create our Database.

Updating Startup.cs

The first thing we have to do is to add the EntityFramework support and our ApplicationDbContext implementation to our application startup class. Open the Startup.cs file and update the ConfigureServices method in the following way (new lines are highlighted):

```
public void ConfigureServices(IServiceCollection services)
    {
        services.AddMvc();

        // Add EntityFramework support for SqlServer.
        services.AddEntityFrameworkSqlServer();

        // Add ApplicationDbContext.
        services.AddDbContext<ApplicationDbContext>(options =>
options.UseSqlServer(Configuration.GetConnectionString("DefaultConnection")
)
                );
    }
```

The new code will also require the following namespace references:

```
using Microsoft.EntityFrameworkCore;
using TestMakerFreeWebApp.Data;
```

Adding the Initial Migration

Open a **PowerShell** Command Prompt and navigate through the project's root folder, which is as follows in our example:

```
C:\Projects\TestMakerFree\TestMakerFreeWebApp\
```

Once there, type the following command to add the first migration:

```
dotnet ef migrations add "Initial" -o "Data\Migrations"
```

 The optional -o parameter can be used to change the location where the migration code-generated files will be created; if we don't specify it, a root-level /Migrations/ folder will be created and used as default. Since we put all the EntityFrameworkCore classes into the /Data/ folder, it's advisable to store migrations there as well.

The command should give the *on-screen* output below:

Wait for the migration to be created, and then type the following to apply it:

```
dotnet ef database update
```

Once done, open the **Server Object Explorer** and verify that the `TestMakerFree` Database has been created, along with all the relevant tables:

 If you've used migrations before, you might be asking why we didn't use the Visual Studio's *Package Manager Console* to execute these commands. The reason is simple--unfortunately, doing this won't work, because the commands need to be executed within the project root folder, which is not where the *Package Manager Console* commands are executed. It is also unknown whether that behavior will change in the near future.

If we go back to Visual Studio and take a look at our project's **Solution Explorer**, we can see that there's a new `/Data/Migrations/` folder containing the EF Core *code-generated* files.

The "No executable found matching command dotnet-ef" error

At the time of writing, there's a nasty issue affecting most .NET Core-based Visual Studio projects that can prevent the `dotnet ef` command from working properly. More specifically, you can be prompted by the following error message when trying to execute that command:

```
No executable found matching command "dotnet-ef"
```

If you experience this issue, try to check the following:

- Double-check that you properly added the `Microsoft.EntityFrameworkCore.Tools` and the `Microsoft.EntityFrameworkCore.Tools.DotNet` package libraries (as explained earlier), as they are required for the command to work
- Ensure that you are issuing the `dotnet ef` command in the project's root folder-- the same one that also contains the `<ProjectName>.csproj` file; it won't work anywhere else

If both of these checks hit their marks, try this workaround--right-click on the project's root folder, select **Edit <ProjectName>.csproj** to open that file to edit in Visual Studio, and look for the following element:

```
<ItemGroup>
  <DotNetCliToolReference Include="Microsoft.EntityFrameworkCore.Tools"
  Version="2.0.1" />
  <DotNetCliToolReference
Include="Microsoft.EntityFrameworkCore.Tools.DotNet" Version="2.0.0" />
</ItemGroup>
```

 Alternatively, you can also edit the `<ProjectName>.csproj` file with a text editor such as *Notepad++*; just ensure that you reload your project when you're done.

The `<ItemGroup>` element is just a container here; you need to look for the highlighted lines. Needless to say, the **Version** value will change when using a different or more recent EF Core release. Be aware that these elements can have a slightly different syntax.

However, they definitely need to be there; if you can't find them, you will know why the `dotnet ef` command is not working. Fix that unwanted behavior by manually adding them to your project configuration file. They *must* we wrapped within an `<ItemGroup>` block, so you can either put them together in a group with other `<DotNetCliToolReference>` elements (if there is at least one), or add a whole net `<ItemGroup>` block.

As soon as you update your project configuration file, restart Visual Studio (or reload the project), and then try to execute the `dotnet ef` command again from the project's root folder. In the unlikely case that you end up with some NuGet package conflicts, you can try issuing the `dotnet update` command from the project's root folder to fix them; right after that, reload your project and try to execute the `dotnet ef` command again.

 A lot more can be said regarding this issue, but doing that will bring us too far from the scope of this book. If you want to know more, you can take a look at the article I wrote about it while working on this book at `https://goo.gl/Ki6mdb`.

Understanding Migrations

Before going ahead, it would be useful to say a few words explaining what *Code-First Migrations* actually are and the advantages we gain by using them.

Whenever we're developing an application and defining a Data Model, we can be sure that it will change a number of times for many good reasons: new requirements from the product owner, optimization processes, consolidation phases, and so on. A bunch of properties will be added, deleted, or have their type changed. Chances are, sooner or later, we'll be adding new entities as well, and/or changing their relation pattern according to our ever-changing needs.

Each time we do something like that, we'll also put our Data Model out of sync with its underlying, *Code-First* generated Database. This won't be a problem when we're debugging our app within a development environment, because that scenario usually allows us to recreate the Database from scratch whenever the project changes.

Upon deploying the application into production, we'll be facing a whole different story; as long as we're handling real data, dropping and recreating our Database won't be an option anymore. This is what the *Code-First Migrations* feature is meant to address: giving the developer a chance to alter the Database schema without having to drop/recreate the whole thing.

We won't dig more into this topic; Entity Framework Core is a world of its own, and addressing it in detail is out of the scope of this book. If you want to learn more, we suggest you start with the official EF Core MS documentation at `https://docs.microsoft.com/en-us/ef/core/`.

Implementing a Data Seed strategy

We have created the Database, yet it's still completely empty. In order to test it against our existing application, it will be useful to find an easy way of adding some sample data programmatically.

In the most recent *Entity Framework* versions, up to and including EF6, it was possible to do that using the `DbMigrationsConfiguration.Seed()` method. Unfortunately, though, migrations configuration doesn't exist in EF Core; this seems to be more of an implementation choice than a lack of features, since the seeding task can now be performed directly within the `Startup.cs` file.

If you're interested in reading the discussion leading to that conclusion, we strongly suggest you take a look at the following URL, pointing to the issue #3070 of the Entity Framework Core repository on GitHub:

`https://github.com/aspnet/EntityFramework/issues/3070`

Although this is definitely true, there is still some controversy going on between the EF Core developers community regarding that specific aspect. The absence of a high-level API and/or a consolidated pattern to run seeding after applying migrations is indeed something that should be addressed somehow, as executing such a delicate task during application run creates a number of issues, and it doesn't seem to be a viable solution in most scenarios.

Creating a DbSeeder class

Let's start by adding a `DbSeeder.cs` static class to the `/Data/` folder. This class will use the `ApplicationDbContext` to create some sample entities and save them to our Database; doing that will take a considerable amount of code, hence it might be useful to split the various class components into `#region` blocks so that we can better understand the various steps.

Let's start with the `Public Methods` region, which will contain the methods that we want to make available from external classes:

```
[...]

#region Public Methods
public static void Seed(ApplicationDbContext dbContext)
{
    // Create default Users (if there are none)
    if (!dbContext.Users.Any()) CreateUsers(dbContext);

    // Create default Quizzes (if there are none) together with their
      set of Q&A
    if (!dbContext.Quizzes.Any()) CreateQuizzes(dbContext);
}
#endregion

[...]
```

As we can see, the region contains a single `Seed()` method that will accept an `ApplicationDbContext` parameter and launch a couple of private methods-- `CreateUsers()` and `CreateQuizzes()`--which will actually get the job done. These will be addressed in the `Seed Methods` region below.

We implemented the `Seed()` method using a conservative approach, as it will be executed each and every time our Data Model changes. We don't want any user or quiz to be added twice, so we ensure that all entities are not already present in the Database before adding them.

The *Seed Methods* region is quite long, so we'll split it into two parts, one for each method; let's start with `CreateUsers()`:

```
[...]

#region Seed Methods
private static void CreateUsers(ApplicationDbContext dbContext)
{
    // local variables
    DateTime createdDate = new DateTime(2016, 03, 01, 12, 30, 00);
    DateTime lastModifiedDate = DateTime.Now;

    // Create the "Admin" ApplicationUser account (if it doesn't exist
                                                    already)
    var user_Admin = new ApplicationUser()
    {
        Id = Guid.NewGuid().ToString(),
```

```
                UserName = "Admin",
                Email = "admin@testmakerfree.com",
                CreatedDate = createdDate,
                LastModifiedDate = lastModifiedDate
        };

        // Insert the Admin user into the Database
        dbContext.Users.Add(user_Admin);

#if DEBUG
        // Create some sample registered user accounts (if they don't exist
                                                        already)
        var user_Ryan = new ApplicationUser()
        {
            Id = Guid.NewGuid().ToString(),
            UserName = "Ryan",
            Email = "ryan@testmakerfree.com",
            CreatedDate = createdDate,
            LastModifiedDate = lastModifiedDate
        };

        var user_Solice = new ApplicationUser()
        {
            Id = Guid.NewGuid().ToString(),
            UserName = "Solice",
            Email = "solice@testmakerfree.com",
            CreatedDate = createdDate,
            LastModifiedDate = lastModifiedDate
        };

        var user_Vodan = new ApplicationUser()
        {
            Id = Guid.NewGuid().ToString(),
            UserName = "Vodan",
            Email = "vodan@testmakerfree.com",
            CreatedDate = createdDate,
            LastModifiedDate = lastModifiedDate
        };

        // Insert sample registered users into the Database
        dbContext.Users.AddRange(user_Ryan, user_Solice, user_Vodan);
#endif
        dbContext.SaveChanges();
    }

    [...]
```

This method will create the *Admin* user, plus a set of sample registered users: *Ryan, Solice,* and *Vodan.* Each user comes with his own unique ID (in **Guid** format) and credentials set; these will definitely be useful for the login and authentication tests that will come in the future.

Before moving ahead, let's spend a moment looking at the `#if...` `#endif` conditional block that we used here, which is a C# pre-processor directive, also known as a **conditional compilation directive**. This means that the wrapped code will be compiled only if the given condition matches. The DEBUG switch will be `True` for *release builds* and `False` for *debug builds*, thus allowing us to use two different behaviors for our testing environment and for production. Since we don't want to create the sample users in our production environment, we've put that part of code inside a conditional compilation block that is executed only when the application is running in Debug mode.

Here's the second part of the `Seeds Method` region:

```
[...]

private static void CreateQuizzes(ApplicationDbContext dbContext)
{
    // local variables
    DateTime createdDate = new DateTime(2016, 03, 01, 12, 30, 00);
    DateTime lastModifiedDate = DateTime.Now;

    // retrieve the admin user, which we'll use as default author.
    var authorId = dbContext.Users
        .Where(u => u.UserName == "Admin")
        .FirstOrDefault()
        .Id;

#if DEBUG
    // create 47 sample quizzes with auto-generated data
    // (including questions, answers & results)
    var num = 47;
    for (int i = 1; i <= num; i++)
    {
        CreateSampleQuiz(
            dbContext,
            i,
            authorId,
            num - i,
            3,
            3,
            3,
            createdDate.AddDays(-num));
    }
```

```
#endif

    // create 3 more quizzes with better descriptive data
    // (we'll add the questions, answers & results later on)
    EntityEntry<Quiz> e1 = DbContext.Quizzes.Add(new Quiz()
    {
        UserId = authorId,
        Title = "Are you more Light or Dark side of the Force?",
        Description = "Star Wars personality test",
        Text = @"Choose wisely you must, young padawan: " +
                "this test will prove if your will is strong enough " +
                "to adhere to the principles of the light side of the
                                                    Force " +
                "or if you're fated to embrace the dark side. " +
                "No you want to become a true JEDI, you can't possibly
                                                    miss this!",
        ViewCount = 2343,
        CreatedDate = createdDate,
        LastModifiedDate = lastModifiedDate
    });

    EntityEntry<Quiz> e2 = DbContext.Quizzes.Add(new Quiz()
    {
        UserId = authorId,
        Title = "GenX, GenY or Genz?",
        Description = "Find out what decade most represents you",
        Text = @"Do you feel confortable in your generation? " +
                "What year should you have been born in?" +
                "Here's a bunch of questions that will help you to find
                                                    out!",
        ViewCount = 4180,
        CreatedDate = createdDate,
        LastModifiedDate = lastModifiedDate
    });

    EntityEntry<Quiz> e3 = DbContext.Quizzes.Add(new Quiz()
    {
        UserId = authorId,
        Title = "Which Shingeki No Kyojin character are you?",
        Description = "Attack On Titan personality test",
        Text = @"Do you relentlessly seek revenge like Eren? " +
                "Are you willing to put your like on the stake to
                            protect your friends like Mikasa? " +
                "Would you trust your fighting skills like Levi "+
                "or rely on your strategies and tactics like Arwin? " +
                "Unveil your true self with this Attack On Titan
                                        personality test!",
        ViewCount = 5203,
```

```
            CreatedDate = createdDate,
            LastModifiedDate = lastModifiedDate
        });

    // persist the changes on the Database
    DbContext.SaveChanges();
}
#endregion

[...]
```

The preceding `CreateQuizzes()` method adds a total of 50 sample quizzes to the Database. As we can see, 47 of them come with questions, answers, and results, thanks to the `CreateSampleQuiz()` utility method (which we'll see in a bit), while the other three feature a more realistic title and text contents, yet they come out empty. We did that on purpose, as we plan to manually add their questions, answers, and results with our Angular app in the subsequent chapters.

Last but not least comes the `Utility Methods` region:

```
[...]

#region Utility Methods
/// <summary>
/// Creates a sample quiz and add it to the Database
/// together with a sample set of questions, answers & results.
/// </summary>
/// <param name="userId">the author ID</param>
/// <param name="id">the quiz ID</param>
/// <param name="createdDate">the quiz CreatedDate</param>
private static void CreateSampleQuiz(
    ApplicationDbContext dbContext,
    int num,
    string authorId,
    int viewCount,
    int numberOfQuestions,
    int numberOfAnswersPerQuestion,
    int numberOfResults,
    DateTime createdDate)
{
    var quiz = new Quiz()
    {
        UserId = authorId,
        Title = String.Format("Quiz {0} Title", num),
        Description = String.Format("This is a sample description for
                                        quiz {0}.", num),
        Text = "This is a sample quiz created by the DbSeeder class for
```

```
                                            testing purposes. " +
            "All the questions, answers & results are auto-
                                        generated as well.",
        ViewCount = viewCount,
        CreatedDate = createdDate,
        LastModifiedDate = createdDate
    };
    dbContext.Quizzes.Add(quiz);
    dbContext.SaveChanges();

    for (int i = 0; i < numberOfQuestions; i++)
    {
        var question = new Question()
        {
            QuizId = quiz.Id,
            Text = "This is a sample question created by the DbSeeder
                        class for testing purposes. " +
                "All the child answers are auto-generated as well.",
            CreatedDate = createdDate,
            LastModifiedDate = createdDate
        };
        dbContext.Questions.Add(question);
        dbContext.SaveChanges();

        for (int i2 = 0; i2 < numberOfAnswersPerQuestion; i2++)
        {
            var e2 = dbContext.Answers.Add(new Answer()
            {
                QuestionId = question.Id,
                Text = "This is a sample answer created by the DbSeeder
                                class for testing purposes. ",
                Value = i2,
                CreatedDate = createdDate,
                LastModifiedDate = createdDate
            });
        }
    }

    for (int i = 0; i < numberOfResults; i++)
    {
        dbContext.Results.Add(new Result()
        {
            QuizId = quiz.Id,
            Text = "This is a sample result created by the DbSeeder
                                class for testing purposes. ",
            MinValue = 0,
            // max value should be equal to answers number * max answer
                                                value
```

```
                MaxValue = numberOfAnswersPerQuestion * 2,
                CreatedDate = createdDate,
                LastModifiedDate = createdDate
            });
        }
    dbContext.SaveChanges();
    }
#endregion

[...]
```

Here lies the `CreateSampleQuiz()` method implementation, which adds a new quiz to the Database, along with a configurable tree of questions, answers, and results for the quiz itself.

Before going further, it's important to note how this method, which is called no less than 47 times by `CreateQuizzes()`, makes a good use of the `dbContext.SaveChanges()` command. This is how we tell our `ApplicationDbContext` instance to persist all the pending changes to the Database. This is quite resource intensive; however, we need to do that to retrieve the `Id` key of the quizzes and questions we add, which we need to properly create the **Quiz** > **Questions** > **Answers** and **Quiz** > **Results** relationships. The `dbContext.SaveChanges()` method performs actual `INSERT` queries under the Entity Framework hood, so it can be *resource-intensive* if we run it multiple times. Luckily enough, the whole *data-seed* process will happen only once, so it won't impact the overall performance of our application.

The `DbSeeder.cs` class features an impressive amount of code, yet there's nothing to worry about as it's full of repeating tasks. However, it does make good use of the various features made available by our `ApplicationDbContext` class and its `DbContext` base class.

If you want to know more about `DbContext`, you can check out the official API at `https://docs.microsoft.com/en-US/ef/core/api/microsoft.entityframeworkcore.dbcontext.`

Adding the DbSeeder to Startup.cs

Our next task will be to add the `DbSeeder` to our `Startup` class. Since it's a static class, we will be able to use it anywhere, but we need an instance of our `ApplicationDbContext`; it would be great to get that using *Dependency Injection.*

Theoretically speaking, we can add a new parameter in the `Configure()` method, as follows:

```
[...]

public void Configure(IApplicationBuilder app, IHostingEnvironment env,
    ApplicationDbContext dbContext)
{
    [...]

    DbSeeder.Seed(dbContext);
}

[...]
```

This will indeed instantiate it through DI and get it done without drawbacks. However, we really don't want to alter the `Configure` method default parameter list, even if it won't affect our application.

We can achieve the same outcome in a less-intrusive fashion with a few more lines of code:

```
[...]

public void Configure(IApplicationBuilder app, IHostingEnvironment env)
{
    [...]

    // Create a service scope to get an ApplicationDbContext instance
            using DI
    using (var serviceScope =
        app.ApplicationServices.GetRequiredService<IServiceScopeFactory>
        ().CreateScope())
    {
        var dbContext =
        serviceScope.ServiceProvider.GetService<ApplicationDbContext>();
        // Create the Db if it doesn't exist and applies any pending
                                            migration.
        dbContext.Database.Migrate();
        // Seed the Db.
        DbSeeder.Seed(dbContext);
    }
}

[...]
```

Append the highlighted snippet at the end of the Startup class `Configure` method, and then add an import reference to the following required namespace at the start of the `Startup.cs` file:

```
[...]
using Microsoft.Extensions.DependencyInjection;
[...]
```

We're now good to go.

Seeding the Database

We're now ready to seed our Database. As we have hooked the `DbSeeder.Seed()` method to the `Startup` class, it'll be as easy as executing our app once by pressing *F5*: this will be enough to let the seeder work its magic. If we did everything correctly, our Database should be populated in no time. In order to check that, we can follow these steps:

1. Open the **Server Object Explorer** panel.
2. Expand the nodes up to our `TestMakerFree` Database.
3. Right-click on the **dbo.Quizzes** table and select **View Data**.

We should see something like the following:

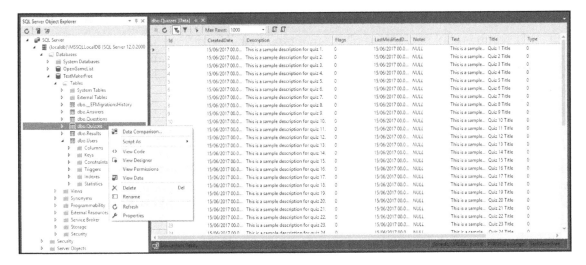

Updating the QuizController

Last but not least, we need to make some changes to the `QuizController` to make it use the `ApplicationDbContext` to retrieve data instead of those *Dummy Data Provider* strategies we implemented back in `Chapter 2`, *Backend with .NET Core*.

In order to do that, the first thing we need to do is to find an efficient way to map each `Quiz` entity to a corresponding `QuizViewModel` object, as our new Data Provider won't generate them anymore. We can achieve such a result in a number of ways, including the following:

- Adding a `Helper Method`, such as `GetQuizViewModel(Quiz quiz)`, thus handling the mapping manually with a few lines of code
- Adding a `Constructor Method` to the `QuizViewModel` itself, such as `QuizViewModel(Quiz quiz)`, doing pretty much the same thing as the aforementioned helper method
- Adding one of the many **Object-to-Object Auto-Mapping Tools** freely available via NuGet and configuring it to handle the mapping automatically whenever we need it

We'll definitely go for the latter.

Introducing Mapster

ASP.NET features a lot of object-to-object mapping tools, `AutoMapper` being the most used and acknowledged one; you're free to use the one you like the most and/or are most used to. For the purpose of this book, we'll use **Mapster** because it's lightweight, simple to use, and often performs better than its big brothers.

Installation

From **Solution Explorer**, right-click on the **TestMakerFreeWebApp** project and select **Manage NuGet Packages**. Ensure that the **Browse** tab is selected, and then type `Mapster` into the search box and press Enter. Select the appropriate result and press the **Install** button to add it.

Ensure that you select a stable version; for the purpose of this book, we'll use **Mapster 3.1.1**, which is currently the latest stable one. As always, you're free to choose any other release as long as you remember the disclaimer in Chapter 1.

For those who prefer to use the *NuGet Package Manager Console*, here's the one liner:

```
PM> Install-Package Mapster -Version 3.1.1
```

Basic usage

Like most mappers, **Mapster** can do its job in a number of different and convenient ways.

Let's start with the most basic usage, where a source object can be directly mapped to a destination object:

```
var destObject = sourceObject.Adapt<TDestination>();
```

Alternatively, we can instantiate a mapper by ourselves (or get it through *Dependency Injection*):

```
IAdapter adapter = new Adapter();
var destObject = adapter.Adapt<TDestination>(sourceObject);
```

All achieve the same result using a static method:

```
var destObject = TypeAdapter.Adapt<TDestination>;
```

All mappings can be either configured *on-the-fly*--during the mapping itself--or globally, using the `TypeAdapterConfig` static class, which also features a fluent and readable syntax:

```
TypeAdapterConfig<TSource, TDestination>
    .NewConfig()
    .Ignore(dest => dest.IgnoreThisProperty)
    .Map(dest => dest.MergeProperty1And2,
        src => string.Format("{0}{1}", src.Property1, src.Property2));
```

However, where **Mapster** really shines is the speed. Arguably 2.5 times faster than `AutoMapper`, it's twice as fast as other better known alternatives out there.

Those who want to know more about *Mapster* and how to use it are encouraged to visit the official project repo on GitHub at `https://github.com/chaowlert/Mapster`.

Updating the QuizController

Now that we know how to use **Mapster**, we can upgrade our `QuizController` accordingly. Open the `QuizController.cs` file and perform the following changes (new/updated lines are highlighted):

```
using System;
using Microsoft.AspNetCore.Mvc;
using Newtonsoft.Json;
using TestMakerFreeWebApp.ViewModels;
using System.Collections.Generic;
using System.Linq;
using TestMakerFreeWebApp.Data;
using Mapster;

namespace TestMakerFreeWebApp.Controllers
{
    [Route("api/[controller]")]
    public class QuizController : Controller
    {
        #region Private Fields
        private ApplicationDbContext DbContext;
        #endregion

        #region Constructor
        public QuizController(ApplicationDbContext context)
        {
            // Instantiate the ApplicationDbContext through DI
            DbContext = context;
        }
        #endregion Constructor


        #region RESTful conventions methods
        /// <summary>
        /// GET: api/quiz/{id}
        /// Retrieves the Quiz with the given {id}
        /// </summary>
        /// <param name="id">The ID of an existing Quiz</param>
        /// <returns>the Quiz with the given {id}</returns>
        [HttpGet("{id}")]
        public IActionResult Get(int id)
        {
            var quiz = DbContext.Quizzes.Where(i => i.Id ==
              id).FirstOrDefault();
            return new JsonResult(
                quiz.Adapt<QuizViewModel>(),
                new JsonSerializerSettings()
```

```
            {
                Formatting = Formatting.Indented
            });
    }

    /// <summary>
    /// Adds a new Quiz to the Database
    /// </summary>
    /// <param name="m">The QuizViewModel containing the data to
    ///                  insert</param>
    [HttpPut]
    public IActionResult Put(QuizViewModel m)
    {
        throw new NotImplementedException();
    }


    /// <summary>
    /// Edit the Quiz with the given {id}
    /// </summary>
    /// <param name="m">The QuizViewModel containing the data to
    ///                              update</param>
    [HttpPost]
    public IActionResult Post(QuizViewModel m)
    {
        throw new NotImplementedException();
    }


    /// <summary>
    /// Deletes the Quiz with the given {id} from the Database
    /// </summary>
    /// <param name="id">The ID of an existing Test</param>
    [HttpDelete("{id}")]
    public IActionResult Delete(int id)
    {
        throw new NotImplementedException();
    }
    #endregion

    #region Attribute-based routing methods
    /// <summary>
    /// GET: api/quiz/latest
    /// Retrieves the {num} latest Quizzes
    /// </summary>
    /// <param name="num">the number of quizzes to retrieve</param>
    /// <returns>the {num} latest Quizzes</returns>
    [HttpGet("Latest/{num:int?}")]
    public IActionResult Latest(int num = 10)
    {
```

```csharp
            var latest = DbContext.Quizzes
                .OrderByDescending(q => q.CreatedDate)
                .Take(num)
                .ToArray();
            return new JsonResult(
                latest.Adapt<QuizViewModel[]>(),
                new JsonSerializerSettings()
                {
                    Formatting = Formatting.Indented
                });
    }


    /// <summary>
    /// GET: api/quiz/ByTitle
    /// Retrieves the {num} Quizzes sorted by Title (A to Z)
    /// </summary>
    /// <param name="num">the number of quizzes to retrieve</param>
    /// <returns>{num} Quizzes sorted by Title</returns>
    [HttpGet("ByTitle/{num:int?}")]
    public IActionResult ByTitle(int num = 10)
    {
        var byTitle = DbContext.Quizzes
            .OrderBy(q => q.Title)
            .Take(num)
            .ToArray();
        return new JsonResult(
            byTitle.Adapt<QuizViewModel[]>(),
            new JsonSerializerSettings()
            {
                Formatting = Formatting.Indented
            });
    }


    /// <summary>
    /// GET: api/quiz/mostViewed
    /// Retrieves the {num} random Quizzes
    /// </summary>
    /// <param name="num">the number of quizzes to retrieve</param>
    /// <returns>{num} random Quizzes</returns>
    [HttpGet("Random/{num:int?}")]
    public IActionResult Random(int num = 10)
    {
        var random = DbContext.Quizzes
            .OrderBy(q => Guid.NewGuid())
            .Take(num)
            .ToArray();
        return new JsonResult(
            random.Adapt<QuizViewModel[]>(),
```

```
                        new JsonSerializerSettings()
                        {
                            Formatting = Formatting.Indented
                        });
                }
            #endregion
        }
    }
```

We did a lot of changes here:

- At the start of the file, we added a reference to the `TestMakerFreeWebApp.Data` and `Mapster` required namespaces.
- We added a private `DbContext` member, which we assign through DI in a new `constructor` method.
- We used the `DbContext` to change the behavior of all our data-retrieval methods: `Get`, `Latest`, `ByTitle`, and `Random`. We got rid of the Dummy Data Provider and used `ApplicationDbContext` instead, meaning that all the quiz data will now be fetched from our Database from now on.
- We used the `.Adapt<TDestination>` method of **Mapster** to map the *Quiz* entity to the `QuizViewModel` class anywhere; note how we even mapped *Quiz* arrays into `QuizViewModel` arrays, as the library supports them too.

Testing the Data Provider

Before moving further, it's time to perform a final test to check whether everything we did up to this point--*ApplicationDbContext, Code-First Database Initialization, Data Migrations, Data Seed*, and *Data Mapping*--is working as expected.

To do that, just launch the application in *debug* mode by pressing the *F5* key. If everything has been implemented properly, you should be presented with a *Home Page* similar to this:

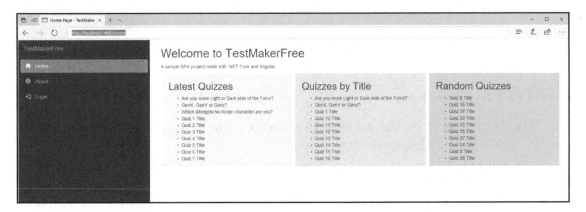

Although it doesn't seem too different from what we already had by the end of `Chapter 3`, *Frontend with Angular*, we know that a lot of stuff changed under the hood. For example, our application is now equipped with a persistent Database built on top of a real Data Model handled by an EF-powered, migrations-aware `DbContext` available through *Dependency Injection* upon a *per-request* scope.

Suggested topics

Data Model, Data Provider, ADO.NET, Object-Relational Mapper, Entity Framework Core, Code-First, Database-First, Model-First, Entity Class, Data Annotations, DbContext, CRUD Operations, Data Migration, Dependency Injection (DI), ORM Mapping, and Mapster.

Summary

We started this chapter by enumerating a number of things we couldn't implement due to our *Dummy Data Provider* limitations; in order to overcome these, we chose to replace it with a real Data Provider built upon a persistent Database.

Entity Framework Core seemed an obvious choice to get what we want, so we added its relevant packages to our project; we briefly enumerated the available *Data Modeling* approaches and resorted to using *Code-First* due to its flexibility.

Right after that, we proceeded to create our entity classes--`ApplicationUser`, `Quiz`, `Question`, `Answer` and `Result`--along with a set of relationships taking advantage of the renowned Entity Framework Core's *Convention over Configuration* approach. Then, we built our `ApplicationDbContext` class accordingly.

After completing our Data Model, we chose the Database Engine, quickly resorting to the Visual Studio's default MSSQL `LocalDb` instance; we added the connection string to the `appsettings.json` file and passed it to `ApplicationDbContext` through the `Setup` class. Doing this allowed us to add our first migration using the `dotnet ef` tool using **PowerShell** and, once done, use *Code-First* to generate our Database accordingly.

We didn't want to leave our Database empty, so we implemented a `DbSeeder` static class to seed it with some sample data; we learned how our `ApplicationDbContext` instance can be used within a static class, thanks to the ASP.NET Core *Dependency Injection* approach; doing that took a reasonable, yet well spent, amount of time.

Finally, we switched back to the `QuizController` class and updated it to make it use the new Data Provider, replacing the outdated one; in order to do this in the best possible way, we also installed **Mapster**, a fast and easy-to-use ORM mapping tool that we used to successfully perform some *Model-to-ViewModel* mapping tasks.

After completing all these tasks, we ran our application in **Debug** mode to verify that everything was still working as intended. The `HomeView` is very similar to the one we had at the end of Chapter 3, *Frontend with Angular*, yet a lot of things changed on the *backend*. Our application is now ready to grow the way we want it to.

5
Client-Server Interactions

In the previous chapter, we replaced our dummy data provider with a real data provider built upon the Entity Framework Core using the Code-First approach. Now that we have data persistence, we're ready to entrust our users with the ability to interact with our application; this means that we can implement some much needed stuff, such as the following:

- **Authentication-related features**: Login form, access control, *server-side* sessions, and so on
- **CRUD operations for all our entities**: Creating/updating a quiz along with its questions/answers/results sets, taking a quiz, and so on

In this chapter, we will take care of the latter by adding a number of *client-server* interactions handled by standard HTTP requests/response chains; the authentication features will be addressed in a separate chapter later on.

Add, update, and delete quizzes

The first thing we'll do is to implement the add, update, and delete methods for our Web API's QuizController. We'll adhere to RESTful conventions and good practices, using the proper HTTP verb for each scenario: POST to create, PUT to update, and DELETE to delete.

Updating QuizController

Remember the #region RESTful conventions methods in our `QuizController.cs` file? It's time to update its contents to support CRUD operations on `Quiz` entities.

Here's the new code (new and updated lines are highlighted):

```
[...]

#region RESTful conventions methods
/// <summary>
/// GET: api/quiz/{id}
/// Retrieves the Quiz with the given {id}
/// </summary>
/// <param name="id">The ID of an existing Quiz</param>
/// <returns>the Quiz with the given {id}</returns>
[HttpGet("{id}")]
public IActionResult Get(int id)
{
    var quiz = DbContext.Quizzes.Where(i => i.Id == id)
        .FirstOrDefault();

    // handle requests asking for non-existing quizzes
    if (quiz == null)
    {
        return NotFound(new
        {
            Error = String.Format("Quiz ID {0} has not been found", id)
        });
    }

    return new JsonResult(
        quiz.Adapt<QuizViewModel>(),
        new JsonSerializerSettings()
        {
            Formatting = Formatting.Indented
        });
}

/// <summary>
/// Adds a new Quiz to the Database
/// </summary>
/// <param name="model">The QuizViewModel containing the data to
insert</param>
[HttpPut]
public IActionResult Put([FromBody]QuizViewModel model)
{
```

```
    // return a generic HTTP Status 500 (Server Error)
    // if the client payload is invalid.
    if (model == null) return new StatusCodeResult(500);

    // handle the insert (without object-mapping)
    var quiz = new Quiz();

    // properties taken from the request
    quiz.Title = model.Title;
    quiz.Description = model.Description;
    quiz.Text = model.Text;
    quiz.Notes = model.Notes;

    // properties set from server-side
    quiz.CreatedDate = DateTime.Now;
    quiz.LastModifiedDate = quiz.CreatedDate;

    // Set a temporary author using the Admin user's userId
    // as user login isn't supported yet: we'll change this later on.
    quiz.UserId = DbContext.Users.Where(u => u.UserName == "Admin")
        .FirstOrDefault().Id;

    // add the new quiz
    DbContext.Quizzes.Add(quiz);
    // persist the changes into the Database.
    DbContext.SaveChanges();

    // return the newly-created Quiz to the client.
    return new JsonResult(quiz.Adapt<QuizViewModel>(),
            new JsonSerializerSettings()
            {
                Formatting = Formatting.Indented
            });
}

/// <summary>
/// Edit the Quiz with the given {id}
/// </summary>
/// <param name="model">The QuizViewModel containing the data to
update</param>
[HttpPost]
public IActionResult Post([FromBody]QuizViewModel model)
{
    // return a generic HTTP Status 500 (Server Error)
    // if the client payload is invalid.
    if (model == null) return new StatusCodeResult(500);

    // retrieve the quiz to edit
```

```
        var quiz = DbContext.Quizzes.Where(q => q.Id ==
                    model.Id).FirstOrDefault();

        // handle requests asking for non-existing quizzes
        if (quiz == null)
        {
            return NotFound(new
            {
                Error = String.Format("Quiz ID {0} has not been found",
                    model.Id)
            });
        }

        // handle the update (without object-mapping)
        //    by manually assigning the properties
        //    we want to accept from the request
        quiz.Title = model.Title;
        quiz.Description = model.Description;
        quiz.Text = model.Text;
        quiz.Notes = model.Notes;

        // properties set from server-side
        quiz.LastModifiedDate = quiz.CreatedDate;

        // persist the changes into the Database.
        DbContext.SaveChanges();

        // return the updated Quiz to the client.
        return new JsonResult(quiz.Adapt<QuizViewModel>(),
                new JsonSerializerSettings()
                {
                    Formatting = Formatting.Indented
                });
    }

    /// <summary>
    /// Deletes the Quiz with the given {id} from the Database
    /// </summary>
    /// <param name="id">The ID of an existing Test</param>
    [HttpDelete("{id}")]
    public IActionResult Delete(int id)
    {
        // retrieve the quiz from the Database
        var quiz = DbContext.Quizzes.Where(i => i.Id == id)
            .FirstOrDefault();

        // handle requests asking for non-existing quizzes
        if (quiz == null)
```

```
        {
            return NotFound(new
            {
                Error = String.Format("Quiz ID {0} has not been found", id)
            });
        }

        // remove the quiz from the DbContext.
        DbContext.Quizzes.Remove(quiz);
        // persist the changes into the Database.
        DbContext.SaveChanges();

        // return an HTTP Status 200 (OK).
        return new OkResult();
    }
    #endregion

    [...]
```

It goes without saying--yet we're still saying it--that these changes require the using TestMakerFree.Data reference at the beginning of the file.

The preceding source code contains some comments that will help explain the implementation details of what we just did. Nonetheless, it will be useful to focus on the following highlights:

- We updated our already-implemented Get method so that it will be able to handle requests pointing to non-existing items. Although this is not strictly related to what we're doing now, we took the chance to do that while we were there.
- We implemented the Put, Post, and Delete methods to make them actually perform the expected *server-side* operations to add, update, and delete a quiz instead of throwing a NotImplementedException, like they were doing since Chapter 2, *Backend with .NET Core*.
- We added the [FromBody] parameter attribute to the Put and Post methods signatures; we did this to tell .NET Core to fetch the QuizViewModel sent by our Angular app--in JSON format--from the request body.
- We used the Adapt<TDestination>() feature from the Mapster ORM library at the end of the Put and Post methods to return a new QuizViewModel to the client built upon the created/modified Quiz.

Also, note how we didn't use `Mapster` to populate the `Quiz` entity from the `QuizViewModel` in the `Post` method, as we have chosen to manually treat, check, and assign each property separately there; we did that to gain more control over these changes, separating the properties that the user is allowed to modify from those who should be set from *server-side* only.

We should also spend a few moments talking about what we didn't do here: no error-handling strategies, no validation or integrity checks on user-input values, no authentication, just to name a few. This isn't a robust, *production-ready* code yet, and we need to be fully aware of that. There's nothing wrong with it; we're still in the development phase, after all, and we'll refine these aspects once we get a good grip on all the features we still need to know.

Adapting the client

Now that our server-side `QuizController` supports the four basic CRUD functions, we can upgrade our Angular client to make use of them.

Adding QuizEditComponent

Let's start with making our users aware that they can create their own quizzes.

Navigate to the `/ClientApp/app/components/navmenu/` folder, open the `navmenu.component.html` file, and append the following `<li>` element to the end of the existing `<ul>` (new lines are highlighted):

```
[...]

<ul class='nav navbar-nav'>
    <li [routerLinkActive]="['link-active']">
        <a [routerLink]="['/home']">
            <span class='glyphicon glyphicon-home'></span> Home
        </a>
    </li>
    <li [routerLinkActive]="['link-active']">
        <a [routerLink]="['/about']">
            <span class='glyphicon glyphicon-info-sign'></span> About
        </a>
    </li>
    <li [routerLinkActive]="['link-active']">
        <a [routerLink]="['/login']">
```

```
            <span class='glyphicon glyphicon-log-in'></span> Login
        </a>
    </li>
    <li [routerLinkActive]="['link-active']">
        <a [routerLink]="['/quiz/create']">
            <span class='glyphicon glyphicon-log-in'></span> Create
                Quiz
        </a>
    </li>
</ul>

[...]
```

Needless to say, we also need to update our Angular app's `RouterModule` to add the relevant route accordingly--along with the references to the component that will handle it--in the `app.module.shared.ts` file:

```
[...]

import { QuizListComponent } from './components/quiz/quiz-list.component';
import { QuizComponent } from './components/quiz/quiz.component';
import { QuizEditComponent } from './components/quiz/quiz-edit.component';
import { AboutComponent } from './components/about/about.component';

[...]

declarations: [
    AppComponent,
    NavMenuComponent,
    HomeComponent,
    QuizListComponent,
    QuizComponent,
    QuizEditComponent,
    AboutComponent,
    LoginComponent,
    PageNotFoundComponent
],

[...]

RouterModule.forRoot([
    { path: '', redirectTo: 'home', pathMatch: 'full' },
    { path: 'home', component: HomeComponent },
    { path: 'quiz/create', component: QuizEditComponent },
    { path: 'quiz/:id', component: QuizComponent },
    { path: 'about', component: AboutComponent },
    { path: 'login', component: LoginComponent },
    { path: '**', component: PageNotFoundComponent }
```

```
])

[...]
```

Ensure that you add the new `quiz/create` rule above the `quiz/:id` one, or the request will be handled by the latter! That `:id` keyword we used there is a *catch-all* and hence it will accept numbers and strings.

Saving the file with these changes will immediately raise a TS to compile warning, as there isn't a `QuizEditComponent` class out there. Let's fix that by adding a `quiz-edit.component.ts` file within the `/ClientApp/app/components/quiz/` folder with the following code:

```typescript
import { Component, Inject, OnInit } from "@angular/core";
import { ActivatedRoute, Router } from "@angular/router";
import { HttpClient } from "@angular/common/http";

@Component({
    selector: "quiz-edit",
    templateUrl: './quiz-edit.component.html',
    styleUrls: ['./quiz-edit.component.css']
})

export class QuizEditComponent {
    title: string;
    quiz: Quiz;

    // this will be TRUE when editing an existing quiz,
    // FALSE when creating a new one.
    editMode: boolean;

    constructor(private activatedRoute: ActivatedRoute,
        private router: Router,
        private http: HttpClient,
        @Inject('BASE_URL') private baseUrl: string) {

        // create an empty object from the Quiz interface
        this.quiz = <Quiz>{};

        var id = +this.activatedRoute.snapshot.params["id"];
        if (id) {
            this.editMode = true;

            // fetch the quiz from the server
            var url = this.baseUrl + "api/quiz/" + id;
            this.http.get<Quiz>(url).subscribe(res => {
```

```
                    this.quiz = res;
                    this.title = "Edit - " + this.quiz.Title;
                }, error => console.error(error));
            }
            else {
                this.editMode = false;
                this.title = "Create a new Quiz";
            }
        }

    onSubmit(quiz: Quiz) {
        var url = this.baseUrl + "api/quiz";

        if (this.editMode) {
            this.http
                .post<Quiz>(url, quiz)
                .subscribe(res => {
                    var v = res;
                    console.log("Quiz " + v.Id + " has been updated.");
                    this.router.navigate(["home"]);
                }, error => console.log(error));
        }
        else {
            this.http
                .put<Quiz>(url, quiz)
                .subscribe(res => {
                    var q = res;
                    console.log("Quiz " + q.Id + " has been created.");
                    this.router.navigate(["home"]);
                }, error => console.log(error));
        }
    }

    onBack() {
        this.router.navigate(["home"]);
    }
}
```

As always, we're also adding the `quiz-edit.component.html` template file:

```
<h2>{{title}}</h2>
<div class="quiz-edit">
    <div>
        <label for="title">Quiz title:</label>
        <br />
        <input type="text" id="title" [(ngModel)]="quiz.Title"
         placeholder="choose a title..." />
    </div>
```

```
<div>
    <label for="description">Quiz description:</label>
    <br />
    <input type="text" id="description"
     [(ngModel)]="quiz.Description" placeholder="enter a
      description..." />
</div>
<div>
    <label for="text">Quiz informative text:</label>
    <br />
    <textarea id="text" [(ngModel)]="quiz.Text" placeholder="enter
      a text..."></textarea>
</div>
<div>
    <input *ngIf="editMode" type="button" value="Apply Changes"
          (click)="onSubmit(quiz)" />
    <input *ngIf="!editMode" type="button" value="Create the Quiz!"
          (click)="onSubmit(quiz)" />
    <input type="button" value="Cancel" (click)="onBack()" />
</div>
</div>
```

Also, we're adding the `quiz-edit.component.css` stylesheet file:

```
.quiz-edit input[type="text"],
.quiz-edit textarea {
    min-width: 500px;
}
```

The code is well documented as it has a lot of comments explaining what we're doing here and there. However, let's give it a quick overview:

- The first thing to note is that we used the `QuizEditComponent` name, not `QuizCreateController`; the reason we did that is easily understandable by looking at the source code, we'll use the same component to handle either the *Create a new Quiz* feature--with a PUT request to our `QuizController`--or the *Edit an existing Quiz* feature--with a POST one. Doing that will save us a tremendous amount of development time, at the cost of some *if-then-else* conditional directives in the component class and template files; the whole purpose of the `editMode` internal property is to help us perform these switches wherever we need them.

- We already know most of the Angular classes, services, and decorators that we used here--Inject, HttpClient, Router, ActivatedRoute, and so on; no need to repeat ourselves here, we already know why they're here.
- We added three different UI buttons to our template file, but only two of them will be visible at the same time, depending on whether the component works in editMode or not. We did that trick using the *ngIf directive, which is another extremely useful tool in the *Angular Template Syntax* shed. As we can easily see, it can be used to conditionally add or remove any element from the DOM as long as we feed it with any property or expression returning a Boolean value.

Activating the Edit mode

We're now able to launch our QuizEditController in Create mode from the **Create a Quiz** NavMenu link; however, there's currently no way to access the Edit mode yet. The most logical way to do that would probably be from the QuizComponent; the user will navigate from the quiz list(s) to a specific quiz, then--assuming that it's the author--would see a button to access the Quiz Edit view.

To implement such behavior, open the quiz.component.html template file and add the following code (new lines are highlighted):

```html
<div *ngIf="quiz" class="quiz">
    <h2>{{quiz.Title}}</h2>
    <ul>
        <li>
            <label>Title:</label>
            <input [(ngModel)]="quiz.Title" placeholder="Insert the
            title..." />
        </li>
        <li>
            <label>Description:</label>
            <textarea [(ngModel)]="quiz.Description"
            placeholder="Insert a suitable description..."></textarea>
        </li>
    </ul>
    <div>
        <input type="button" value="Edit" (click)="onEdit()" />
    </div>
</div>
```

Once done, add the `onEdit()` method implementation to the `quiz.component.ts` file in the following way:

```
[...]

onEdit() {
    this.router.navigate(["quiz/edit", this.quiz.Id]);
}

[...]
```

The preceding code should be added just below the `constructor` method of the `QuizComponent` class.

Event handlers versus router links

It's worth nothing that instead of adding an `<input>` element and binding its click action to a event-handler `delegate` method like we just did, we could've done the following:

```
<a [routerLink]="['/quiz/edit', quiz.Id]"
```

This is the same approach taken by the `NavMenuComponent` with the menu entries: just a plain anchor ID `QueryString` parameter. Both approaches will get the job done, hence we're free to use whatever we like the most.

 A big advantage of the `anchor/routerLink` method is that everything happens on the template, arguably making it easier and faster to lay it down; conversely, the `input/click` method is more versatile, as the `delegate` method enables the developer to do virtually anything, as we'll get to see in the next paragraph.

Adding the Edit route

Last but not least, we need to add the Edit route to the `AppModule` class. Open the `/ClientApp/app/app.module.shared.ts` file and add the following:

```
[...]

RouterModule.forRoot([
    { path: '', redirectTo: 'home', pathMatch: 'full' },
    { path: 'home', component: HomeComponent },
    { path: 'quiz/create', component: QuizEditComponent },
    { path: 'quiz/edit/:id', component: QuizEditComponent },

[...]
```

Implementing the Delete feature

Before going further, we can take the chance to add a **Delete Quiz** button to our QuizController and bind it to another event-handler method that will take care of the client-server interactions required to actually execute the delete action.

Let's start with creating the button in the quiz.component.html template file; we can put it just below the Edit button:

```
[...]

<div>
    <input type="button" value="Edit" (click)="onEdit()" />
    <input type="button" value="Delete this Quiz" (click)="onDelete()" />
</div>

[...]
```

Once done, add the following onDelete() method implementation in the quiz.component.ts file, right below the onEdit() method:

```
[...]

onDelete() {
    if (confirm("Do you really want to delete this quiz?")) {
        var url = this.baseUrl + "api/quiz/" + this.quiz.Id;
        this.http
            .delete(url)
            .subscribe(res => {
                console.log("Quiz " + this.quiz.Id + " has been
                deleted.");
                this.router.navigate(["home"]);
            }, error => console.log(error));
    }
}

[...]
```

There's nothing new here, except for the good old JavaScript confirm() technique that we threw in to prevent users from accidentally deleting a quiz; that popup is as ugly as it was in the 90s, but it's still a good time/value deal when we're in a hurry, even in Angular!

A word on Observables

We're definitely making a good use of the Angular `HttpClient`--as would be expected from any decent *server-side* fed SPA. Although it's not advisable to waste too much space talking about it, we should definitely spend a few words on its new abstraction pattern based upon **Observables**. One of the most relevant differences with the previous approach is that Observables have a lazy behavior by design, meaning that they won't fire unless there is a valid subscription issued by a `.subscribe()` function call.

This is a major perspective switch from the AngularJS **Promises**, that will execute right off the bat, regardless of how the client code will use their result afterward. Another important difference involves the `.subscribe()` function, which will be fired upon completion of the add task of `ItemService`. In Angular, subscriptions are designed to work just like a standard `.then()` or `.complete()` function featured in most async-based JavaScript libraries (AngularJS/Promises, JQuery/AJAX, and so on), with the key difference that they are also bound to the `Observable` itself; this means that they won't just trigger once and resolve, but they will be executed each and every time the `Observable` completes its task(s) until it ceases to exist, unless they get cancelled by calling the `.unsubscribe()` function method on their `Observable`.

That said, we can easily note that the minimalistic `HTTP` requests we've been implementing are hardly a good example to demonstrate the advantages of this behavior as most of these `Observables` will fire only once; to better see the difference with the previous approaches, we will have to implement some truly reactive functionalities such as Search with Autocomplete, Websockets, Push Notifications, Instant Messaging, and similar stuff.

First client-server test

With all these new additions, our Angular-based SPA should be able to show at least a glimpse of its true potential; let's perform a full surface test before adding questions, answers, and results to the loop.

This is how our **Home** view should appear now:

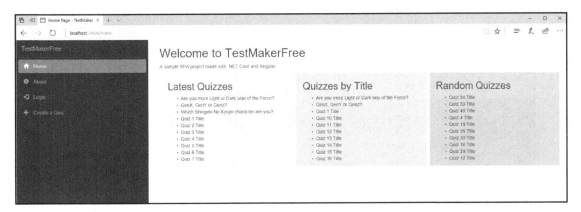

The new **Create a Quiz** NavMenu link is there, just as expected; by clicking on that, we will be brought to the Quiz Edit view:

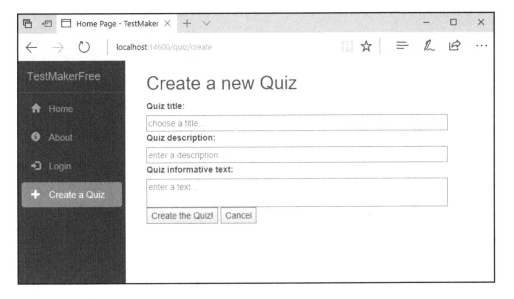

As we can see, the `QuizEditComponent` is working as we would expect when the `editMode` switch is set to `FALSE`, prompting the user to create a new quiz. Let's fill the fields with some sample data, as shown in this screenshot:

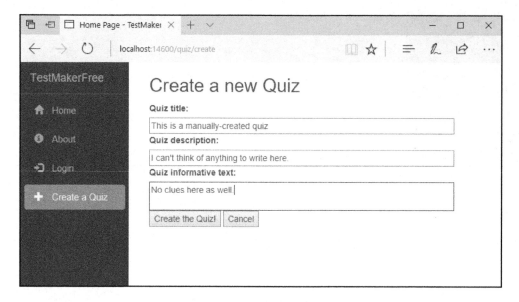

Once done, click on the **Create a Quiz** button to see what happens:

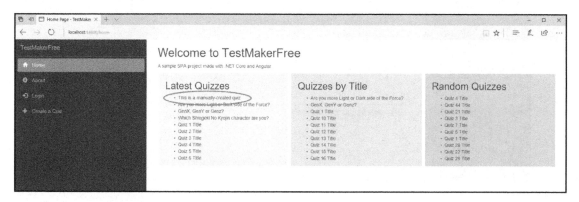

Here's our new boy, it worked!

We can now create new quizzes; let's see whether we can edit the existing ones as well. From the **Home** view, click on the quiz we just added to access the Quiz view:

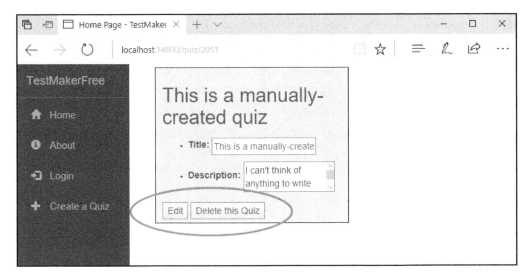

From here, we can test whether our **Edit** and **Delete this Quiz** buttons work. Clicking on the first one will bring us to the Edit Quiz view:

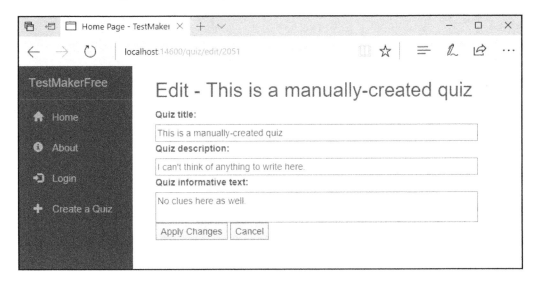

We can try to change some string values here and see whether the changes are reflected in the Database; we can even place some debug symbols within our *client-side* and *server-side* code to see how the request will be issued by the Angular app, received by .NET Core, and eventually handled within the `Delete` action method of `QuizController` through our EF Core's `ApplicationDbContext` instance.

When we're done, go back to the Quiz view and click on the **Delete the Quiz** button; the delete confirmation popup should appear to check whether we're really sure about that:

Click on **Cancel** first, then click on the **Delete this Quiz** button again and click on **OK** to let the app work its magic and then bring you back to the **Home** view. From there, we should be able to see that the newly created quiz is gone for good.

The client-server workflow

Everyone should have already figured it out by now, yet it can still be useful to recap the interactions workflow between the client-side and the server-side components of our app:

- The user can create a new quiz using the **Create a Quiz** button from the navigation menu; as soon as they click on it, it will navigate to the `QuizEditComponent`. The component will run in Create mode since the `editMode` internal property value will be set to `FALSE` within the constructor. Once there, he can create a new quiz and confirm the operation by clicking on the **Create the Quiz** button; as soon as they do that, the Angular `HttpClient` returns an `Observable` object ready to issue a `PUT` request call to the server-side API. That call will be handled by the `QuizController`, which will create the quiz within the database using an instance of the `ApplicationDbContext` class obtained through dependency injection.

- Alternatively, the user can select an already-existing quiz from one of the lists in the Home view and navigate to the corresponding Quiz view; from there, he can choose to **Edit** or **Delete** that quiz using one of the available buttons. From there, these two things can happen:

    - If the user clicks on the **Edit** button, the application will fire the `onEdit()` event-handler `delegate` method, which will route the user to the `QuizEditComponent`; this time the component will run in Edit mode, as the `editMode` property will be `TRUE`. The user can change one or more values and confirm them by clicking on the **Apply Changes** button; as soon as they do that, the Angular `HttpClient` returns an `Observable` object ready to issue a `POST` request call to the server-side API. This call will be handled by the `QuizController`, which will persist the applied changes to the database using an instance of the `ApplicationDbContext` class obtained through dependency injection.

    - If the user clicks on the **Delete** button, the application will fire the `onDelete()` event-handler `delegate` method, which will use the Angular `HttpClient` to return an `Observable` object ready to issue a `DELETE` request call to the server-side API. The call will be handled by the `QuizController`, which will delete the quiz from the database using an instance of the `ApplicationDbContext` class obtained through dependency injection.

Note how the various `Observable` objects we're using to handle the `HTTP` responses will immediately fire thanks to the fluent `.subscribe()` call issued by the calling method, creating an asynchronous thread that will always take care of the following tasks:

- **In case of success**, re-route the user to the Home view, not before outputting the good news in the console log
- **In case of failure**, output the error in the console log

It's also worth noting how the Angular framework reinitializes the Home view--along with all the `ItemListComponent` elements--each time the user is sent back to the *Home* view so that he'll be able to see the changes he just made using the **create**, **edit**, and **delete** features immediately after they occur.

Questions, answers, and results

We just did an excellent job with our quizzes, but it's still not enough to allow our users to actually create--or even take!--a quiz; we're still missing questions, answers, and results.

In the following paragraphs, we'll do our best to bring them up to speed.

Server-side tasks

Remember all those controllers that we set up back in `Chapter 2`, *Backend with .NET Core*? We have been neglecting them for a while, with the sole exception of the `QuizController`; it's definitely time to atone.

QuestionController

Let's start with `QuestionController`. Here's the code that will put it back on track (new/updated lines are highlighted):

```
using System;
using Microsoft.AspNetCore.Mvc;
using Newtonsoft.Json;
using TestMakerFreeWebApp.ViewModels;
using System.Collections.Generic;
using System.Linq;
using TestMakerFreeWebApp.Data;
using Mapster;
```

```
namespace TestMakerFreeWebApp.Controllers
{
    [Route("api/[controller]")]
    public class QuestionController : Controller
    {
        #region Private Fields
        private ApplicationDbContext DbContext;
        #endregion

        #region Constructor
        public QuestionController(ApplicationDbContext context)
        {
            // Instantiate the ApplicationDbContext through DI
            DbContext = context;
        }
        #endregion

        #region RESTful conventions methods
        /// <summary>
        /// Retrieves the Question with the given {id}
        /// </summary>
        /// <param name="id">The ID of an existing Question</param>
        /// <returns>the Question with the given {id}</returns>
        [HttpGet("{id}")]
        public IActionResult Get(int id)
        {
            var question = DbContext.Questions.Where(i => i.Id == id)
                .FirstOrDefault();

            // handle requests asking for non-existing questions
            if (question == null)
            {
                return NotFound(new
                {
                    Error = String.Format("Question ID {0} has not been
                    found", id)
                });
            }

            return new JsonResult(
                question.Adapt<QuestionViewModel>(),
                new JsonSerializerSettings()
                {
                    Formatting = Formatting.Indented
                });
        }

        /// <summary>
```

```
/// Adds a new Question to the Database
/// </summary>
/// <param name="model">The QuestionViewModel containing the
        data to insert</param>
[HttpPut]
public IActionResult Put([FromBody]QuestionViewModel model)
{
    // return a generic HTTP Status 500 (Server Error)
    // if the client payload is invalid.
    if (model == null) return new StatusCodeResult(500);

    // map the ViewModel to the Model
    var question = model.Adapt<Question>();

    // override those properties
    //   that should be set from the server-side only
    question.QuizId = model.QuizId;
    question.Text = model.Text;
    question.Notes = model.Notes;

    // properties set from server-side
    question.CreatedDate = DateTime.Now;
    question.LastModifiedDate = question.CreatedDate;

    // add the new question
    DbContext.Questions.Add(question);
    // persist the changes into the Database.
    DbContext.SaveChanges();

    // return the newly-created Question to the client.
    return new JsonResult(question.Adapt<QuestionViewModel>(),
        new JsonSerializerSettings()
        {
            Formatting = Formatting.Indented
        });
}

/// <summary>
/// Edit the Question with the given {id}
/// </summary>
/// <param name="model">The QuestionViewModel containing the
     data to update</param>
[HttpPost]
public IActionResult Post([FromBody]QuestionViewModel model)
{
    // return a generic HTTP Status 500 (Server Error)
    // if the client payload is invalid.
    if (model == null) return new StatusCodeResult(500);
```

```
    // retrieve the question to edit
    var question = DbContext.Questions.Where(q => q.Id ==
                model.Id).FirstOrDefault();

    // handle requests asking for non-existing questions
    if (question == null)
    {
        return NotFound(new
        {
            Error = String.Format("Question ID {0} has not been
            found", model.Id)
        });
    }

    // handle the update (without object-mapping)
    //    by manually assigning the properties
    //    we want to accept from the request
    question.QuizId = model.QuizId;
    question.Text = model.Text;
    question.Notes = model.Notes;

    // properties set from server-side
    question.LastModifiedDate = question.CreatedDate;

    // persist the changes into the Database.
    DbContext.SaveChanges();

    // return the updated Quiz to the client.
    return new JsonResult(question.Adapt<QuestionViewModel>(),
        new JsonSerializerSettings()
        {
            Formatting = Formatting.Indented
        });
}

/// <summary>
/// Deletes the Question with the given {id} from the Database
/// </summary>
/// <param name="id">The ID of an existing Question</param>
[HttpDelete("{id}")]
public IActionResult Delete(int id)
{
    // retrieve the question from the Database
    var question = DbContext.Questions.Where(i => i.Id == id)
        .FirstOrDefault();

    // handle requests asking for non-existing questions
    if (question == null)
```

```
        {
            return NotFound(new
            {
                Error = String.Format("Question ID {0} has not been
                found", id)
            });
        }

        // remove the quiz from the DbContext.
        DbContext.Questions.Remove(question);
        // persist the changes into the Database.
        DbContext.SaveChanges();

        // return an HTTP Status 200 (OK).
        return new OkResult();
    }
    #endregion

    // GET api/question/all
    [HttpGet("All/{quizId}")]
    public IActionResult All(int quizId)
    {
        var questions = DbContext.Questions
            .Where(q => q.QuizId == quizId)
            .ToArray();
        return new JsonResult(
            questions.Adapt<QuestionViewModel[]>(),
            new JsonSerializerSettings()
            {
                Formatting = Formatting.Indented
            });
    }
  }
}
```

There's nothing new here, as we stick to the same pattern that we already used for the QuizController; we retrieve an ApplicationDbContext instance through dependency injection, and we use it throughout all our methods to get, insert, update, and delete our entities. We can see the usual references to the namespaces we already know, such as our TestMakerFree.Data provider and the Mapster package library.

There are some minor differences here and there, such as the `quizId` property that we use to enforce our one-to-many relationship between a quiz and its questions; a good example would be the `All()` action method when we get to retrieve all the questions related to a given `quizId`.

AnswerController

The `AnswerController` won't be much different, at least for the time being:

```
using System;
using Microsoft.AspNetCore.Mvc;
using Newtonsoft.Json;
using TestMakerFreeWebApp.ViewModels;
using System.Collections.Generic;
using System.Linq;
using TestMakerFreeWebApp.Data;
using Mapster;

namespace TestMakerFreeWebApp.Controllers
{
    [Route("api/[controller]")]
    public class AnswerController : Controller
    {
        #region Private Fields
        private ApplicationDbContext DbContext;
        #endregion

        #region Constructor
        public AnswerController(ApplicationDbContext context)
        {
            // Instantiate the ApplicationDbContext through DI
            DbContext = context;
        }
        #endregion

        #region RESTful conventions methods
        /// <summary>
        /// Retrieves the Answer with the given {id}
        /// </summary>
        /// <param name="id">The ID of an existing Answer</param>
        /// <returns>the Answer with the given {id}</returns>
        [HttpGet("{id}")]
        public IActionResult Get(int id)
        {
            var answer = DbContext.Answers.Where(i => i.Id == id)
                .FirstOrDefault();
```

```csharp
            // handle requests asking for non-existing answers
            if (answer == null)
            {
                return NotFound(new
                {
                    Error = String.Format("Answer ID {0} has not been
                    found", id)
                });
            }

            return new JsonResult(
                answer.Adapt<AnswerViewModel>(),
                new JsonSerializerSettings()
                {
                    Formatting = Formatting.Indented
                });
        }

        /// <summary>
        /// Adds a new Answer to the Database
        /// </summary>
        /// <param name="model">The AnswerViewModel containing the data
        ///     to insert</param>
        [HttpPut]
        public IActionResult Put([FromBody]AnswerViewModel model)
        {
            // return a generic HTTP Status 500 (Server Error)
            // if the client payload is invalid.
            if (model == null) return new StatusCodeResult(500);

            // map the ViewModel to the Model
            var answer = model.Adapt<Answer>();

            // override those properties
            //    that should be set from the server-side only
            answer.QuestionId = model.QuestionId;
            answer.Text = model.Text;
            answer.Notes = model.Notes;

            // properties set from server-side
            answer.CreatedDate = DateTime.Now;
            answer.LastModifiedDate = answer.CreatedDate;

            // add the new answer
            DbContext.Answers.Add(answer);
            // persist the changes into the Database.
            DbContext.SaveChanges();
```

```
        // return the newly-created Answer to the client.
        return new JsonResult(answer.Adapt<AnswerViewModel>(),
            new JsonSerializerSettings()
            {
                Formatting = Formatting.Indented
            });
}

/// <summary>
/// Edit the Answer with the given {id}
/// </summary>
/// <param name="model">The AnswerViewModel containing the data
///     to update</param>
[HttpPost]
public IActionResult Post([FromBody]AnswerViewModel model)
{
    // return a generic HTTP Status 500 (Server Error)
    // if the client payload is invalid.
    if (model == null) return new StatusCodeResult(500);

    // retrieve the answer to edit
    var answer = DbContext.Answers.Where(q => q.Id ==
                model.Id).FirstOrDefault();

    // handle requests asking for non-existing answers
    if (answer == null)
    {
        return NotFound(new
        {
            Error = String.Format("Answer ID {0} has not been
            found", model.Id)
        });
    }

    // handle the update (without object-mapping)
    //    by manually assigning the properties
    //    we want to accept from the request
    answer.QuestionId = model.QuestionId;
    answer.Text = model.Text;
    answer.Value = model.Value;
    answer.Notes = model.Notes;

    // properties set from server-side
    answer.LastModifiedDate = answer.CreatedDate;

    // persist the changes into the Database.
    DbContext.SaveChanges();
```

```
                // return the updated Quiz to the client.
                return new JsonResult(answer.Adapt<AnswerViewModel>(),
                    new JsonSerializerSettings()
                    {
                        Formatting = Formatting.Indented
                    });
        }


        /// <summary>
        /// Deletes the Answer with the given {id} from the Database
        /// </summary>
        /// <param name="id">The ID of an existing Answer</param>
        [HttpDelete("{id}")]
        public IActionResult Delete(int id)
        {
            // retrieve the answer from the Database
            var answer = DbContext.Answers.Where(i => i.Id == id)
                .FirstOrDefault();

            // handle requests asking for non-existing answers
            if (answer == null)
            {
                return NotFound(new
                {
                    Error = String.Format("Answer ID {0} has not been
                found", id)
                });
            }

            // remove the quiz from the DbContext.
            DbContext.Answers.Remove(answer);
            // persist the changes into the Database.
            DbContext.SaveChanges();

            // return an HTTP Status 200 (OK).
            return new OkResult();
        }
        #endregion

        // GET api/answer/all
        [HttpGet("All/{questionId}")]
        public IActionResult All(int questionId)
        {
            var answers = DbContext.Answers
                .Where(q => q.QuestionId == questionId)
                .ToArray();
            return new JsonResult(
                answers.Adapt<AnswerViewModel[]>(),
```

```
                        new JsonSerializerSettings()
                        {
                            Formatting = Formatting.Indented
                        });
                }
            }
        }
```

We can see a couple of new things here:

- The `quizId` property that has been replaced with the `questionId` to comply with the relationship between the `Answer` entity and its parent `Question`
- In the `Post()` action method, where we're not using the object mapping, we had to manually set the `Value` property of the updated answer

ResultController

Last but not least, here comes the `ResultController` (most relevant lines are highlighted):

```
using System;
using Microsoft.AspNetCore.Mvc;
using Newtonsoft.Json;
using TestMakerFreeWebApp.ViewModels;
using System.Collections.Generic;
using System.Linq;
using TestMakerFreeWebApp.Data;
using Mapster;

namespace TestMakerFreeWebApp.Controllers
{
    [Route("api/[controller]")]
    public class ResultController : Controller
    {
        #region Private Fields
        private ApplicationDbContext DbContext;
        #endregion

        #region Constructor
        public ResultController(ApplicationDbContext context)
        {
            // Instantiate the ApplicationDbContext through DI
            DbContext = context;
        }
        #endregion

        #region RESTful conventions methods
```

```
/// <summary>
/// Retrieves the Result with the given {id}
/// </summary>
/// <param name="id">The ID of an existing Result</param>
/// <returns>the Result with the given {id}</returns>
[HttpGet("{id}")]
public IActionResult Get(int id)
{
    var result = DbContext.Results.Where(i => i.Id == id)
        .FirstOrDefault();

    // handle requests asking for non-existing results
    if (result == null)
    {
        return NotFound(new
        {
            Error = String.Format("Result ID {0} has not been
            found", m.Id)
        });
    }

    return new JsonResult(
        result.Adapt<ResultViewModel>(),
        new JsonSerializerSettings()
        {
            Formatting = Formatting.Indented
        });
}

/// <summary>
/// Adds a new Result to the Database
/// </summary>
/// <param name="model">The ResultViewModel containing the data
///     to insert</param>
[HttpPut]
public IActionResult Put([FromBody]ResultViewModel model)
{
    // return a generic HTTP Status 500 (Server Error)
    // if the client payload is invalid.
    if (model == null) return new StatusCodeResult(500);

    // map the ViewModel to the Model
    var result = model.Adapt<Result>();

    // override those properties
    // that should be set from the server-side only
    result.CreatedDate = DateTime.Now;
    result.LastModifiedDate = result.CreatedDate;
```

```
        // add the new result
        DbContext.Results.Add(result);
        // persist the changes into the Database.
        DbContext.SaveChanges();

        // return the newly-created Result to the client.
        return new JsonResult(result.Adapt<ResultViewModel>(),
            new JsonSerializerSettings()
            {
                Formatting = Formatting.Indented
            });
    }

    /// <summary>
    /// Edit the Result with the given {id}
    /// </summary>
    /// <param name="model">The ResultViewModel containing the data
        to update</param>
    [HttpPost]
    public IActionResult Post([FromBody]ResultViewModel model)
    {
        // return a generic HTTP Status 500 (Server Error)
        // if the client payload is invalid.
        if (model == null) return new StatusCodeResult(500);

        // retrieve the result to edit
        var result = DbContext.Results.Where(q => q.Id ==
                    model.Id).FirstOrDefault();

        // handle requests asking for non-existing results
        if (result == null)
        {
            return NotFound(new
            {
                Error = String.Format("Result ID {0} has not been
              found", m.Id)
            });
        }

        // handle the update (without object-mapping)
        // by manually assigning the properties
        // we want to accept from the request
        result.QuizId = model.QuizId;
        result.Text = model.Text;
        result.MinValue = model.MinValue;
        result.MaxValue = model.MaxValue;
        result.Notes = model.Notes;
```

```
        // properties set from server-side
        result.LastModifiedDate = result.CreatedDate;

        // persist the changes into the Database.
        DbContext.SaveChanges();

        // return the updated Quiz to the client.
        return new JsonResult(result.Adapt<ResultViewModel>(),
            new JsonSerializerSettings()
            {
                Formatting = Formatting.Indented
            });
}


/// <summary>
/// Deletes the Result with the given {id} from the Database
/// </summary>
/// <param name="id">The ID of an existing Result</param>
[HttpDelete("{id}")]
public IActionResult Delete(int id)
{
    // retrieve the result from the Database
    var result = DbContext.Results.Where(i => i.Id == id)
        .FirstOrDefault();

    // handle requests asking for non-existing results
    if (result == null)
    {
        return NotFound(new
        {
            Error = String.Format("Result ID {0} has not been
            found", m.Id)
        });
    }

    // remove the quiz from the DbContext.
    DbContext.Results.Remove(result);
    // persist the changes into the Database.
    DbContext.SaveChanges();

    // return an HTTP Status 200 (OK).
    return new OkResult();
}
#endregion

// GET api/result/all
[HttpGet("All/{quizId}")]
public IActionResult All(int quizId)
```

```
            {
                var results = DbContext.Results
                    .Where(q => q.QuizId == quizId)
                    .ToArray();
                return new JsonResult(
                    results.Adapt<ResultViewModel[]>(),
                    new JsonSerializerSettings()
                    {
                        Formatting = Formatting.Indented
                    });
            }
        }
    }
```

This code will definitely raise some compiler warnings due to the fact that there are no
MinValue and/or MaxValue properties in the ResultViewModel class (yet); let's fill the
gap by adding them both in the ResultViewModel.cs file (new lines are highlighted):

```
[...]

#region Properties
public int Id { get; set; }
public int QuizId { get; set; }
public string Text { get; set; }
public int? MinValue { get; set; }
public int? MaxValue { get; set; }
public string Notes { get; set; }
[DefaultValue(0)]
public int Type { get; set; }
[DefaultValue(0)]
public int Flags { get; set; }
[JsonIgnore]
public DateTime CreatedDate { get; set; }
public DateTime LastModifiedDate { get; set; }
#endregion

[...]
```

This will fix the warning and allow the compiler to successfully build our code. We already
explained the purpose of these properties when we worked on the Result entity back in
Chapter 4, *Data Model with Entity Framework Core*, so we won't repeat ourselves here.

BaseApiController

Our .NET Web API controllers get their job done; however, they're all affected by a noticeable flaw--the amount of duplicate code we used to make them all behave in the same way, although with different entities. More specifically, this means the following:

- They all have a `DbContext` property and a constructor that retrieves it through dependency injection
- They all create a number of `JsonSerializerSettings` objects configured in the same way

This is a rather common issue when working with the MVC pattern, where the same interfaces and approaches are often adopted multiple times and within different controllers.

Luckily enough, repeating a behavior doesn't necessarily mean repeating the code; we can easily cut these dupes with the help of a Base class.

 Those who are already familiar with the C# class inheritance mechanism will definitely know the purpose of a Base class and how to use it. In the unlikely case that you aren't, just think of it as a parent class that can be created to allow a number of other derived classes to inherit all the members, properties, and behaviors defined there. This pattern is extremely popular in object-oriented programming, although the semantics may vary from language to language; for example, in Java, a Base class is called **Superclass**, while the derived classes are known as **Subclasses**.

Let's try to put together a Base class for our web API controllers that will take care of the repeating tasks summarized earlier. From **Solution Explorer**, right-click on the /Controllers/ folder and add a new `BaseApiClontroller.cs` class file with the following code:

```
using System;
using Microsoft.AspNetCore.Mvc;
using Newtonsoft.Json;
using System.Collections.Generic;
using System.Linq;
using TestMakerFreeWebApp.Data;
using Mapster;

namespace TestMakerFreeWebApp.Controllers
{
    [Route("api/[controller]")]
    public class BaseApiController : Controller
```

```
    {
        #region Constructor
        public BaseApiController(ApplicationDbContext context)
        {
            // Instantiate the ApplicationDbContext through DI
            DbContext = context;

            // Instantiate a single JsonSerializerSettings object
            // that can be reused multiple times.
            JsonSettings = new JsonSerializerSettings()
            {
                Formatting = Formatting.Indented
            };

        }
        #endregion

        #region Shared Properties
        protected ApplicationDbContext DbContext { get; private set; }
        protected JsonSerializerSettings JsonSettings { get; private
                                                              set; }

        #endregion
    }
}
```

Implementing BaseApiController

The next thing to do is to derive the `QuizController`, `QuestionController`, `AnswerController`, and `ResultController` from this `BaseApiController` class, so they can inherit the shared properties and get rid of a lot of duplicate code; let's start with the `QuizController`.

Open the `QuizController.cs` file and perform the following changes (updated lines are highlighted):

```
[...]

namespace TestMakerFreeWebApp.Controllers
{
    public class QuizController : BaseApiController
    {
        #region Constructor
        public QuizController(ApplicationDbContext context)
            : base(context) { }
        #endregion

[...]
```

As we can see, we removed the following:

- The `[Route("api/[controller]")]` attribute, since it's already present in the `BaseApiController`; all the Base class attributes will be inherited by the derived classes as well
- The Private Members region, thus shrinking the constructor to a minimal amount

Once done, scroll down to the end of the `Get(id)` action method and update its return value in the following way (updated lines are highlighted):

```
[...]

    return new JsonResult(
        quiz.Adapt<QuizViewModel>(),
        JsonSettings);

[...]
```

Replace all the other `JsonSerializerSettings()` instances created on the fly with the `JsonSettings` property to further reduce the amount of source code lines.

Once done with the `QuizController`, we need to perform these two changes on all the other Web API controllers as well--`QuestionController`, `AnswerController`, and `ResultController`--all except `HomeController`. For obvious space reasons, we won't do that here, leaving such a task to the reader; the things to do are identical anyway.

 IMPORTANT: Ensure not to inherit the `BaseApiController` class within your `HomeController`, as this is not a web API Controller; it has its specific set of server-side routing rules to serve the start page; doing that will prevent your app from running properly.

Client-side tasks

The server-side part of the job has been done; it's time to switch to Angular and integrate all these new features within the GUI.

Adding the interfaces

Let's start with defining our client-side interfaces to handle questions, answers, and results; from **Solution Explorer**, right-click on the `/ClientApp/app/interfaces/` folder and create the TypeScript files with the appropriate names and contents described here:

- `question.ts`: Here's the code for the `question.ts` file:

```
interface Question {
    Id: number;
    QuizId: number;
    Text: string;
}
```

- `answer.ts`: Here's the `answer.ts` file:

```
interface Answer {
    Id: number;
    QuestionId: number;
    Text: string;
    Value: number;
}
```

- `result.ts`: Here's the `result.ts` file:

```
interface Result {
    Id: number;
    QuizId: number;
    Text: string;
    MinValue?: number;
    MaxValue?: number;
}
```

Note how we also included the foreign-key properties to retrieve the **Quiz** or **Question** *parent*, as we'll use them in our client app soon enough.

QuestionListComponent

The first thing we'll do is to implement a `QuestionListComponent` that will show a list of questions for any given quiz; once done, we'll add it to our already-existing `QuizEditComponent`, thus enabling our users to view, create, edit, and/or delete them from the same place where they can edit the details of the parent quiz.

Start with creating the `/ClientApp/app/components/question/` folder, then right-click on it and add the `question-list.component.ts` file with the following content (relevant lines are highlighted):

```
import { Component, Inject, Input, OnChanges, SimpleChanges } from
"@angular/core";
import { Router } from "@angular/router";
import { HttpClient } from "@angular/common/http";

@Component({
    selector: "question-list",
    templateUrl: './question-list.component.html',
    styleUrls: ['./question-list.component.css']
})

export class QuestionListComponent implements OnChanges {
    @Input() quiz: Quiz;
    questions: Question[];
    title: string;

    constructor(private http: HttpClient,
        @Inject('BASE_URL') private baseUrl: string,
        private router: Router) {

        this.questions = [];
    }

    ngOnChanges(changes: SimpleChanges) {
        if (typeof changes['quiz'] !== "undefined") {

            // retrieve the quiz variable change info
            var change = changes['quiz'];

            // only perform the task if the value has been changed
            if (!change.isFirstChange()) {
                // execute the Http request and retrieve the result
                this.loadData();
            }
        }
    }

    loadData() {
        var url = this.baseUrl + "api/question/All/" + this.quiz.Id;
        this.http.get<Question[]>(url).subscribe(res => {
            this.questions = res;
        }, error => console.error(error));
    }
```

```
    onCreate() {
        this.router.navigate(["/question/create", this.quiz.Id]);
    }

    onEdit(question: Question) {
        this.router.navigate(["/question/edit", question.Id]);
    }

    onDelete(question: Question) {
        if (confirm("Do you really want to delete this question?")) {
            var url = this.baseUrl + "api/question/" + question.Id;
            this.http
                .delete(url)
                .subscribe(res => {
                    console.log("Question " + question.Id + " has been
                     deleted.");

                    // refresh the question list
                    this.loadData();
                }, error => console.log(error));
        }
    }
}
```

Once done, follow up with the `question-list.component.html` **template** file:

```html
<h3>Questions</h3>
<div *ngIf="questions.length > 0">
    <table class="questions">
        <thead>
            <tr>
                <th>Text</th>
                <th>Options</th>
            </tr>
        </thead>
        <tbody>
            <tr *ngFor="let question of questions">
                <td>{{question.Text}}</td>
                <td><input type="button" value="Edit"
                        (click)="onEdit(question)" />
                    <input type="button" value="Delete"
                        (click)="onDelete(question)" /></td>
            </tr>
        </tbody>
    </table>
</div>
<div *ngIf="questions.length == 0">
    This quiz has no questions (yet):
```

```
        click the <strong>Add a new Question</strong> button to add the first
    one!
    </div>
    <input type="button" value="Add a new Question" (click)="onCreate()" />
```

Also, follow up with the `question.list.component.css` style sheet file:

```
table.questions {
    min-width: 500px;
}
```

We've got lot of new stuff here; let's see how it works.

By looking at the class implementation, we can see how we're expecting to receive a `quiz` property, which will most likely come from the parent component--the `quiz-edit.component.ts` file. Since it will come from there, we had to use the `@Input()` decorator to authorize the binding. The `quiz` property will be used within the `loadData()` method to assemble the URL for the server-side API to retrieve all the existing questions for the current quiz; as usual, that request will be issued by the Angular `HttpClient`, just like we did a number of times earlier.

However, it's difficult to miss that we're taking a different approach here. The news is the `loadData()` method itself, which is not called in the constructor phase, nor in the `ngOnInit()` life cycle hook we used in the past; we can clearly see that it's executed within the `ngOnChanges()` method, which is something we have never heard of.

Introducing ngOnChanges()

The `ngOnChanges()` method is nothing less than another life cycle hook that will trigger each time Angular sets a data-bound input property. We had to use it instead of the constructor or `ngOnInit()` methods for a rather obvious reason: we can't load the questions unless the parent `quiz` property is available, so we need to postpone the `Http` call until the parent component sets it. Since the quiz is also retrieved with an asynchronous `Http` call by the parent component, we had to find a way to tell our `QuestionListComponent` when the data-bound property is actually updated.

The following schema should help you better visualize the issue:

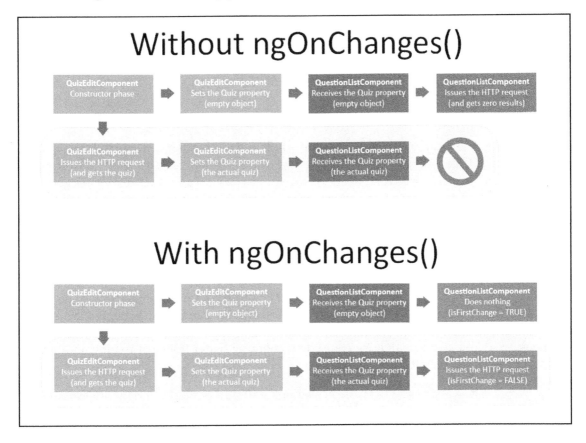

The rounded rectangle with gray background is the asynchronous thread where the QuizEditComponent retrieves the quiz using the HttpClient.

By looking at the upper portion of the preceding schema, we can see how, without using ngOnChanges(), the QuestionListComponent will issue a completely useless Http call trying to get the questions of an empty quiz object, thus getting zero results. Besides, when the quiz is actually retrieved, it won't do anything because there are no triggers that can tell that the quiz object value has been changed; long story short, we will never get these questions.

The lower portion of the schema tells a whole different story: there are no useless Http calls at the end of the constructor-based life cycle, as the isFirstChange() method that we put within our ngOnChanges() implementation will return TRUE, giving us a good reason to ignore the event and do nothing. Later on, when the parent's async call will complete and the quiz will be set, that same method will return FALSE, giving the green flag for issuing the Http call the right way--or, rather, at the right time.

Why bother?

Wait a minute... why did we have to pass the whole quiz **object**, since we're only using it to get the quiz ID? Can't we just forget about it as a whole and just pass the quiz ID from the QuizEditController? We won't need to wait for any async call, as we're already getting it from the route! Why should we complicate the task with all this ngOnChanges() fuzz?

This is a legitimate question, especially now that the app is still in its embryonic stage, we can definitely afford to have a component that will serve all the available questions for a given quiz without knowing anything about the quiz itself, other than its ID. We can even say that, for the time being, working with the quiz ID and forgetting about the rest would be the right thing to do here. However, there will be other scenarios where we will need to have more information from our source object--or from our parent component--than those we can fetch from the parent route. Sooner or later, we'll definitely hit one of them; when it happens, we'd love to know that we could do something better than just issuing another Http call and re-fetch it all from scratch.

 The ngOnChanges() life cycle hook will be a powerful tool in our Angular arsenal; learning how it works and how to use it can be a great help to overcome a number of nasty concurrency issues between components and is definitely a great addition in our Angular knowledge. For further information regarding it, we strongly suggest that you refer the following URL addresses from the Angular official documentation:

```
https://angular.io/api/core/OnChanges
https://angular.io/guide/lifecycle-hooks#onchanges
```

The template file

Let's come back to the QuestionListComponent template file. Once again, we made good use of the *ngIf directive to show a different <div> element depending on if the quiz has at least one question or not; the former contains a table where we iterate through the questions and show them accordingly, while the latter hosts a classic "empty contents" info message that the users will see where the quiz contains no questions (yet).

We also added three input buttons that will fire some `delegate` methods defined in the `QuestionListComponent` class: `onAdd`, `onEdit`, and `onDelete`. Their names are quite self-explanatory, hence we already know what to expect from them. Note how the `Delete` event handler is the only one that performs its task firsthand, while the other two will just route the user away. None of these routes is handled yet, but we'll fix this soon enough.

Adding the references

As always, before we can use the component, we need to add it to the `AppModule` class. Open the `app.module.shared.ts` file and add the following highlighted lines in the `import` list and the `declarations` array:

```
[...]

import { QuizListComponent } from './components/quiz/quiz-list.component';
import { QuizComponent } from './components/quiz/quiz.component';
import { QuizEditComponent } from './components/quiz/quiz-edit.component';
import { QuestionListComponent } from './components/question/question-list.component';

[...]

    declarations: [
        AppComponent,
        NavMenuComponent,
        HomeComponent,
        QuizListComponent,
        QuizComponent,
        QuizEditComponent,
        QuestionListComponent,

[...]
```

As soon as we do that, we can add our new component to the `quiz-edit.component.ts` file using its `<question-list>` selector. A good place to put it will be right after the `<div>` element containing the quiz command buttons:

```
[...]

<div>
    <input *ngIf="editMode" type="button" value="Apply Changes"
(click)="onSubmit(quiz)" />
    <input *ngIf="!editMode" type="button" value="Create the Quiz!"
(click)="onSubmit(quiz)" />
    <input type="button" value="Cancel" (click)="onBack()" />
</div>
```

```
<question-list [quiz]="quiz" *ngIf="editMode"></question-list>
```

[...]

Again, this is just standard stuff: the one-way data-binding to the quiz object that we've talked about for a long time early on, and a *ngIf directive that will ensure that the child component will be shown only when the parent works in Edit mode.

QuestionEditComponent

Now, it's time to create the QuestionEditComponent, along with its required routes and references. To do that, right-click on the /ClientApi/api/components/question/ folder and add the question-edit.component.ts file with the following content (relevant lines are highlighted):

```
import { Component, Inject, OnInit } from "@angular/core";
import { ActivatedRoute, Router } from "@angular/router";
import { HttpClient } from "@angular/common/http";

@Component({
    selector: "question-edit",
    templateUrl: './question-edit.component.html',
    styleUrls: ['./question-edit.component.css']
})

export class QuestionEditComponent {
    title: string;
    question: Question;

    // this will be TRUE when editing an existing question,
    // FALSE when creating a new one.
    editMode: boolean;

    constructor(private activatedRoute: ActivatedRoute,
        private router: Router,
        private http: HttpClient,
        @Inject('BASE_URL') private baseUrl: string) {

        // create an empty object from the Quiz interface
        this.question = <Question>{};

        var id = +this.activatedRoute.snapshot.params["id"];

        // check if we're in edit mode or not
        this.editMode = (this.activatedRoute.snapshot.url[1].path ===
            "edit");
```

```
if (this.editMode) {

    // fetch the quiz from the server
    var url = this.baseUrl + "api/question/" + id;
    this.http.get<Question>(url).subscribe(res => {
        this.question = res;
        this.title = "Edit - " + this.question.Text;
    }, error => console.error(error));
}
else {
    this.question.QuizId = id;
    this.title = "Create a new Question";
}
}

onSubmit(question: Question) {
    var url = this.baseUrl + "api/question";

    if (this.editMode) {
        this.http
            .post<Question>(url, question)
            .subscribe(res => {
                var v = res;
                console.log("Question " + v.Id + " has been
                updated.");
                this.router.navigate(["quiz/edit", v.QuizId]);
            }, error => console.log(error));
    }
    else {
        this.http
            .put<Question>(url, question)
            .subscribe(res => {
                var v = res;
                console.log("Question " + v.Id + " has been
                 created.");
                this.router.navigate(["quiz/edit", v.QuizId]);
            }, error => console.log(error));
    }
}

onBack() {
    this.router.navigate(["quiz/edit", this.question.QuizId]);
}
}
```

Pay attention to the highlighted lines, as we're using a different way to choose between activating the Edit mode or not. The reason is that we can't rely on the mere presence of the ID in this component, because--as we're about to see-- even the Create mode route will ship one: the ID of the parent quiz, which we need to actually create the question.

Once done, follow up with the `question-edit.component.html` template file:

```html
<h2>{{title}}</h2>
<div class="question-edit">
    <div>
        <label for="text">Question text:</label>
        <br />
        <textarea id="text" [(ngModel)]="question.Text"
          placeholder="enter a suitable text..."></textarea>
    </div>
    <div>
        <input *ngIf="editMode" type="button" value="Apply Changes"
          (click)="onSubmit(question)" />
        <input *ngIf="!editMode" type="button" value="Create the
          Question!" (click)="onSubmit(question)" />
        <input type="button" value="Cancel" (click)="onBack()" />
    </div>

    <answer-list *ngIf="editMode" [question]="question"></answer-list>

</div>
```

The preceding highlighted line shows how we're already setting up things for the upcoming `AnswerListComponent` that we will implement in a short while; the overall approach is identical to `<question-list>`, which we already used in the `QuizEditComponent`.

Finally, here's the `question-edit.component.css` style sheet file:

```css
.question-edit textarea {
    min-width: 500px;
}
```

There's nothing new here, as we're using the same pattern we successfully pulled off to handle the **Quiz | Questions** one-to-many relationship.

References and routes

We already know that we have to add every component to the `app.module.shared.ts` file's `import` list and `declarations` array, so we won't explain how to do it again; let's just do it as we already did a number of other times.

While we're there, let's add the missing routes as well to the `RouterModule`, just after the quiz ones:

```
[...]
{ path: 'quiz/create', component: QuizEditComponent },
{ path: 'quiz/edit/:id', component: QuizEditComponent },
{ path: 'quiz/:id', component: QuizComponent },
{ path: 'question/create/:id', component: QuestionEditComponent },
{ path: 'question/edit/:id', component: QuestionEditComponent },
{ path: 'about', component: AboutComponent },

[...]
```

We can easily note a big difference between the `quiz/create` and the `question/create/:id` routes--the latter will require an `:id` parameter, just like the `question/edit/:id` counterpart. We already explained the reason earlier, but it can't hurt to repeat it here--the Create mode will need to know the `QuizId` when issuing the `Put Http` call to the `QuestionController`, as it's a required property of the `Question` Entity.

AnswerListComponent

After all we did with the questions, implementing the answer-related components will be a walk in the park! Jokes aside, this is pretty much the same code with some minimal differences. As a matter of fact, it will be even easier, as we won't have to struggle with child components; we'll just need to implement the `ngOnChanges()` life cycle hook again, since we have no parent changes to detect.

Anyway, here's the deal: from **Solution Explorer**, create the `/ClientApi/app/components/answer/` folder and right-click on it to add the following `answer-list.component.ts` class file:

```
import { Component, Inject, Input, OnChanges, SimpleChanges } from
"@angular/core";
import { Router } from "@angular/router";
import { HttpClient } from "@angular/common/http";

@Component({
    selector: "answer-list",
```

```
    templateUrl: './answer-list.component.html',
    styleUrls: ['./answer-list.component.css']
})

export class AnswerListComponent implements OnChanges {
    @Input() question: Question;
    answers: Answer[];
    title: string;

    constructor(private http: HttpClient,
        @Inject('BASE_URL') private baseUrl: string,
        private router: Router) {

        this.answers = [];
    }

    ngOnChanges(changes: SimpleChanges) {
        if (typeof changes['question'] !== "undefined") {

            // retrieve the question variable change info
            var change = changes['question'];

            // only perform the task if the value has been changed
            if (!change.isFirstChange()) {
                // execute the Http request and retrieve the result
                this.loadData();
            }
        }
    }

    loadData() {
        var url = this.baseUrl + "api/answer/All/" + this.question.Id;
        this.http.get<Answer[]>(url).subscribe(res => {
            this.answers = res;
        }, error => console.error(error));
    }

    onCreate() {
        this.router.navigate(["/answer/create", this.question.Id]);
    }

    onEdit(answer: Answer) {
        this.router.navigate(["/answer/edit", answer.Id]);
    }

    onDelete(answer: Answer) {
        if (confirm("Do you really want to delete this answer?")) {
            var url = this.baseUrl + "api/answer/" + answer.Id;
```

```
              this.http
                  .delete(url)
                  .subscribe(res => {
                      console.log("Answer " + answer.Id + " has been
                                                        deleted.");

                      // refresh the question list
                      this.loadData();
                  }, error => console.log(error));
          }
      }
  }
```

Follow this with the `answer-list.component.html` **template file:**

```
<h3>Answers</h3>
<div *ngIf="answers.length > 0">
    <table class="answers">
        <thead>
            <tr>
                <th>Text</th>
                <th>Value</th>
                <th></th>
            </tr>
        </thead>
        <tbody>
            <tr *ngFor="let answer of answers">
                <td>{{answer.Text}}</td>
                <td>{{answer.Value}}</td>
                <td><input type="button" value="Edit"
                        (click)="onEdit(answer)" />
                    <input type="button" value="Delete"
                        (click)="onDelete(answer)" /></td>
            </tr>
        </tbody>
    </table>
</div>
<div *ngIf="answers.length == 0">
    This questions has no answers (yet):
    click the <strong>Add a new Answer</strong> button to add the first
one!
</div>
<input type="button" value="Add a new Answer" (click)="onCreate()" />
```

Then, follow it with the `answer-list.component.css` style sheet file:

```
table.answers {
    min-width: 500px;
}
```

Before moving further, don't forget to add the `AnswerListComponent` to the `app.module.shared.ts` file--just like we did a number of times already.

AnswerEditComponent

The `AnswerEditComponent` is so much similar to the `QuestionEditComponent`--at least for the time being--that we can just copy and paste the `question-edit.component.ts` file, rename it as `answer-edit.component.ts`, and perform the following changes:

- Replace **Question** with **Answer** and **question** with **answer**
- Replace **Quiz** with **Question** and **quiz** with **question**

Ensure that you follow the given order; also, if you plan to do it automatically, don't forget to activate the case-sensitive switch from within your text editor to avoid screwing up the source code!

 We were able to do that because we used the same naming conventions for everything, from the Web API server-side routes to to the CSS classes; however, exploiting find and replace in this way is hardly a good behavior, and we only do that because we don't want to overburden this book with source code samples. We strongly suggest the reader to take this chance to try implementing the `AnswerEditComponent` with the acquired knowledge instead of using the copy and replace trick, as it will be a great exercise to check whether they properly understand everything.

The same trick can be done for the `answer-edit.component.css` style sheet file; conversely, the template file requires some additional work.

The template file

Each time we add a new answer, we need to give it a score value. The best thing we can do to properly handle this is to add a `<select>` element to the `AnswerEditComponent` template file so that the active user can pick a number from a list of allowed values.

Here's the full `answer-edit.component.html` template file, with the relevant code highlighted:

```html
<h2>{{title}}</h2>
<div class="answer-edit">
    <div>
        <label for="text">Answer text:</label>
        <br />
        <textarea id="text" [(ngModel)]="answer.Text"
         placeholder="enter a suitable text..."></textarea>
    </div>

    <div>
        <label for="value">Score Value:</label>
        <br />
        <select id="value" name="value" [(ngModel)]="answer.Value">
            <option *ngFor="let num of [-5,-4,-3,-2,-1,0,1,2,3,4,5]"
            [value]="num">{{num}}</option>
        </select>
    </div>

    <div>
        <input *ngIf="editMode" type="button" value="Apply Changes"
         (click)="onSubmit(answer)" />
        <input *ngIf="!editMode" type="button" value="Create the
        Answer!" (click)="onSubmit(answer)" />
        <input type="button" value="Cancel" (click)="onBack()" />
    </div>
</div>
```

By doing so, our users will be able to give each answer a value from a minimum of −5 to a maximum of 5. Needless to say, this is just an example; we're free to let the user pick the number they want by setting wider boundaries or by replacing the `<select>` element with an `<input type="number" />` element; as always, the choice is ours.

References and routes

As for the references and routes, we already know what to do. Let's just emphasize the routing aspect, as this is the only thing that might not throw an immediate exception if we do something wrong, thus taking more time to fix in case of an error:

```
[...]
{ path: 'question/edit/:id', component: QuestionEditComponent },
{ path: 'answer/create/:id', component: AnswerEditComponent },
{ path: 'answer/edit/:id', component: AnswerEditComponent },
{ path: 'about', component: AboutComponent },

[...]
```

ResultListComponent

Instead of implementing the `ResultListComponent` from scratch, we can give another try to the copy-rename-replace trick we used in the previous paragraph, taking the `QuestionListComponent` as the source. Create the `/ClientApi/api/components/result/` folder, then copy paste the `question-list.component.ts` and `question-list.component.css` files there, renaming them as `result-list.component` accordingly.

Once done, perform the following case-sensitive find and replace tasks:

- Replace **Question** with **Result**
- Replace **question** with **result**

Alternatively, the reader can try to implement them both by himself and make additional changes, along with the following `result-list.component.html` template file that requires some additional work (relevant lines highlighted):

```
<h3>Results</h3>
<div *ngIf="results.length > 0">
    <table class="results">
        <thead>
            <tr>
                <th>Text</th>
                <th>Min. Value</th>
                <th>Max. Value</th>
                <th>Options</th>
            </tr>
        </thead>
        <tbody>
            <tr *ngFor="let result of results">
```

```
            <td>{{result.Text}}</td>
            <td *ngIf="result.MinValue === null">N/A</td>
            <td *ngIf="result.MinValue !== null">
            {{result.MinValue}}</td>
            <td *ngIf="result.MaxValue === null">N/A</td>
            <td *ngIf="result.MaxValue !== null">
            {{result.MaxValue}}</td>
            <td><input type="button" value="Edit"
                        (click)="onEdit(result)" />
                <input type="button" value="Delete"
                        (click)="onDelete(result)" /></td>
          </tr>
        </tbody>
    </table>
</div>
<div *ngIf="results.length == 0">
    This quiz has no results (yet):
    click the <strong>Add a new Result</strong> button to add the first
one!
</div>
<input type="button" value="Add a new Result" (click)="onCreate()" />
```

We're dealing with `MinValue` and `MaxValue` here, which we defined as `nullable` numbers. We can just use `{{result.MinValue}}` and `{{result.MaxValue}}` within a `<td>` block, just like we did with the preceding `{{result.Text}}`; it would have worked, showing an empty string in case of null; however, since we wanted to show a custom *N/A* string instead, we used some `*ngIf` directives to get a more readable result.

Reference and routes

Open the `quiz-edit.component.html` template file and implement the `ResultListComponent` as a sub-component in the following way, right after the `<question-list>` element (new line highlighted):

```
[...]

    <question-list *ngIf="editMode" [quiz]="quiz"></question-list>

    <result-list *ngIf="editMode" [quiz]="quiz"></result-list>

[...]
```

Right after that, open the `app.module.shared.ts` file and add the usual import references, declarations, and routes:

```
[...]

import { AnswerEditComponent } from './components/answer/answer-
edit.component';
import { ResultListComponent } from './components/result/result-
list.component';
import { ResultEditComponent } from './components/result/result-
edit.component';
import { AboutComponent } from './components/about/about.component';

[...]

    declarations: [

[...]

        AnswerEditComponent,
        ResultListComponent,
        ResultEditComponent,
        AboutComponent,

[...]

        RouterModule.forRoot([

[...]

            { path: 'answer/edit/:id', component: AnswerEditComponent
                                                                   },
            { path: 'result/create/:id', component: ResultEditComponent
                                                                   },
            { path: 'result/edit/:id', component: ResultEditComponent
                                                                   },
            { path: 'about', component: AboutComponent },

[...]
```

As we can see, we also took the chance to add the references and routes for the upcoming `ResultEditComponent`, which is coming in the next paragraph.

ResultEditComponent

Once again, our copy-rename-replace trick can save us some valuable time--and space. Copy and paste the `question-edit.component.ts` and CSS files to the `/ClientApi/api/components/result/` folder, rename them as `result-edit.component`, and perform the same case-sensitive find and replace tasks we used the last time:

- Replace **Question** with **Result**
- Replace **question** with **result**

As always, the wise reader should take the chance to manually implement the `ResultEditComponent` instead.

Once the class and style sheet files are ready, create the `result-edit.component.html` template file from scratch in that same folder and fill it with the following code (relevant lines are highlighted):

```
<h2>{{title}}</h2>
<div class="result-edit">
    <div>
        <label for="text">Result text:</label>
        <br />
        <textarea id="text" [(ngModel)]="result.Text"
            placeholder="enter a suitable text..."></textarea>
    </div>

    <div>
        <label for="MinValue">Minimum Score Value:</label>
        <br />
        <input type="number" id="MinValue" name="MinValue"
            [(ngModel)]="result.MinValue" />
    </div>

    <div>
        <label for="MaxValue">Maximum Score Value:</label>
        <br />
        <input type="number" id="MaxValue" name="MaxValue"
            [(ngModel)]="result.MaxValue" />
    </div>

    <div>
        <input *ngIf="editMode" type="button" value="Apply Changes"
                            (click)="onSubmit(result)" />
        <input *ngIf="!editMode" type="button" value="Create the
                    Result!" (click)="onSubmit(result)" />
```

```
            <input type="button" value="Cancel" (click)="onBack()" />
    </div>

</div>
```

As we can see, we had to handle the `MinValue` and `MaxValue` unique properties of the `Result` interface. We already faced a similar scenario with the `Value` property in the `AnswerEditComponent` template file; however, this time we chose a different approach because these properties are meant to host `nullable` numeric values. The `<input type="number />` is a good compromise here, as it will prevent users from inputting non-numeric values while also accepting an empty value, which will be treated as `null` by our code.

Full-scale test

We can't possibly say that we were slacking off here! After a tremendous amount of work, it's time to perform a final client-server test to ensure that everything is working as expected.

Just a quick consideration before we start: it's been a while from our last client-server test, and we changed a whole lot of things. It's very important to understand that receiving some compiler, runtime, or GUI-related errors here will be perfectly normal, especially if we performed some find-replace as we did (not) suggest to. Whenever this happens, it will only mean that we missed something on the way. Don't lose the grip, read the error messages, use the built-in debugger, check up your source code, and do your best to find the issue; if you can't figure it out, try to "unmount" some component by removing the references; this will greatly help you understand what's actually working and where the problem lies. Always keep in mind that the code is never wrong, yet also don't forget that you're in control here.

Run the application in *debug* mode by pressing *F5* and wait from the **Home** view to load. Once done, click on one of the available quiz items; ensure that you choose one of the auto generated ones, because we need it to have **questions**, **answers**, and **results**:

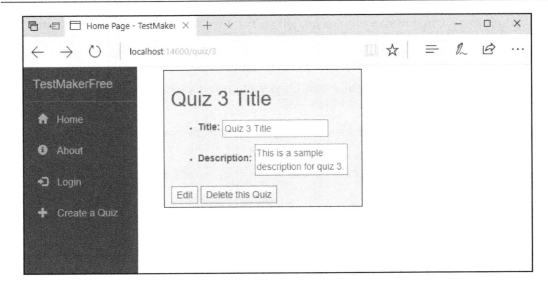

Here's our beloved (yet still ugly) Quiz view. From there, left-click on the **Edit** button and see what happens:

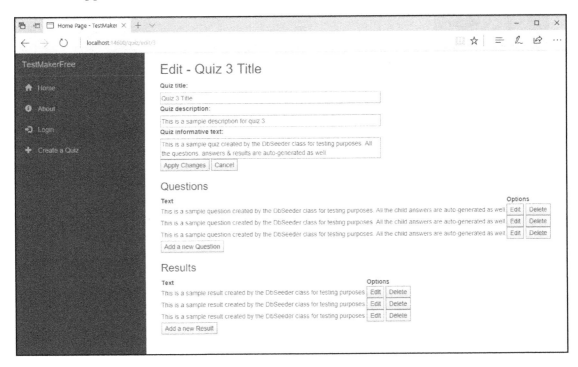

We'll admit that it can definitely look a lot better. Yet it works! We got the quiz data, the questions list and the results list, which means that our `QuestionListComponent` and `ResultQuizComponent` are actually doing their job.

From here, we can click on the **Add a new Question** button to check out if the `QuestionEditComponent` is working as well:

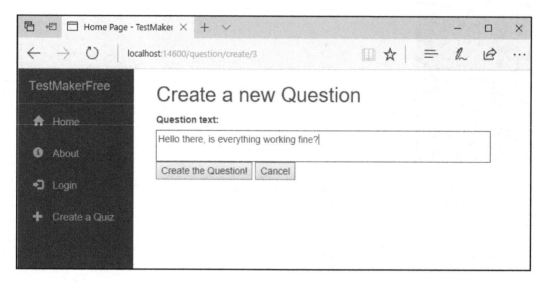

Fill it with some sample data (as in the preceding screenshot), and then click on the **Create the Question** button to get routed back to the Quiz Edit view:

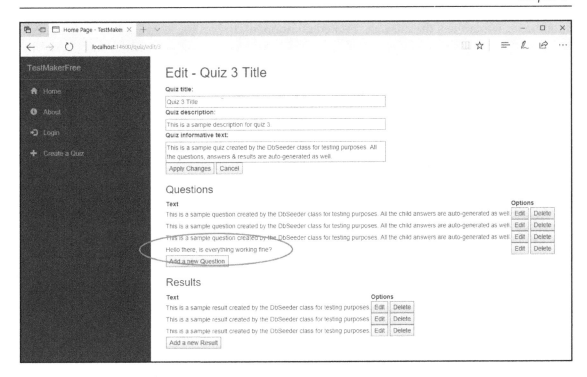

As expected, the new question is there; now we can use it to test the Edit mode of `QuestionEditComponent`. Left-click on the **Edit** button to its right to access it:

From here, we can test the answers-related component; the `AnswerListComponent` seems to be working fine already, so we can click on the **Add a new Answer** button and check out the `AnswerEditComponent` in Create mode:

From here, we can fill in the values and then issue the **Create the Answer** command; we'll get routed back to the `AnswerEditComponent`, where the `AnswerListComponent` should behave according to our actions:

So far, so good; now we should test the `AnswerEditComponent` in Edit mode to confirm that it also works. Once done, we can navigate backward using the **Cancel** button and delete what we just did to test the **Delete** functionalities provided by the answers and questions listing components. We should see the answer and the question disappear from the listings as soon as we confirm our choice.

Last but not least, we need to test the result-related components and repeat the same steps to ensure that everything is working fine on that part as well:

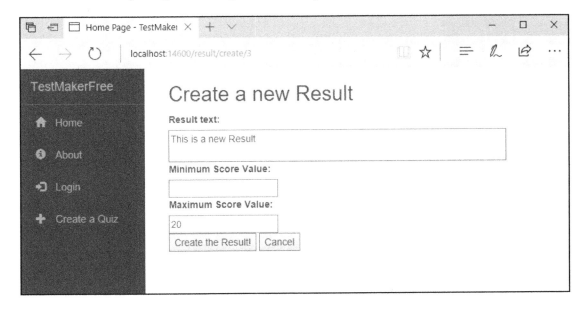

Since we're dealing with `nullable` values here, it's important to check for them too; in the preceding example, we're trying to create a new result without lower bounds--a null `MinValue`--and a `MaxValue` of 20. Our `ResultListComponent` should be able to handle it without problems, as we can see by clicking on the **Create the Result** button:

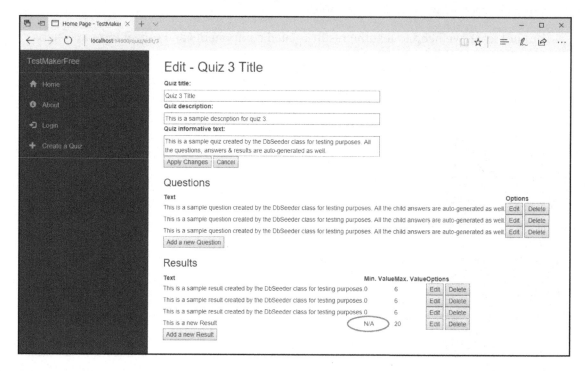

Here comes our custom N/A string. Now we just have to **Edit** the new result to test the `ResultEditComponent` in Edit mode; once done, **Delete** it and get ready for the next chapter.

Suggested topics

RESTful conventions, `HTTP` **verbs**, `HTTP` **status**, `Observables`, `OnChanges/ngOnChanges`, Life cycle Hooks, Base, and Derived classes

Summary

Before moving further, let's do a quick recap of what we did throughout this chapter.

We started working on the server-side aspects of our project. Having replaced the fake data provider with a real one, we made good use of it by implementing the `Put`, `Post`, and `Delete` action methods within our .NET Web API Controllers, mapping our Entities to their respective ViewModels--and the other way around--with the help of the `Mapster` package library. However, we shortly acknowledged the fact that we were writing a lot of duplicate code; in order to reduce this, we implemented a `BaseApiController` class that we used to do some common and repeating tasks, such as making the `DbContext` available through dependency injection and providing a handy `JsonSettings` property. We then derived all our web API controllers from that class and trimmed their source code accordingly.

Right after that, we switched to the client side and implemented the components required to run the new APIs within our Angular app; we started with the `QuizEditComponent`, on which we put a lot of effort to make it able to spin in two ways--Create mode and Edit mode--so that we could use it to add new quizzes as well as update the existing ones. We also updated the `AppModule` to add the required references, dependencies, and routes.

After a quick client-server test, we moved to the `QuestionListComponent`, where we also spent some time to understand the capabilities of the `ngOnChanges()` life cycle hook and learn how to better use it to suit our present and future needs; then, we switched to the `QuestionEditComponent`, where we were able to leverage the knowledge previously acquired when working with the quiz counterpart.

From there, it wasn't much more than a walk in the park, as we already knew what to do with the missing Angular components: `AnswerListComponent`, `AnswerEditComponent`, `ResultListComponent`, and `ResultEditComponent`; although they did have something unique, such as `<select>` elements and `nullable` values, implementing these components was mostly an opportunity to retrace our steps and get a good grip on what we previously did.

After all these changes, we felt the urge to do another round of client-server tests; we spent some good time playing with our SPA, adding, updating, and deleting our entities. After all the hardwork, we can definitely say that we did a good job; our application is working fine, and it's already packed with interesting features built upon a consolidated set of client-server interactions. If only the UI wasn't so ugly. Luckily enough, the following chapter will greatly help us overcome that.

6
Style Sheets and UI Layout

Up to this point, we have done our best to keep the layout as simple as we could so that we could focus entirely on the server-side and client-side coding aspects of our app: .NET Core Web API Controllers, Angular components, C#, and TypeScript. Keeping the layout to a minimum is generally a wise approach when we're learning something new; it also has a few downsides though, the biggest one being the blatant fact that our application is rather unattractive, to say the least: there is no user, client, or customer who wouldn't say that... or worse.

How bad is it, doc?

It almost entirely depends on what we're planning to do with the project we've been working on; as we just said, while we're working our way through tutorials, demos, or sample projects, it's not bad at all, for at least a couple of good reasons:

- We will greatly benefit from keeping our focus on .NET and Angular, leaving the rest for later; applying styles is something that we can easily do whenever we feel like it, even if we don't have a decent grip on style sheet language already
- It's generally a good idea to restrain ourselves from doing any relevant style implementation until we can fully understand where and how to do that conveniently; to put it in other words, we shouldn't do styles until we find a suitable approach for doing that within the given scenario and/or environment

That's why we chose to take this path in the first place; we're definitely in the learning phase, after all. On top of that, we gladly sat upon the minimalistic, yet rather functional layout shipped with the .NET MVC with Angular Visual Studio template that we chose to adopt.

However, since we planned to build a production-ready native web application, we can't restrain ourselves from applying some custom styling any longer; there's no way that our imaginary product owner will be satisfied otherwise. It's time to dress our (mostly) naked doll and make it as pretty as we can.

Introducing LESS

If you've worked with style sheets within the last few years, there's no chance you won't have heard of **LESS**; however, for the sake of those who didn't, let's take a few words to talk about it. Before getting to that though, we must briefly introduce the concepts of style sheet language and **Cascading Style Sheets** (**CSS**).

 This paragraph is mostly aimed at those who have never used LESS before. If you have some experience with LESS already or feel like you don't need to know anything else about why we'll use it, you might as well skip it entirely and jump to the next paragraph: Install and Configure LESS.

Style sheet languages

A style sheet language, also known as style language, is a programming language used to define the presentation layer's UI design rules of a structured document. We can think of it as a skin or a theme that we can apply to a logical item (the structured document) to change its appearance. For example, we can make it look blue, red, or yellow; we can make the characters bigger or smaller and thinner or wider; we can change the text spacing, alignment, and flow; and so on.

Using dedicated style sheet languages gives developers the chance to separate the presentation layer's **code and structure** (respectively JavaScript and HTML) from the **UI design rules**, thus enforcing the **separation of concerns** (**SoC**) principle within the presentation layer itself.

When it comes to web pages, web applications, and anything else that mostly uses HTML, XHTML, XML, and other markup language-based documents, the most important style sheet language undoubtedly is CSS.

CSS

It was December 17, 1996, when the **World Wide Web Consortium** (**W3C**) released the official W3C CSS Recommendation for the style sheet language that would be known as **CSS1**. CSS2 came less than two years later (May 1998), while its revised version, CSS2.1, took considerably more time (June 2011).

Starting from CSS3, things started to become more complex, since the W3C ditched the single, monolithic specification approach by splitting it into separate documents called **modules**, each one of them following its very own publishing, acceptance, and recommendation history. Starting in 2012, with four of these (Media Queries, Namespaces, Selectors, and Color) being published as formal recommendations and full CSS2.1 backward-compatibility, CSS3 quickly became the most adopted style sheet language standard for the development of new websites.

CSS code sample

Regardless of their version, each adding new features while maintaining backward compatibility with the previous one(s), CSS sticks to the following syntax:

```
<selector> [sub-selector] [sub-sub-selector] {
    <property>: <value>;
    <another-property>: <value>;
    <yet-another-property>: <value>;
    [...]
}
```

This translates as follows:

```
.quiz {
    margin: 5px;
    padding: 5px 10px;
    border: 1px solid black;
    background-color: #dddddd;
    width: 300px;
}
```

We've seen this code before; it's a class we added in our application's `quiz.component.ts` file in a previous chapter. It basically says that any HTML element with the **quiz** CSS class assigned will have a light-gray background color, a black, solid, and pixel-wide border, no margin against the surrounding elements, and a certain amount of padding between its borders and the content. To assign a CSS class to an HTML element, use the `class` attribute in the following way:

```
<div class="quiz"> [...some content...] </div>
```

If the attribute already exists, additional CSS classes can be assigned by separating them with a single space:

```
<div class="quiz otherClass someOtherClass"> [...some content...] </div>
```

Simple enough, isn't it?

What is LESS and why use it?

LESS is a cascading style sheet preprocessor; we can think of it as a server-side script for CSS files, enabling us to do a number of things that CSS doesn't support (yet), just like PHP and/or ASP can do for an HTML page. The following diagram should help us better understand the concept:

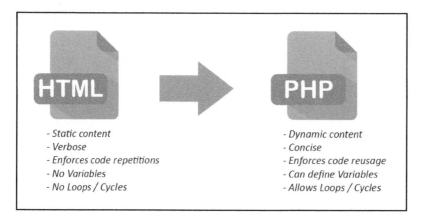

These are the main advantages of using a hypertext preprocessor instead of writing raw **HTML** pages; we're talking about **PHP**, but the same goes for ASP.NET Web Forms, Razor, and basically everything else.

The following are the advantages of using **LESS** instead of writing raw **CSS** files:

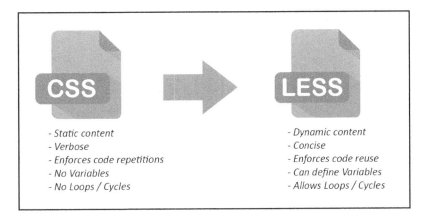

As we can see, they serve the exact same purpose in terms of assisting, improving, and enhancing the development effort.

Making the switch from static style sheets to dynamic style sheets is just as easy as switching from static HTML pages to PHP or ASP dynamic pages; they both feature a nested metalanguage that can extend the base static language in a pure backward-compatible fashion. This means that a valid CSS file is also a valid LESS file, just as a valid HTML file is also a valid PHP or ASP file.

There are also some key differences between hypertext preprocessors and style sheet preprocessors, the most important being how web servers deal with them. Hypertext preprocessors such as PHP and ASP are compiled by the web server upon each request; the web server compiles them on the fly and then serves the resulting HTML for each request-response flow. Conversely, style sheet preprocessor files are usually compiled into standard CSS files before being published; in other words, the web service doesn't know about the existence of these files, as it just serves the resulting CSS-compiled result.

This also means that using a style sheet preprocessor will have no performance impact on the server, unless we choose to install some experimental and still highly inefficient handlers, extensions, modules, or client-side scripts that will compile the source files on the fly.

IMPORTANT NOTE: From now on, we'll take for granted that the reader has a decent knowledge of CSS files, syntax, selectors, and their common use within HTML pages. If this is not the case, we strongly suggest that you learn the core CSS concepts before going further, using the Learning CSS website, maintained and hosted by W3C, featuring a massive number of useful guides, tutorials, and articles:

```
https://www.w3.org/Style/CSS/learning.
```

Variables

Among the most valuable LESS features, there is **variable** support. This is a brief example of what we can do with it:

```less
// Variables can be declared as such:
@link-color: #red;
@link-color-hover: lightcoral;

// And then they can be referenced like this:
a, span. link {
    color: @link-color;
}

a:hover, span.link:hover {
    color: @link-color-hover;
}
```

As you might have noticed, double-slash style (//) inline comments are supported as well, while CSS only allows the slash-asterisk (/**/) syntax.

Import directives

Another LESS key feature is the capability of importing other CSS and LESS files. If we're familiar with the standard CSS @import, we know that it can only be used at the beginning of the file to issue the loading of an external CSS file. With LESS, we can do the following:

```less
// look for a style.less file and process + import its contents.
@import "style";

// look for a style.less file and process + import its contents.
@import "style.less";

// look for a style.css file and import its contents (no processing).
@import "style.css";
```

Note that the behavior depends on the imported file extension. These defaults can be overridden with the following `options` switches:

```
// link/use a Less file without including it in the output.
@import (reference) "something.less";

// include the file in the output without processing it.
@import (inline) "something.less";

// pretend this is a LESS file, regardless of the extension.
@import (less) "something.css";

// pretend this is a CSS file, regardless of the extension.
@import (css) "something.less";

// never include this file more than once (default behavior).
@import (once) "something.less";

// always include this file in the output, even multiple times.
@import (multiple) "something.less";

// do not break the compile operation if the file is not found.
@import (optional) "something.less";
```

If we need to specify multiple `options` within a single `@import` statement, we can do that by separating each one of them with a comma:

```
// take it as a LESS file, import once, skip if not found.
@import (less,once,optional) "something.css";
```

Nested selectors

We will be able to nest selectors within other selectors, thus making our code more succinct and readable. Just to use a quick example, consider this:

```
quiz-list {
    border: 0;
    margin: 0;
    padding: 0;
    vertical-align: top;
    display: block;
}

quiz-list.latest {
        background-color: #f6f6f6;
}
```

```
quiz-list.latest h3 {
    background-image: url(/img/latest-icon.png);
}
```

We can shrink this into something like the following:

```
quiz-list {
    border: 0;
    margin: 0;
    padding: 0;
    vertical-align: top;
    display: block;
    &amp;.latest {
        // the &amp; char represents the current selector parent.
        // in this scenario, it stands for: item-list.latest.
        background-color: #f6f6f6;
        h3 {
            background-color: @color-latest;
            background-image: url(/img/latest-icon.png);
        }
    }
}
```

It might not be such a big deal for small-scale CSS files, yet it's a great readability improvement for big ones.

Mixins

Being able to not repeat ourselves is a key principle of all computer programming languages; however, it's not easy to respect that within standard CSS files, because we will often be forced to write something like this:

```
.button-s {
    background-color: blue;
    border: 1px solid black;
    border-radius: 5px;
    font-family: Verdana;
    font-size: 0.8em;
    width: 100px;
}

.button-m {
    background-color: blue;
    border: 1px solid black;
    border-radius: 5px;
    font-family: Verdana;
    font-size: 1em;
```

```
        width: 200px;
    }

    .button-l {
        background-color: blue;
        border: 1px solid black;
        border-radius: 5px;
        font-family: Verdana;
        font-size: 1.2em;
        width: 300px;
    }
```

With LESS, we can shrink it into this:

```
    .button-s {
        background-color: blue;
        border: 1px solid black;
        border-radius: 5px;
        font-family: Verdana;
        font-size: 0.8em;
        width: 100px;
    }

    .button-m {
        .button-s;
        font-size: 1em;
        width: 200px;
    }

    .button-l {
        .button-s;
        font-size: 1.2em;
        width: 300px;
    }
```

In other words, a mixin is a selector reference within another selector. That's another great feature that can save us a lot of time whenever we're dealing with large CSS files.

Extend pseudo-class

Another great feature is the LESS :extend pseudo-class, which can be used to apply all properties of a class to another class, optionally including, using the all keyword, all the child classes and pseudo-classes. To use a quick example, take the following CSS code:

```
.link {
    color: white;
    background-color: blue;
}

.link:before {
    content: ">";
}

.link-red {
    color: white;
    background-color: red;
}

.link-red:before {
    content: ">";
}
```

This can be conveniently written this way using LESS:

```
.link {
    color: white;
    background-color: blue;
    :before {
        content: ">";
    }
}

.link-red {
    &amp; :extend(.link all);
    background-color: red;
}
```

Note how, since we've used the all keyword, we don't have to repeat the :before pseudo-class of the base .link selector, as it will be applied to .link-red as well.

LESS docs and support

We won't go any further than that with LESS, as it will take us far from the scope of this book. From now on, we'll take for granted that everything that we'll do with it will be acknowledged and understood.

For the sake of simplicity, we won't use anything different from what we briefly introduced in the previous chapters; however, we strongly suggest that you take a look at the advanced features (parametric mixins, functions, loops, guards, and more) as soon as you have the chance; they can hardly fail to pay off. You can learn more about them from the LESS official webpage at http://lesscss.org/.

SASS, Stylus, and other alternatives

As most readers probably know, or can easily imagine, LESS is not the only style sheet preprocessor language out there. As a matter of fact, it was released more than two years after **Systematically Awesome Style Sheets (Sass)**, also known as **SCSS**, which had served the exact same purpose since 2007. Sass can offer basically the same set of features as LESS and came out first, so why shouldn't it be used instead?

Truth be told, no one will ever get fired for picking **Sass** or other viable alternatives, such as Stylus and Switch CSS, instead of LESS. We're free to choose the style sheet preprocessor we like the most, as long as we can use it without issues, meaning that our development framework--Visual Studio, for example--is able to support it. Luckily enough, all of them are now widely supported by many Visual Studio Extensions, so it won't make any significant difference.

Here's a list of some of the best extension tools that will provide support for LESS, Sass and/or other preprocessors:

- **Web Compiler** by *Mads Kristensen*, an all-around tool to compile LESS, Sass, Stylus, JSX and CoffeeScript directly within the Visual Studio **Solution Explorer** (right-click | **Web Compiler** | **Compile File**).
- **LESS Compiler** by *Mads Kristensen*, a lightweight alternative to the above which uses the official Node.js-based LESS compiler with no setup. Once installed, it will show a neat overlay in the lower-right corner of any LESS file opened with Visual Studio giving the developer the chance to turn the compile feature ON or OFF for the whole project and/or for the current file only; it doesn't support Sass.
- **CompileSass** by *Sam Rueby*, another lightweight alternative that looks for all files with the .scss extension and compiles them in the background using LibSass, resulting in fast compile times; it doesn't support LESS.

Any of these tools will do, as long as it supports the standard you want to use; that said, for the purpose of this book, we'll pick LESS over Sass and other alternatives because we find it more straightforward, easy to use, and slightly more suited for a Windows environment than its counterparts, at least for now; we'll also install the **LESS Compiler** tool, so our LESS sources will be automatically compiled into CSS files on each build in the most lightweight way.

Implementing LESS

LESS happens to be written in JavaScript, so installing it can be as easy as downloading the official `less.js` JavaScript library, linking it to our `/Views/Home/Index.cshtml` page, and letting its magic work without having to set up anything else.

Should we do that, then? Not a chance. As we said earlier, delegating the compilation task on the client side will be highly inefficient, especially in a client-intensive Angular-based SPA. Not to mention the fact that we already have **Webpack** that will automatically compile, optimize, and pack all our CSS classes together in a single file.

Given our scenario, the best thing we can possibly do without changing our current Angular files and Webpack configuration is the following:

1. Install the aforementioned LESS Compiler extension tool and configure it to automatically build LESS files.
2. Rename all our existing CSS files with LESS files with the same name, as CSS files are also LESS files.
3. Update the existing code to take full advantage of the features and syntax provided by LESS.

That's it, we won't have to change anything in Angular, as our components will always point to the compiled file, the one ending with the `.css` prefix. We also don't have to worry about minify, uglify, and/or merge these files, as these tasks are already handled by **Webpack** using our current configuration.

That said, let's get to work.

Installing LESS compiler

Installing an extension tool on Visual Studio is quite easy; from the topmost menu, select **Tools | Extensions and Updates**, and then click to the **Online** item tree to the left. Once there, start a search using the LESS Compiler keyword and locate the **LESS Compiler** by *Mads Kristensen*:

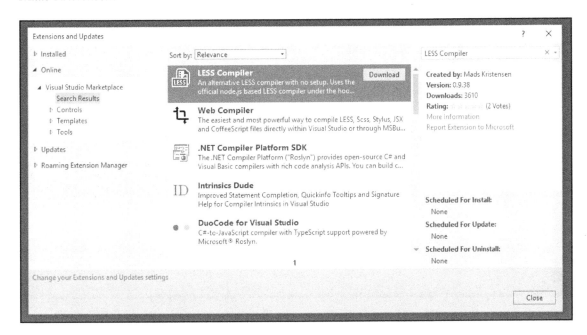

During the installation phase, you will be asked to quit and restart Visual Studio, so be sure to save everything before doing it.

Starting with the 2017 release, Visual Studio won't prompt you for an immediate restart like it used to do in the past; it will just inform you that the new tool(s) will be installed once all VS windows are closed, meaning that you will need to manually close all the active Visual Studio instances to launch the *VSIX* installer and perform the setup. Although this is perfectly understandable behavior, it might be negatively affected by some blocking VS-related processes--commonly MSBuild.exe--that can manage to survive even after a full Visual Studio shutdown. If that's the case, use the **Task Manager** to locate the offending processes within the process list and manually kill them to release the VSIX lock.

Once done, use the **Solution Explorer** to navigate to the
`/AppClient/app/components/app/app.component.css` file and rename it to
`app.component.less`. A warning popup will appear, informing you that the file can
become unusable and asking for a confirm; choose **YES**, and then open the new file.

You should see something like the following:

See the HUD-like screen near the lower-right corner? This is how the **LESS Compiler** tells
us about what it will do upon build, either globally and for the currently opened file; both
settings can be changed by clicking on them. For our specific purposes, we just need to
change the **Project** settings value from `Off` to `On`. Do that, and then update the file content
by adding a single comment on top in the following way:

```less
// our first LESS file

@media (max-width: 767px) {
    /* On small screens, the nav menu spans the full width of the screen.
Leave a space for it. */
    .body-content {
        padding-top: 50px;
    }
}
```

Once done, **Save** your file and look at the **Solution Explorer** to see what happens. The LESS compiler should automatically detect the updated content and compile the file accordingly; after a couple seconds, you should see something like this:

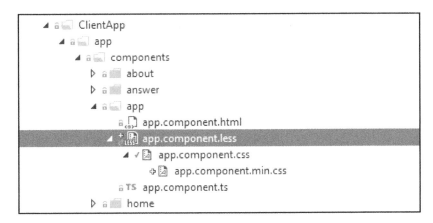

That's it, our `.less` source file has been compiled into its corresponding `.css` and `.min.css` files. If we open them, we can see how the first one hosts the human-readable version of the CSS-compatible code, while the latter contains the minified version. From now on, it will happen automatically upon **Save**, so we can just forget about it and concentrate on our styling.

Before continuing, rename all the other component's CSS files to give them the `.less` extension like we just did with the `app.component.css` file; we'll do that anyway sooner or later, hence it's better to get it over and done with.

Compiling LESS files with Webpack

Alternatively, we can also change our existing Webpack configuration to make it compile the LESS files into CSS. This can be done in the following way:

1. Add a less loader to our existing Webpack configuration file.
2. Rename all our existing CSS files with LESS files with the same name.
3. Reference the `less` files in the components instead of the `css` ones.

Choosing this path will require installing the Webpack less-loader using NuGet:

```
npm install --save-dev less-loader less
```

Then, it will require adding the appropriate rule in the `webpack.config.js` file in the following way:

```
[...]

  module: {
      rules: [

[...]

        {
            test: /\.less$/,
            use: [{
                loader: "style-loader" // creates style nodes from JS
                                                              strings
            }, {
                loader: "css-loader" // translates CSS into CommonJS
            }, {
                loader: "less-loader" // compiles Less to CSS
            }]
        }

[...]
```

Such a method is absolutely viable; on top of that, since it will seamlessly integrate with the Webpack workflow, it will even save us the trouble of installing a separate tool. However, we didn't choose it because we wanted to actually be able to see the transformation between LESS and CSS syntax, which is a great deal for learning purposes.

DIY versus framework-based styling

Now that we have converted all our static CSS files into dynamic LESS scripts, we can definitely take the chance to replace the quick'n'dirty styling that we put together for demonstration purposes, only with something better. However, before doing that, we need to choose which of these we want to do:

1. Keep the Bootstrap framework that was shipped by our ASP.NET Core MVC with Angular template.
2. Replace it with another frontend framework such as **Foundation**, **Pure**, **Skeleton**, **UIKit**, and **Materialize**.
3. Remove it and also avoid any framework-based alternative, thus adopting a pure do-it-yourself approach.

The first two options share the same approach: leverage our styling on a consolidated environment used by thousands of developers; no matter which variant we'll choose, we'll end up walking on solid ground. The latter, however, is an entirely different pair of shoes. Anyone who is into CSS design is well aware of such a debate, which we can summarize in the following single phrase:

> *Should we build our own grid-based responsive layout or use a responsive design framework instead?*

The answer is not that simple because either alternative has its set of advantages. Let's try to perform a quick recap of the most relevant arguments.

Do-it-yourself approach

The most classic approach: we build our very own grid-based layout, featuring a custom set of resizing faster and/or vector set of images and icon files, following the responsive design good practices and guidelines as issued by the famous *Ethan Marcotte 2010* article published in the *A List Apart* blog:

```
http://alistapart.com/article/responsive-web-design.
```

Also follow the subsequent, improved theories and patterns described in his following brief book (*Responsive Web Design*, A Book Apart, 2011).

Pros

- **Faster loading times**, as we will be able to only code, add, and/or include what we need
- **Unique design** (all framework-based websites are supposed to look the same)

Cons

- **Can be quite hard to handle**, unless we're true CSS3/MediaQuery experts
- **Slow development**, due to the massive amount of required tests for all the existing platforms (browsers, operating systems, and mobile devices)
- **Hard to keep it updated** to the latest standards since there will be no one who will bother to test or improve that code other than us

Framework-based approach

This is the common approach nowadays, where we start from a consolidated, widely-accepted UI frontend framework such as Bootstrap, Foundation, Pure or Materialize, and customize it to suit our needs. The word customizing can mean a number of things here, from picking a skin to completely changing the structural behavior of most classes, depending on how much we want to customize the results and/or how much time we are allowed to spend doing that.

Pros

- **Development speed**: These frameworks are a time-saver, as we will be able to use reliable, cross-browser compatible code blocks instead of coding everything from scratch.
- **Consistency**: One of the biggest frontend framework achievements is that they make designers and developers speak the same language, as they will both be able to acknowledge, understand, and apply their changes to the project in a consistent way.
- **Community support**: Each framework has a huge support community, meaning that we'll receive free code samples, support, and updates for as long as we need to. This can be huge, especially if we want to achieve good results without having to commit too much into cross-browser, responsive CSS design.

Cons

- **Limited knowledge**: We didn't write that code, so we won't always be able to understand what we're doing and why the stuff we're using behaves like that
- **Performance heavy**: Even the most lightweight and modular framework will undoubtedly be packed with a lot of stuff we won't be using in our project; these contents will be sent by the web server and loaded by the client anyway
- **Updating issues**: Whenever an improved build of the framework is out, we will have to choose between updating it and taking the risk of breaking something, and not updating it and risking losing the bug fixes and the added/improved support for the new CSS standards

Conclusions

As we can see, both ways can be viable depending on our specific scenario; therefore, the decision between going with a custom grid and adopting a framework-based one should be made on a case-by-case basis.

That said, after our non-exhaustive analysis, we think that adopting a frontend framework might be a good call for our project; we'll also keep Bootstrap for the task, since it happens to be one of the most suited ones for native web applications based on Angular, as we'll be able to see in the following paragraphs.

It's worth noting that by choosing Bootstrap, we're ditching a great alternative that will surely pave its way in the upcoming months; we're talking about `material2`, also known as **Angular Material**, a top-notch component library based upon material design. The only reason we didn't pick it is that the project is still in beta in Q3 2017. Whoever is bold enough to try that can ditch this chapter entirely and step into that pair of shoes by looking at the official project page at `https://material.angular.io/` or look at their source code repository on GitHub, at `https://github.com/angular/material2`.

Working with Bootstrap

Luckily enough, Bootstrap 3.3.7--the latest *stable* release at the time of writing--is already installed in our project, thanks to the *ASP.NET Core MVC with Angular* template we chose to use back in `Chapter 1`, *Getting Ready*. Whoever knows how it looks can easily understand how it couldn't be otherwise, since its classes are being used anywhere in our Angular HTML templates!

For those who'll ask why we didn't use Bootstrap 4 here, at the time of writing, the v4 is still in alpha (4.0.0.alpha6) and is still subject to a relevant amount of breaking API changes. Although there are a lot of early adopters willing to use it these days, there's no way we can adopt it within this book. The reader is encouraged to try it out as soon as he'll think it's time, as long as he won't forget the disclaimers we wrote back in `Chapter 1`, *Getting Ready*.

Changing the theme

To be precise, we're currently using the Bootstrap default theme; the first thing we can do is to change it with something slightly less common all over the world. There's a ton of free and commercial alternatives available; however, it will be wise to stick to the open source world, at least for now; luckily enough, there's a great open source Bootstrap theme collection available as an NPM package that we can easily use.

From **Solution Explorer**, open the package.json file and add the following highlighted one right below the reference to the bootstrap package:

```
[...]

"bootstrap": "3.3.7",
"bootswatch": "3.3.7",
"css": "2.2.1",

[...]
```

As soon as we click on **Save**, Visual Studio will download the package through NPM into the project's /node_modules/ folder.

To actually change the theme, we need to change the bootstrap.css file that will be fetched by Webpack and used to compile the distribution files. To do that, use the **Solution Explorer** to expand the tree node to the left of the webpack.config.js file to show the nested webpack.config.vendor.js file:

Open that nested file and change this single highlighted line:

```
const nonTreeShakableModules = [
    'bootstrap',
    'bootswatch/flatly/bootstrap.css',
    'es6-promise',
    'es6-shim',
```

```
'event-source-polyfill',
'jquery',
];
```

 From that line, we can see how we're committing to the Bootswatch's **Flatly** theme; in case we don't like it, or if we want to try a different one before choosing, we can go to the *Bootswatch* project's official site and take a look at the other available themes at `https://bootswatch.com/`.

Rebuild the Webpack vendor config file

Now we need to force **Webpack** to recompile the vendor configuration file, because that's not something it does automatically. To do that, we have three options:

- Delete the `/wwwroot/dist/` folder
- Update the `.csproj` project configuration file to do that on each build
- Create a batch file

Let's see each one of them in detail.

Delete the /wwwroot/dist/ folder

If we take a look at our project configuration file--the `projectName.csproj` in the project's root folder--we can see that the Webpack vendor configuration file is built in debug mode only if the `/wwwroot/dist/` folder doesn't exist:

```
[...]

<Target Name="DebugRunWebpack" BeforeTargets="Build" Condition="
'$(Configuration)' == 'Debug' And !Exists('wwwroot\dist') ">
  <!-- Ensure Node.js is installed -->
  <Exec Command="node --version" ContinueOnError="true">
    <Output TaskParameter="ExitCode" PropertyName="ErrorCode" />
  </Exec>
  <Error Condition="'$(ErrorCode)' != '0'" Text="Node.js is required to
build and run this project. To continue, please install Node.js from
https://nodejs.org/, and then restart your command prompt or IDE." />

  <!-- In development, the dist files won't exist on the first run or when
cloning to
       a different machine, so rebuild them if not already present. -->
  <Message Importance="high" Text="Performing first-run Webpack build..."
/>
  <Exec Command="node node_modules/webpack/bin/webpack.js --config
```

```
webpack.config.vendor.js" />
  <Exec Command="node node_modules/webpack/bin/webpack.js" />
</Target>

[...]
```

Therefore, we can just delete the /dist/ folder to trigger the build.

Update the .csproj file

In case we're looking for a more automatic way of doing the same thing, we can always remove the second condition within the .csproj file to always compile the file:

```
[...]

<Target Name="DebugRunWebpack" BeforeTargets="Build" Condition="
'$(Configuration)' == 'Debug' ">

[...]
```

However, that will definitely have a negative impact on the project's overall build time during debug.

Create the update-webpack.bat file

The batch file can be a viable alternative if we don't want to delete the /dist/ folder while also avoiding to slowing down our build process.

From **Solution Explorer**, create a new file within the project's root folder, name it as update-webpack.bat, and fill it with the following contents:

```
cd %~dp0
node node_modules/webpack/bin/webpack.js --config webpack.config.vendor.js
```

The first line tells the file to change the execution folder to the directory hosting the batch file itself; that will allow the batch file to be executed from anywhere, including the Windows GUI with a double-click. The second and last line executes Webpack, passing the webpack.config.vendor.js configuration file as a parameter.

Once done, navigate through the project's root folder and type the following to execute the file:

```
> update-webpack
```

You should be able to tell that everything went okay by looking at the white, green, and yellow output lines:

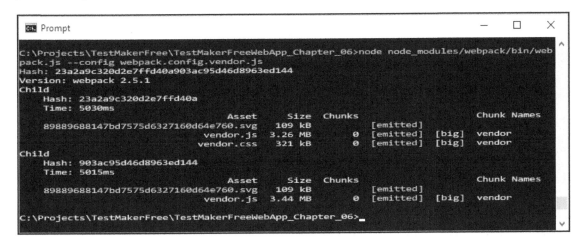

That's it, the only downside is that we'll have to rerun the batch file everytime we change something in the `webpack.config.vendor.js` file; luckily enough, that won't happen much.

If you don't like the Command Prompt and/or you're looking for a shortcut to run scripts, batches, and executable files within the Visual Studio GUI, check out the great and free **Command Task Runner** tool by *Mads Kristensen* available through NuGet. For additional information, visit `https://marketplace.visualstudio.com/items?itemName=MadsKristensen.CommandTaskRunner`.

Testing the new theme

Now that we changed and (re)compiled the vendor file, we are entitled to give our project a **Run** and test our new Bootstrap "Flatly" theme:

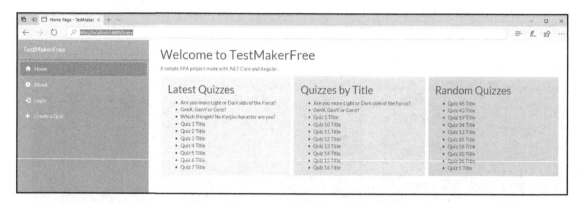

It seems like it works. Don't worry, we know it's still ugly! That was just the first step.

Revising the UI structure

Before diving into the UI layout of each component, we should now spend some valuable time to revise our app's overall UI structure; it basically means that we'll add some HTML elements and also take the chance to apply or update some bootstrap default classes.

AppComponent

Let's start with some small changes in the `app.component.html` template file, which hosts the main skeleton (new/updated lines are highlighted):

```html
<div class='container-fluid'>
    <div class='row'>
        <nav class="navbar header-content">
            <div class="container-fluid">
                <div class="navbar-header">
                    <a [routerLink]="['/home']">
                        <img src="/dist/res/img/logo.svg"
                          alt="TestMakerFree" />
                    </a>
                </div>
                <quiz-search class="search-header" placeholder="Search
                  for a quiz..."></quiz-search>
```

```
            </div>
        </nav>
    </div>
    <div class='row'>
        <div class='col-sm-3'>
            <nav-menu></nav-menu>
        </div>
        <div class='col-sm-9 body-content'>
            <router-outlet></router-outlet>
        </div>
    </div>
</div>
```

Also, in its LESS style sheet file:

```less
.header-content {
    position: fixed;
    top: 0;
    left: 0;
    right: 0;
    z-index: 1;
    height: 85px;
    background-color: #f4f4f4;
    border-bottom: 1px solid #dedede;

    .navbar-header {
        text-align: left;
    }

    img {
        height: 80px;
        margin: 3px 0 0 8px;
    }
}

.body-content {
    margin-top: 100px;
}

@media (max-width: 767px) {
    .header-content {
        .navbar-header {
            text-align: center;
        }
    }

    .body-content {
        padding-top: 50px;
```

```
        }
    }
```

We can easily see that we added a new `<div class="row">` element here, which contains some header-related content. Among the sub-elements, there are two new items that we've never seen before; the `logo.svg` file and the `<quiz-search>` element, which obviously refers to a `QuizSearchComponent` that doesn't even exist yet. Worry not, as we'll introduce them both in a short while.

NavMenuComponent

Moving on to the `NavMenuComponent`, here's the updated part of the `navmenu.component.html` template file:

```
[...]

<div class='navbar-header'>
    <button type='button' class='navbar-toggle'
        data-toggle='collapse' data-target='.navbar-collapse'>
        <span class='sr-only'>Toggle navigation</span>
        <span class='icon-bar'></span>
        <span class='icon-bar'></span>
        <span class='icon-bar'></span>
    </button>
    <quiz-search class="search-navmenu" placeholder="Type here..."></quiz-
search>
</div>

[...]
```

Note how we just changed a single line, replacing the previous `<a>` link to the **Home** view with another instance of that still non-existent `QuizSearchComponent`.

As for the `navmenu.component.less` style sheet file, here's the updated content:

```
.main-nav {
    position: fixed;
    top: 85px;
    left: 0;
    right: 0;
    z-index: 1;

    li {
        a {
            cursor: pointer;
        }
```

```
        .glyphicon {
            margin-right: 10px;
        }

        &amp;.link-active a,
        &amp;.link-active a:hover,
        &amp;.link-active a:focus {
            background-color: #4189C7;
            color: white;
        }
    }
}

@media (min-width: 768px) {
    .main-nav {
        top: 100px;
        width: calc(~"25% - 30px");
        min-width: 180px;

        .navbar {
            border-radius: 0 15px 15px 0;
            border-width: 0px;
            height: 100%;

            a {
                width: 100%;
                white-space: nowrap;
                overflow: hidden;
                text-overflow: ellipsis;
            }

            ul {
                float: none;
            }

            li {
                float: none;
                font-size: 15px;
                margin: 6px;

                a {
                    padding: 10px 16px;
                    border-radius: 4px;
                }
            }
        }

        .navbar-header {
```

```
        float: none;
    }

    .navbar-collapse {
        padding: 0px;
    }
  }
}
```

There's nothing relevant here, except for some minor restyling. For obvious reasons, we can't waste more pages explaining what these CSS lines actually do; we'll be able to see the results soon enough.

QuizSearchComponent

The time has come to unveil `QuizSearchComponent`. As you would expect, it's nothing more than a new Angular component that we can add within the already existing `/ClientApp/app/components/quiz/` folder.

Here's the `quiz-search.component.ts` class file:

```
import { Component, Input } from "@angular/core";

@Component({
    selector: "quiz-search",
    templateUrl: './quiz-search.component.html',
    styleUrls: ['./quiz-search.component.css']
})

export class QuizSearchComponent {
    @Input() class: string;
    @Input() placeholder: string;
}
```

Also, here's the `quiz-search.component.html` template file:

```
<form class="navbar-form navbar-left {{class}}" role="search">
    <div class="form-group">
        <input type="text" class="form-control"
placeholder="{{placeholder}}">
    </div>
    <button type="submit" class="btn btn-default">Submit</button>
</form>
```

As we can see, the class and template files are nothing new; we should already know how these `class` and `placeholder` input properties work and how they will be used to programmatically give custom values to the `{{class}}` and `{{placeholder}}` interpolation endpoints in the template file.

The real deal here is the `quiz-search.component.less` style sheet file:

```less
.navbar-form {
    &amp;.search-header {
        display: none;
    }

    &amp;.search-navmenu {
        display: block;
        border: 0;
        margin: 2px 0 0 0;
        padding: 5px;
        float: left;
        width: calc(~"100% - 80px");
        max-width: calc(~"100% - 80px");
        min-width: 250px;

        .form-group {
            float: left;
            margin: 0 10px 0 0;

            input[type="text"] {
                width: 180px;
            }
        }
    }
}

@media (min-width: 768px) {
    .navbar-form {
        &amp;.search-header {
            display: block;
            margin: 20px 0 0 20px;
        }

        &amp;.search-navmenu {
            display: none;

            input[type="text"] {
                width: 180px;
            }
        }
```

```
    }
}
```

Note how we used the LESS selector-nesting feature to define two very different behaviors for the `search-header` and `search-navmenu` classes; we did that because we wanted the two `QuizSearchComponent` instances to have their own distinctive layout and behavior. We'll see more about them in a short while.

Registering QuizSearchComponent

As always, don't forget to register the `QuizSearchComponent` within the `app.module.shared.ts` file:

```
[...]

import { QuizSearchComponent } from './components/quiz/quiz-
search.component';

[...]

@NgModule({
    declarations: [

[...]

        QuizSearchComponent,

[...]
```

The logo SVG file

Last but not least, let's spend a couple of words on that `logo.svg` file, that we used as source of the `<img>` element that we placed within the header container of `AppComponent`.

Truth be told, it's just something that we put together with Inkscape to give our app a distinctive branding style. You can find it at `http://www.testmakerfree.com/dist/res/img/logo.svg`.

Alternatively, you can find it in this book's GitHub official repository. Anyway, here it is:

The font we used here is called **White Pine** and was released back in 2015 under the SIL Open Fonts license by its maker, *Anna London*, whom we would like to thank for the awesome work. You can download it for free from her official blog at `http://www.annalondon.com/blog/design/whitepine/`.

If you do, don't forget to thank her with a tweet or a Facebook share!

A quick test

Let's take a quick break to see the result of our work until now. Press *F5* to run the project in debug mode and get ready to see something like this:

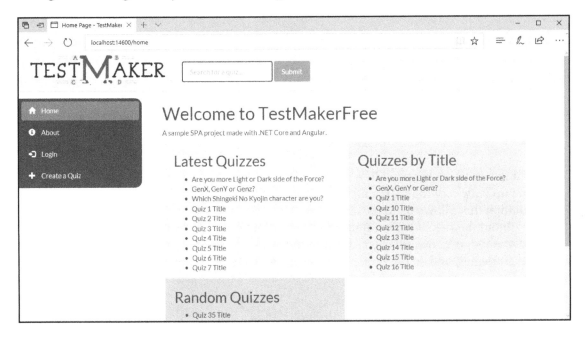

Not bad at all! We'll not win a prize for this layout, that's for sure, yet we came up with something more original than the Bootstrap defaults. However, we're still far from done; in the upcoming chapters, we'll bring the party to the inner components as well.

Styling the components

Before diving into the depths of our Angular app, it might be the case to ask ourselves a quick question about what we just did in the style sheet file of `QuizSearchComponent`. Is there a reason why we put the `search-header` and `search-navmenu` classes there? Couldn't we place them in the `AppComponent` and `NavMenuComponent` LESS files to handle everything from the parents, thus leaving the child without a dedicated style sheet?

To properly answer such questions, we need to understand how Angular handles its components and their style sheet files; the best way to do that is to introduce a whole new concept called **CSS Encapsulation**, which will greatly help us in styling our components.

CSS encapsulation

What is **encapsulation**? Among the many good answers that can be easily found around the web, the one given by the software engineer *Edward V. Berard* is perhaps the most exhaustive one:

> *The concept of encapsulation as used in an object-oriented context is not essentially different from its dictionary definition. It still refers to building a capsule, in the case a conceptual barrier, around some collection of things.*

 The quote comes from the "*Abstraction, Encapsulation, and Information Hiding* article by *Edward V. Berard*." The whole article text can be found at `http://www.tonymarston.co.uk/php-mysql/abstraction.txt`.

When thinking about encapsulation in object-oriented programming, the best example we can come up with is probably the concept of namespacing. Namespaces are a basic form of encapsulation that allows us to recycle/reuse the same property, method, and function names without the risk of hitting name conflicts; other good examples are the local variables within a method, the class instances built within a `using` statement block, the threading isolation strategies, and so on.

CSS encapsulation has always been one of the web developer's most wanted dreams. The reason for that is simple to understand: the ability to style a specific component without affecting the others, or to restrict the scope of some CSS selectors without the risk of overwriting something more general, is definitely something that will save a lot of work.

The great news here is that Angular provides CSS encapsulation as a built-in feature. That's it. There's nothing we need to do, it's already there, in our current components. We can easily confirm that by launching our project in *debug* mode and looking at the generated HTML code using a DOM inspector--such as the one shipped with **Edge**, that can be activated by pressing *F12*.

Here's the evidence:

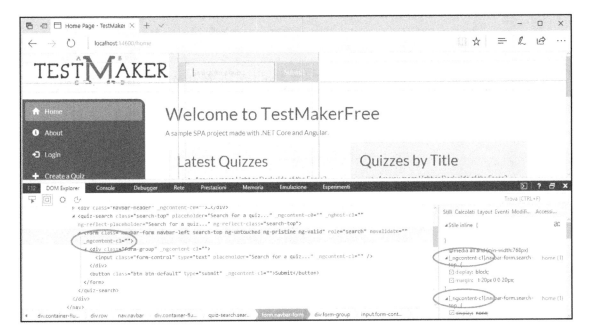

As we can see, Angular automatically inserts a custom HTML5 attribute to all the elements within the component; that attribute will then be prepended to each CSS selector, thus acting like a pseudo-namespace that will restrict the scope of those styles to that component only.

It goes without saying that these custom attributes should never be used by the developer, as their names are autogenerated by Angular, and thus are often subject to changes.

Native encapsulation using Shadow DOM

As an alternative to the **CSS Encapsulation**, Angular also features another great *namespace-like* feature using its unique **Shadow DOM** implementation.

Explaining what the Shadow DOM actually is in a few words is another impossible task, yet we'll try to do that nonetheless; Shadow DOM is one of the four **Web Component** standards, along with HTML Templates, Custom Elements, and HTML Imports. It allows whoever uses it (the developer or the underlying framework) to hide DOM logic behind other elements, thus enabling--among many other things--CSS scoping and DOM encapsulation.

 If you want to know more about *Web Component* and *Shadow DOM*, we strongly suggest that you read this awesome article by *Eric Bidelman* at `https://developers.google.com/web/fundamentals/architecture/building-components/shadowdom`.

To cut it short, Angular can (optionally) use the Shadow DOM to wrap any given component into a dedicated rendering context, thus isolating it from the rest of the DOM; as a result, all the CSS stylings will also be encapsulated into that limited scope.

This optional feature is called **Native Encapsulation** and can be activated using the `ViewEncapsulation` enum within the `@Component` part of the component class file.

Let's give it a try within our `quiz-search.component.ts` file (new lines are highlighted):

```
import { Component, Input, ViewEncapsulation } from "@angular/core";

@Component({
    selector: "quiz-search",
    templateUrl: './quiz-search.component.html',
    styleUrls: ['./quiz-search.component.css'],
    encapsulation: ViewEncapsulation.Native
})

export class QuizSearchComponent {
    @Input() class: string;
    @Input() placeholder: string;
}
```

We can see the results by giving our project another run and inspecting the HTML, like we did earlier:

It's worth noting that this time we had to use Google Chrome, since it's the only web browser supporting native Shadow DOM as of today. Trying to do that with Edge will result in the following error:

```
TypeError: Object doesn't support property or method
'createShadowRoot'
```

We can see how the rendering engine wrapped our component's contents within a **#shadow-root** pseudo-element containing all the stylings. By looking at the rendering results, we can easily note that this alternative approach is way more drastic than the default one; the component is completely isolated, hence it doesn't inherit the *Bootstrap* default styles and just outputs as standard HTML.

We definitely don't want to use this behavior, hence we will need to *rollback* the changes we made on our `QuizSearchComponent` class; however, before doing that, let's do one more quick test.

Disable encapsulation

Both of these encapsulation features can be disabled on a per-component basis using the `ViewEncapsulation.None` switch in the following way:

```
import { Component, Input, ViewEncapsulation } from "@angular/core";

@Component({
    selector: "quiz-search",
    templateUrl: './quiz-search.component.html',
    styleUrls: ['./quiz-search.component.css'],
    encapsulation: ViewEncapsulation.None
})

export class QuizSearchComponent {
    @Input() class: string;
    @Input() placeholder: string;
}
```

With `ViewEncapsulation.None`, neither the HTML5 attribute nor the #**shadow-root** element will be used; this basically means that all the CSS classes defined for that component will be shared among all the other components and applied globally, just like the good old CSS cascading rules we're well aware of.

This behavior can be useful to propagate some general-purpose CSS styling from high-level components; that's not the case of our `QuizSearchComponent`, so let's perform a quick source code rollback by deleting all the references to the `ViewEncapsulation` enum from the class file's `import` list and `@Component` section and deep dive into our inner components' restyling task.

HomeComponent

The next thing to do is to give a quick restyling to the `HomeComponent`.

Let's start with the `home.component.html` template file:

```
<div class="row">
    <div class="col-lg-4">
        <quiz-list class="latest"></quiz-list>
    </div>
    <div class="col-lg-4">
        <quiz-list class="byTitle"></quiz-list>
    </div>
    <div class="col-lg-4">
        <quiz-list class="random"></quiz-list>
```

```
        </div>
    </div>
```

We removed the sample title/subtitle we used back in Chapter 1, *Getting Ready*, and added some Bootstrap's grid system classes to ensure that the quiz-list elements will be properly stacked when using smaller-resolution devices.

 For additional information on the Bootstrap grid system, check out
https://getbootstrap.com/docs/3.3/css/#grid.

Once done, jump to the home.component.less style sheet file and remove everything, leaving only a brief comment to remember why the file is empty:

```
// nothing to do here
```

That's it.

QuizListComponent

This component plays a key role in our Angular app and desperately needs a better layout; we'll change a lot of things here to make it more enjoyable.

Open the quiz-list.component.html template file and perform the following changes (new/updated lines are highlighted):

```
<div class="panel panel-primary {{class}}">
    <div class="panel-heading">
        <span class="glyphicon"></span>
        <h4>{{title}}</h4>
    </div>
    <div class="panel-body">
        <ul class="list-group">
            <li class="list-group-item"
                *ngFor="let quiz of quizzes"
                [class.selected]="quiz === selectedQuiz"
                (click)="onSelect(quiz)">
                <img src="https://lorempixel.com/50/50/?random=
                {{quiz.Id}}"
                    alt="{{quiz.Title}}" class="img-circle" />
                <span>{{quiz.Title}}</span>
            </li>
        </ul>
    </div>
</div>
```

As we can see, the underlying logic didn't change; we still have a `*ngFor` cycle that iterates through the **quizzes** array, pulls out a **quiz** object `ent`, and uses its properties to build an HTML unordered list. We just wrapped it with a Bootstrap panel to ensure that it will have a properly-styled container; if we take a closer look at **line 1**, we can see how we also added the `{{class}}` interpolation directive to ensure that the container panel will have the same class attribute value given to that `QuizListComponent` instance by its parent component, as previously seen in the `HomeComponent` template file.

Other than that, we also added a random image using `lorempixel.com`, a *free-of-charge* web service that can be used to fetch placeholders images for sample layouts.

 Note how we're adding a `random` GET parameter to each `HTTP` request to the `lorempixel.com` service with the `{{quiz.Id}}` as value; we did that to prevent the web browser from caching these images, which is a common scenario when requesting the same URL multiple times from the same page.

Also, here's the `quiz-list.component.less` style sheet file:

```less
.panel {
    margin-bottom: 12px;

    .panel-heading {
        color: #fefefe;

        .glyphicon {
            float: right;
            font-size: 41px;
            color: #d6d6d6;
        }
    }

    .panel-body {
        padding: 0;

        .list-group {
            margin: 0;

            .list-group-item {
                padding: 6px;
                overflow: auto;
                cursor: pointer;

                &:hover {
                    background-color: #dae9f5;
```

```
            &amp;:before {
                display: inline-block;
                font-family: 'Glyphicons Halflings';
                content: "\e013";
                float: right;
                font-size: 30px;
                margin: 4px 5px 0 0;
                color: #60a777;
            }
        }

        img {
            display: block;
            float: left;
            width: 50px;
            height: 50px;
            background-color: #ffffff;
            border: 1px solid #707d8c;
            padding: 2px;
            margin: 0 6px 0 0;
        }
    }
    }
}

&amp;.latest {
    border-color: #384a5d;

    .panel-heading {
        background-color: #384a5d;

        .glyphicon:before {
            content: "\e162";
        }
    }
}

&amp;.byTitle {
    border-color: #4b657f;

    .panel-heading {
        background-color: #4b657f;

        .glyphicon:before {
            content: "\e151";
        }
    }
}
```

```
&amp;.random {
    border-color: #617992;

    .panel-heading {
        background-color: #617992;

        .glyphicon:before {
            content: "\e104";
        }
    }
}
}
```

These style sheet rules are quite complex, so it might be worthwile spending a couple of words on them; again, we used the LESS nested selectors feature, which allows us to encapsulate children selectors within their parent set of rules. We defined a single "main" `.panel` selector, which basically contains the following things:

- A very limited set of rules that will be applied to the selector itself (the "margin-bottom" single line)
- A `.panel-heading` child selector, containing the generic configuration for the panel heading DIV element; these rules will be applied to any `QuizListComponent` instance's template, regardless of the `class` attribute value
- A `.panel-body` child selector, containing the generic configuration for the panel body DIV element; again, these rules will be applied to all `QuizListComponent` instances
- A set of selectors relative by itself--`&amp;.latest`, `&amp;.byTitle`, and `&amp;.random`; these rules will be applied only to the `QuizListComponent` instance with that specific `class`, thus ensuring a different styling for each different class

The last bullet might be quite difficult to get; to better understand it, let's perform a quick recap to understand how the `&amp;` ampersand selector actually works. If we recall correctly, it represents the current selector's parent, meaning that the `&amp;.latest`, `&amp;.byTitle`, and `&amp;.random` selectors--along with their "children" --will be CSS-compiled to `.panel.latest`, `.panel.byTitle`, and `.panel.random`, and so on, right?

That's right, we can easily confirm that by looking at the autogenerated `quiz-list.component.css` file:

```css
[...]

.panel.latest {
  border-color: #384a5d;
}
.panel.latest .panel-heading {
  background-color: #384a5d;
}
.panel.latest .panel-heading .glyphicon:before {
  content: "\e162";
}
.panel.byTitle {
  border-color: #4b657f;
}

[...]

.panel.random {
  border-color: #617992;
}

[...]
```

By looking at that, we can acknowledge that only one of these selectors will be applied to each single `QuizListComponent` instance, depending on the class specified upon their initialization in the `HomeComponent` template file:

```html
[...]
<quiz-list class="latest"></quiz-list>
[...]
<quiz-list class="byTitle"></quiz-list>
[...]
<quiz-list class="random"></quiz-list>
[...]
```

This is certain since we explicitly put that same class in the `quiz-list.component.html` template file's container `<div>` element using the `{{class}}` interpolation directive:

```
<div class="panel panel-primary {{class}}">
```

```
[...]
```

This concludes our journey through the `QuizListComponent` files, at least for now.

 We would like to talk a bit more about the other styling rules we used within the LESS file, but we can't do that without compromising on the book length; the reader can easily understand their purpose by tracking their respective selectors using the browser's DOM inspector.

Another UI test

Performing a quick test after all this hardwork is more than advisable. Press *F5* to run the project in debug mode and check out the greatly-revised **Home** view:

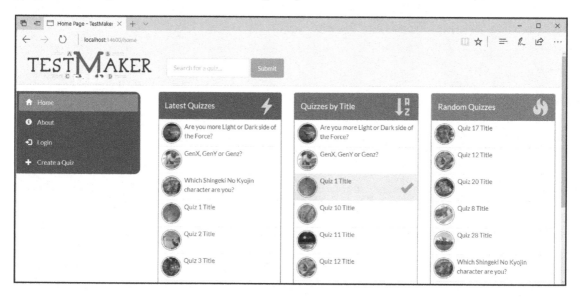

We're finally getting something decent out there; we even added a not-so-terrible *mouseover* effect showing a green check to the right of each quiz whenever the pointer goes on it.

The technique we used to fetch the autogenerated images works so well that all the repeating quizzes share the same image, just like they were actually related to that quiz! This is precisely why we used the `quiz.Id` property value to seed the random `GET` parameter that we used to trick the browser's cache; that way, any repeating quiz will have the same image URL used before, which will be hit by the browser's cache and served instead of a new one.

The UI layout is viable enough even if we reduce the browser's window size to 1,024 pixels, emulating the viewport of a common tablet:

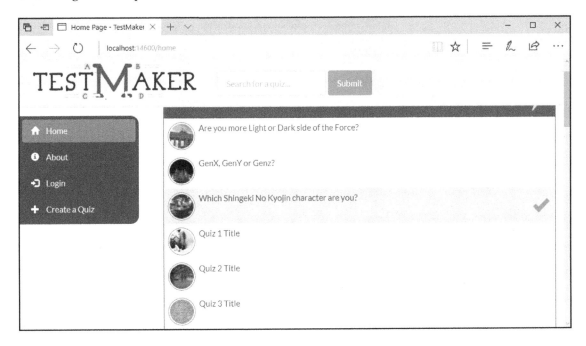

The Bootstrap *grid-system* keeps scaling well down to smartphone-like resolutions, where the second `QuizSearchComponent` kicks its way in and the NavMenu collapses to the top, with the panels stacked right below it:

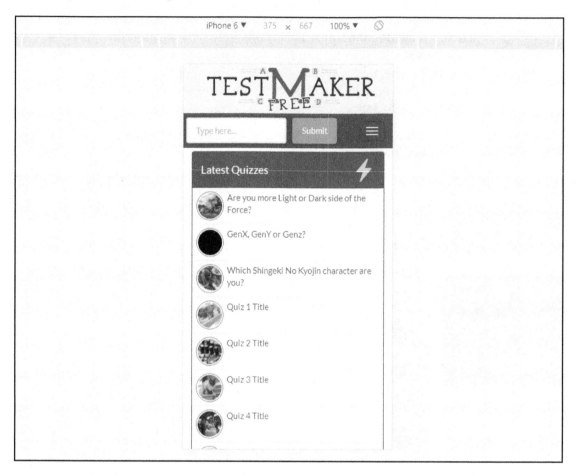

Given these results, we can't be anything but happy; however, our job isn't done yet, as we still have a lot of components requiring immediate attention; let's move on to the next one.

QuizComponent

Here's another component with a terrible layout; let's do our best to improve it.

Here's the new `quiz.component.html` template file:

```
<div class="quiz">
    <div class="quiz-details">
        <div class="quiz-image">
            <img src="https://lorempixel.com/150/150/?random=
                {{quiz.Id}}"
                    alt="{{quiz.Title}}" class="img-circle">
        </div>
        <div class="quiz-info-block">
            <div class="quiz-heading">
                <h2>{{quiz.Title}}</h2>
                <span class="help-block">{{quiz.Description}}</span>
                <!--<span class="help-block">Created by User # on
                {{quiz.CreatedDate}}</span>-->
            </div>

            <ul class="navigation">
                <li class="active">
                    <a data-toggle="tab" href="#description">
                        <span class="glyphicon glyphicon-user"></span>
                          Description
                    </a>
                </li>
                <li>
                    <a data-toggle="tab" href="#stats">
                        <span class="glyphicon glyphicon-stats"></span>
                          Stats
                    </a>
                </li>
                <li>
                    <a data-toggle="tab" href="#share">
                        <span class="glyphicon glyphicon-share-alt">
                  </span>
                          Share
                    </a>
                </li>
            </ul>
            <div class="quiz-body">
                <div class="tab-content">
                    <div id="description" class="tab-pane active">
                        {{quiz.Text}}
                    </div>
                    <div id="stats" class="tab-pane">
```

```
                    TO-DO
              </div>
              <div id="share" class="tab-pane">
                    TO-DO
              </div>
          </div>
      </div>

      <div class="commands">
          <a [routerLink]="['/quiz', quiz.Id, 'take']"
            class="btn btn-success">
            <span class="glyphicon glyphicon-education"></span>
              Take the Test!
          </a>
          <a [routerLink]="['/home']"
            class="btn btn-default">
            <span class="glyphicon glyphicon-backward"></span>
              Back
          </a>
          <div class="edit">
              <input type="button" value="Edit"
                      (click)="onEdit()"
                      class="btn btn-sm btn-warning" />
              <input type="button" value="Delete"
                      (click)="onDelete()"
                      class="btn btn-sm btn-danger" />
          </div>
      </div>
    </div>
  </div>
</div>
```

Also, here's the `quiz.component.less` style sheet file:

```
.quiz {
    position: relative;
    padding: 0;
    text-align: center;
    width: 80%;

    @media (max-width: 767px) {
        width: 100%;
    }

    .quiz-details {
        .quiz-image {
            position: relative;
            z-index: 1;
```

```
        width: 100%;
        text-align: center;

        img {
            width: 150px;
            height: 150px;
            clear: both;
            margin: auto;
            position: relative;
            background-color: #ffffff;
            border: 1px solid #707d8c;
            padding: 2px;
        }
}

.quiz-info-block {
    width: 100%;
    border-radius: 20px;
    position: absolute;
    top: 80px;
    background: #f0f0f0;
    z-index: 0;
    padding: 60px 0 30px 0;

    .quiz-heading {
        width: 100%;
        text-align: center;
        margin: 10px 0 0;
    }

    .navigation {
        margin: 20px 15px 0px 15px;
        padding: 0;
        list-style: none;
        border-bottom: 1px solid #a3aab1;

        li {
            display: inline-block;
            margin: 0 0 -6px 0;
            padding: 0;

            a {
                background: transparent;
                border-radius: 10px 10px 0 0;
                padding: 10px 30px;
                float: left;
            }
```

```
            &amp;.active a {
                background: #4189C7;
                color: #fff;
            }
        }
    }

.quiz-body {
    padding: 20px 20px 30px 20px;

    .tab-content {
        h4 {
            width: 100%;
            margin: 10px 0;
            color: #333;
        }
    }
}

.commands {
    border-top: 1px solid #dddddd;
    width: 80%;
    padding: 15px 0 0 0;
    margin: 15px auto 0 auto;

    .btn {
        min-width: 140px;
        margin: 0 10px;
    }

    .edit {
        border-top: 1px solid #dddddd;
        width: 80%;
        padding: 15px 0 0 0;
        margin: 15px auto 0 auto;
    }
        }
    }
    }
}
```

There's nothing new here; as usual, we dropped some Bootstrap default classes and added a couple of new things here and there, such as the **Back** button--to route back our users to the **Home** view. We also took the chance to implement the `lorempixel.com` placeholder image here, this time with a bigger size (150 px), as expected for a detail page.

Testing it up

Let's test it without further ado by pressing *F5*:

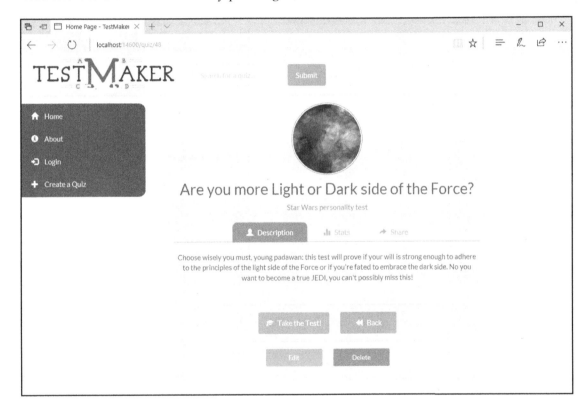

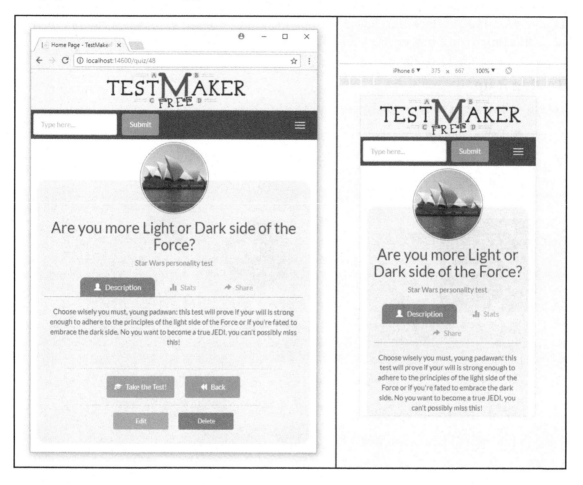

Not bad at all, it's time to proceed to the next task.

QuizEditComponent

Here's the most complex Angular component we made so far; luckily enough, we can get it over with a handful of default Bootstrap styles.

As always, let's start with the `quiz-edit.component.html` **template file:**

```html
<div class="quiz-edit">
    <h2>{{title}}</h2>
    <div class="form-group">
        <label for="title">Quiz title:</label>
        <br />
        <input type="text" id="title"
               [(ngModel)]="quiz.Title"
               placeholder="choose a title..."
               class="form-control"
               />
    </div>
    <div class="form-group">
        <label for="description">Quiz description:</label>
        <br />
        <input type="text" id="description"
               [(ngModel)]="quiz.Description"
               placeholder="enter a description..."
               class="form-control"
               />
    </div>
    <div class="form-group">
        <label for="text">Quiz informative text:</label>
        <br />
        <textarea id="text"
                  [(ngModel)]="quiz.Text"
                  placeholder="enter a text..."
                  class="form-control"
                  ></textarea>
    </div>
    <div class="form-group commands">
        <input *ngIf="editMode" type="button"
               value="Apply Changes"
               (click)="onSubmit(quiz)"
               class="btn btn-success"
               />
        <input *ngIf="!editMode" type="button"
               value="Create the Quiz!"
               (click)="onSubmit(quiz)"
               class="btn btn-success"
               />
        <input type="button"
               value="Cancel"
               (click)="onBack()"
               class="btn btn-default"
               />
    </div>
```

```
<question-list *ngIf="editMode" [quiz]="quiz"></question-list>

<result-list *ngIf="editMode" [quiz]="quiz"></result-list>

</div>
```

Then, we'll follow up with the `quiz-edit.component.less` style sheet file:

```less
.quiz-edit {
    width: 80%;

    @media (max-width: 767px) {
        width: 100%;
    }

    textarea {
        min-height: 100px;
    }

    .commands {
        margin-top: 20px;
    }
}
```

Question, answer, and result components

The `QuizEditComponent` features a lot of subcomponents that deserve some love as well; however, we don't want to waste more and more book pages on them, hence we'll just give some the most relevant tips here about what needs to be done, leaving the actual styling to the reader; trying to emulate the following screenshots can be a great exercise to try our LESS-based skills on the field.

 As always, those who really don't want to bother with that can always pull the Chapter 6, *Style Sheets and UI Layout*, source code from the official GitHub repository of this book. That's entirely up to the reader.

Buttons and icons

As we could easily see, one of the most important things to do in order to de-uglify our components is applying the default Bootstrap classes to our <input type="button">, <input type="submit">, <button>, and <a> elements. Let's take the following template:

```
[...]

<div *ngIf="questions.length == 0">
    This quiz has no questions (yet):
    click the <strong>Add a new Question</strong> button to add the first
one!
</div>
<input type="button"
        value="Add a new Question"
        (click)="onCreate()"
        class="btn btn-sm btn-primary"
        />
```

The above code is taken from the question-list.component.html template file: as we can see, we're using the btn-sm and btn-primary button classes here, as we want the button to be smaller than the **Apply Changes** and **Cancel** main buttons within the parent component; for buttons and button-like links placed within a table row it's generally wise to use the btn-xs class to save even more space.

Also, as per our internal convention, we're going to use the btn-primary class when *adding* something new, btn-warning and btn-danger for *edit* and *delete* operations and btn-success for *saving* our stuff; that said, you're free to change it and do as you wish: just remember that repeating the same colors for the same editing tasks will greatly help our users to understand what they need to do while navigating through the various views.

Another thing we can do to improve our button's look and feel is decorate them with some fancy icons, just like we did a number of times already: Bootstrap allows us to easily achieve such result thanks to the *Glyphicon Halfling* set, a great icon library that is available free of charge--as long as we use it through Bootstrap. Using these icons is just as simple as adding a single <span> element with the appropriate glyphicon class.

If we need to do that on `<input>` elements, that can't contain children:

```
<input type="button" value="Add a new Question"
        (click)="onCreate()" class="btn btn-sm btn-primary" />
```

We can replace them with `<button>` elements in the following way:

```
<button (click)="onCreate()" class="btn btn-sm btn-primary">
    <span class="glyphicon glyphicon-plus-sign"></span>
    Add a new Question
</button>
```

Repeat these tricks for all the **input** and **button** elements throughout all the various question, answer and result control's templates and you should be good to go.

Tables and DIVs

Other than buttons, we also have to apply the proper Bootstrap styles to our `<table>` elements:

```
<h3>Questions</h3>
<div *ngIf="questions.length > 0">
    <div class="table-responsive">
        <table class="table table-hover questions">

[...]
```

Here we added the `.table` and `.table-hover` classes to the `<table>` element, and also wrapped it up within a new `<div class="table-responsive">` element: the classes will affect the table look and feel, while the container element--as the name implies --will give responsive features to our table; more specifically, the table will scroll horizontally on small devices (under 768 px) if there's no way to resize its contents within the browser's viewport.

The Bootstrap default table requires little or no styling: however since our Bootstrap template hides the `<th>` borders by default, it's not a bad idea to restore them to improve their readability. We can do that with a simple CSS rule:

```
.table thead  tr  th {
    border-bottom: 2px solid #ecf0f1;
}
```

No need to use LESS for this, unless we don't want to apply more custom rules on these tables.

Forms and inputs

Styling a form in Bootstrap is also very easy, we just have to add the `.form-group` class to the container `<form>` or `<div>` and the `.form-control` class to each input-type element:

```
<h2>{{title}}</h2>
<div class="question-edit">
    <div class="form-group">
        <label for="text">Question text:</label>
        <br />
        <textarea id="text"
                [(ngModel)]="question.Text"
                placeholder="enter a suitable text..."
                class="form-control"
                ></textarea>
    </div>

    [...]
```

Jumping to the LESS style sheet file, it won't hurt to increase the height of the text areas-- to increase their overall usability--and also put a limit to the horizontal spanning of some specific elements, such as the right panel (for *high-res* viewports) and the `<select>`:

```
.answer-edit {
    width: 80%;

    @media (max-width: 767px) {
        width: 100%;
    }

    textarea {
        min-height: 100px;
    }

    select {
        max-width: 200px;
    }

    .commands {
        margin-top: 20px;
    }
}
```

That's about it.

If we want to further improve what we've done, or test some more Bootstrap classes, we can always take a look at the official Bootstrap form-styling documentation at the Bootstrap official site:

`http://getbootstrap.com/`.

Full-scale layout test

Restyling our app components will take a considerable amount of time, but the rules to follow are few and easy to implement, so we should have no issues--as long as we understood how to properly use LESS.

As soon as we think we're done, we should definitely perform a full-scale test to ensure that the new layout is working well. If we followed our rules, we should be able to see something close to the following screenshots:

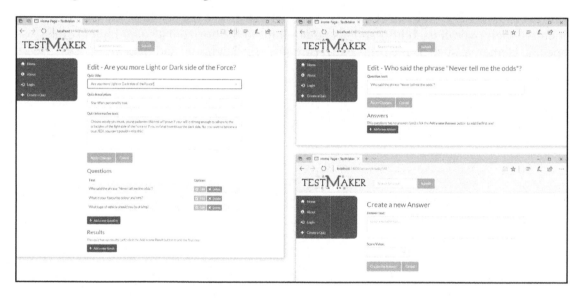

You can find the source code for all these screenshots in the official GitHub repo shipped with this book. That said, those who came up with a different outcome are encouraged to keep their own result for the following chapters and try to make it work with the new stuff that will come, as it would definitely translate into a better learning experience.

This puts an end to our work; we're done with the restyling, at least for the time being. From now on, we'll use the acquired knowledge to properly style our components while adding and/or implementing them.

Suggested topics

Style sheet language, SoC, CSS, CSS3, LESS, Sass , Stylus, Switch CSS, Material Design, Bootstrap, Bootswatch, CSS3 Parent Selector, grid system, SVG, mobile-friendly, mobile-first, CSS encapsulation, and Shadow DOM

Summary

We started this chapter admitting that our ultra-minimalistic UI/UX approach wouldn't work for a potentially shippable product that our Native Web Application should eventually become. Having acknowledged that fact, we added a LESS-based custom style sheet file to our project. Before doing that, for the benefit of those not familiar with the style sheet preprocessor approach, we spent some time enumerating some of the LESS main advantages.

Right after adding the first `.less` file to our project, we had to choose between keeping Bootstrap, switching it for an alternative client-side framework such as Foundation or Pure, or adopting to a full do-it-yourself approach. We briefly enumerated some pros and cons of each alternative, then we opted for keeping Bootstrap 3, mostly because of its great *mobile-friendly* grid system and ease of use.

In an attempt to distinguish our SPA look and feel from the default Angular template we replaced the default bootstrap skin with a bootswatch theme: in order to do that we had to perform some modifications on our NPM and Webpack configuration files to download and compile the new theme in the most appropriate way.

We then started to apply some Bootstrap and custom styling to the existing components. We started with the main app and NavMenu components, then quickly moved to the **Home** view and the `QuizListComponent` instances contained there; we also spent some valuable time learning the basics of CSS Encapsulation and Shadow DOM and how they can be enabled and disabled in Angular to set a limited scope on our styling rules.

Right after the **Home** view we focused on the `QuizComponent` and `QuizEditComponent`: once done, we chose to let the reader do the rest, not before giving him some useful advise about the styling rules to follow.

Now that our SPA finally got a decent look we can continue our journey into .NET Core and Angular, dealing with some advanced concepts such as data validation, authentication, unit testing and more: these will be the topics of the upcoming chapters.

7
Forms and Data Validation

In this chapter, we'll mostly deal with **Forms**. As we most certainly know, HTML forms are one of the most important and delicate aspects of any business application. Nowadays, forms are used to fulfill almost any task involving user-submitted data, such as registering or logging in to a website, issuing a payment, reserving a hotel room, ordering a product, performing, and retrieving search results, and more.

If we were asked to define a form from a developer's perspective, we would come out with the statement *a form is a UI-based interface that allows authorized users to enter data that will be sent to a server for processing*. The moment we accept this definition, two additional considerations should come into mind:

- Each form should provide a data-entry experience good enough to efficiently guide our users through the expected workflow, otherwise they won't be able to properly use it
- Each form, as long as it brings potentially insecure data to the server, can have a major security impact in terms of data integrity, data security, and system security, unless the developer possesses the required *know-how* to adopt and implement the appropriate countermeasures

These two phrases provide a good summary of what we'll do in this chapter; we'll do our best to guide our users into submitting the data in the most appropriate way, and we'll also learn how to properly check these input values to prevent, avoid, and/or minimize a wide spectrum of integrity and security threats. It's also important to understand that these two topics are frequently intertwined with each other; hence, we'll often deal with them at the same time.

Data validation

If we take a look at our current .NET Core with Angular project, we can see how there's good news and there's bad news: the good news is that we already have some decent forms in place--the `QuizEditComponent`, `QuestionEditComponent`, `AnswerEditComponent`, and `ResultEditComponent` are nothing more, nothing less than wrappers for forms. They also provide a rather good-looking user experience since the restyling performed in Chapter 6, *Style Sheets and UI Layout*, do we really need anything else?

The answer is yes. When we first laid down these forms back in Chapter 5, *Client-Server Interactions*, we entirely skipped the part in which we were supposed to validate the user-submitted data, postponing that task to a not-so-distant future; we don't even have a proper `<form>` element in our templates! Well, guess what? The time has finally come.

Forms in Angular

Let's try to summarize the most blatant shortages of our current form-less approach:

- We cannot keep track of the global form state, there's no way we can tell whether the form is valid or not, if some required fields are missing and so on
- We have no easy way to display error messages to the user to let them know what they have to do to make the form valid
- We do not verify the input data, we just collect them into objects, and then serialize and toss them to the server without thinking twice

Sure, we can easily work around most of these issues by implementing some custom methods within our form-based components; we can throw some `isValid()`, `isNumber()` and so on here and there, and then hook them up to our template syntax and show/hide the validation messages with the help of `*ngIf`, `*ngFor`, and the likes. However, it will definitely be a horrible way to address our problem; we didn't choose a feature-rich client-side framework such as Angular to work that way.

Luckily enough, we have no reason to do that, since Angular provides us with a couple of alternative strategies to deal with these common form-related scenarios: **Template-Driven Forms** and **Model-Driven (or Reactive) Forms**. Both of them are thigh-coupled with the framework and thus extremely viable; they both belong to the `@angular/forms` library and also share a common set of form control classes. However, they also have their own specific sets of features, along with their pros and cons, that can ultimately lead us to choose one of them. Let's try to quickly summarize these differences.

Template-Driven forms

If you come from AngularJS, there's a high chance that the Template-Driven approach will ring a bell or two. As the name implies, Template-Driven forms host most of the logic in the template code; working with a Template-Driven form means to build the form in the `.html` template file, to data bind the various input fields to a `ngModel` instance, and use a dedicated `ngForm` object, related to the whole form and containing all the inputs, each one of them being accessible through their name, to perform the required validity checks.

To better understand it, here's how a Template-Driven form looks:

```
<form novalidate autocomplete="off" #form="ngForm">
    <input type="text" name="title" value="" required
        placeholder="Insert a title..."
        [(ngModel)]="quiz.Title" #title="ngModel"
        />

    <span *ngIf="(title.touched || title.dirty) &&
     title.errors?.required">
        Title is a required field: please enter a valid title.
    </span>

    <button name="btnSubmit"
        (click)="onSubmit()"
        [disabled]="form.invalid">
        Submit
    </button>

</form>
```

As we can see, we can access any element, including the form itself, with some convenient aliases--the attributes with the # sign--and check for their current states to create our own validation workflow. These states are provided by the framework and will change in real time depending on various things; **touched**, for example, becomes TRUE when the control has been visited at least once, **dirty**, as opposite of **pristine**, means that the control value has changed, and so on. We used both of them in the preceding example, because we want our validation message to be shown only if the user moves his focus to the <input name="qName"> and then goes away, leaving it blank by either deleting its value or not setting it.

These are Template-Driven forms in a nutshell; let's try to summarize the pros and cons of this approach:

The pros

- *Template-Driven* forms are *very easy to write*. We can recycle most of our HTML knowledge (assuming that we have any); on top of that, if we came from AngularJS, we already know how well we can make them work once we've mastered the technique.
- They are also rather easy to read and understand, at least from an HTML point of view; we have a plain, understandable HTML structure containing all the input fields and validators, one after another. Each element will have a name, a two-way binding with the underlying ngModel, and (possibly) a Template-Driven logic built upon aliases hooked to other elements that we can also see, or to the form itself.

The cons

- *Template-Driven* forms require a lot of HTML code, which can be rather difficult to maintain and is generally more error-prone than pure TypeScript.
- For the same reason, these forms cannot be unit tested. We have no way to test their validators or to ensure that the logic we implemented will work, other than running an end-to-end test with our browser, which is hardly ideal for complex forms.
- Their readability will quickly drop as we add more and more validators and input tags; keeping all their logic within the template might be fine for small forms, but it doesn't scale well when dealing with complex data items.

Ultimately, we can say that Template-Driven forms might be the way to go when we need to build small forms with simple data validation rules, where we can benefit more from their simplicity. On top of that, they are quite similar to the template code we already have in place; we can replace our container DIVs with <form> elements, decorate our input fields with aliases, throw in some validators handled by *ngIf statements, and we will be set in (almost) no time.

However, the lack of unit testing and the HTML code bloat that they will eventually produce will eventually lead us toward the alternative approach.

 For additional information on *Template-Driven* forms, we highly recommend you to read the official Angular documentation at https://angular.io/guide/forms.

Model-Driven/Reactive forms

The Model-Driven approach was specifically added in Angular 2+ to address the known limitations of the Template-Driven forms; the forms implemented with this alternative method are known as Model-Driven forms or Reactive forms.

The main difference here is that (almost) nothing happens in the template, which acts as a mere reference of a TypeScript object--the form model--that gets instantiated and configured programmatically within the component class.

To better understand the overall concept, let's try to rewrite the previous form in a Model-Driven/Reactive way (the relevant parts are highlighted):

```
<form [formGroup]="form" (ngSubmit)="onSubmit()">

    <input formControlName="title" required />

    <span *ngIf="(form.get('title').touched || form.get('title').dirty)
        && form.get('title').errors?.required">
        Title is a required field: please enter a valid title.
    </span>

    <button type="submit" name="btnSubmit"
        [disabled]="form.invalid">
        Submit
    </button>

</form>
```

Here's the underlying form model that we will define in the component class file (the relevant parts are highlighted):

```
import { FormGroup, FormControl, ReactiveFormsModule, Validators } from
'@angular/forms';

class ModelFormComponent implements OnInit {
  form: FormGroup;

  ngOnInit() {
    this.form = new FormGroup({
        title: new FormControl()
    });
  }
}
```

Let's try to understand what's happening here:

- The `form` property is an instance of `FormGroup` and represents the form itself
- `FormGroup`, as the name suggests, is a container of form controls sharing the same purpose; as we can see, the `form` itself acts as a `FormGroup`, which means that we can nest `FormGroup` objects inside other `FormGroups` (we didn't do that in our sample, though)
- Each data input element in the form template--in the preceding code, `name`--is represented by an instance of `FormControl`
- Each `FormControl` instance encapsulates the related control's current state, such as valid, invalid, touched, and dirty, including its actual value
- Each `FormGroup` instance encapsulates the state of each child control, meaning that it will be valid only if/when all its children are also valid

Also note that we have no way to access the `FormControls` directly, like we were doing in Template-Driven forms; we have to retrieve them using the `.get()` method of the main `FormGroup`, which is the form itself.

At first glance, the `Model-Driven` template doesn't seem much different from the `Template-Driven` one; we still have a `form` element, an `input` element hooked to a `span` validator, and a submit button; on top of that, checking the state of the input elements takes a bigger amount of source code, as they have no aliases we can use. Where's the real deal?

To help us visualize the difference, let's look at the following diagrams; here's a scheme depicting how **Template-Driven Forms** work:

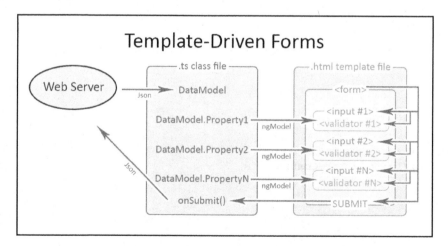

By looking at the arrows we can easily see that, in **Template-Driven Forms**, everything happens in the template; the HTML form elements are directly bound to the component **Data Model** represented by a property filled with an asynchronous HTML request to the web server, such as the `quiz: Quiz` in our `QuizEditComponent` file. That *Data Model* will get updated as soon as the user changes something, unless some validator prevents them from doing that. If we think about it, we can easily understand how there isn't a single part of the whole workflow that happens to be under our control; Angular handles everything by itself, using the information found in the data bindings defined within our template. This is what *Template-Driven* actually means.

Let's now take a look at the **Model-Driven Forms** (or *Reactive Forms*) approach:

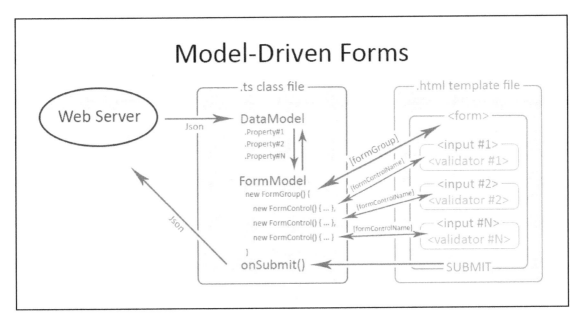

As we can see, the arrows depicting the **Model-Driven** Forms workflow tell a whole different story. They show how the data flows between the component *Data Model*--which we get from the web server--and a UI-oriented *form model* that retains the states and the values of the HTML form (and its children input elements) presented to the user. This means that we'll be able to get in the middle between the data and the form control objects and perform a number of tasks firsthand: push and pull data, detect and react to user changes, implement our own validation logic, perform unit tests, and so on.

Instead of being superseded by a template that's not under our control, we can track and influence the workflow programmatically, since the *form model* that calls the shots is also a TypeScript class; that's what *Model-Driven* is about. This also explains why they are also called **Reactive Forms**--an explicit reference to the *Reactive* programming style that favors explicit data handling and change management throughout the workflow.

For additional information on *Model-Driven/Reactive* Forms, we highly recommend you to read the official Angular documentation at https://angular.io/guide/reactive-forms.

Enough with the theory; it's time to empower our components with some Reactive forms.

Our first Reactive form

The first thing we have to do to start working with Reactive Forms is to add a reference to the ReactiveFormsModule in the AppModule class.

Adding ReactiveFormsModule

From **Solution Explorer**, open the app.module.shared.ts file and add the following (new lines are highlighted):

```
import { NgModule } from '@angular/core';
import { CommonModule } from '@angular/common';
import { FormsModule, ReactiveFormsModule } from '@angular/forms';

[...]

    imports: [
        CommonModule,
        HttpClientModule,
        FormsModule,
        ReactiveFormsModule,

[...]
```

That's it, now we're good to go.

Updating QuizEditComponent

The QuizEditComponent features a very simple yet perfectly working form, hence it's perfect to become our guinea pig.

Open the quiz-edit.component.ts file and update it in the following way (new lines are highlighted):

```
import { Component, Inject, OnInit } from "@angular/core";
import { FormGroup, FormControl, FormBuilder, Validators } from
'@angular/forms';

[...]

export class QuizEditComponent {
    title: string;
    quiz: Quiz;
    form: FormGroup;

[...]

    constructor(private activatedRoute: ActivatedRoute,
        private router: Router,
        private http: HttpClient,
        private fb: FormBuilder,
        @Inject('BASE_URL') private baseUrl: string) {

        // create an empty object from the Quiz interface
        this.quiz = <Quiz>{};

        // initialize the form
        this.createForm();

        var id = +this.activatedRoute.snapshot.params["id"];
        if (id) {
            this.editMode = true;

            // fetch the quiz from the server
            var url = this.baseUrl + "api/quiz/" + id;
            this.http.get<Quiz>(url).subscribe(result => {
                this.quiz = result;
                this.title = "Edit - " + this.quiz.Title;

                // update the form with the quiz value
                this.updateForm();

[...]
```

Here's a summary of what we did here:

- We added a reference to the @angular/form components we'll use within the class
- We added the form: FormGroup class property that will host our Form Model
- We injected the fb: FormBuilder object that will be used to create and update the Form Model
- We added two calls to a couple of new internal methods--createForm() and updateForm()--which will respectively initialize and update the Form Model

Now we need to add these two new methods; scroll down until you reach the onSubmit() method and put these code lines right before it:

```
createForm() {
    this.form = this.fb.group({
        Title: ['', Validators.required],
        Description: '',
        Text: ''
    });
}

updateForm() {
    this.form.setValue({
        Title: this.quiz.Title,
        Description: this.quiz.Description || '',
        Text: this.quiz.Text || ''
    });
}
```

These two methods are quite self-explanatory; they both use the FormBuilder instance to respectively initialize the Form Model and set its values using the Data Model. As we can see by looking at the updated constructor source code, the createForm() method is called before the Data Model is retrieved from the web server, while updateForm() is executed as soon as the HttpClient gets the job done.

We're not done yet; we also need to perform some minor, yet very important changes to the onSubmit() method itself. Here's the updated code (new/updated lines are highlighted):

```
[...]

onSubmit() {

    // build a temporary quiz object from form values
    var tempQuiz = <Quiz>{};
    tempQuiz.Title = this.form.value.Title;
```

```
tempQuiz.Description = this.form.value.Description;
tempQuiz.Text = this.form.value.Text;

var url = this.baseUrl + "api/quiz";

if (this.editMode) {

    // don't forget to set the tempQuiz Id,
    // otherwise the EDIT would fail!
    tempQuiz.Id = this.quiz.Id;

    this.http
        .post<Quiz>(url, tempQuiz)
        .subscribe(res => {
            this.quiz = res;
            console.log("Quiz " + this.quiz.Id + " has been
            updated.");
            this.router.navigate(["home"]);
        }, error => console.log(error));
}
else {
    this.http
        .put<Quiz>(url, tempQuiz)
        .subscribe(res => {
            var v = res;
            console.log("Quiz " + v.Id + " has been created.");
            this.router.navigate(["home"]);
        }, error => console.log(error));
}
}

[...]
```

The source code comments should help understand what we just did. However, let's quickly review the changes we made:

- We removed the `quiz` parameter from the `onSubmit()` method signature, as we won't need it anymore; in Model-Driven Forms, we need to work with the Form Model, leaving the Data Model immutable.
- We created a `tempQuiz` local instance, filling it with the values retrieved by the Form Model. It's worth noting that we also had to set its `Id` in case of `this.editMode`, otherwise the PUT request would fail, being the `Id` field obviously required for edits; we retrieved it directly from the Data Model, since we never put it in the Form Model, as we don't need it there.

- We passed the new `tempQuiz` instance as the new source parameter for our PUT and POST HTTP request calls.

We're done with the class file. Now we need to change the `quiz-edit.component.html` template file as well (new/updated lines are highlighted):

```html
<div class="quiz-edit">
    <h2>{{title}}</h2>
    <form [formGroup]="form" (ngSubmit)="onSubmit()">
        <div class="form-group">
            <label for="title">Quiz title:</label>
            <br />
            <input type="text" id="title"
                   formControlName="Title" required
                   placeholder="choose a title..."
                   class="form-control" />
        </div>
        <div class="form-group">
            <label for="description">Quiz description:</label>
            <br />
            <input type="text" id="description"
                   formControlName="Description"
                   placeholder="enter a description..."
                   class="form-control" />
        </div>
        <div class="form-group">
            <label for="text">Quiz informative text:</label>
            <br />
            <textarea id="text"
                      formControlName="Text"
                      placeholder="enter a text..."
                      class="form-control"></textarea>
        </div>
        <div class="form-group commands">
            <button *ngIf="editMode" type="submit"
                [disabled]="form.invalid"
                class="btn btn-success">
                Apply Changes
            </button>
            <button *ngIf="!editMode" type="submit"
                    [disabled]="form.invalid"
                    class="btn btn-success">
                Create the Quiz!
            </button>
            <button *ngIf="!editMode" type="submit"
                    (click)="onBack()"
                    class="btn btn-default">
```

```
                Cancel
            </button>
        </div>
    </form>

    <question-list *ngIf="editMode" [quiz]="quiz"></question-list>

    <result-list *ngIf="editMode" [quiz]="quiz"></result-list>

</div>
```

We wrapped our DIVs within a `<form>` element and used the `[formGroup]` and `formControlName` template attributes to connect the form and its input fields to the *Form Model*. We also made some important modification to our buttons, removing `(click)="onSubmit(quiz)"`--which is called by the form itself without the attribute--and adding `[disabled]="form.invalid"` to prevent the user from performing a submit when the form has an invalid *state*.

That's it, we just upgraded our previous Template-Driven form into a brand-new Model-Driven form; now that we took the first steps into the Reactive path, we can add some validators to further improve its usability, consistency, and robustness.

Adding validators

As a matter of fact, we already added a basic validator to the `createForm()`:

```
[...]
        Title: ['', Validators.required],
[...]
```

This will definitely make Angular aware of the fact that the quiz Form Model will never be **valid** as long as there's an empty Title, which is precisely what we want since Title is a required field.

Let's quickly test it out. Launch the project in debug mode, navigate through a quiz, click on the **Edit** button, and try to entirely remove the existing Title:

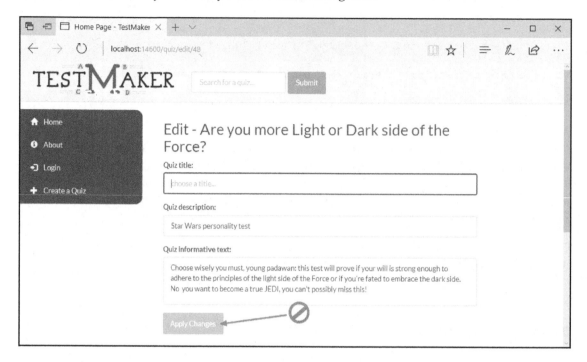

It works! It seems that we're unable to submit the form as long as the **Title** textbox is empty.

The only missing thing here is a visual warning of some sort, otherwise there's a high chance that the user won't understand what he has to do. We can easily fill the gap with the help of some neat Bootstrap classes; open the `quiz-edit.component.html` template file and update it with the following highlighted lines:

```
[...]

<div class="form-group"
    [ngClass]="{ 'has-error has-feedback' :
form.get('Title').errors?.required }">
    <label for="title">Quiz title:</label>
    <br />
    <input type="text" id="title"
            formControlName="Title" required
            placeholder="choose a title..."
            class="form-control"
            />
    <span *ngIf="form.get('Title').errors?.required"
```

```
            class="glyphicon glyphicon-remove form-control-feedback"
            aria-hidden="true"></span>
        <div *ngIf="(form.get('Title').dirty
                || form.get('Title').touched)
                && form.get('Title').errors?.required"
            class="help-block">
            Title is a required field: please insert a valid title.
        </div>
    </div>
</div>

[...]
```

Once done, if we repeat our previous test, we should see something like this:

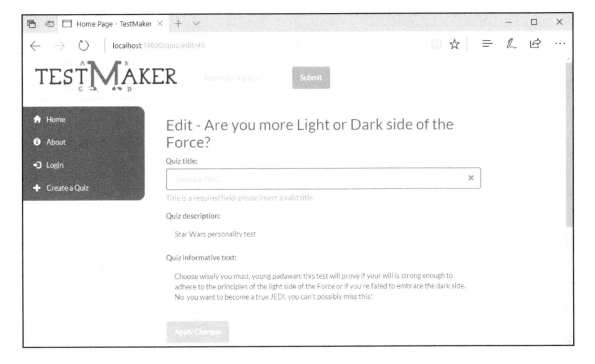

We're definitely sending some relevant signals here; now we can be sure that our users will find out what to do.

Adding shortcuts

If we take another look at our brand new validator template, we can see a certain amount of code bloat; the `form.get('Title')` method is called no less than five times, and all those long lines pose a serious threat to our template's readability. Is there a way to address that?

As a matter of fact, there is--whenever we feel like we're writing too much code or repeating a complex task too many times, we can create one or more helper methods within our component class to centralize the underlying logic. In our specific scenario, we can add these methods to the `QuizEditComponent` class:

```
// retrieve a FormControl
getFormControl(name: string) {
    return this.form.get(name);
}

// returns TRUE if the FormControl is valid
isValid(name: string) {
    var e = this.getFormControl(name);
    return e && e.valid;
}

// returns TRUE if the FormControl has been changed
isChanged(name: string) {
    var e = this.getFormControl(name);
    return e && (e.dirty || e.touched);
}

// returns TRUE if the FormControl is invalid after user changes
hasError(name: string) {
    var e = this.getFormControl(name);
    return e && (e.dirty || e.touched) && !e.valid;
}
```

The comments are self-explanatory, so there's nothing more to say. These helper methods grant us the chance to shrink our previous validation code, as follows:

```
<div class="form-group"
        [ngClass]="{ 'has-error has-feedback' : hasError('Title') }">
    <label for="title">Quiz title:</label>
    <br />
    <input type="text" id="title"
            formControlName="Title" required
            placeholder="choose a title..."
            class="form-control" />
    <span *ngIf="hasError('Title')
        class="glyphicon glyphicon-remove form-control-feedback"
```

```
            aria-hidden="true"></span>
    <div *ngIf="hasError('Title')"
            class="help-block">
        Title is a required field: please insert a valid title.
    </div>
</div>
```

Much better.

Our first Reactive form is now complete; from now on, this will be our standard approach whenever we need to implement a form. However, we still have to bring the remaining form-based components--`QuestionEditComponent`, `AnswerEditComponent`, and `ResultEditComponent`--up to Reactive speed. Luckily enough, we'll just have to play the same music, at least for the most part.

Upgrading components

In this section, we will upgrade the other Angular components, providing them with the Reactive forms they need.

QuestionEditComponent

The `QuestionEditComponent` poses no threat; its form structure is even simpler than `QuizEditComponent`. For this very reason, it can be a perfect exercise for the reader; all it takes is to retrace the steps of what we already did and repeat the exact same tasks. The `form` property, the injected `fb: FormBuilder`, the `createForm()`, and `updateForm()` methods, the `tempQuestion` instance to use within the `onSubmit()` method, and so on.

Just remember to set the `QuizId` variable to the `tempQuestion` instance, as the Entity Framework Data Provider will need it to create and/or update the question:

```
[...]

onSubmit() {

    // build a temporary question object from form values
    var tempQuestion = <Question>{};
    tempQuestion.Text = this.form.value.Text;
    tempQuestion.QuizId = this.question.QuizId;

[...]
```

Moving to the template file, it's all about adding the `<form>` element, changing the submit buttons, and using the `[formGroup]` and `formControlName` accordingly, instead of the existing `[(ngModel)]`. The only significant difference is the fact that we'll have a required `<textarea>` element instead of an `<input type="text">`, yet the things to do are still the same.

Last but not least, remember to append the helper methods to the component class: `getFormControl()`, `isValid()`, and so on; otherwise, we won't be able to use the shortcuts in the template file.

As always, those who don't feel like practicing with the Angular code by themselves can just download the `Chapter 7`, *Forms and Data Validation*, source code from the book's official GitHub repository.

At the end of the day, we should be able to see something like this:

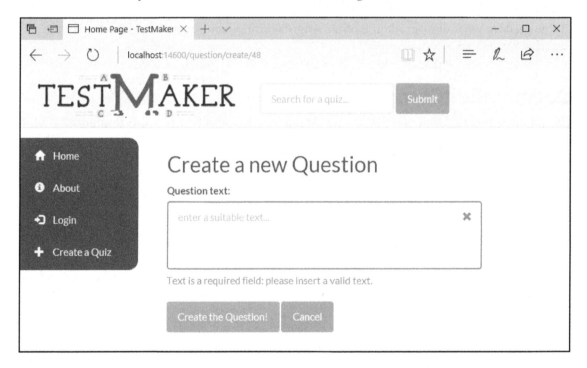

AnswerEditComponent

The same recommendation will also work for the `AnswerEditComponent` upgrade; the only real difference here is the answer's `Value` numeric property, which will require some specific code in the component's class file:

```
[...]

createForm() {
    this.form = this.fb.group({
        Text: ['', Validators.required],
        Value: [0,
            [Validators.required,
            Validators.min(-5),
            Validators.max(5)]
        ]
    });
}

[...]
```

Also, it will require some specific code in the template file:

```
[...]

<div class="form-group"
    [ngClass]="{ 'has-error has-feedback' : hasError('Value') }">
    <label for="value">Score Value:</label>
    <br />
    <select id="value"
            formControlName="Value" required
            class="form-control">
        <option *ngFor="let num of [-5,-4,-3,-2,-1,0,1,2,3,4,5]"
                [value]="num">
            {{num}}
        </option>
    </select>
    <div *ngIf="hasError('Value')"
        class="help-block">
        Please select a valid number between -5 and 5.
    </div>
</div>

[...]
```

As we can see, we added *three* different validators within the Form Model's Value property; we did that because we want to receive a required value that is also not smaller *than* −5 and not bigger than 5. Whenever any of these conditions fails, the Form Model will become invalid.

Wait a minute, we already provide the user with a <select> element filled with predetermined values from −5 to +5; should we really lose our valuable time in validating such input?

As a matter of fact, we should; validation isn't something that can be delegated to input elements, regardless of how they're supposed to work. That <select> can be replaced with another input type, and/or be rendered as something that can also accept empty or different values; we chose the Reactive pattern because we want to perform the validation logic to our Form Model, right? The HTML form elements have nothing to do with it, and they definitely can't give us the control that we crave for.

Anyway, since we added that validator, we can take the chance to improve the form UX by adding a Pick a value option to the <select> itself:

```
<select id="value"
        formControlName="Value" required
        class="form-control">
    <option value="">Pick a value...</option>
    <option *ngFor="let num of [-5,-4,-3,-2,-1,0,1,2,3,4,5]"
            [value]="num">
        {{num}}
    </option>
</select>
```

We put the new option on top of the other ones to ensure that it will be shown when the user creates a new answer. However, for that to happen, we also need to change the new answer's default value from zero to empty string:

```
createForm() {
    this.form = this.fb.group({
        Text: ['', Validators.required],
        Value: ['',
            [Validators.required,
            Validators.min(-4),
            Validators.max(5)]
        ]
    });
}
```

The last thing to do is perform a minor update to the `Answer` interface to make it able to handle a nullable number:

```
interface Answer {
    Id: number;
    QuestionId: number;
    Text: string;
    Value?: number;
}
```

Truth be told, updating the `Answer` interface is not strictly necessary; TypeScript 2.x doesn't enforce strict null-checking in variables, unless we explicitly enable it by adding the `"strictNullChecks": true` directive to the `compilerOptions` section of `tsconfig.json`. However, learning how to properly handle nullable and non-nullable types can be a great way to better understand the various implications of what we're doing.

As soon as we have done everything, we can run our project in debug mode, navigate through an existing question, and click on the **Add a new Answer** button; once there, give focus and leave focus to the form controls to see the results of our hard work:

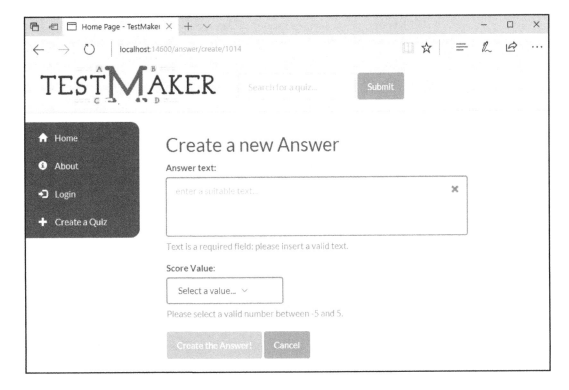

ResultEditComponent

The `ResultEditComponent` can also be upgraded just like the previous ones; yet, it features another slightly different logic--the `MinValue` and `MaxValue` properties, both of them having a nullable number type. The scenario is similar to the `AnswerEditComponent` Value property, which we faced in the previous paragraph, except that we now have two `<input type="number">` instead of a single `<select>`.

Luckily enough, it doesn't change how we can handle it in the component template file:

```
[...]

<div class="form-group"
        [ngClass]="{ 'has-error has-feedback' : hasError('MinValue')
                                                }">
    <label for="MinValue">Minimum Score Value:</label>
    <br />
    <input type="number" id="MinValue" name="MinValue"
            formControlName="MinValue"
            class="form-control"
            />
    <span *ngIf="hasError('MinValue')"
        class="glyphicon glyphicon-remove form-control-feedback"
        aria-hidden="true"></span>
    <div *ngIf="hasError('MinValue')"
            class="help-block">
        Insert a numeric value, or leave it blank to match everything
                        up to MaxValue.
    </div>
</div>

<div class="form-group"
        [ngClass]="{ 'has-error has-feedback' : hasError('MaxValue') }">
    <label for="MaxValue">Maximum Score Value:</label>
    <br />
    <input type="number" id="MaxValue" name="MaxValue"
            formControlName="MaxValue"
            class="form-control"
            />
    <span *ngIf="hasError('MaxValue')"
        class="glyphicon glyphicon-remove form-control-feedback"
        aria-hidden="true"></span>
    <div *ngIf="hasError('MaxValue')"
            class="help-block">
        Insert a numeric value, or leave it blank to match everything
                        up to MinValue.
    </div>
```

```
</div>

[...]
```

Also, in the class file (relevant lines are highlighted):

```
[...]

createForm() {
    this.form = this.fb.group({
        Text: ['', Validators.required],
        MinValue: ['', Validators.pattern(/^\d*$/)],
        MaxValue: ['', Validators.pattern(/^\d*$/)]
    });
}

updateForm() {
    this.form.setValue({
        Text: this.result.Text,
        MinValue: this.result.MinValue || '',
        MaxValue: this.result.MaxValue || ''
    });
}

[...]
```

The only new thing here is the `Validator.pattern`, which accepts a string or a regex that will be matched against the control value, to give it a valid or invalid status accordingly.

If we want to test these validators, we can temporarily change the `MinValue` and/or `MaxValue` input type to `text`, then go back to the form, insert a non-numeric value, and see what happens:

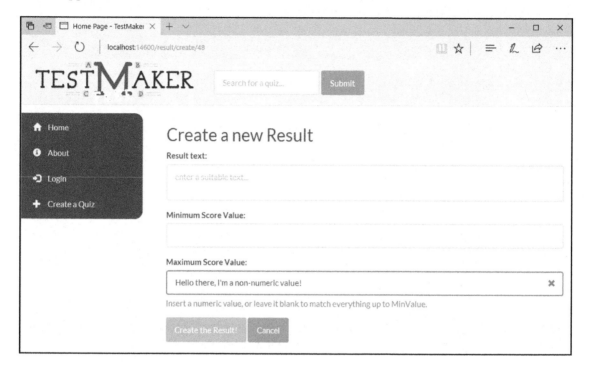

This was the last form-based component requiring attention; now that we've learned the technique, we'll use it for all of our future forms.

Debugging and testing

Before moving on to the next big topic, we should really spend some of our valuable time to understand some key concepts related to form debugging. As said before, one of the advantages granted by the Model-Driven approach is the fact that it allows us to have granular control on our form elements; how can we use these features to our advantage and translate them into writing a more robust code? In the following paragraphs, we'll try to address this question by showing some useful techniques that can be used to gain more control over our forms.

A look at the Form Model

We've talked a lot about the Form Model lately, yet we still haven't seen it once. It would greatly help to have it on screen while developing the form templates, especially if it can be updated in real time as we play with the form inputs and controls.

Here's a convenient HTML snippet containing the Template Syntax required to let it happen:

```
<div class="panel panel-info"
     style="margin-top: 20px;">
  <div class="panel-heading">Form debug info</div>
  <div class="panel-body">
      <p><strong>Form value:</strong></p>
      <div class="help-block">
          {{ form.value | json }}
      </div>
      <p><strong>Form status:</strong></p>
      <div class="help-block">
          {{ form.status | json }}
      </div>
  </div>
</div>
```

We can put this snippet below any of our form-based components, for example, the `QuestionEditComponent`, to obtain the following result:

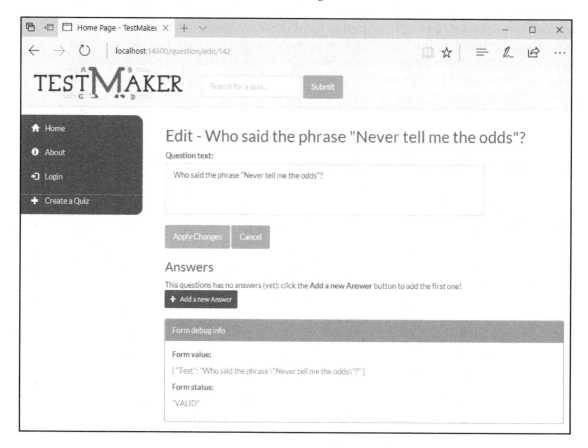

Pretty useful, right? If we play with the form a bit, we can see how the values contained in the **Form debug info** panel will change as we change the input controls; something like that will definitely come in handy when dealing with complex forms.

The pipe operator

By looking at the highlighted lines of the preceding source code, we can see how we used the *pipe* operator (|), which is another useful tool coming from the Angular Template Syntax.

To quickly summarize what it does, we can say the following: the `pipe` operator allows the use of some transformation functions that can be used to perform various tasks such as format strings, join array elements into a string, uppercase/lowercase a text, and sort a list. Here are the pipes that come *built-in* with Angular: `DatePipe`, `UpperCasePipe`, `LowerCasePipe`, `CurrencyPipe`, `PercentPipe`, and `JsonPipe`; these are all available for use in any template. Needless to say, we used the latter in the preceding script to transform the `form.value` and `form.status` objects into readable JSON strings.

 It's worth noting that we can also chain multiple pipes and define custom pipes; however, we don't need to do that for the time being and talking about such a topic will bring us far from the scope of this chapter. If you want to know more about pipes, we strongly suggest you to read the official Angular documentation at `https://angular.io/guide/pipes`.

Reacting to changes

One of the reasons we chose the Reactive approach was to be able to react to the changes issued by the user. We can do that by subscribing to the `valueChanges` property exposed by the `FormGroup` and `FormControl` classes, which returns a RxJS Observable that emits the latest values.

Truth be told, we've been using Observables since `Chapter 3`, *Frontend with Angular*, when we did subscribe to the `get()` method of `HttpClient` to handle the `HTTP` response received by the web server for the first time; we extensively used them again in `Chapter 5`, *Client-Server Interactions*, when we had to implement the support for the `put()` and `post()` methods as well, and we still use them wherever and whenever we need to fetch the JSON data that feeds our Data Model interfaces and Form Model objects. Now, we'll use them to demonstrate how we can perform custom operations whenever the user changes something within a form.

Observing the Observable

Once again the `QuestionEditComponent` will be our lab rat; open its TypeScript class file and update it with the following highlighted lines:

```
[...]

export class QuestionEditComponent {
    title: string;
    question: Question;
    form: FormGroup;
```

```
        activityLog: string;

[...]

createForm() {
    this.form = this.fb.group({
        Text: ['', Validators.required]
    });

    this.activityLog = '';
    this.log("Form has been initialized.");

    // react to form changes
    this.form.valueChanges
        .subscribe(val => {
            if (!this.form.dirty) {
                this.log("Form Model has been loaded.");
            }
            else {
                this.log("Form was updated by the user.");
            }
        });
}

log(str: string) {
    this.activityLog += "["
        + new Date().toLocaleString()
        + "] " + str + "<br />";
&gt;}

[...]
```

In the preceding code, we provided our Form Model with a simple, yet effective logging feature that will register any change activity performed by the framework and/or by the user.

As we can see, all the logic has been put within the createForm() function, because this is where the Form Model gets initialized--along with the Observable we need to monitor. The log() function is just a shortcut to append a basic timestamp to the log activity string and add it to the activityLog local variable in a centralized way.

In order to enjoy our new logging feature to the fullest, we have to find a way to put the `activityLog` on screen. To do that, open the `QuestionEditComponent` template file and add the following highlighted lines to our existing `Form debug info` panel:

```
<div class="panel panel-info"
    style="margin-top: 20px;">
    <div class="panel-heading">Form debug info</div>
    <div class="panel-body">
        <p><strong>Form value:</strong></p>
        <div class="help-block">
            {{ form.value | json }}
        </div>
        <p><strong>Form status:</strong></p>
        <div class="help-block">
            {{ form.status | json }}
        </div>
        <p><strong>Form activity log:</strong></p>
        <div class="help-block">
            <span *ngIf="activityLog"
                [innerHTML]="activityLog"></span>
        </div>
    </div>
</div>
```

That's it, now the activity log will be shown in a truly Reactive way.

It's worth noting that we didn't use the double-curly braces of interpolation here, but we went straight for the `[innerHTML]` directive instead. The reason for that is very simple--the interpolation strips the HTML tags from the source string; hence, we would've lost the `<br />` tag that we used in the `log()` function to separate all log lines with a line feed. If not for that, we would have used the `{{ activityLog }}` syntax instead.

All we need to do now is to test our new activity log. To do so, run the project in debug mode, go straight to `QuestionEditComponent` by editing an already-existing question, play with the form fields, and see what happens in the **Form debug info** panel:

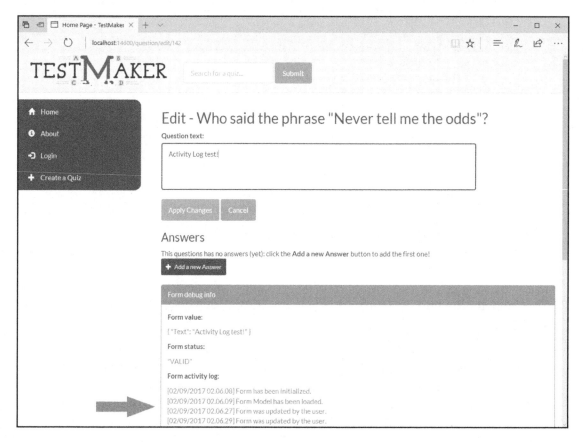

The first log should trigger automatically right after the Form Model initialization, which should happen quite fast; the second log should also trigger automatically as soon as the `HttpClient` retrieves the question JSON and the Form Model gets updated. Then, the form will log any update performed by the user; all we can do is change the text area, yet that's more than enough for our humble reactivity test to complete successfully.

Extending the activity log

Reacting to the Form Model changes is not the only thing we can do; we can extend our subscriptions to observe any form control as well. Here's a further upgrade we can perform on our current activity log implementation to demonstrate that:

```
[...]

// react to changes in the form.Text control
this.form.get("Text")!.valueChanges
    .subscribe(val => {
        if (!this.form.dirty) {
            this.log("Text control has been loaded with initial
                values.");
        }
        else {
            this.log("Text control was updated by the user.");
        }
    });

[...]
```

Place the preceding code at the end of the `createForm()` method, right below the Form Model subscription we implemented early on; this will add further log lines within the Form activity log, all related to the changes occurred in the `Text` component.

What we just did here is more than enough to demonstrate the wonders of the `valueChanges` Observable property; let's move on to the next topic.

> We can definitely keep the **Form debug info** panel in the `QuestionEditComponent` template for further reference, yet there's no need to copy/paste it within the other form-based components' templates or anywhere else.

Client-side debugging

Another great advantage of Observables is that we can use them to debug a good part of the whole Reactive workflow by placing **breakpoints** within our subscriptions source code. To quickly demonstrate this, just add a Visual Studio breakpoint on our latest subscription, as follows:

```
76
77          // react to changes in the form.Text control
78          this.form.get("Text")!.valueChanges
79              .subscribe(val => {
80                  if (!this.form.dirty) {
81                      this.log("Text control has been loaded with initial values.");
82                  }
83                  else {
84                      this.log("Text control was updated by the user.");
85                  }
86              });
87          }
88
```

Once done, run the project in debug mode and navigate to the `QuestionEditComponent`; the breakpoint will be hit as soon as the Form Module will be loaded, since the **Text** control will be updated as well, and also every time we perform a change to that control. Whenever it happens, we'll be able to use all the Visual Studio debugging tools and features that are available on client-side debugging, such as Watch, Local, Immediate Window, Call Stack, and more.

 As of today, client-side debugging isn't supported by **Microsoft Edge** browser; you can do that natively in **Internet Explorer** and, starting with Visual Studio 2017, **Google Chrome**. For additional information about client-side debugging with Google Chrome, we strongly suggest that you read the following post on the official MSDN blog:

https://blogs.msdn.microsoft.com/webdev/2016/11/21/client-side-debugging-of-asp-net-projects-in-google-chrome/

Forms unit testing

The **Form debug info** panel can be very useful during development, especially if we adapt the activity log feature from time to time to better suit our needs; the client-side debugging feature powered by Visual Studio is even better, because this allows us to scope into TypeScript variables, subscriptions, and initializers in a truly efficient way. Not to mention the fact that the *server-side* compilation provided by TypeScript + WebPack + WebPackMiddleware will shield us from most syntax, semantic, and logical programming errors, freeing us from the pests of script-based programming, at least for the most part.

However, what about test-driven development? What if we want to test our forms against some specific use cases? Is there a way we can mock our control's and model's behavior and perform Unit Tests?

The answer is yes; more specifically, thanks to the Reactive approach we chose, we'll be able to unit test our forms just like the rest of our client app using the various open source testing frameworks shipped and/or supported by Angular--Jasmine, Karma, and Protractor--as well as its very own native test environment called Angular testing utilities. We'll talk more about that in `Chapter 9`, *Advanced Topics*.

Suggested topics

Template-Driven Forms, Model-Driven Forms, Reactive Forms, Data Validation, Angular Validators, Angular Pipes, Double-curly Braces of Interpolation, RxJS, Observables, Client-Side Debugging, Test-Driven Development (TDD), Unit Testing, Jasmine, Karma, Protractor, and Angular testing utilities

Summary

This chapter was entirely dedicated to Angular forms. We started clarifying what a form actually is and enumerated the features it needs to have in order to fulfill its duties, grouping them into two main requirements: providing a good user experience and properly handling the submitted data.

We then turned our focus to the Angular framework and to the two form design models it offers: the Template-Driven approach, mostly inherited from AngularJS, and the Model-Driven or Reactive alternative. We took some valuable time to analyze the pros and cons provided by both of them, and then we performed a detailed comparison of the underlying logic and workflow. At the end of the day, we chose to embrace the Reactive way of doing things, as it gives more control to the developer and enforces a more consistent separation of duties between the Data Model and the Form Model.

Right after that, we went from theory to practice by testing our acquired knowledge on our client app's `QuizEditComponent`: we upgraded our previous, loosely Template-Driven form with a brand new Reactive form with improved UI and UX; we also added the data validation logic by making good use of the Angular Template Syntax in conjunction with the classes and directives granted by Angular's `ReactiveFormsModule`. Once done, we did the same with all our other form-based components--`QuestionEditComponent`, `AnswerEditComponent`, and `ResultEditComponent`--leaving the implementation to the reader, yet highlighting all the noticeable differences between them.

At the end of the upgrade process, we moved our first steps toward the world of form debugging and testing, using some of the most interesting features of the Model-Driven approach to fulfill a number of useful tasks: showing the JSON-serialized Form Model and form status on screen, subscribing to the Observables exposed by the form to react to user changes, using these subscriptions to hook the Visual Studio client-side debugger to the Reactive workflow, and so on.

Eventually, we spent a few words introducing the concepts of unit testing and test-driven development, which will be addressed in `Chapter 9`, *Advanced Topics*.

8

Authentication and Authorization

Generally speaking, the term authentication refers to any process of verification that someone, be it a human being or an automated system, is who (or what) it claims to be. This is also true within the context of the **World Wide Web** (**WWW**), where that same word is mostly used to denote any technique used by a website or service to collect a set of login information from a user agent, typically a web browser, and authenticate them using a membership and/or identity service.

Authentication should never be confused with authorization, as it is a different process and is in charge of a very different task. To give a quick definition, we can say that the purpose of authorization is to confirm that the requesting user is allowed to have access to the action they want to perform. In other words, while authentication is about who they are, authorization is about what they're allowed to do.

To better understand the distance between these two apparently similar concepts, we can think of two real-world scenarios:

- A free, yet registered account trying to gain access to a paid or premium only service or feature; this is a common example of authenticated, yet not authorized access; we know who they are, yet they're not allowed to go there
- An anonymous user trying to gain access to a publicly available page or file; this is an example of non-authenticated, yet authorized access; we don't know who they are, yet they can access public resources just like everyone else

To auth, or not to auth

As a matter of fact, implementing **authentication** and/or **authorization** logic isn't mandatory for most web-based applications or services; there are a number of websites that still don't do that, mostly because they serve contents that can be accessed by anyone at any time. This used to be pretty common among most corporate, marketing, and informative websites until some years ago; that was before their owners learned how important it is to build a network of registered users and how much these loyal contacts are worth nowadays.

We don't need to be experienced developers to acknowledge how much the WWW has changed in the last few years; each and every website, regardless of its purpose, has an increasing and more or less legitimate interest in tracking their users nowadays, giving them the chance to customize their navigation experience, interacting with their social networks, collecting email addresses, and so on. None of the preceding can be done without an authentication mechanism of some sort.

There are billions of websites and services that require authentication to work properly, as most of their content and/or intents depend upon the actions of registered users: forums, blogs, shopping carts, subscription-based services, and even collaborative tools such as wikis (including ours).

Long story short, the answer is yes; as long as we want to have users performing CRUD operations within our client app, there is no doubt that we should implement some kind of authentication and authorization procedure. If we're aiming for a production-ready SPA with, we definitely want to know who our users are in terms of name and email address. It is the only way to determine who will be able to view, add, update, or delete our valued quizzes, not to mention perform administrative-level tasks, keep track of our users, and so on.

Authentication

Since the origin of the WWW, the vast majority of authentication techniques rely upon **HTTP/HTTPS implementation standards**, and all of them work more or less in the following way:

1. A non-authenticated user-agent asks for a content that cannot be accessed without some kind of permissions.
2. The web application returns an authentication request, usually in form of an HTML page containing an empty web form to complete.

3. The user-agent fills up the web form with their credentials, usually a username and a password, and then sends it back with a `POST` command, which is most likely issued by a click on a **Submit** button.

4. The web application receives the `POST` data and calls the aforementioned server-side implementation that will try to authenticate the user with the given input and return an appropriate result.

5. If the result is successful, the web application will authenticate the user and store the relevant data somewhere, depending on the chosen authentication method: sessions/cookies, tokens, signatures, and so on (we'll talk about it later on). Conversely, the result will be presented to the user as a readable outcome inside an error page, possibly asking them to try again, contact an administrator, or something else.

This is still the most common approach nowadays. Almost all websites we can think of are using it, albeit with a number of big or small differences regarding security layers, state management, JWT, or other RESTful tokens, basic or digest access, single sign-on properties, and more.

Third-party authentication

Being forced to have a potentially different username and password for each website visit can be frustrating, other than requiring the users to develop custom password storage techniques that might lead to security risks. In order to overcome this issue, a wide amount of IT developers started to look around for an alternative way to authenticate users that could replace the standard authentication technique based upon usernames and passwords with an authentication protocol based upon trusted third-party providers.

The rise and fall of OpenID

Among the first successful attempts to implement a thid-party authentication mechanism was the first release of **OpenID**, an open and decentralized authentication protocol promoted by the non-profit OpenID Foundation. Available since 2005, it was quickly and enthusiastically adopted by some big players such as Google and StackOverflow, who originally based their authentication providers upon it.

Here's how it works in a few words:

- Whenever our application receives an OpenID authentication request, it opens a transparent connection interface through the requesting user and a trusted, third-party authentication provider (for example, the **Google Identity Provider**); the interface can be a popup, an AJAX, populated modal windows, or an API call, depending on the implementation
- The user sends his username and password to the aforementioned third-party provider, who performs the authentication accordingly and communicates the result to our application by redirecting the user to where he came from, along with a security token that can be used to retrieve the authentication result
- Our application consumes the token to check the authentication result, authenticating the user in case of success or sending an error response in case of failure

Despite the great enthusiasm between 2005 and 2009, with a good amount of relevant companies publicly declaring their support for OpenID and even joining the foundation--including PayPal and Facebook--the original protocol didn't live up to the great expectations: legal controversies, security issues and, most importantly, the massive popularity surge of the social networks with their improper--yet working--*OAuth-based* social logins within the 2009-2012 period basically killed it.

 Those who don't know what OAuth is, have some patience; we'll get there soon enough.

OpenID Connect

In a desperate attempt to keep their flag alive after the takeover of the *OAuth/OAuth2* social logins, the OpenID foundation released the "third generation" of the OpenID technology in February 2014; this was called OpenID Connect.

Despite the name, the new installment has little or nothing to do with their ancestors; it's merely an authentication layer built upon the OAuth2 authorization protocol. In other words, it's little more than a standardized interface to help developers using OAuth2 as an authentication framework in a less improper way, which is kind of funny, considering that OAuth2 played a major role in taking out OpenID 2.0 in the first place.

The choice to move to OpenID Connect was quite sad in 2014 and it still is as of today; however, after more than three years, we can definitely say that--despite its undeniable limitations--OpenID Connect can still provide a useful, standardized way to obtain user identity. It allows developers to request and receive information about authenticated users and sessions using a convenient, RESTful-based JSON interface; it features an extensible specification that also supports some promising optional features such as encryption of identity data, auto discovery of OpenID providers, and even session management. In short, it's still useful enough to be used instead of relying on pure OAuth2.

For additional information about OpenID, we strongly suggest that you read the following specifications from the OpenID Foundation official website:

OpenID Connect
`http://openid.net/specs/openid-connect-core-1_0.html.`

OpenID 2.0 to OpenID Connect migration guide
`http://openid.net/specs/openid-connect-migration-1_0.html.`

Authorization

In most standard implementations, including those featured by ASP.NET, the authorization phase kicks in right after the authentication, and it's mostly based on permissions or roles; any authenticated user might have their own set of permissions and/or belong to one or more roles, and thus be granted access to a specific set of resources. These *role-based* checks are usually set by the developer in a declarative fashion within the application source code and/or configuration files.

Authorization, like we said, shouldn't be confused with authentication, despite the fact that it can be easily exploited to perform an implicit authentication as well, especially when it's delegated to a third-party actor.

Third-party authorization

The best known third-party authorization protocol nowadays is the 2.0 release of *OAuth*, also known as **OAuth2**, which supersedes the former release (**OAuth 1** or simply **OAuth**) originally developed by *Blaine Cook* and *Chris Messina* in 2006.

We already talked a lot about it for good reasons; **OAuth 2** has quickly become the industry-standard protocol for authorization and is currently used by a gigantic amount of community-based websites and social networks, including Google, Facebook, and Twitter. It basically works like this:

- Whenever an existing user requests a set of permissions to our application via OAuth, we open a transparent connection interface between them and a third-party authorization provider that is trusted by our application (for example, Facebook)
- The provider acknowledges the user and, if they have the proper rights, responds by entrusting them with a temporary, specific access key
- The user presents the access key to our application and will be granted access

We can clearly see how easy it is to exploit this authorization logic for authentication purposes as well; after all, if Facebook says I can do something, shouldn't it also imply that I am who I claim to be? Isn't that enough?

The short answer is no. It might be the case for Facebook, because their **OAuth 2** implementation implies that the subscriber receiving the authorization must have authenticated himself to Facebook first; however, this assurance is not written anywhere. Considering how many websites are using it for authentication purposes, we can assume that Facebook won't likely change their actual behavior, yet we have no guarantees about it.

Theoretically speaking, these websites can split their authorization system from their authentication protocol at any time, thus leading our application's authentication logic to an unrecoverable state of inconsistency. More generally, we can say that presuming something is from something else is almost always a bad practice, unless that assumption lies upon very solid, well-documented, and (most importantly) highly guaranteed grounds.

Proprietary versus third-party

Theoretically speaking, it's possible to entirely delegate the authentication and/or authorization tasks to existing external, third-party providers such as those we mentioned before; there are a lot of web and mobile applications that proudly follow this route nowadays. There are a number of undeniable advantages in using such an approach, including the following:

- **No user-specific DB tables/data models**, just some provider-based identifiers to use here and there as reference keys.

- **Immediate registration**, since there's no need to fill in a registration form and wait for a confirmation email--no username, no password. This will be appreciated by most users and will probably increase our conversion rates as well.
- **Little or no privacy issues**, as there's no personal or sensitive data on the application server.
- **No need to handle usernames and passwords** and implement automatic recovery processes.
- **Fewer security-related issues** such as form-based hacking attempts or brute-force login attempts.

Of course, there are also some downsides:

- **There won't be an actual user base**, so it will be difficult to get an overview of active users, get their email address, do statistics, and so on
- **The login phase might be resource-intensive**, since it will always require an external, back and forth secure connection with a third-party server
- **All users will need to have (or open) an account with the chosen third-party provider(s)** in order to log in
- **All users will need to trust our application** because the third-party provider will ask them to authorize it for accessing their data
- **We will have to register our application with the provider** in order to be able to perform a number of required or optional tasks, such as receiving our public and secret keys, authorizing one or more URI initiators, and choosing the information we want to collect

Taking all these pros and cons into account, we can say that relying on third-party providers might be a great time-saving choice for small-scale apps, including ours; however, building our own account management system seems to be the only way to overcome the aforementioned governance and control-based flaws undeniably brought by that approach.

In this book, we'll explore both these routes, in an attempt to get the most--if not the best--of both worlds. In this chapter, we'll create an **internal membership provider** that will handle authentication and provide its very own set of authorization rules; in the following chapter, we'll further leverage that same implementation to demonstrate how we can give our users the chance to log in using a sample third-party auth provider (Facebook) and use its SDK and API to fetch the data that we need to create our corresponding internal users, thanks to the built-in features provided by the *ASP.NET Core Identity* package.

Proprietary auth with .NET Core

The authentication patterns made available by ASP.NET Core are basically the same as supported by the previous versions of ASP.NET:

- **No authentication**, if we don't feel like implementing anything or if we want to use (or develop) a self-made auth interface without relying upon the *ASP.NET Core Identity* system
- **Individual user accounts**, when we set up an internal database to store user data using the standard *ASP.NET Identity* interface
- **Azure Active Directory**, which implies using a token-based set of API calls handled by the **Azure AD Authentication Library (ADAL)**
- **Windows authentication**, only viable for local-scope applications within Windows domains or Active Directory trees

All these approaches--excluding the first one--are handled by **ASP.NET Core Identity**, a membership system that allows us to add authentication and authorization functionalities to our application. With **ASP.NET Core Identity**, we can easily implement a login mechanism that will allow our users to create an account and login with a username and a password. On top of that, we can also give them the chance to use an external login provider--as long as it's supported by the framework; as of today, the list of available providers includes Facebook, Google, Microsoft Account, Twitter, and more.

Setting up the .NET Core Identity

In Chapter 1, *Getting Ready*, when we created our .NET Core project, we made the choice to go with an empty project featuring no authentication. That was because we didn't want Visual Studio to install the **ASP.NET Core Identity** within our application's startup files right from the start. However, now that we'll use it, we need to manually perform the required setup steps.

Configuring the Identity service

Enough with the theory, let's put the plan into action. Open the Startup.cs file and add the following highlighted lines:

```
[...]

// This method gets called by the runtime. Use this method to add services
to the container.
```

```
public void ConfigureServices(IServiceCollection services)
{
    services.AddMvc();

    // Add EntityFramework support for SqlServer.
    services.AddEntityFrameworkSqlServer();

    // Add ApplicationDbContext.
    services.AddDbContext<ApplicationDbContext>(options =>
options.UseSqlServer(Configuration["Data:DefaultConnection:ConnectionString
"])
        );

    // Add ASP.NET Identity support
    services.AddIdentity<ApplicationUser, IdentityRole>(
        opts =>
        {
            opts.Password.RequireDigit = true;
            opts.Password.RequireLowercase = true;
            opts.Password.RequireUppercase = true;
            opts.Password.RequireNonAlphanumeric = false;
            opts.Password.RequiredLength = 7;
        })
        .AddEntityFrameworkStores<ApplicationDbContext>();
}

[...]
```

It's just like we did in `Chapter 4`, *Data Model with Entity Framework Core,* when we added the support for *Entity Framework* and registered the `ApplicationDbContext` in the **Dependency Injection (DI)** container; while we were there, we also took the chance to override some of the default password policy settings to demonstrate how we can configure the Identity service to suit our needs.

Note that the use of the `IdentityRole` class will require a reference to the `Microsoft.AspNetCore.Identity` namespace near the top of the file:

```
[...]

using Microsoft.Extensions.DependencyInjection;
using TestMakerFreeWebApp.Data;
using Microsoft.AspNetCore.Identity;

[...]
```

Extending the ApplicationUser

The next thing to do is to empower our `ApplicationUser` model class with all the features required by the ASP.NET Core Identity service to use it for auth purposes. Luckily enough, the package comes with a built-in `IdentityUser` base class that can be used to extend our own, thus granting it all that we need.

To do that, navigate to the `/Data/Models/` folder, edit the `ApplicationUser.cs` file, and update it in the following way:

```
[...]

public class ApplicationUser : IdentityUser

[...]
```

Again, this will require a `using Microsoft.AspNetCore.Identity` on top.

As soon as we apply the changes and save the file, the Visual Studio Error List panel should show three warnings about the `UserName`, `Id`, and `Email` properties of our new model; apparently, these properties are now in conflict with three members already existing in the base class with the same names. As a matter of fact, we did that on purpose when we first created the model back in Chapter 4, *Data Model with Entity Framework Core*; we knew that this moment would eventually come, hence we named these properties with the exact same names of those being in the `UserIdentity` base class. Thanks to that decision, we can now fix our model by simply commenting out the offending properties in the following way:

```
[...]

#region Properties
//[Key]
//[Required]
//public string Id { get; set; }

//[Required]
//[MaxLength(128)]
//public string UserName { get; set; }

//[Required]
//public string Email { get; set; }

public string DisplayName { get; set; }

[...]
```

Alternatively, we can also entirely delete them; they won't be needed anymore.

Upgrading the DbContext

In order to support the *ASP.NET Core Identity* service, our `ApplicationDbContext` class needs to be updated as well.

Open the `Data/ApplicationDbContext.cs` class file and perform the following changes:

1. Add a `using` reference to `Microsoft.AspNetCore.Identity.EntityFrameworkCore`, as required by the new base class:

   ```
   using Microsoft.AspNetCore.Identity.EntityFrameworkCore;
   ```

2. Change the base class from `DbContext` to `IdentityDbContext<ApplicationUser>`:

   ```
   [...]

   public class ApplicationDbContext :
   IdentityDbContext<ApplicationUser>

   [...]
   ```

3. Remove the `DbSet<ApplicationUser> Users` property, as the `IdentityDbContext` base class that we just inherited already has it built in:

   ```
   [...]

   #region Properties
   // public DbSet<ApplicationUser> Users { get; set; }
   public DbSet<Quiz> Quizzes { get; set; }

   [...]
   ```

Revising the DbSeeder

Now that our `ApplicationUser` model class is inheriting the `IdentityUser` base class, we most likely broke the seeding mechanism we set up back in Chapter 4, *Data Model with Entity Framework Core*. However, it's not a big deal; we can take the chance to create some sample roles, since we can now make good use of them.

The first thing we need to do is to provide our DbSeeder class with a UserManager and a RoleManager, as they are the required Microsoft.AspNetCore.Identity handler classes to properly work with users and roles. We can inject them using DI within the service scope we defined in the Startup.cs file back in Chapter 4, *Data Model with Entity Framework Core,* and then pass them to the DbSeed.Seed() method, just like we did with the DbContext.

These are the changes to apply to the Startup.cs file (new and changed parts are highlighted):

```
[...]

// Create a service scope to get an ApplicationDbContext instance using DI
using (var serviceScope =
app.ApplicationServices.GetRequiredService<IServiceScopeFactory>().CreateSc
ope())
{
    var dbContext =
    serviceScope.ServiceProvider.GetService<ApplicationDbContext>();
    var roleManager =
    serviceScope.ServiceProvider.GetService<RoleManager<IdentityRole>>
    ();
    var userManager =
  serviceScope.ServiceProvider.GetService<UserManager<ApplicationUser>>
    ();
    // Create the Db if it doesn't exist and applies any pending
    migration.
    dbContext.Database.Migrate();
    // Seed the Db.
    DbSeeder.Seed(dbContext, roleManager, userManager);
}

[...]
```

Once done, we can open our /Data/DbSeeder.cs file and update the Seed() method accordingly:

```
[...]

public static Seed(
    ApplicationDbContext dbContext,
    RoleManager<IdentityRole> roleManager,
    UserManager<ApplicationUser> userManager
    )
{

    // Create default Users (if there are none)
```

```
    if (!dbContext.Users.Any())
    {
        CreateUsers(dbContext, roleManager, userManager)
            .GetAwaiter()
            .GetResult();
    }

    // Create default Quizzes (if there are none) together with their
        set of Q&A
    if (!dbContext.Quizzes.Any()) createQuizzes(dbContext);
}

[...]
```

Other than the expected references to the `RoleManager` and `UserManager`, we can easily see that we did something else. Specifically, we changed the way we're executing the `CreateUsers()` method; instead of simply invoking it, we're now using `GetAwaiter()` to get an awaiter object that will await the completion of its task, followed by a `GetResult()` that will end the wait and return the resulting value (which is `null` in our case) and return to the main execution context.

This is a rather common way to deal with async tasks from a synchronous context; that's good to know, yet why did we do? Are we planning to change `CreateUsers()` into an async method returning a `Task`?

The answer is yes, that's precisely what we're about to do. The reason is simple--since most of the `roleManager` and `userManager` method are asynchronous, the best way to invoke them would be from an `async` method. This leaves us with two possible routes: go async all the way up to the `Configure()` method within the `Startup.cs` file, or block it somehow. We went for the latter options, along with some important caveats that we'll briefly introduce at the end of this section.

The next step involves upgrading the `CreateUsers` method:

```
[...]

private static async Task CreateUsers(
    ApplicationDbContext dbContext,
    RoleManager<IdentityRole> roleManager,
    UserManager<ApplicationUser> userManager)
{
    // local variables
    DateTime createdDate = new DateTime(2016, 03, 01, 12, 30, 00);
    DateTime lastModifiedDate = DateTime.Now;

    string role_Administrator = "Administrator";
```

```
    string role_RegisteredUser = "RegisteredUser";

    //Create Roles (if they doesn't exist yet)
    if (!await roleManager.RoleExistsAsync(role_Administrator))
    {
        await roleManager.CreateAsync(new
          IdentityRole(role_Administrator));
    }
    if (!await roleManager.RoleExistsAsync(role_RegisteredUser))
    {
        await roleManager.CreateAsync(new
            IdentityRole(role_RegisteredUser));
    }

    // Create the "Admin" ApplicationUser account
    var user_Admin = new ApplicationUser()
    {
        SecurityStamp = Guid.NewGuid().ToString(),
        UserName = "Admin",
        Email = "admin@testmakerfree.com",
        CreatedDate = createdDate,
        LastModifiedDate = lastModifiedDate
    };
    // Insert "Admin" into the Database and assign the "Administrator"
      and "RegisteredUser" roles to him.
    if (await userManager.FindByNameAsync(user_Admin.UserName) == null)
    {
        await userManager.CreateAsync(user_Admin, "Pass4Admin");
        await userManager.AddToRoleAsync(user_Admin,
        role_RegisteredUser);
        await userManager.AddToRoleAsync(user_Admin,
         role_Administrator);
        // Remove Lockout and E-Mail confirmation.
        user_Admin.EmailConfirmed = true;
        user_Admin.LockoutEnabled = false;
    }

#if DEBUG
    // Create some sample registered user accounts
    var user_Ryan = new ApplicationUser()
    {
        SecurityStamp = Guid.NewGuid().ToString(),
        UserName = "Ryan",
        Email = "ryan@testmakerfree.com",
        CreatedDate = createdDate,
        LastModifiedDate = lastModifiedDate
    };
```

```
var user_Solice = new ApplicationUser()
{
    SecurityStamp = Guid.NewGuid().ToString(),
    UserName = "Solice",
    Email = "solice@testmakerfree.com",
    CreatedDate = createdDate,
    LastModifiedDate = lastModifiedDate
};

var user_Vodan = new ApplicationUser()
{
    SecurityStamp = Guid.NewGuid().ToString(),
    UserName = "Vodan",
    Email = "vodan@testmakerfree.com",
    CreatedDate = createdDate,
    LastModifiedDate = lastModifiedDate
};

// Insert sample registered users into the Database and also assign
  the "Registered" role to him.
if (await userManager.FindByNameAsync(user_Ryan.UserName) == null)
{
    await userManager.CreateAsync(user_Ryan, "Pass4Ryan");
    await userManager.AddToRoleAsync(user_Ryan,
    role_RegisteredUser);
    // Remove Lockout and E-Mail confirmation.
    user_Ryan.EmailConfirmed = true;
    user_Ryan.LockoutEnabled = false;
}
if (await userManager.FindByNameAsync(user_Solice.UserName) ==
    null)
{
    await userManager.CreateAsync(user_Solice, "Pass4Solice");
    await userManager.AddToRoleAsync(user_Solice,
    role_RegisteredUser);
    // Remove Lockout and E-Mail confirmation.
    user_Solice.EmailConfirmed = true;
    user_Solice.LockoutEnabled = false;
}
if (await userManager.FindByNameAsync(user_Vodan.UserName) == null)
{
    await userManager.CreateAsync(user_Vodan, "Pass4Vodan");
    await userManager.AddToRoleAsync(user_Vodan,
    role_RegisteredUser);
    // Remove Lockout and E-Mail confirmation.
    user_Vodan.EmailConfirmed = true;
    user_Vodan.LockoutEnabled = false;
}
```

```
#endif
    await dbContext.SaveChangesAsync();
}

[...]
```

As we can see, we made some relevant changes here:

- As expected, we added the `async` modifier to the method signature and changed the return type from `void` to `Task`; we already know the reason, and we'll tell more about that in a short while, so let's go ahead for now.
- We used the newly-added `roleManager` object instance to create two sample roles: `Administrator` and `RegisteredUser`.
- We replaced the existing `DbContext.Add` and `DbContext.AddRange` method calls with those provided by the `userManager` object instance; this allowed us to specify a password that will be automatically hashed.
- We removed the programmatic `Id</kbd> Guid assignment for each user, as the Guid will be autogenerated by the userManager.CreateUserAsync() method, and replaced it with a new SecurityStamp property, also accepting a Guid. This is one of the many properties shipped by the IdentityUser base class, and it's required when creating a new user.`

> The `Administrator` and `RegisteredUser` roles we just implemented here will be the core of our authorization mechanism; all of our users will be assigned to at least one of them. Note how we assigned both of them to the **admin** user, to make him be able to do everything a standard user can do, plus more: all the other users only have the latter, so they'll be unable to perform any administrative-level task--as long as they're not provided with the `Administrator` role.

With this, we're done updating our project's classes. Before going further, it might be wise to issue a whole project rebuild to ensure that we're not getting build errors within our code.

A word on async tasks, awaits, and deadlocks

To better explain what we did with the `CreateUsers()` method of the `DbSeeder` class, we should spend a few words about the concept async tasks.

Whoever knows the basics of thread programming within legacy ASP.NET knows well that you should never even think about blocking an async task. The reason isn't always immediate to explain and understand, yet we'll try to give it a shot. One of the first thing you should learn when working with sync methods invoking async tasks in ASP.NET is that when the top-level method awaits a task, its current execution context gets blocked until the task completes. This won't be a problem, unless that context allows only one thread to run at a time, which is precisely the case of the `AspNetSynchronizationContext`. If we combine these two things together, we can easily see that blocking an async method returning a task will expose our application to a high risk of deadlock. A deadlock, from a software development perspective, is a dreadful situation that occurs whenever a process or thread enters a waiting state indefinitely, usually because the resource it's waiting for is held by another waiting process. In any legacy ASP.NET web application, we'll face a deadlock every time we're blocking a task, simply because that task, in order to complete, will require the same execution context of the invoking method, which is kept blocked by that method until the task completes!

After hearing this terrifying story, there's definitely something that we should ask ourselves: why in the hell have we chosen to block the `CreateUsers()` method in the first place! Are we nuts or what?

As a matter of fact, we're not using legacy ASP.NET here; we're using .NET Core. Luckily enough, .NET Core dropped the former pattern based upon the `SynchronizationContext` for a contextless approach layered upon a versatile, deadlock-resilient thread pool. To keep it simple, we have nothing to worry about when using `GetAwaiter().GetResult()`, `.Wait`, `.Result`, or any other blocker; the only real downside in doing so is that we will lose all the benefits brought by asynchronous programming, such as performances and scalability. However, we can definitely live without them within the single request that will trigger the execution of our `DbSeeder` class in the whole application's lifetime.

For additional information regarding threads, async tasks, awaits, and asynchronous programming in ASP.NET we highly recommend that you check out the outstanding articles written by *Stephen Cleary* on the topic, which will greatly help you understand some of the most tricky and complex scenarios that can fall upon our heads when developing with these technologies. Some of them have been written a while ago, yet they never really age:

```
https://blogs.msdn.microsoft.com/pfxteam/2012/04/12/asyncawait-
faq/.
http://blog.stephencleary.com/2012/07/dont-block-on-async-code.
html.
https://msdn.microsoft.com/en-us/magazine/jj991977.aspx.
https://blog.stephencleary.com/2017/03/aspnetcore-
synchronization-context.html.
```

Updating the database

It's time to create a new migration and reflect the code changes to the database by taking advantage of the code-first approach we chose in `Chapter 4`, *Data Model with Entity Framework Core*.

Adding the identity migration

To do that, open a command line or Powershell prompt and go to our project's root folder, then write the following:

```
dotnet ef migrations add "Identity" -o "Data\Migrations"
```

A new migration should then be added to the project:

The new migration files will be autogenerated in the `\Data\Migrations\` folder.

Applying the migration

The next thing to do is to apply the new migration to our Database and update the existing data accordingly. Since we updated our `DbSeeder` class to support the new changes, the best thing we can do is to let it repopulate our database accordingly. Unfortunately, we know perfectly well that as long as there are some existing users in the database tables, the `CreateUsers()` method won't even run. This leaves us with two options:

- **Upgrade the existing database**, then manually delete all users; if we do that, the *DbSeeder* will recreate them all on the first run using the ASP.NET Core Identity interface
- **Drop and recreate the database** entirely, so the `DbSeeder` will kick in and repopulate everything--users, quizzes, questions, and so on--on the first run

Option #1 - update

The former route should be the most reasonable one, except it can cause some data loss or other consistency issues due to the fact that our `ApplicationDbContext` and `ApplicationUser` classes experienced some major changes. Although Entity Framework should be able to handle everything properly, it will mostly depend on what we did to our data during the various CRUD tests we performed in the last three chapters.

> The risk of data loss is also stated by the yellow message *"An operation was scaffolded that may result in the loss of data..."* shown by the Command Prompt upon completing the migration task; if we look at the preceding screenshot, we can clearly see it (third line from the bottom).

If we want to take this route, we can start issuing this command:

```
dotnet ef database update
```

Once done, without running the project, do the following:

1. Open the **SQL Server Object Explorer** in Visual Studio.
2. Navigate to the **TestMakerFree** database and expand it.
3. Right-click on the **dbo.Users** table and select **View Data**.
4. Delete all the existing rows (select them all, and then *right-click* | **Delete**).

Option #2 - drop and recreate

If we go for option #2, we will lose all our existing data; however, it will be recreated by the `DbSeeder` at the first run, so we'll only lose what we did during our CRUD-based tests during the last three chapters.

> Although it might seem a horrible way to fix things, that's definitely not the case; we're still in the development phase, hence we can definitely allow a full database refresh.

Should we choose to take this bus, here are the commands to use:

```
dotnet ef database drop
dotnet ef database update
```

The drop command should ask for a **Y/N** confirmation before proceeding; when it does, hit the y key and let it happen. When the drop and the update tasks are both done, we can run our project in debug mode and wait for the DbSeeder to kick in and do its magic; once done, we should have an updated database with *.NET Core Identity* support.

Seeding the data

Regardless of the option we chose to update the database, we now have to repopulate it. Run the project in debug mode and let the DbSeeder work its magic; as soon as you're able to see the Home view full of quizzes, go to the **SQL Server Object Explorer** in Visual Studio, navigate to the **TestMakerFree** database, and check for the presence of the following:

- Six new DB tables: AspNetRoleClaims, AspNetRoles, AspNetUserClaims, AspNetUserLogins, AspNetUserRoles, and AspNetUserTokens
- Four rows within the Users table: Solice, Vodan, Ryan, and of course, Admin
- A whole lot of new columns in the *Users* table: from AccessFailedCount to TwoFactorEnabled:

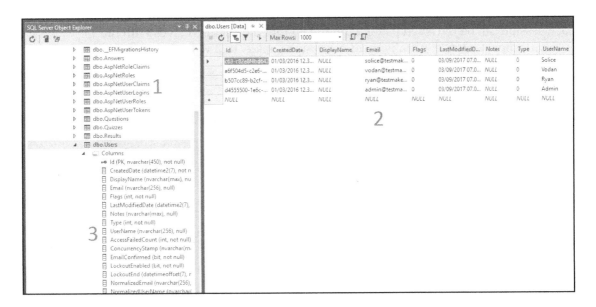

Bingo! Our *ASP.NET Core Identity* service is up, running, and fully integrated with our data model; now we just need to implement it within our controllers and hook it up with our Angular client app.

Authentication methods

Now that we have updated our database to support the .NET Core Identity authentication workflow and patterns, we should choose which authentication method to implement.

As we most certainly know, the HTTP protocol is *stateless*, meaning that whatever we do during a request/response cycle will be lost before the subsequent request, including the authentication result. The only way we have to overcome this is to store that result somewhere, along with all its relevant data, such as user ID, login date/time, and last request time.

Sessions

Since a few years ago, the most common and traditional method to do that was to store this data on the server using either a memory-based, disk-based, or external session manager. Each session can be retrieved using a unique ID that the client receives with the authentication response, usually inside a session cookie, that will be transmitted to the server on each subsequent request.

Here's a brief diagram showing the **Session-Based Authentication Flow**:

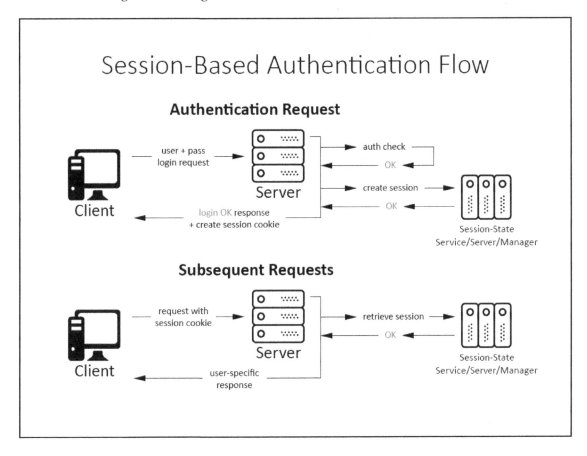

This is still a very common technique used by most web applications. There's nothing wrong with adopting this approach, as long as we are okay with its widely acknowledged downsides, such as the following:

- **Memory issues**: Whenever there are many authenticated users, the web server will consume more and more memory. Even if we use a file-based or external session provider, there will nonetheless be an intensive IO, TCP, or socket overhead.
- **Scalability issues**: Replicating a session provider in a scalable web farm might not be an easy task and will often lead to bottlenecks or wasted resources.

- **Cross-domain issues**: Session cookies behave just like standard cookies, so they cannot be easily shared among different origins/domains. These kinds of problems can often be solved with some workarounds, yet they will often lead to insecure scenarios to make things work.
- **Security issues**: There is a wide and detailed literature of security-related issues involving sessions and session cookies: XSS attacks, cross-site request forgery, and a number of other threats that won't be covered here for the sake of simplicity. Most of them can be mitigated by some countermeasures, yet they can be difficult to handle for first-hand developers.

As these issues arose over the years, there's no doubt that most analysts and developers put effort into figuring out different approaches.

Tokens

Token-based authentication has been increasingly adopted by single-page applications and mobile apps in the last few years for a number of undeniably good reasons that we'll try to briefly summarize here.

The most important difference between session-based authentication and token-based authentication is that the latter is *stateless*, meaning that we won't be storing any user-specific information on the server memory, database, session provider, or other data containers of any sort.

This single aspect solves most of the downsides that we pointed out earlier for session-based authentication. We won't have sessions, so there won't be an increasing overhead; we won't need a session provider, so scaling will be much easier. Also, for browsers supporting `LocalStorage`, we won't be even using cookies, so we won't get blocked by *cross-origin* restrictive policies and, hopefully, we'll get around most security issues.

Here's a typical **Token-Based Authentication Flow**:

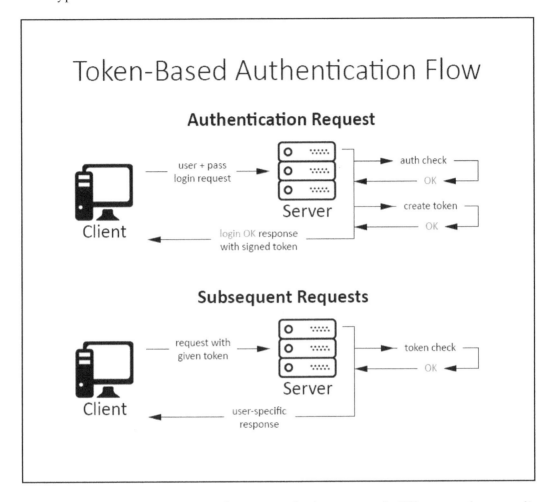

In terms of client-server interaction, these steps don't seem much different to the preceding diagram; apparently, the only difference is that we'll be issuing and checking tokens instead of creating and retrieving sessions. The real deal is happening (or not happening) at server-side level. We can immediately see that the token-based auth flow does not rely upon a stateful session-state server, service or manager. This will easily translate into a considerable boost in terms of performance and scalability.

Signatures

This is a method used by most modern API-based cloud-computing and storage services, including **Amazon Web Services (AWS)**. In contrast with session-based and token-based approaches, that rely upon a transport layer that can be theoretically accessed by/exposed to a third-party attacker, signature-based authentication performs a hash of the whole request using a previously shared `private` key. This ensures that no intruder or man-in-the-middle can ever act as the requesting user, as they won't be able to sign the request.

Two-factor

This is the standard `authentication` method used by most banking and financial accounts, being arguably the most secure one. The implementation may vary, but it always relies upon the following base workflow:

- The user performs a standard login with a username and password
- The server identifies the user and prompts them with an additional, user-specific request that can be only satisfied by something obtained or obtainable through a different channel: an OTP password sent by SMS, a unique authentication card with a number of answer codes, a dynamic PIN generated by a proprietary device or a mobile app, and so on
- If the user gives the correct answer, they get authenticated using a standard session-based or token-based method

Conclusions

After reviewing all these authentication methods, we'll use a token-based authentication approach featuring **JSON Web Tokens (JWT)**, as it seems the most viable one for our specific scenario.

JWT is a JSON-based open standard explicitly designed for native web applications, available in multiple languages, such as .NET, Python, Java, PHP, Ruby, JavaScript/NodeJS, and PERL. We're choosing it because it's becoming a de facto standard for token authentication, as it's natively supported by most technologies.

 For specific details about JWT, we recommend reading `https://jwt.io/`.

Implementing JWT authentication

In order to handle JWT-based token authentication, we need to properly set up the ASP.NET Core Identity service to ensure that it will handle these tasks:

- **Generate** a JWT token upon each username/password `POST` request coming from our clients
- **Validate** any JWT token coming with `HTTP` requests by looking at the headers of the request itself

That said, the first thing to do is define the required steps we need to take care of:

1. Add and configure the authentication service in the `Startup.cs` file.

2. Update the `appsettings.json` and `appsettings.Development.json` files to store the required JWT security information (issuer and security key).

3. Create a `TokenController` that will accept `POST` requests carrying the user credentials (username and password), validate them, and generate JWT tokens accordingly.

4. Create an Angular `LoginComponent` with a Model-Driven login form to allow our users to perform the login.

5. Create an Angular `AuthService` that will handle login/logout and store the JWT token so it can be reused.

6. Find a way to add the JWT Bearer token (if present) to the `headers` block of each request.

Sounds like a plan...let's do this! It goes without saying that the first three tasks affect the server-side part of our web application and are therefore meant to be done using .NET Core, while the remaining three are mostly related to our client-side Angular app.

Add the auth service to the .NET Core Startup class

Those coming from ASP.NET Core 1.x should remember that in order to configure authorization, we had to register and configure the auth middleware within the `Configure` method in the `Startup` class; each authentication scheme did require its own dedicated section to initialize and configure with the relevant settings--cookie names, URI endpoints, and so on.

In ASP.NET Core 2.x, the approach is slightly different: the authentication process is now configured via *services*, hence we have to register each scheme--along with its configuration settings--in the `ConfigureServices` method within the `Startup.cs` file. We still have to add the `AuthenticationMiddleware` to the `HTTP` request pipeline, but it's the only thing we have to do there.

From **Solution Explorer**, open the `Startup.cs` file, navigate through the `ConfigureServices` method and append the following lines, just below the *Add ASP.NET Identity support* block:

```
[...]

using Microsoft.AspNetCore.Authentication.JwtBearer;
using Microsoft.IdentityModel.Tokens;
using System.Text;

[...]

// Add Authentication with JWT Tokens
services.AddAuthentication(opts =>
{
    opts.DefaultScheme = JwtBearerDefaults.AuthenticationScheme;
    opts.DefaultAuthenticateScheme =
JwtBearerDefaults.AuthenticationScheme;
    opts.DefaultChallengeScheme = JwtBearerDefaults.AuthenticationScheme;
})
.AddJwtBearer(cfg =>
{
    cfg.RequireHttpsMetadata = false;
    cfg.SaveToken = true;
    cfg.TokenValidationParameters = new TokenValidationParameters()
    {
        // standard configuration
        ValidIssuer = Configuration["Auth:Jwt:Issuer"],
        ValidAudience = Configuration["Auth:Jwt:Audience"],
        IssuerSigningKey = new SymmetricSecurityKey(
```

```
                Encoding.UTF8.GetBytes(Configuration["Auth:Jwt:Key"])),
                ClockSkew = TimeSpan.Zero,

                // security switches
                RequireExpirationTime = true,
                ValidateIssuer = true,
                ValidateIssuerSigningKey = true,
                ValidateAudience = true
            };
        });

        [...]
```

What we did here was to add the authentication support, configuring the default authentication schemes, and added the JWT authentication type. Note how we split the JWT Bearer configuration settings into two parts: the standard configuration, where we have set up the required settings, and the security switches, which can be optionally set to `false` to ease the debug process--in case the token fails to validate--to quickly understand the failure reason(s).

 Note that in ASP.NET Core 2.x, multiple auth types can now be chained using fluent code syntax, so we can even accept something else beside JWT tokens; we'll make good use of this convenient feature later on.

Don't miss the highlighted lines in the preceding code; they're supposed to fetch something from the `AppSettings` configuration file that doesn't exist yet, but will do soon.

We're not done with the `Startup.cs` file; we still need to add the authentication middleware to the HTTP pipeline. Scroll down to the `Configure` method and add the following highlighted lines right before the MVC middleware:

```
        [...]

        // Add the AuthenticationMiddleware to the pipeline
        app.UseAuthentication();

        app.UseMvc(routes =>

        [...]
```

Now we're done.

Updating the AppSettings files

The next thing to do is to add those missing `AppSettings` values that we're already looking for in the `Startup` class. Open the `appsettings.json` file and add the following lines to the existing JSON configuration object (new lines are highlighted):

```
[...]

{
  "Data": {
    "DefaultConnection": {
      "ConnectionString": "Data Source=(localdb)\\MSSQLLocalDB;Initial
Catalog=TestMakerFree;Integrated Security=True;
MultipleActiveResultSets=True"
    }
  },
  "Auth": {
    "Jwt": {
      "Issuer": "http://www.testmakerfree.com/",
      "Audience": "http://www.testmakerfree.com/",
      "Key": "---insert-your-own-key-here---"
      "TokenExpirationInMinutes": 86400
    }
  },
  "Logging": {

[...]
```

For demonstration purposes, we did set the `TokenExpirationInMinutes` with a value of 60 days; you're highly encouraged to opt for a shorter value for any production-wise scenario!

These settings will be good for the published version of our app, but won't work in our local development environment. To fix that, open the `appsettings.Development.json` file and add the alternative configuration:

```
[...]

  "Auth": {
    "Jwt": {
      "Issuer": "http://localhost:14600/",
      "Audience": "http://localhost:14600/",
    }
  },

[...]
```

This uses the same keys, but different issuer.

The TokenController

The next step will be to add a `TokenController` to issue and refresh tokens. Ideally speaking, it will be a good idea to inherit it from the `BaseApiController` base class we put together back in Chapter 5, *Client-Server Interactions*, so we can access our `ApplicationDbContext`. However, we will definitely need even more than that; since we'll be working with users, it would be nice to also have an (injected) instance of that `UserManager` class we did use when working on our `DbSeeder` class. On top of that, we'll definitely need to access the JWT configuration values we put in the `AppSettings` files a moment ago.

In order to have access to all these objects, we can choose between three possible approaches:

1. Inject all this stuff in the `TokenController` constructor.
2. Upgrade our existing `BaseApiController` class, empowering it with the DI object instances we need.
3. Create another base controller class, similar to `BaseApiController` but with more stuff, and inherit the `TokenController` from it.

The former approach is viable enough, yet it has a minor issue--if we work on the `TokenController` only, we'll lose the chance to get the job done in advance for all the other controllers who will need that new stuff later on. For this very reason, the other two approaches seem to be more efficient; with that in mind, in order to keep our code base as thin as possible, we'll go with option #2.

Upgrading the BaseApiController

Here's the new source code with the new DI-injected instances (new/updated lines are highlighted):

```
using System;
using Microsoft.AspNetCore.Mvc;
using Newtonsoft.Json;
using System.Collections.Generic;
using System.Linq;
using TestMakerFreeWebApp.Data;
using Mapster;
using Microsoft.AspNetCore.Identity;
```

```csharp
using Microsoft.Extensions.Configuration;

namespace TestMakerFreeWebApp.Controllers
{
    [Route("api/[controller]")]
    public class BaseApiController : Controller
    {
        #region Constructor
        public BaseApiController(
            ApplicationDbContext context,
            RoleManager<IdentityRole> roleManager,
            UserManager<ApplicationUser> userManager,
            IConfiguration configuration
            )
        {
            // Instantiate the required classes through DI
            DbContext = context;
            RoleManager = roleManager;
            UserManager = userManager;
            Configuration = configuration;

            // Instantiate a single JsonSerializerSettings object
            // that can be reused multiple times.
            JsonSettings = new JsonSerializerSettings()
            {
                Formatting = Formatting.Indented
            };

        }
        #endregion

        #region Shared Properties
        protected ApplicationDbContext DbContext { get; private set; }
        protected RoleManager<IdentityRole> RoleManager { get; private
            set; }
        protected UserManager<ApplicationUser> UserManager { get;
            private set; }
        protected IConfiguration Configuration { get; private set; }
        protected JsonSerializerSettings JsonSettings { get; private
            set; }
        #endregion
    }
}
```

After all the DI we've been through, we can easily understand what we did here, so let's go ahead.

Reflecting the upgrade on the affected controllers

Needless to say, these changes to the `BaseApiController` will break all the derived controllers; in order to fix that, replace their constructor in the following way (new/changed lines are highlighted):

```
[...]

#region Constructor
public QuizController(
    ApplicationDbContext context,
    RoleManager<IdentityRole> roleManager,
    UserManager<ApplicationUser> userManager,
    IConfiguration configuration
    )
    : base(context, roleManager, userManager, configuration) { }
#endregion

[...]
```

These changes are valid for the `QuizController` class; the same exact code will also fix the `AnswerController`, `QuestionController`, and `ResultController` code, as long as we remember to change the controller name in the constructor. Once done, our code will be able to compile again, and we'll be free to proceed with the main dish.

Adding the TokenController

From **Solution Explorer**, right-click on the `/Controllers/` folder and select **Add | New Item**, expand the ASP.NET Core node to the left, pick the `Web API Controller` class, call it `TokenController.cs`, and click on **OK** to create it. Here's the full source code of the new controller class (relevant lines are highlighted):

```
using System;
using System.Collections.Generic;
using System.Linq;
using System.Threading.Tasks;
using Microsoft.AspNetCore.Mvc;
using System.Reflection.Metadata;
using TestMakerFreeWebApp.ViewModels;
using TestMakerFreeWebApp.Data;
using Microsoft.AspNetCore.Identity;
using System.IdentityModel.Tokens.Jwt;
using System.Security.Claims;
using Microsoft.Extensions.Configuration;
using Microsoft.IdentityModel.Tokens;
```

```
using System.Text;

namespace TestMakerFreeWebApp.Controllers
{
    public class TokenController : BaseApiController
    {
        #region Private Members
        #endregion Private Members

        #region Constructor
        public TokenController(
            ApplicationDbContext context,
            RoleManager<IdentityRole> roleManager,
            UserManager<ApplicationUser> userManager,
            IConfiguration configuration
            )
            : base(context, roleManager, userManager, configuration) {
            }
        #endregion

        [HttpPost("Auth")]
        public async Task<IActionResult>
         Jwt([FromBody]TokenRequestViewModel model)
        {
            // return a generic HTTP Status 500 (Server Error)
            // if the client payload is invalid.
            if (model == null) return new StatusCodeResult(500);

            switch (model.grant_type)
            {
                case "password":
                    return await GetToken(model);
                default:
                    // not supported - return a HTTP 401 (Unauthorized)
                    return new UnauthorizedResult();
            }
        }

        private async Task<IActionResult>
           GetToken(TokenRequestViewModel model)
        {
            try
            {
                // check if there's an user with the given username
                var user = await
                UserManager.FindByNameAsync(model.username);
                // fallback to support e-mail address instead of
                                username
```

```
if (user == null && model.username.Contains("@"))
    user = await
    UserManager.FindByEmailAsync(model.username);


if (user == null
    || !await UserManager.CheckPasswordAsync(user,
    model.password))
{
    // user does not exists or password mismatch
    return new UnauthorizedResult();
}

// username & password matches: create and return the
 Jwt token.

DateTime now = DateTime.UtcNow;

// add the registered claims for JWT (RFC7519).
// For more info, see
  https://tools.ietf.org/html/rfc7519#section-4.1
var claims = new[] {
    new Claim(JwtRegisteredClaimNames.Sub, user.Id),
    new Claim(JwtRegisteredClaimNames.Jti,
     Guid.NewGuid().ToString()),
    new Claim(JwtRegisteredClaimNames.Iat,
        new
    DateTimeOffset(now).ToUnixTimeSeconds().ToString())
    // TODO: add additional claims here
};

var tokenExpirationMins =
    Configuration.GetValue<int>
     ("Auth:Jwt:TokenExpirationInMinutes");
var issuerSigningKey = new SymmetricSecurityKey(
Encoding.UTF8.GetBytes(Configuration["Auth:Jwt:Key"]));

var token = new JwtSecurityToken(
    issuer: Configuration["Auth:Jwt:Issuer"],
    audience: Configuration["Auth:Jwt:Audience"],
    claims: claims,
    notBefore: now,
    expires:
   now.Add(TimeSpan.FromMinutes(tokenExpirationMins)),
    signingCredentials: new SigningCredentials(
        issuerSigningKey,
     SecurityAlgorithms.HmacSha256)
);
```

```
                    var encodedToken = new
                    JwtSecurityTokenHandler().WriteToken(token);

                    // build & return the response
                    var response = new TokenResponseViewModel()
                    {
                        token = encodedToken,
                        expiration = tokenExpirationMins
                    };
                    return Json(response);
                }
                catch (Exception ex)
                {
                    return new UnauthorizedResult();
                }
            }
        }
    }
```

Despite the remarkable amount of code, the `TokenController` does nothing really special. The comments already explain most of the tasks, yet it can't hurt to quickly summarize what we did:

- The whole workflow is triggered by the `Auth()` action method, which will intercept a `POST HTTP` request containing a set of parameters depicted in the `TokenRequestViewModel` class, which we'll see in a short while. This is the information that we expect when a client service is asking for a JWT token; we'll talk more about it later on.

- The `Jwt` method will check the `GrantType` parameter value; in case of the password, it will execute the `GetToken` internal method that will generate a new token, otherwise it will respond with a **HTTP error 500** and quit.

- The `GetToken` method is where most of the magic takes place; it checks the username and password that came with the `POST` request against our identity data and, depending on the result, either generates a token and returns it within a JSON object built upon the `TokenResponseViewModel` class--which we'll be seeing shortly--or quits with an **HTTP error 401 Unauthorized**.

As we can easily guess, our new `TokenController` won't compile unless we add the two `ViewModel` classes that we mentioned as well for this very reason; the next step will be to add them.

The TokenRequestViewModel

Let's start adding the former one, that contains the parameters that will come from the client when trying to authenticate itself. From **Solution Explorer**, right-click on the /ViewModels/ folder and add a new TokenRequestViewModel.cs file with the following content:

```csharp
using Newtonsoft.Json;

namespace TestMakerFreeWebApp.ViewModels
{
    [JsonObject(MemberSerialization.OptOut)]
    public class TokenRequestViewModel
    {
        #region Constructor
        public TokenRequestViewModel()
        {

        }
        #endregion

        #region Properties
        public string grant_type { get; set; }
        public string client_id { get; set; }
        public string client_secret { get; set; }
        public string username { get; set; }
        public string password { get; set; }
        #endregion
    }
}
```

The TokenResponseViewModel

Once done, perform the same steps to add the TokenResponseViewModel, which is the POCO class hosting the parameters returned to the client by the server after a successful login:

```csharp
using Newtonsoft.Json;

namespace TestMakerFreeWebApp.ViewModels
{
    [JsonObject(MemberSerialization.OptOut)]
    public class TokenResponseViewModel
    {
        #region Constructor
        public TokenResponseViewModel()
```

```
        {

        }
        #endregion

        #region Properties
        public string token { get; set; }
        public int expiration { get; set; }
        #endregion
    }
}
```

This concludes the ASP.NET Core part of our job. Before switching to Angular, we can spend some valuable time to briefly test it using Postman.

Testing with Postman

For those who don't know it, **Postman** is a lightweight REST client that can be used to test basically any HTTP API; in our specific scenario, we can use it to send custom GET, POST, PUT, or DELETE HTTP requests to our app and see how our server-side .NET Core controllers will handle them.

 Postman can be installed either as a standalone app or a Chrome extension; both versions have the same features and will work in the same way, so we're free to choose what we like the most. In this example, we'll use the *stand-alone* app that can be downloaded from the https://www. getpostman.com/ official website. If you prefer to use the Chrome extension, you can find it at https://chrome.google.com/webstore/ detail/postman/fhbjgbiflinjbdggehcddcbncdddomop.

Once installed, run the application (or the Chrome extension) and wait for the animated splash screen to take its course; right after that, you'll be presented with a welcome screen, when you'll be asked to sign up for a free account or go straight to the app. Registration isn't mandatory to do what we have to do, so we're free to choose what we want; both routes will eventually take us to the main application screen.

From there, we can set up a basic POST HTTP request to test our TokenController in the following way:

- Select the **Builder** tab from the top of the main screen; a multi-panel, browser-like window should appear, with something resembling an address bar near the upper panel's top and a flat tab panel right below it.

- Select **POST** from the drop-down list to the left of the address bar, then type in the following address to the immediate right:
  `http://localhost:<port>/api/token/auth`. Do not press *Enter* and don't click on the **Send** button yet.
- Select **Body** from the tab panel just below the address bar; a checkbox list should appear. Activate the **raw** checkbox, and then select **JSON (application/json)** from the drop-down list to the right.
- Type the following code within the text area right below the checkbox list:

```
{
  "username":"Admin",
  "password":"Pass4Admin",
  "grant_type":"password"
}
```

If we did everything correctly, our **Postman** screen should look just like the one depicted in the following screenshot:

If everything is looking good, switch to Visual Studio, run the project in *debug* mode, and wait for the *Home* view to appear; as soon as you see the quiz listings, switch back to **Postman** and click on the blue **Send** button to the right of the address bar and look to the **Response** panel. If everything worked out well, we should be able to see our JWT Token wrapped in a JSON object:

```
{
    "token":
"eyJhbGciOiJIUzI1NiIsInR5cCI6IkpXVCJ9.eyJpc3MiOiJsb2NhbGhvc3QiLCJzdWIiOiJBZ
G1pbiIsImp0aSI6ImViMTQxOGFiLTRhMzgtNGIxNS1iMzA4LWY0ZmIwODI2NDZiZiIsImlhdCI6
MTUwNDUwMDM3NSwibmJmIjoxNTA0NTAwMzc1LCJleHAiOjE1MDQ1MDM5NzV9.2XFA3Y243Tpfr_
c_NusduQvdHLztt2vevzttd_Y5YnI",
    "expiration": 60
}
```

This is the HTTP response body returned by the Auth() action method of our TokenController; we can also take a look at the headers by selecting the appropriate tab within that screen.

In the unlikely case that we're not getting the expected result, we can use the server-side debug features of Visual Studio to see what happens behind the scenes until we figure it out.

As soon as we're done with **Postman**, we can finally switch to the other REST client we're expected to connect our *ASP.NET Identity* service with--our beloved Angular SPA.

Angular login form

Ideally, the next step would be to add a proper login form to the currently not implemented-*yet* LoginComponent, which has been around as an empty skeleton since Chapter 3, *Frontend with Angular*. However, before doing that, we need to provide our Angular SPA with a TokenResponse interface--to handle the TokenResponseViewModel in a strongly-typed fashion--and an AuthService class where we will centralize all the auth-related methods, such as login, logout, and isLoggedIn.

The TokenResponse interface

From **Solution Explorer**, right-click on the /ClientApp/app/services/ folder and add a token.response.ts TypeScript file with the following content:

```
interface TokenResponse {
    token: string,
    expiration: number
}
```

The AuthService class

This will be our first Angular service; we should be excited!

From **Solution Explorer**, navigate to the /ClientApp/app/ folder and create a /services/ subfolder within it. Right-click on the new folder and add an auth.service.ts TypeScript file; then, fill it with the following code (relevant lines are highlighted):

```
import { EventEmitter, Inject, Injectable, PLATFORM_ID } from
"@angular/core";
import { isPlatformBrowser } from '@angular/common';
import { HttpClient, HttpHeaders } from "@angular/common/http";
import { Observable } from "rxjs";
import 'rxjs/Rx';

@Injectable()
export class AuthService {
    authKey: string = "auth";
    clientId: string = "TestMakerFree";

    constructor(private http: HttpClient,
        @Inject(PLATFORM_ID) private platformId: any) {
    }

    // performs the login
    login(username: string, password: string): Observable<boolean> {
        var url = "api/auth/jwt";
        var data = {
            username: username,
            password: password,
            client_id: clientId,
            // required when signing up with username/password
            grant_type: "password",
            // space-separated list of scopes for which the token is
             issued
```

```
                scope: "offline_access profile email"
        };

        return this.http.post<TokenResponse>(url, data)
            .map((res) => {
                let token = res && res.token;
                // if the token is there, login has been successful
                if (token) {
                    // store username and jwt token
                    this.setAuth(res);
                    // successful login
                    return true;
                }

                // failed login
                return Observable.throw('Unauthorized');
            })
            .catch(error => {
                return new Observable<any>(error);
            });
    }
}
```

The highlighted lines do reveal the hot stuff here:

- The isPlatformBrowser is an Angular function that, when fed with an instance of the PLATFORM_ID token obtained through DI, returns **true** if the execution context represents a browser platform: this is something we'll need to know very soon.
- The real magic happens within the login() method, which is in charge of issuing the HTTP POST request to the Auth method of our TokenController and performing the authentication using the username and password received by the caller. If the login happens, the relevant data (username and token) will be saved in the browser's localStorage--via the setAuth() method, which we'll see in a while--and the method will return true, otherwise it will throw an error that that will be handled by the caller accordingly.

Now that we understand how the login() method works, we can add the remaining logic. Append the following content below the previous code, just before the end of the class:

```
[...]

// performs the logout
logout(): boolean {
    this.setAuth(null);
    return true;
```

```
    }

    // Persist auth into localStorage or removes it if a NULL argument is given
    setAuth(auth: TokenResponse | null): boolean {
        if (isPlatformBrowser(this.platformId)) {
            if (auth) {
                localStorage.setItem(
                    this.authKey,
                    JSON.stringify(auth));
            }
            else {
                localStorage.removeItem(this.authKey);
            }
        }
        return true;
    }

    // Retrieves the auth JSON object (or NULL if none)
    getAuth(): TokenResponse | null {
        if (isPlatformBrowser(this.platformId)) {
            var i = localStorage.getItem(this.authKey);
            if (i) {
                return JSON.parse(i);
            }
        }
        return null;
    }

    // Returns TRUE if the user is logged in, FALSE otherwise.
    isLoggedIn(): boolean {
        if (isPlatformBrowser(this.platformId)) {
            return localStorage.getItem(this.authKey) != null;
        }
        return false;
    }

    [...]
```

As we can see by looking at the preceding code, we added three methods that will actually access the localStorage: setAuth(), getAuth(), and isLoggedIn(). The first one is in charge of the insert, update, and delete operations; the second will retrieve the auth JSON object (if any); and the last one can be used to check whether the current user is authenticated or not without having to JSON.parse the entire object again. There's also a fourth method--logout()--which is basically a shortcut for setAuth(null).

It's worth noting how all these methods will only provide access to the localStorage if the executing context is a browser platform: this is what isPlatformBrowser and

PLATFORM_ID are there for. This is just a safety net that prevents our code from creating potential issues with the *server-side prerendering* of our angular app performed by ASP.NET Core, which won't be able to deal properly with browser-specific features and *browser types*. This JavaScript coding approach is called *isomorphic* and it's a required pattern when developing an *Angular Universal* application, which is expected to run on *client-side* and *server-side*.

For more info about **Angular Universal** and **isomorphic JavaScript** check out the following resources:
https://universal.angular.io
http://isomorphic.net/javascript
https://github.com/angular/universal#angular-universal

For those who have never heard of it, the localStorage object is part of HTML5's Web Storage API; more specifically, it's a local caching object that keeps its content with no given expiration date. That's a great way to store our JWT-related JSON response, as we want to keep it even when the browser is closed. Before doing that, we choose to convert it into a string using JSON.stringify, since not all localStorage browser implementations can store JSON-type objects flawlessly. It's also worth mentioning that, instead of relying on the localStorage, we can use the sessionStorage object, that stores data only until the currently active session ends. However, that will mean deleting the token whenever the user closes the specific browser tab, which is hardly a desirable behavior for a SPA.

It's worth noting how all these methods will only provide access to the localStorage if the executing context is a browser platform: this is what isPlatformBrowser and PLATFORM_ID are there for. This is just a safety net that prevents our code from creating potential issues with the *server-side prerendering* of our angular app performed by ASP.NET Core, which won't be able to deal properly with browser-specific features and *browser types*. For more info about this specific topic, check out the Angular Universal paragraph in Chapter 9, *Advanced Topics*.

This quick localStorage implementation might be good for our sample SPA, but it could raise some performance issues in request-intensive scenarios as it gets the job done in a *synchronous* way, just like the *localStorage API* natively does. In case we want to adopt a better approach we can use the clever angular-async-local-storage NPM package by *Cyrille Tuzi*, which wraps the whole API into *RxJS Observables* to be homogeneous with the Angular way of doing things. For more info about this brilliant project, check out the following URL: https://www.npmjs.com/package/angular-async-local-storage

Updating the AppModule

As always, we won't be able to use the AuthService unless we add the required reference to the AppModule class. Open the app.module.shared.ts file and update it by adding the following highlighted lines:

```
[...]

import { RouterModule } from '@angular/router';
import { AuthService } from './services/auth.service';
import { AppComponent } from './components/app/app.component';

[...]

imports: [
    CommonModule,
    HttpClientModule,
    FormsModule,
    ReactiveFormsModule,
    RouterModule.forRoot([
        { path: '', redirectTo: 'home', pathMatch: 'full' },
        { path: 'home', component: HomeComponent },
        { path: 'quiz/create', component: QuizEditComponent },
        { path: 'quiz/edit/:id', component: QuizEditComponent },
        { path: 'quiz/:id', component: QuizComponent },
        { path: 'question/create/:id', component: QuestionEditComponent
                                },
        { path: 'question/edit/:id', component: QuestionEditComponent
                                },
        { path: 'answer/create/:id', component: AnswerEditComponent },
        { path: 'answer/edit/:id', component: AnswerEditComponent },
        { path: 'result/create/:id', component: ResultEditComponent },
        { path: 'result/edit/:id', component: ResultEditComponent },
        { path: 'about', component: AboutComponent },
        { path: 'login', component: LoginComponent },
        { path: '**', component: PageNotFoundComponent }
    ])
],
providers: [
    AuthService
]

[...]
```

That's it.

The new LoginComponent

From **Solution Explorer**, navigate to the `/ClientApp/app/components/login/` folder and open the `login.component.ts` file; replace the current content with this brand-new login form:

```
<div class="login-container">
    <img id="login-img" class="login-img"
        src="//ssl.gstatic.com/accounts/ui/avatar_2x.png" />
    <h2 class="login-title">{{title}}</h2>
    <form [formGroup]="form"
          (ngSubmit)="onSubmit()"
          class="login-form">
        <div *ngIf="form.errors?.auth"
            class="error-panel help-block">
            {{form.errors.auth}}
        </div>
        <div class="form-group"
            [ngClass]="{ 'has-error has-feedback' :
             hasError('Username') }">
            <input type="text" required
                   formControlName="Username"
                   class="form-control"
                   placeholder="Username or Email address" />
            <span *ngIf="hasError('Username')"
                class="glyphicon glyphicon-remove form-control-
                feedback"
                aria-hidden="true"></span>
            <div *ngIf="hasError('Username')"
                 class="help-block">
                Please insert a valid username or e-mail address.
            </div>
        </div>
        <div class="form-group"
            [ngClass]="{ 'has-error has-feedback' :
                hasError('Password') }">
            <input type="password" required
                   formControlName="Password"
                   class="form-control"
                   placeholder="Password" />
            <span *ngIf="hasError('Password')"
                class="glyphicon glyphicon-remove form-control-
                            feedback"
                aria-hidden="true"></span>
            <div *ngIf="hasError('Password')"
                 class="help-block">
                Please insert a password.
            </div>
        </div>
```

```
            </div>
            <div class="checkbox">
                <label><input type="checkbox" name="remember"
                    value="remember" />Remember me</label>
            </div>
            <button type="submit"
                    [disabled]="form.invalid"
                    class="btn btn-md btn-success btn-block btn-signin">
                Sign in
            </button>
        </form>
        <div class="login-link">
            <a href="#">
                Forgot the password?
            </a>
        </div>
    </div>
</div>
```

The preceding source code resembles the other form-based templates, with a small difference: we added a validation message for the whole form, that will trigger in case of `this.form.error?.auth`. We'll understand it better in a short while, when we'll take a look at the TypeScript class file; for now, let's just take for granted that it will be shown whenever that error will be raised, making the form invalid.

Here's the `login.component.ts` class file (relevant lines are highlighted):

```
import { Component, Inject } from "@angular/core";
import { FormGroup, FormControl, FormBuilder, Validators } from
'@angular/forms';
import { Router } from "@angular/router";
import { AuthService } from '../../services/auth.service';

@Component({
    selector: "login",
    templateUrl: "./login.component.html",
    styleUrls: ['./login.component.css']
})

export class LoginComponent {
    title: string;
    form: FormGroup;

    constructor(private router: Router,
        private fb: FormBuilder,
        private authService: AuthService,
        @Inject('BASE_URL') private baseUrl: string) {
```

```
        this.title = "User Login";

        // initialize the form
        this.createForm();

    }

    createForm() {
        this.form = this.fb.group({
            Username: ['', Validators.required],
            Password: ['', Validators.required]
        });
    }

    onSubmit() {
        var url = this.baseUrl + "api/token/auth";
        var username = this.form.value.Username;
        var password = this.form.value.Password;

        this.authService.login(username, password)
            .subscribe(res => {
                // login successful

                // outputs the login info through a JS alert.
                // IMPORTANT: remove this when test is done.
                alert("Login successful! "
                    + "USERNAME: "
                    + username
                    + " TOKEN: "
                    + this.authService.getAuth()!.token
                );

                this.router.navigate(["home"]);
            },
            err => {
                // login failed
                console.log(err)
                this.form.setErrors({
                    "auth": "Incorrect username or password"
                });
            });
    }

    onBack() {
        this.router.navigate(["home"]);
    }

    // retrieve a FormControl
```

```
getFormControl(name: string) {
    return this.form.get(name);
}

// returns TRUE if the FormControl is valid
isValid(name: string) {
    var e = this.getFormControl(name);
    return e && e.valid;
}

// returns TRUE if the FormControl has been changed
isChanged(name: string) {
    var e = this.getFormControl(name);
    return e && (e.dirty || e.touched);
}

// returns TRUE if the FormControl is invalid after user changes
hasError(name: string) {
    var e = this.getFormControl(name);
    return e && (e.dirty || e.touched) && !e.valid;
}
}
```

The highlighted lines show how we're using our new `AuthService` object instance--which we inject through DI--to attempt the login tasks and returning the result. Note that we also implemented a temporary JavaScript `alert()` to show the successful login information right before routing back the user to the Home view; we'll remove it as soon as we see that everything works as expected.

 It's worth noting that the `authService.login()` method is returning an *Observable* with a value of `true` or `false` depending on result; by subscribing to that Observable, the `LoginComponent` class is able to tell how the login went and set the `form.errors.auth` value accordingly; that's precisely the error that will trigger the global validator message we configured earlier.

Last but not least, here's the new content of the LESS file. Note that we never added a `login.component.less` file to the project before, hence we'll have to create it from scratch:

```
.login-container {
    max-width: 600px;
    padding: 40px 40px;
    background-color: #F7F7F7;
    margin: 0 0 25px 0;
    border-radius: 10px;
```

```
        border: 1px solid #eee;

        .login-img {
            width: 96px;
            height: 96px;
            margin: 0 auto 10px;
            display: block;
            border-radius: 50%;
        }

        .login-title {
            margin: 15px 0;
            text-align: center;
            font-size: 1.5em;
            color: #444;
        }

        .login-link {
            margin-top: 10px;
            text-align: center;
        }

        .login-form {
            .form-group {
                margin-bottom: 8px;
            }

            .error-panel {
                color: #e74c3c;
                text-align: center;
            }
        }
    }

@media (max-width: 767px) {
    .login-container {
        width: 100%;
    }
}
```

First login test

Although we're not done yet, it's now a good time to perform a first login test. This will definitely help us better visualize what we're doing and also understand what we're still missing.

Before proceeding with the login, it's strongly advisable to place some debugging breakpoints to cover the following key spots of our app:

1. At the beginning of the onSubmit method of LoginComponent, that occurs when the <form> is submitted (Angular).
2. At the beginning of the Login method of AuthService, that will issue the HTTP POST request (Angular).
3. At the beginning of the Auth() method of TokenController, that will receive the POST, validate the credentials against the ASP.NET Identity DB tables and respond accordingly (ASP.NET).
4. Within the map method of AuthService, which will handle the result of the HTTP POST asynchronously (Angular).
5. Within the subscribe method of LoginComponent, which will redirect the user to the *Home* view or set up a form validation error depending on the login result (Angular).

Once done, run the project in debug mode and click on the **Login** menu item in the panel to the left; you should see something like the following:

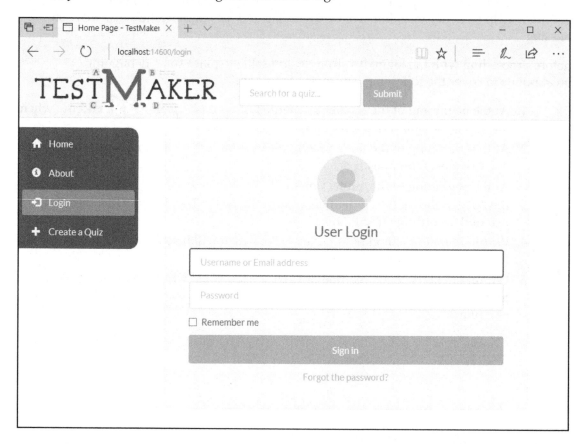

To be completely honest, the **Remember me** and **Forgot the password?** functions are not working yet, but we'll fix those in due time. For now, let's focus on the actual login phase. Start with a non-existing username, such as `TestUser`; type in any password, click on the **Sign in** button and get ready to go through all the breakpoints. In this phase, we need to do our best to check each single variable to ensure that everything is working fine.

At the end of the whole process, we should receive an error message just like the following one:

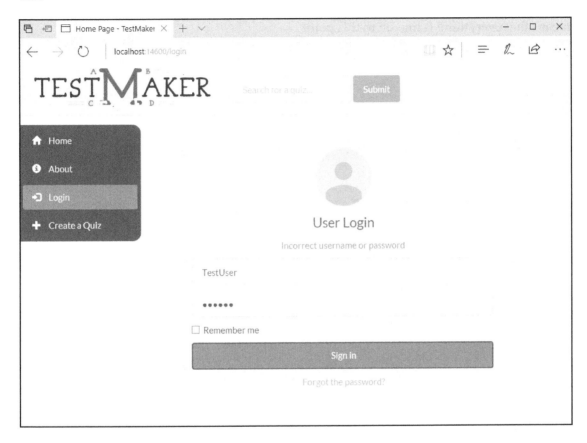

That's perfectly fine, since we used a non-existing user! Right after that, repeat the whole cycle, this time with an existing user--such as **Admin**--yet with a wrong password. Carefully watch what happens as the underlying code goes on and checks that the password mismatch scenario will be properly handled by each one of our server-side and client-side actors.

Eventually, repeat the same task, this time using a valid username/password combination from those we've put into the `DbSeeder` , such as: username **Vodan**, password **Pass4Vodan**. This time you should be able to see the following JavaScript popup, which means that everything is fine up to this point:

As soon as we see that it works, it could be wise to go back to the `login.component.ts` file and remove the annoying JavaScript `alert()`, which we only used for demonstration purposes; we don't need it anymore.

If something goes wrong and we don't get the expected result, we can use the debug features of Visual Studio to find out the issue. Once done, we can check the offending code against the sources contained in this book-- or, even better, in the official GitHub repo--and fix it accordingly.

Adding the token to the HTTP request header

Like we said, we're not done yet; now that we've got the token, we need to find the proper way to pass it along with each `HTTP` request, otherwise our server-side ASP.NET controllers wouldn't be able to know that we did authenticate ourselves and that we're authorized to access some potentially restricted resources. To put it in other words, we need to tweak our current `HTTP` service to make it add our JWT token in the header portion of all our HTTP calls.

There are at least three possible ways to obtain that:

1. Update all of our Angular Components that issue `HTTP` requests to make them add the JWT token to the request header before each call.
2. Create a custom service that wraps the Angular `HttpClient` and make it append the JWT token to the headers before performing the requests.
3. Implement a `HTTP interceptor` that will act right before any request will be sent and make it append the JWT token to the headers before releasing it.

The latter option has been made available since Angular 4.3 with the release of the new `HttpClient`--which we've been proudly using since `Chapter 3`, *Frontend with Angular*, -- and is probably the most elegant, robust, and effective way to do what we want.

The AuthInterceptor class

In a nutshell, `HttpInterceptors` are something that we can use to perform modifications to our HTTP requests in a global, centralized way. The most common use case for that pattern is to automatically attach auth information to requests before they're being sent, which is definitely our scenario.

Intercepting HTTP requests has always been possible in AngularJS, yet it has been a missing feature of the new Angular 2+, thus forcing most developers into working, yet unsatisfying workarounds such as the aforementioned HTTP wrappers, helper functions returning custom Headers, and so on. With the release of Angular 4.3, the gap has been filled, thanks to the introduction of the `HttpInterceptor` interface, which is what we'll use to create our own `AuthInterceptor` class.

From **Solution Explorer**, right-click on the `/ClientApp/app/services/` folder, add the `auth.interceptor.ts` TypeScript file, and fill it with the following contents:

```
import { Injectable, Injector } from "@angular/core";
import { HttpHandler, HttpEvent, HttpInterceptor, HttpRequest } from
"@angular/common/http";
import { AuthService } from "./auth.service";
```

```
import { Observable } from "...........",

@Injectable()
export class AuthInterceptor implements HttpInterceptor {

    constructor(private injector: Injector) { }

    intercept(
        request: HttpRequest<any>,
        next: HttpHandler): Observable<HttpEvent<any>> {

        var auth = this.injector.get(AuthService);
        var token = (auth.isLoggedIn()) ? auth.getAuth()!.token : null;
        if (token) {
            request = request.clone({
                setHeaders: {
                    Authorization: `Bearer ${token}`
                }
            });
        }
        return next.handle(request);
    }
}
```

As we can see, our custom interceptor implements the `HttpInterceptor` interface and its `intercept` method, accepting the `HttpRequest` and `HttpHandler` parameters; inside the method, we clone the original request--which is immutable, thus can't be altered directly-- and add the authorization header containing our token, which we retrieve through the `getToken()` method of our `AuthService` class. Note how, once we're done, we pass the request to the next handler in the stack; a great feature of `HttpInterceptor` is that they can be easily chained, as we'll see in the next paragraph.

Adding the HttpInterceptor in the AppModule

It goes without saying that our `AuthInterceptor` class will only work if we properly configure it within our `AppModule` class. To do that, open the `app.module.shared.ts` file and add the following (new code highlighted):

```
[...]

import { HttpClientModule, HTTP_INTERCEPTORS } from '@angular/common/http';
import { RouterModule } from '@angular/router';

import { AuthService } from './services/auth.service';
import { AuthInterceptor } from './services/auth.interceptor';
```

```
[...]

providers: [
    AuthService,
    {
        provide: HTTP_INTERCEPTORS,
        useClass: AuthInterceptor,
        multi: true
    }
]

[...]
```

If we did everything correctly, now the token should be automatically added to each HTTP request. We can easily test it from the server side by placing a breakpoint at the start of the QuizController.GetLatest() method, that gets called each time the Home view is accessed:

```
154
155    #region Attribute-based routing methods
156    /// <summary>
157    /// GET: api/quiz/latest
158    /// Retrieves the {num} latest Quizzes
159    /// </summary>
160    /// <param name="num">the number of quizzes to retrieve</param>
161    /// <returns>the {num} latest Quizzes</returns>
162    [HttpGet("Latest/{num:int?}")]
163    public IActionResult Latest(int num = 10)
164    {
165        var latest = DbContext.Quizzes
166            .OrderByDescending(q => q.CreatedDate)
167            .Take(num)
168            .ToArray();
169        return new JsonResult(
170            latest.Adapt<QuizViewModel[]>(),
171            JsonSettings);
172    }
173
```

We can then run our application in debug mode and see what happens upon the first `HTTP` request:

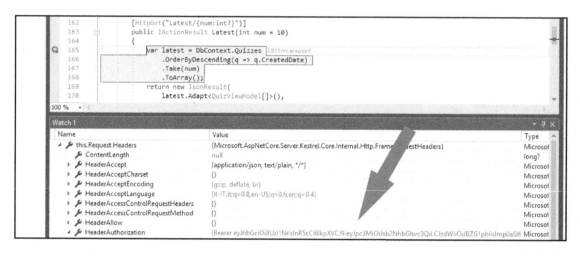

By looking into the `Request.Headers.HeaderAuthorization` property--using the Visual Studio's **Watch** window--we should be able to see our token, the same that we got back from our `TokenController` a short while ago, unless we cleared our browser's `localStorage`; in case we did that, all we need to do is visit the Login view again and perform a new login to get another token, and then try again.

As soon as we see the Bearer token, before leaving that breakpoint and ending the debug session, we should also check out the `this.User.Identity.IsAuthenticated` property, which should be set to `true` --meaning that our user has been successfully authenticated using the token.

Enforcing authorization

Now that we can be sure that our JWT-based auth implementation is working as expected, we need to define some testable auth-based navigation patterns and access rules that will allow us to differentiate the logged-in user from the anonymous one, preventing the latter from either seeing and doing something that he shouldn't be allowed to. Needless to say, we need to handle them on the client side and also on the server side.

It's actually easy to do that, since we already have some Angular components that should be made accessible to authenticated users only and vice versa--along with the .NET Core controllers they use under the hood; let's see how we can pull off that task.

Adapting the client

Let's start by updating the main menu navigation bar.

NavMenuComponent

From the `/ClientApp/app/components/navmenu/` folder, open the
`navmenu.component.ts` file and update it in the following way:

```
import { Component } from '@angular/core';
import { AuthService } from '../../services/auth.service';

@Component({
    selector: 'nav-menu',
    templateUrl: './navmenu.component.html',
    styleUrls: ['./navmenu.component.css']
})
export class NavMenuComponent {
    constructor(public auth: AuthService) {
    }
}
```

This will give us access to the `authService` instance (obtained through DI), which we can use to determine whether the current user is logged in or not.

It's worth noting that we made the `auth` instance member `public` instead of `private`. We did that because we plan to use it within the component's template file, like we'll see in a short while. Although the template is part of the component, it will be compiled as a separate class in the **Ahead-of-Time (AOT)** compilation scenario, which will be the case whenever we'll want to deploy our web app in production. For this very reason, as a general rule-of-thumb, it's always wise to set a public access level to these members--as long as we'll use them within the template file.

Right after that, open the `navmenu.component.html` template file and change its content accordingly:

```
[...]

<li *ngIf="!this.auth.isLoggedIn()"
    [routerLinkActive]="['link-active']">
    <a [routerLink]="['/login']">
        <span class='glyphicon glyphicon-log-in'></span> Login
    </a>
</li>
```

```
<li *ngIf="this.auth.isLoggedIn()"
    [routerLinkActive]="['link-active']">
    <a [routerLink]="['/quiz/create']">
        <span class='glyphicon glyphicon-plus'></span> Create a Quiz
    </a>
</li>

[...]
```

What we did here was to use a couple of *ngIf directives to selectively show or hide our content depending on whether the currently active user is logged in or not. More specifically, we don't want to display the Login link to an already logged-in user, and we also want to prevent anonymous users from accessing the *Create a Quiz* view.

While we are here, we can take the chance to give our logged-in users the chance to log out by adding a dedicated **Logout** button in the following way:

```
[...]

<li *ngIf="this.auth.isLoggedIn()">
    <a (click)="logout()">
        <span class='glyphicon glyphicon-log-out'></span> Logout
    </a>
</li>

[...]
```

We can put that <li> element anywhere within the unordered list; however, the most logical place would be just below the sibling element hosting the **Login** button link. Once done, we need to go back to the navmenu.component.ts file and add an appropriate method to handle the newly-added logout feature:

```
import { Component } from '@angular/core';
import { Router } from "@angular/router";
import { AuthService } from '../../services/auth.service';


@Component({
    selector: 'nav-menu',
    templateUrl: './navmenu.component.html',
    styleUrls: ['./navmenu.component.css']
})
export class NavMenuComponent {
    constructor(
        public auth: AuthService,
        private router: Router
    ) {
```

```
        }

    logout(): boolean {
        // logs out the user, then redirects him to Home View.
        if (this.auth.logout()) {
            this.router.navigate([""]);
        }
        return false;
    }
}
```

By looking at the highlighted code, we can see how we also had to retrieve the `Router` class (as always, through DI) to be able to redirect the logged-out user back to the Home view.

QuizComponent

The `QuizComponent` also features some **Edit** and **Delete** buttons that we should definitely hide from the sight of any non-logged in user.

Again, we need to open the `quiz.component.ts` file and do what it takes to add the `AuthService` class to the loop:

```
[...]

import { AuthService } from '../../services/auth.service';

[...]

constructor(private activatedRoute: ActivatedRoute,
    private router: Router,
    private http: HttpClient,
    public auth: AuthService,
    @Inject('BASE_URL') private baseUrl: string) {

[...]
```

We then use it to conditionally hide the `Edit` and `Delete` buttons in the `quiz.component.html` template file:

```
[...]

<div *ngIf="auth.isLoggedIn()" class="edit">
    <input type="button" value="Edit"
            (click)="onEdit()"
            class="btn btn-sm btn-warning" />
    <input type="button" value="Delete"
```

```
                    (click)="onDelete()"
                    class="btn btn-sm btn-danger" />
    </div>

    [...]
```

That's basically it.

Again, we chose to make the `auth` instance member `public` instead of `private`, since we're also using it in the template file; that way, we can ensure that it will be found even in an AOT compilation scenario.

> Before moving on to the server-side part, it would be wise to perform a quick UI test to ensure that everything is working properly. This can be easily done by launching the application in *debug* mode, perform some login and logout tasks using our existing users--*Admin, Solice, Ryan,* and *Vodan*--and see how the `NavMenuComponent` and `QuizComponent` will react.

Shielding the server

Now that our client is more or less ready, it's time to shield our .NET API controllers from unauthorized requests as well. We can easily do that using the `[Authorize]` attribute, which can be used to restrict access to any controller and/or controller method we don't want to open to unauthorized access.

To implement the required authorization behavior, it can be wise to use it on the `Put`, `Post` and `Delete` methods of all our `BaseApiController` extended classes, as follows:

```
[...]

[HttpPut]
[Authorize]
public IActionResult Put([FromBody]QuizViewModel model)

[...]

[HttpPost]
[Authorize]
public IActionResult Post([FromBody]QuizViewModel model)

[...]

[HttpDelete("{id}")]
```

```
[Authorize]
public IActionResult Delete(int id)

[...]
```

The preceding code is taken from the `QuizController`, but we need to perform the exact same upgrade on `QuestionController`, `AnswerController`, and `ResultController` as well. Don't forget to add the following required namespace reference at the beginning of each of these files:

```
using Microsoft.AspNetCore.Authorization;
```

Now all these action methods are protected against unauthorized access, as they will accept only requests coming from logged-in users/clients with a valid JWT token; those who don't have it will receive a **401 - Unauthorized HTTP error response**.

Retrieving the current user ID

Before closing the `QuizController` file, we should take the chance to remove that phony `item.UserId` value override we defined back in Chapter 5, *Client-Server Interactions*, when we had no authentication mechanism in place. The offending lines are still lying within the `Put()` method implementation:

```
[...]
// Set a temporary author using the Admin user's userId
// as user login isn't supported yet: we'll change this later on.
quiz.UserId = DbContext.Users.Where(u => u.UserName == "Admin")
    .FirstOrDefault().Id;

[...]
```

Now that we're working with real authenticated accounts, we can easily retrieve the current `userID`; if we remember correctly, we did actually put it in the JWT token claims, as we can see by taking another quick look at the `GetToken()` method of the `TokenController` class:

```
[...]

var claims = new[] {
    new Claim(JwtRegisteredClaimNames.Sub, user.Id),
    new Claim(JwtRegisteredClaimNames.Jti, Guid.NewGuid().ToString()),

[...]
```

This means that we can retrieve it in the following way (updated code is highlighted):

```
[...]

// retrieve the current user's Id
quiz.UserId = User.FindFirst(ClaimTypes.NameIdentifier).Value;

[...]
```

Let's perform this change and move on.

 This minor update should be enough for now. However, it won't work when dealing with external providers, as they will put their own data in these claims. Retrieving our local `UserId` in such scenarios will require some additional work, such as querying a dedicated lookup table; we'll see more about this later on.

Client-server auth test

Before moving further, it's definitely time to perform a client/server interaction test to ensure that our authorization pattern is working as expected.

From the Visual Studio source code editing interface, we can put a breakpoint right below the `Put` method of `QuizController`:

```
51
52      /// <summary>
53      /// Adds a new Quiz to the Database
54      /// </summary>
55      /// <param name="m">The QuizViewModel containing the data to insert</param>
56      [HttpPut]
57      [Authorize]
58      public IActionResult Put([FromBody]QuizViewModel m)
59      {
60          // return a generic HTTP Status 500 (Not Found)
61          // if the client payload is invalid.
62          if (m == null) return new StatusCodeResult(500);
63
64          // map the ViewModel to the Model
65          var quiz = m.Adapt<Quiz>();
66
67          // override those properties
68          //   that should be set from the server-side only
69          quiz.CreatedDate = DateTime.Now;
70          quiz.LastModifiedDate = quiz.CreatedDate;
71
```

Once done, we can launch the application in debug mode, navigate from the *Home* view to the Login view, and authenticate ourselves. Right after that, the **Create a Quiz** menu element should appear, allowing us to click on it.

From there, we can fill in the form with some random text and click on the **Save** button. The form will consequently call the `Put` method of `QuizController`, hopefully triggering our breakpoint. When it happens, open a **Watch** window (**Debug | Windows | Watch | Watch 1**) and check the `this.User.Identity.IsAuthenticated` property value:

```
52          /// <summary>
53          /// Adds a new Quiz to the Database
54          /// </summary>
55          /// <param name="m">The QuizViewModel containing the data to insert</param>
56          [HttpPut]
57          [Authorize]
58          public IActionResult Put([FromBody]QuizViewModel m)
59          {
60              // return a generic HTTP Status 500 (Not Found)
61              // if the client payload is invalid.
62              if (m == null) return new StatusCodeResult(500);  ≤5.943ms elapsed
63
64              // map the ViewMod
65              var quiz = m.Adapt
66
67              // override those
68              //    that should b
69              quiz.CreatedDate =
70              quiz.LastModifiedD
71
72              // retrieve the cu
```

Watch 1

Name	Value
this.User.Identity.IsAuthenticated	true
this.User	{System.Security.Claims.ClaimsPrincipal}

If it's `true`, it means that we've been successfully authenticated. That shouldn't be surprising, since our request already managed to get inside a method protected by an `[Authorize]` attribute.

Suggested topics

Authentication, Authorization, HTTP protocol, Secure Socket Layer, Session State Management, Indirection, Single Sign-On, Azure AD Authentication Library (ADAL), AspNetCore Identity, OpenID, OAuth, IdentityUser, Stateless, Cross-Site Scripting (XSS), Cross-Site Request Forgery (CSRF), Angular HttpClient, Angular HttpInterceptors, LocalStorage, Web Storage API, Server-side prerendering, Angular Universal, Browser Types, Generic Types, JWT Tokens, Claims, Refresh Tokens, and Sliding Sessions.

Summary

At the start of this chapter, we introduced the concepts of authentication and authorization, acknowledging the fact that most applications, including ours, do require a mechanism to properly handle authenticated and non-authenticated clients as well as authorized and unauthorized requests.

We took some time to properly understand the similarities and differences between authentication and authorization as well as the pros and cons of handling these tasks using our own internal provider or delegating them to third-party providers such as Google, Facebook, and Twitter. We also found out that, luckily enough, the `Microsoft.AspNetCore.Identity` framework can be configured to achieve the best of both worlds. To be able to use it, we added the required packages to our project and did what was needed to properly configure them, such as performing some changes in our `ApplicationUser` and `ApplicationDbContext` classes and then adding a new `EntityFrameworkCore` migration to update our database accordingly.

We briefly enumerated the various web-based authentication methods available nowadays: sessions, tokens, signatures, and two-factor strategies of various sorts. After careful consideration, we chose to implement a token-based approach using JSON Web Tokens (JWT), a solid and well-known standard for native web applications.

Implementing JWT within our application took us some time, as we had to take care of a number of steps: writing a dedicated `TokenController` to generate the tokens; set up and configure the required ASP .Net Core middleware needed to validate them; and finally, moving to our Angular client app, creating a **Login** form, an `AuthService` class, and a dedicated `HttpInterceptor` to handle everything on the client side.

Right after that, we implemented the required client-side and server-side authorization rules to protect some of our application views, routes, and APIs from unauthorized access.

All in all, the hand-made authentication and authorization flow we put together in this chapter is pretty much working. However, it lacks some very important features required for a production-ready environment, the most important ones being token expiration and token refresh. We'll learn how to do that in the upcoming chapter, along with other important stuff.

9
Advanced Topics

Our web application is starting to show its true colors. However, there are still some missing features we would like to implement, such as the following ones:

- Token expiration and refresh tokens
- New user registration
- Third-party authentication

In this chapter, we'll do our best to clear all these topics as well.

Token expiration and refresh tokens

When we implemented JWT token authentication in `Chapter 8`, *Third-Party Authentication and External Providers*, we didn't bother much about the token expiration time. We just set its value to an insanely high amount (86,400 minutes, which corresponds to 2 months) and went ahead with the coding. That was great for demonstration purposes, yet it won't be ideal when publishing our project into production. Issuing tokens with such a broad lifespan outside of a test environment will definitely pose a serious security threat. However, we don't want our users to be kicked out and/or lose their auth privileges because the token expires before they're done with their login session; is there a way to drastically reduce the token lifespan while also avoiding the risk of kicking active users out?

The answer is yes; to do so, we have to implement *refresh tokens* in our existing authentication pattern and learn how to properly use them to let our clients renew their tokens in a transparent way. However, before we start working on them, let's spend some valuable time to understand why we need to do that.

A small terminology clarification before we start; from now on, we will refer to the JWT tokens we implemented in `Chapter 8`, *Authentication and Authorization*, as **access tokens**, to distinguish them from the *refresh tokens* that we'll implement now.

What's a refresh token?

As the name implies, a **refresh token** is a special kind of token that can be used to obtain a new access token; the most logical way to use it is when the former access token expires and the client needs a new one to avoid having to perform the login again. Refresh tokens never expire, although they can--and should--be invalidated as soon as they are consumed, for obvious security reasons; on top of that, they also need to be stored properly to ensure that they are not leaked.

Implementing refresh tokens in our current web application won't be hard at all, as long as we perform the following steps:

1. Find a proper way to persist response tokens so that we can add, check, and invalidate them as needed.
2. Add a `refresh_token` property to our `TokenRequestViewModel` and `TokenResponseViewModel` classes, which will be used by the client and the `TokenController` to exchange the refresh token(s) when needed.
3. Update our existing `TokenController` so that it can handle a `refresh_token` request from the client.
4. Update our existing `token.response.ts` TypeScript interface to handle the `refresh_token` property that will be issued by the server.
5. Add a `refreshToken()` method to our Angular client's `AuthService` that we can use to issue a refresh token HTTP request from within our SPA.
6. Add a new `HttpInterceptor` to our Angular client that will automatically understand when the old access token expired and issue a `refresh_token` request to obtain a new one.

As we can easily guess, the first three steps are meant to be done on the server-side part of our web application, while the last three steps are related to the client side.

Choosing an appropriate place to store refresh tokens is mandatory, because we *need* to invalidate them as soon as they are consumed; if we don't, a single refresh token can be used to generate an infinite amount of valid access tokens--each one of them coming with its own refresh token--and we certainly don't want to allow that. We can persist refresh tokens in a number of ways, but--in our specific scenario--the most logical place to save them would be our current database--with a dedicated data model entity.

Server-side tasks

Let's start with the server-side tasks: adding the new entity will also require us to adapt our existing d*ata model* accordingly and--once we're done--update our database using another EF Core migration.

Adding the token entity

From **Solution Explorer**, right-click on the /Data/Models/ folder and add a new Token.ts C# class file, filling it with the following content:

```
using System;
using System.Collections.Generic;
using System.ComponentModel;
using System.ComponentModel.DataAnnotations;
using System.ComponentModel.DataAnnotations.Schema;

namespace TestMakerFreeWebApp.Data
{
    public class Token
    {
        #region Constructor
        public Token()
        {

        }
        #endregion

        #region Properties
        [Key]
        [Required]
        public int Id { get; set; }

        [Required]
        public string ClientId { get; set; }

        [Required]
```

```
            public string Value { get; set; }

            public int Type { get; set; }

            [Required]
            public string UserId { get; set; }

            [Required]
            public DateTime CreatedDate { get; set; }
            #endregion

            #region Lazy-Load Properties
            /// <summary>
            /// The user related to this token
            /// </summary>
            [ForeignKey("UserId")]
            public virtual ApplicationUser User { get; set; }
            #endregion
        }
    }
```

There's nothing new here, just the minimum amount of properties to store the relevant information about the token: the `ClientId`, where it comes from, its `Type`(we'll use a value of `zero` for refresh tokens), its `Value`, the `UserId` it was issued to, and the creation date.

Last but not least, we also implemented the `User` property to take advantage of the EF Core *Lazy-Load* feature, just like we did with the other entities back in `Chapter 4`, *Data Model with Entity Framework Core*. This will require updating the user entity as well.

Upgrading the user entity

Open the `/Data/Models/ApplicationUser.cs` file and add the following `Lazy-Load` property to the end:

```
    [...]

    #region Lazy-Load Properties
    /// <summary>
    /// A list of all the quiz created by this users.
    /// </summary>
    public virtual List<Quiz> Quizzes { get; set; }

    /// <summary>
    /// A list of all the refresh tokens issued for this users.
    /// </summary>
    public virtual List<Token> Tokens { get; set; }
```

```
#endregion

[...]
```

Upgrading ApplicationDbContext

The next thing to do is to update the ApplicationDbContext to properly handle the new entity; open the /Data/ApplicationDbContext.cs file and add the following lines to the end of the OnModelCreating() method:

```
[...]

modelBuilder.Entity<ApplicationUser>().ToTable("Users");
modelBuilder.Entity<ApplicationUser>().HasMany(u => u.Quizzes).WithOne(i =>
i.User);
modelBuilder.Entity<ApplicationUser>().HasMany(u => u.Tokens).WithOne(i =>
i.User);

[...]

modelBuilder.Entity<Result>().ToTable("Results");
modelBuilder.Entity<Result>().Property(i => i.Id).ValueGeneratedOnAdd();
modelBuilder.Entity<Result>().HasOne(i => i.Quiz).WithMany(u => u.Results);

modelBuilder.Entity<Token>().ToTable("Tokens");
modelBuilder.Entity<Token>().Property(i => i.Id).ValueGeneratedOnAdd();
modelBuilder.Entity<Token>().HasOne(i => i.User).WithMany(u => u.Tokens);

[...]

#region Properties
// public DbSet<ApplicationUser> Users { get; set; }
public DbSet<Quiz> Quizzes { get; set; }
public DbSet<Question> Questions { get; set; }
public DbSet<Answer> Answers { get; set; }
public DbSet<Result> Results { get; set; }
public DbSet<Token> Tokens { get; set; }
#endregion Properties

[...]
```

Applying the EF core migration

It's time to use the `dotnet-ef` command-line tool to update our database with the latest changes. Open a command line, navigate to the project's root folder, and type the following commands:

```
dotnet ef migrations add "RefreshTokens" -o "Data\Migrations"
dotnet ef Database update
```

This will create the **Tokens** table and pave the way for all that's yet to come.

Implementing the refresh token

Now that our data model can properly store the refresh tokens, we can move our focus to the Web API, starting with the `ViewModels` that will carry the refresh token from the server to the client and vice versa.

Upgrading TokenResponseViewModel

Open the `/ViewModels/TokenResponseViewModel.cs` file and update it in the following way:

```
[...]

#region Properties
public string token { get; set; }
public int expiration { get; set; }
public string refresh_token { get; set; }
#endregion

[...]
```

This property will be used by our `TokenController` to send the refresh token to the client --along with the access token--upon a successful login.

Upgrading TokenRequestViewModel

Once done, open the `/ViewModels/TokenRequestViewModel.cs` file and perform the following changes:

```
[...]

#region Properties
public string grant_type { get; set; }
public string client_id { get; set; }
```

```
public string client_secret { get; set; }
public string username { get; set; }
public string password { get; set; }
public string refresh_token { get; set; }
#endregion
```

```
[...]
```

This property will be used by our client to send the *refresh token* back to the web server--with the corresponding `grant_type`--to receive a new *access token*.

Upgrading TokenController

Now, we're all set to generate, store, and send the refresh tokens to the clients, and also receive them back. All these tasks will be done within our `TokenController`, which we need to upgrade in a number of ways.

The first thing to do is to handle the `refresh_token` *grant-type* by upgrading the existing `Auth()` action method:

```
[...]

switch (model.grant_type)
{
    case "password":
        return await GetToken(model);
                case "refresh_token":
        return await RefreshToken(model);
    default:
        // not supported - return a HTTP 401 (Unauthorized)
        return new UnauthorizedResult();
}

[...]
```

Right after that, we need to implement the `RefreshToken()` private method we're referencing to:

```
[...]

private async Task<IActionResult> RefreshToken(TokenRequestViewModel model)
{
    try
    {
        // check if the received refreshToken exists for the given
                                                clientId
        var rt = DbContext.Tokens
```

```
                    .FirstOrDefault(t =>
                    t.ClientId == model.clientId
                    && t.Value == model.refreshToken);

            if (rt == null)
            {
                // refresh token not found or invalid (or invalid clientId)
                return new UnauthorizedResult();
            }

            // check if there's an user with the refresh token's userId
            var user = await UserManager.FindByIdAsync(rt.UserId);

            if (user == null)
            {
                // UserId not found or invalid
                return new UnauthorizedResult();
            }

            // generate a new refresh token
            var rtNew = CreateRefreshToken(rt.ClientId, rt.UserId);

            // invalidate the old refresh token (by deleting it)
            DbContext.Tokens.Remove(rt);

            // add the new refresh token
            DbContext.Tokens.Add(rtNew);

            // persist changes in the DB
            DbContext.SaveChanges();

            // create a new access token...
            var response = CreateAccessToken(rtNew.UserId, rtNew.Value);

            // ... and send it to the client
            return Json(response);
        }
        catch (Exception ex)
        {
            return new UnauthorizedResult();
        }
    }

[...]
```

The tasks fulfilled by this new method are well explained in the source code comments; to quickly summarize it, it checks for the existence of the *refresh token* and--if there's nothing odd--proceeds with creating a new one, sending it back to the client as part of a new *access token*.

Needless to say, we also need to implement the `CreateRequestToken()` and `CreateAccessToken()` method mentioned there as well. Here's the first one:

```
[...]

private Token CreateRefreshToken(string clientId, string userId)
{
    return new Token()
    {
        ClientId = clientId,
        UserId = userId,
        Type = 0,
        Value = Guid.NewGuid().ToString("N"),
        CreatedDate = DateTime.UtcNow
    };
}

[...]
```

Also, here's the `CreateAccessToken()` method:

```
[...]

private TokenResponseViewModel CreateAccessToken(string userId, string
refreshToken)
{
    DateTime now = DateTime.UtcNow;

    // add the registered claims for JWT (RFC7519).
    // For more info, see https://tools.ietf.org/html/rfc7519#section-
                                                                  4.1
    var claims = new[] {
        new Claim(JwtRegisteredClaimNames.Sub, userId),
        new Claim(JwtRegisteredClaimNames.Jti,
          Guid.NewGuid().ToString()),
        new Claim(JwtRegisteredClaimNames.Iat,
            new DateTimeOffset(now).ToUnixTimeSeconds().ToString())
        // TODO: add additional claims here
    };

    var tokenExpirationMins =
        Configuration.GetValue<int>
```

```
        ("Auth:Jwt:TokenExpirationInMinutes");
    var issuerSigningKey = new SymmetricSecurityKey(
        Encoding.UTF8.GetBytes(Configuration["Auth:Jwt:Key"]));

    var token = new JwtSecurityToken(
        issuer: Configuration["Auth:Jwt:Issuer"],
        audience: Configuration["Auth:Jwt:Audience"],
        claims: claims,
        notBefore: now,
        expires: now.Add(TimeSpan.FromMinutes(tokenExpirationMins)),
        signingCredentials: new SigningCredentials(
            issuerSigningKey, SecurityAlgorithms.HmacSha256)
    );
    var encodedToken = new JwtSecurityTokenHandler().WriteToken(token);

    return new TokenResponseViewModel()
    {
        token = encodedToken,
        expiration = tokenExpirationMins,
        refresh_token = refreshToken
    };
}

[...]
```

Note how the `CreateAccessToken()` has strong similarities with the source code we used within the `GetToken()` method when we implemented it, back in Chapter 8, *Authentication and Authorization;* that's pretty obvious, since it does the same job--minus adding the `refresh_token`, which we need to support now.

We can easily take two birds with one stone by updating the `GetToken()` method in the following way (updated lines are highlighted):

```
[...]

private async Task<IActionResult> GetToken(TokenRequestViewModel model)
{
    try
    {
        // check if there's an user with the given username
        var user = await UserManager.FindByNameAsync(model.username);
        // fallback to support e-mail address instead of username
        if (user == null && model.username.Contains("@"))
            user = await UserManager.FindByEmailAsync(model.username);

        if (user == null
            || !await UserManager.CheckPasswordAsync(user,
```

```
                       model.password))
    {
        // user does not exists or password mismatch
        return new UnauthorizedResult();
    }

    // username & password matches: create the refresh token
    var rt = CreateRefreshToken(model.client_id, user.Id);

    // add the new refresh token to the DB
    DbContext.Tokens.Add(rt);
    DbContext.SaveChanges();

    // create & return the access token
    var t = CreateAccessToken(user.Id, rt.Value);
    return Json(t);
    }
    catch (Exception ex)
    {
        return new UnauthorizedResult();
    }
    }
}

[...]
```

What we did was to replace the duplicate code with a reference to our new
CreateRefreshToken() and CreateAccessToken() methods. As a result, we gave a
trim to the GetToken() code bloat and also upgraded it to issue the *refresh token* together
with the *access token*.

Client-side tasks

It's time to move to our Angular client and seize the deal; we need to add the
refresh_token property to our existing TokenResponse interface, update our existing
AuthService to give it the ability to refresh tokens, and add a new HttpInterceptor to
be able to understand when we actually need to do that.

Updating the TokenResponse interface

From **Solution Explorer**, navigate to the `/ClientApp/app/interface/` folder, open the `token.response.ts` file, and add the `token_refresh` property, as shown:

```
interface TokenResponse {
    token: string,
    expiration: number,
    refresh_token: string
}
```

This new property is precisely what we need to store the `refresh_token` sent by the server.

Upgrading AuthService

From **Solution Explorer**, navigate to the `/ClientApp/app/services/` folder, open the `auth.service.ts` file, and add the following code to the existing content, after the `login()` method:

```
[...]

// try to refresh token
refreshToken(): Observable<boolean> {
    var url = "api/token/auth";
    var data = {
        client_id: this.clientId,
        // required when signing up with username/password
        grant_type: "refresh_token",
        refresh_token: this.getAuth()!.refresh_token,
        // space-separated list of scopes for which the token is issued
        scope: "offline_access profile email"
    };

    return this.getAuthFromServer(url, data);
}

// retrieve the access & refresh tokens from the server
getAuthFromServer(url: string, data: any): Observable<boolean> {
        return this.http.post<TokenResponse>(url, data)
            .map((res) => {
                let token = res && res.token;
                // if the token is there, login has been successful
                if (token) {
                    // store username and jwt token
                    this.setAuth(res);
```

```
                          // successful login
                          return true;
                      }

                      // failed login
                      return Observable.throw('Unauthorized');
                  })
                  .catch(error => {
                      return new Observable<any>(error);
                  });
          }

      [...]
```

As we can see, the new `refreshToken()` method features a strong resemblance with the `login()` method we implemented back in `Chapter 8`, *Authentication and Authorization*, except for some minor differences; it asks for a different `grant_type`, which also requires sending the `refresh_token` instead of username and password, and it invokes a new `getAuthFromServer()` method to actually retrieve the auth info from the server.

By taking a closer look at the `getAuthFromServer()` implementation, we can see how we can easily call it from the `login()` method as well and get rid of a fair amount of repeating code:

```
      [...]

      login(username: string, password: string): Observable<boolean> {
          var url = "api/token/auth";
          var data = {
              username: username,
              password: password,
              client_id: this.clientId,
              // required when signing up with username/password
              grant_type: "password",
              // space-separated list of scopes for which the token is issued
              scope: "offline_access profile email"
          };

          return this.getAuthFromServer(url, data);
      }

      [...]
```

Our improved `AuthService` is now ready to refresh tokens; we just need to find a way to use the new feature.

Adding AuthResponseInterceptor

We're almost done; the last thing we need to do is to provide our client with a `HttpInterceptor` that will capture the **Http 401 - Unauthorized errors** and try to refresh the access token accordingly. It goes without saying that we need to find a way to have it trigger only once--to avoid endless attempts--and to resend the failed request in case of success.

From **Solution Explorer**, right-click to the `/ClientApp/app/services/` folder and add a new `auth.response.interceptor.ts` TypeScript file, filling it with the following content:

```typescript
import { Injectable, Injector } from "@angular/core";
import { Router } from "@angular/router";
import {
    HttpClient,
    HttpHandler, HttpEvent, HttpInterceptor,
    HttpRequest, HttpResponse, HttpErrorResponse
} from "@angular/common/http";
import { AuthService } from "./auth.service";
import { Observable } from "rxjs";

@Injectable()
export class AuthResponseInterceptor implements HttpInterceptor {

    currentRequest: HttpRequest<any>;
    auth: AuthService;

    constructor(
        private injector: Injector,
        private router: Router
    )
    { }

    intercept(
        request: HttpRequest<any>,
        next: HttpHandler): Observable<HttpEvent<any>> {

        this.auth = this.injector.get(AuthService);
        var token = (this.auth.isLoggedIn()) ?
        this.auth.getAuth()!.token : null;
```

```
        if (token) {
            // save current request
            this.currentRequest = request;

            return next.handle(request)
                .do((event: HttpEvent<any>) => {
                    if (event instanceof HttpResponse) {
                        // do nothing
                    }
                })
                .catch(error => {
                    return this.handleError(error)
                });
        }
        else {
            return next.handle(request);
        }
    }

    handleError(err: any) {
        if (err instanceof HttpErrorResponse) {
            if (err.status === 401) {
                // JWT token might be expired:
                // try to get a new one using refresh token
                console.log("Token expired. Attempting refresh...");
                this.auth.refreshToken()
                    .subscribe(res => {
                    if (res) {
                        // refresh token successful
                        console.log("refresh token successful");

                        // re-submit the failed request
                        var http = this.injector.get(HttpClient);
                        http.request(this.currentRequest).subscribe(
                            result => {
                                // do something
                            }, error => console.error(error)
                        );
                    }
                    else {
                        // refresh token failed
                        console.log("refresh token failed");

                        // erase current token
                        this.auth.logout();

                        // redirect to login page
                        this.router.navigate(["login"]);
```

```
                        }
                }, error => console.log(error));
            }
        }
        return Observable.throw(err);
    }
}
```

That's an impressive amount of TypeScript code, but the included comments should help us properly understand what we did:

- In the `intercept()` method, the first thing we do is check whether there's a token or not; if we don't, there's no need to do anything, otherwise we do two things:
  - Store a reference to the current request in an internal property that can be useful later on
  - Set up an event handler that will call the `handleError()` method in case of HTTP errors

- In the `handleError()` method, we check whether we're dealing with an `HttpErrorResponse` with a status code of **401 - Unauthorized**, which is what we get whenever we attempt to access a controller's action method shielded with the `[Authorize]` attribute using an invalid (expired) access token. If the conditions match, we attempt to refresh the token using the `refreshToken()` method of `AuthService` we implemented a short while ago and subscribe to it, waiting for the outcome:
  - In case of success, we resubmit the request that triggered the response error--which we stored in the `this.currentRequest` local property
  - In case of failure, we perform the logout to clear all the expired tokens from the local storage and then redirect the user back to the login screen

Add the AuthResponseInterceptor in the AppModule

As always, the new interceptor has to be added in the `app.module.shared.ts` file right below the existing one:

```
[...]

import { AuthInterceptor } from './services/auth.interceptor';
import { AuthResponseInterceptor } from
'./services/auth.response.interceptor';

[...]

    providers: [
        AuthService,
        {
            provide: HTTP_INTERCEPTORS,
            useClass: AuthInterceptor,
            multi: true
        },
        {
            provide: HTTP_INTERCEPTORS,
            useClass: AuthResponseInterceptor,
            multi: true
        }
    ]

[...]
```

Testing it up

In order to test up the token refresh feature, we need to (drastically) reduce the access token `ExpirationInMinutes` that we set in the `appsettings.json` and `appsettings.Development.json` files. We can start with a value of 60 for the `appsettings.json` file--as it will be an appropriate time for production--and a temporary 1 value for the `appsettings.Development.json` file so that we'll be able to quickly check out whether what we did actually works.

Once done, we can launch the application in debug mode and wait until we see the **Home** view; from there, it's mandatory that we perform a logout/login before everything else, to ensure that the refresh token will be added to our `localStorage`. As soon as we do that, we can pick an existing quiz from the **Home** view and access the `QuizEditComponent` by clicking on the **Edit** button. Wait a little more than one minute, and then click on the **Apply Changes** button; that should trigger the whole token refresh workflow, which we can easily debug with the Visual Studio interface by placing the appropriate breakpoints within the various .NET Core and Angular methods we have added.

New user registration

Our web application can now authenticate and authorize users just fine, assuming that they are already present in the data model; this can be enough for a testing environment, yet it won't work if we want to put our efforts into production. What if we want to register new users and have them added to the data model along with the sample ones created by the `DbSeeder` class?

In order to implement that, we'll need the following:

- On the *server-side*, add a `UserController`--with a corresponding `UserViewModel`--to handle user registration requests
- On the *client-side*, add a new `RegisterComponent` to our Angular app--with a corresponding account interface--to send these requests, receive the server-side response, and act accordingly

That said, let's see how we can pull it off.

Server-side tasks

We'll start creating the `UserController` and `UserViewModel` on the server side.

UserController

From **Solution Explorer**, right-click to the `/Controllers/` folder, add a new `UserController.cs` C# class, and fill it with the following content:

```
using System;
using System.Threading.Tasks;
using Microsoft.AspNetCore.Mvc;
```

```
using Microsoft.AspNetCore.Identity;
using Microsoft.Extensions.Configuration;
using TestMakerFreeWebApp.ViewModels;
using TestMakerFreeWebApp.Data;
using Mapster;

namespace TestMakerFreeWebApp.Controllers
{
    public class UserController : BaseApiController
    {
        #region Constructor
        public UserController(
            ApplicationDbContext context,
            RoleManager<IdentityRole> roleManager,
            UserManager<ApplicationUser> userManager,
            IConfiguration configuration
            )
            : base(context, roleManager, userManager, configuration) {
                                                          }
        #endregion

        #region RESTful Conventions
        /// <summary>
        /// POST: api/user
        /// </summary>
        /// <returns>Creates a new User and return it accordingly.
                                                    </returns>
        [HttpPost()]
        public async Task<IActionResult> Add([FromBody]UserViewModel
                                                            model)
        {
            // return a generic HTTP Status 500 (Server Error)
            // if the client payload is invalid.
            if (model == null) return new StatusCodeResult(500);

            // check if the Username/Email already exists
            ApplicationUser user = await
                    UserManager.FindByNameAsync(model.UserName);
            if (user != null) return BadRequest("Username already
                                                    exists");

            user = await UserManager.FindByEmailAsync(model.Email);
            if (user != null) return BadRequest("Email already
                                                    exists.");

            var now = DateTime.Now;

            // create a new Item with the client-sent json data
```

```
            user = new ApplicationUser()
            {
                SecurityStamp = Guid.NewGuid().ToString(),
                UserName = model.UserName,
                Email = model.Email,
                DisplayName = model.DisplayName,
                CreatedDate = now,
                LastModifiedDate = now
            };

            // Add the user to the Db with the choosen password
            await UserManager.CreateAsync(user, model.Password);

            // Assign the user to the 'RegisteredUser' role.
            await UserManager.AddToRoleAsync(user, "RegisteredUser");

            // Remove Lockout and E-Mail confirmation
            user.EmailConfirmed = true;
            user.LockoutEnabled = false;

            // persist the changes into the Database.
            DbContext.SaveChanges();

            // return the newly-created User to the client.
            return Json(user.Adapt<UserViewModel>(),
                JsonSettings);
        }
        #endregion
    }
}
```

There's nothing really new here, as we used the same approach for adding quizzes, questions, answers, and results.

UserViewModel

From **Solution Explorer**, right-click to the /ViewModels/ folder, add a new UserViewModel.cs C# class, and fill it with the following content:

```
using Newtonsoft.Json;

namespace TestMakerFreeWebApp.ViewModels
{
    [JsonObject(MemberSerialization.OptOut)]
    public class UserViewModel
    {
```

```
#region Constructor
public UserViewModel()
{

}
#endregion

#region Properties
public string UserName { get; set; }
public string Password { get; set; }
public string Email { get; set; }
public string DisplayName { get; set; }
#endregion
    }
}
```

The view model is also pretty standard; it just contains the fields that we need to create the new user entity and save it to the database.

Client-side tasks

We already know what we need to do in Angular: define a new user interface to reflect the UserViewModel we added on the *server side,* create the RegisterComponent, reference it in the AppModule, add a route to handle user registration and place a link somewhere to make non-logged in users aware about the fact they can create an account if they want to.

Let's do this.

The user interface

From **Solution Explorer**, right-click to the /ClientApp/app/interfaces/ folder and add a user.ts TypeScript file with the following content:

```
interface User {
    Username: string;
    Password: string;
    Email: string;
    DisplayName: string;
}
```

RegisterComponent

From **Solution Explorer**, right-click to the `/ClientApp/app/components/` folder and create a new `/user/` subfolder; right-click to the new folder, add a `register.component.ts` file, and fill it with the following content (the relevant lines are highlighted):

```
import { Component, Inject } from "@angular/core";
import { FormGroup, FormControl, FormBuilder, Validators } from
'@angular/forms';
import { Router } from "@angular/router";
import { HttpClient } from "@angular/common/http";

@Component({
    selector: "register",
    templateUrl: "./register.component.html",
    styleUrls: ['./register.component.css']
})

export class RegisterComponent {
    title: string;
    form: FormGroup;

    constructor(private router: Router,
        private fb: FormBuilder,
        private http: HttpClient,
        @Inject('BASE_URL') private baseUrl: string) {

        this.title = "New User Registration";

        // initialize the form
        this.createForm();

    }

    createForm() {
        this.form = this.fb.group({
            Username: ['', Validators.required],
            Email: ['',
                [Validators.required,
                Validators.email]
            ],
            Password: ['', Validators.required],
            PasswordConfirm: ['', Validators.required],
            DisplayName: ['', Validators.required]
        }, {
            validator: this.passwordConfirmValidator
```

```
        });
    }

onSubmit() {
    // build a temporary user object from form values
    var tempUser = <User>{};
    tempUser.Username = this.form.value.Username;
    tempUser.Email = this.form.value.Email;
    tempUser.Password = this.form.value.Password;
    tempUser.DisplayName = this.form.value.DisplayName;

    var url = this.baseUrl + "api/user";

    this.http
        .put<User>(url, tempUser)
        .subscribe(res => {
            if (res)
            {
                var v = res;
                console.log("User " + v.Username + " has been
                                                    created.");
                // redirect to login page
                this.router.navigate(["login"]);
            }
            else {
                // registration failed
                this.form.setErrors({
                    "register": "User registration failed."
                });
            }
        }, error => console.log(error));
}

onBack() {
    this.router.navigate(["home"]);
}

passwordConfirmValidator(control: FormControl):any {
    let p = control.root.get('Password');
    let pc = control.root.get('PasswordConfirm');
    if (p && pc) {
        if (p.value !== pc.value) {
            pc.setErrors(
                { "PasswordMismatch": true }
            );
        }
        else {
            pc.setErrors(null);
```

```
            }
        }
        return null;
    }

    // retrieve a FormControl
    getFormControl(name: string) {
        return this.form.get(name);
    }

    // returns TRUE if the FormControl is valid
    isValid(name: string) {
        var e = this.getFormControl(name);
        return e && e.valid;
    }

    // returns TRUE if the FormControl has been changed
    isChanged(name: string) {
        var e = this.getFormControl(name);
        return e && (e.dirty || e.touched);
    }

    // returns TRUE if the FormControl is invalid after user changes
    hasError(name: string) {
        var e = this.getFormControl(name);
        return e && (e.dirty || e.touched) && !e.valid;
    }
}
```

We already know how most of the preceding code actually works, as we effectively used it in a number of Model-Driven forms back in Chapter 7, *Forms and Data Validation*; however, there are a couple of things that require further analysis.

Custom validator

As we can see by looking at the highlighted lines, there are two new validators that we used to check the email and password given by the user: the Validators.email--which has obviously been attached to the Email form control--and the passwordConfirmValidator(), which we attached to the whole FormGroup.

The first one is built-in in Angular, while the latter is a custom validator that we put together to compare the Password and PasswordConfirm fields and keep the user informed of their respective value. As we can see, we chose to attach it to the whole form group, because it needs to check two controls at the same time; hence, we need it to trigger whenever either of them changes its value.

The validator itself does nothing fancy; it retrieves the two form controls using the `get()` method, then--if both of them exist--compare their values; if they do match, it sets an error to the `PasswordConfirm` control, otherwise it clears it. Note how we could've set the error globally by adding it on the root form control instead, yet we preferred to turn on the red light over the `PasswordConfirm` control instead; that way, our users will have a better visual hint on what they need to do.

Template and style sheet files

In an effort to keep this chapter small, we'll restrain ourselves from pasting the full contents of the `register.component.html` and `register.component.less` files here; they can be easily downloaded from the book's official GitHub repository.

AppModule

As always, we need to put our new component's references within the `app.module.shared.ts` file. A good place for them would be just below the `LoginComponent` ones:

```
[...]

import { LoginComponent } from './components/login/login.component';
import { RegisterComponent } from './components/user/register.component';

[...]

declarations: [
    [...]
    LoginComponent,
    RegisterComponent,

[...]

RouterModule.forRoot([
    { path: 'login', component: LoginComponent },
    { path: 'register', component: RegisterComponent },

[...]
```

LoginComponent

Now that our `RegisterComponent` is ready, we need to find a proper way to tell that to our users. A good place to start might be adding a **Don't have an account? Click here to create one!** link in the `LoginComponent`. Open the `login.component.html` file and add the following:

```
[...]

<div class="login-link">
    <a href="#">
        Forgot the password?
    </a>
</div>
<div class="login-link">
    <a [routerLink]="['/register']">
        Don't have an account? Click here to create one!
    </a>
</div>

[...]
```

NavMenu

Last but not least, we need to let our users know that they have to navigate to the `LoginComponent` even if they want to create a new account. To do that, open the `navmenu.component.html` template file and update the `Login` label as follows:

```
[...]

<li *ngIf="!auth.isLoggedIn()"
    [routerLinkActive]="['link-active']">
    <a [routerLink]="['/login']">
        <span class='glyphicon glyphicon-log-in'></span> Login /
                                                         Register
    </a>
</li>

[...]
```

Testing it up

To properly test what we just did, we can now launch the application in *debug* mode, perform a **Logout** (if needed) and then click on the **Login/Register** link to access the Login view:

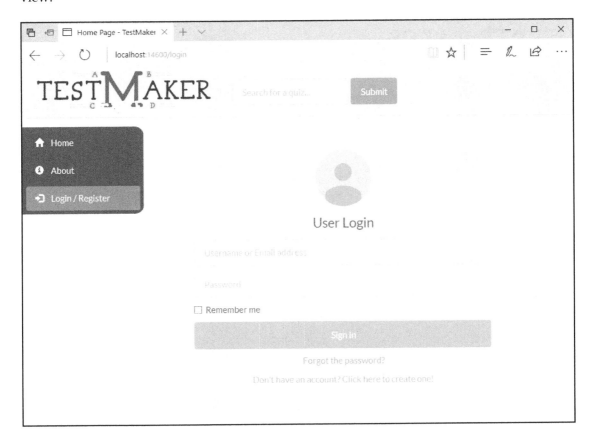

From there, click on the **Don't have an account? Click here to create one!** link to load the
`RegisterComponent` form:

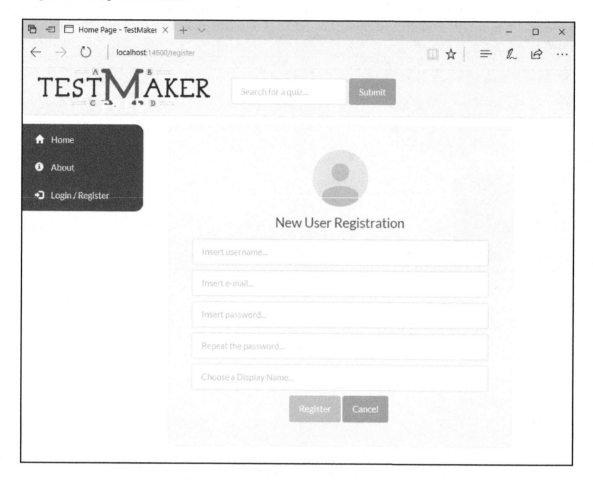

We can then try to fill the form fields, click on the **Register** button, and see what happens;
again, in the (un)likely case that we don't get the expected results, we can use the Visual
Studio debugging interface to inspect both the .NET Core and Angular workflows--with the
help of a bunch of breakpoints in the right places.

Third-party authentication

Allowing users to sign in using their existing credentials is often a great way to drive additional traffic to our applications, as demonstrated by a number of case studies by Google, Facebook, and Twitter.

As you might already know, ASP.NET Core Identity comes with a set of handy packages that will take care of that, saving ourselves from dealing with the relevant amount of complexity of the *OAuth2* authentication flow that we saw back in `Chapter 8`, *Authentication and Authorization*. In this section, we'll demonstrate how we can use its built-in features to implement some external authentication mechanism using a widely known *third-party* provider such as Facebook.

OAuth2 authorization flow

Before we start, let's do a quick recap of how the OAuth2 authorization flow actually works for a standard web application:

1. The user asks the web application to login with the external provider X.
2. The web application prompts the user with a pop-up window containing a page directly hosted by the external provider X, from which they can do the following:
   - Login to X to authenticate themselves there, unless they're not logged in there
   - If/when logged in, authorize the web application to use X as the third-party authentication provider, thus giving it access to the minimum amount of required user information (name, email, and so on) to allow that
3. If the user refuses to either log in to X or to give X the authorization, the popup will close and the authentication process will fail; if they accept, X will send back an OAuth2 access token.
4. The web application will immediately consume that OAuth2 access token to fetch the mentioned user information and use them to either create a new account or login with an existing one, depending on whether this information corresponds to an existing user or not.

This is what happens under the hood, regardless of X being Facebook, Google, Twitter, or anything else. That said, such workflow can be implemented in a number of alternative ways, which can be grouped into two significant approaches (or, to better say, *grant types*):

- Using an **implicit flow**, often handled by a client-side SDK written in JavaScript and made available by the external provider itself
- Using an **explicit flow**, with the help of a set of server-side tools, packages, or libraries made available by the chosen development framework (such as ASP.NET Core), third-party packages, or the external provider itself

The *explicit flow* grant type is also called **authorization code flow**, because it returns a unique *authorization code* that must be used to retrieve the OAuth2 access token, preventing the latter from being directly exposed to the user and to applications that might have access to the user's user agent (such as browsers extensions, installed software, and packet sniffers).

To learn more about the *OAuth2* authorization framework, we strongly suggest reading the following URLs:
Official Page: http://oauth.net/2/.
RFC 6749: https://tools.ietf.org/html/rfc6749.

Implicit flow versus explicit flow

The main difference between the two grant types is all about how the aforementioned *OAuth2 access token* is requested, obtained and handled; in short, how steps 2 and 3 are actually performed.

In a standard **implicit flow**, these steps are entirely performed by the client-side part of our web app--often using a *client-side* SDK such as the *Facebook JavaScript SDK*--and the external provider servers. More specifically:

- The pop-up window (step 2) will directly point to the external provider login/authorization page
- After the login and auth, the OAuth2 access token (step 3) will be directly fetched by the client-side part of our web application and then sent to a dedicated server-side API controller, which will use it to retrieve the user data and perform the account creation/login (step 4)

Conversely, when using an explicit flow grant type such as those provided by `AspNet.Security.OAuth.Providers`, Windows SDK for Facebook, or `OpenIddict`, these same steps take place in the following way:

- The pop-up window (step 2) will point to a server-side intermediate page of our app, which will then redirect the user to the external provider login/authorization page
- After the login and auth, the external provider will redirect the user to a specific callback URL along with an authorization code that will be used by the *server-side* part of our application to retrieve the actual OAuth2 access token (step 3) and then immediately use it to retrieve the user data and perform the account creation/login (step 4)

Either of these approaches is viable enough; however, they both have their pros and cons in terms of security and versatility, depending on the given scenario.

Implicit flow pros and cons

Implementing an **implicit flow** with an official *client-side SDK* released by the third-party provider is *almost* a walk in the park, even in Angular; we just have to find a way to implement a small, yet required amount of external JavaScript within our *client-side* code and load the external JS libraries without messing up the Angular components life cycle--or the page DOM--and we're set.

On top of that, the overall results will most likely look great; the required pop-up window will open (and close) in the best possible way, without size mismatches or other UI/UX issues, and without any hack (that we're aware of).

However, such an approach also comes with a few downsides: our users will be able to receive their access tokens, along with whatever can spy, hack, sniff, or impersonate them; additionally, it will also force us to write a certain amount of dedicated client-side code for each supported provider, which might be far from ideal if we want to support a whole lot of them.

Explicit flow pros and cons

The **explicit flow** approach is the most commonly used in server-side web applications for a number of good reasons: the auth source code is not publicly exposed, the client SecretC confidentiality can be maintained, and the whole process is definitely more secure due to the presence of the *authorization code*, that is nothing less than an additional security layer.

On top of that, in our given scenario, we can rely on an excellent *server-side* tool--the `Microsoft.AspNetCore.Identity` service--which natively supports a wide bunch of external providers, including Facebook, Google, Twitter, and so on. All we need to do is implement a couple of action methods in our existing `TokenController`.

The only real downside about that is the fact that it is still a flow based upon browser redirection, which means that the application must be capable of interacting with the user agent (also known as the web browser); open the login/auth pop-up (with a proper size), receive API authorization codes that are routed through the browser, close that pop-up, and so on. Although this is hardly an issue in standard MVC web applications, it's definitely way more complicated when dealing with Angular and single-page applications; although it can be definitely forced into that, the developer will eventually have to pull off a small, yet consistent number of nasty workarounds; it won't be an out-of-the-box experience, that's for sure.

Conclusions

There's not much to say; both approaches have their pros and cons, hence they're equally useful for the tutorial purposes of this book. That's why we'll implement both of them in order to give the reader the best possible learning experience.

Logging in with Facebook

Let's start with the big whale of the social networks. As we might already know, the *Login with Facebook* feature requires us to create a dedicated *Facebook* app and connect it to our web application using secure endpoints; by doing that, we'll also obtain the `AppId` and `AppSecret` that we can use to perform our first request against Facebook's OAuth2 authentication workflow.

Creating the Facebook app

The first thing we need to do is to create the Facebook app. Doing that is just as easy as following the mentioned steps:

1. Go to the **Facebook Developer** page at `https://developers.facebook.com/`.

   In order to access most of the Facebook Developer page's features, we need to log in using a Facebook Developer Account; to achieve such status, depending on the Facebook policies for your country, you might be asked to verify your identity using a mobile number or a credit card. For detailed information about upgrading your account to a Facebook Developer Account, you can take a look at `https://www.facebook.com/help/167551763306531`.

2. Once inside, click on **Add a New App:**, select **Website**, fill in the required fields, and click on **Create App ID**:

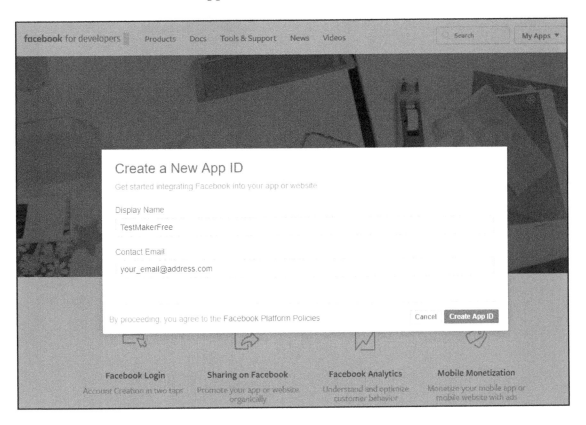

It's worth saying that external provider web platforms are subject to frequent and major changes; the actual pages and forms might be different from those depicted by the screenshots made at the time of writing.

3. As soon as we get past the CAPTCHA, a new Facebook app will be added to our account, and we'll be automatically brought to the **Add Products** selection screen.
4. Once there, we should be able to add a new **Facebook Login** product by selecting the appropriate card and clicking on the **Set Up** button:

We should then be prompted by a wizard-like view where you can choose between various platforms: iOS, Android, Web, and Other; we can choose **Web** and go ahead.

In the following *wizard-like* screen, we'll be asked for our main website URL. Ensure that you specify the development URL there, including the port:

```
http://localhost:14600/
```

This step is very important for both implicit and explicit flows; all the HTTP requests coming from any other URL will be rejected by Facebook. It goes without saying that we'll have to change it as soon as we'll publish our app, but that will go for now.

In the subsequent parts of the wizard, we'll be given the chance to read about the Facebook JavaScript SDK, which is the client-side framework made by Facebook with the intent to provide web developers a standard, easy-to-use interface to implement the whole auth process to their website. Take a good look at those sample code lines, because that's precisely what we'll use when implementing our implicit flow, with some minor changes to make them work in Angular.

Once done, select the **Facebook Login** | **Settings** link from the left menu. From there, we can enter our production and development URIs with the `/auth/signin-facebook` route suffix in the **Valid OAuth Redirect URIs** input field:

We're free to chose a different route if we prefer to, as long as we'll configure it within our web application later on. Anyway, when we're done, we can click on **Save Changes** and go ahead.

 Again, **this is a very important step** for explicit flow only, as implicit flow won't use them; the good news here is that we can specify multiple URIs; hence, we can add the development and production host names right from the start.

By clicking on the **Settings** link in the left navigation menu, we can retrieve the `AppId` and `AppSecret` of our Facebook App--ensure that you write them down--and configure some additional information regarding our *Facebook App*: the *Display Name*, the *App Icon*, the WebSite URL we entered a short while ago, and so on. None of them are required, so we can skip everything and click on the **App Review** link, where we have the chance to make our app available to the public. All we need to do here is to turn the switch **on**:

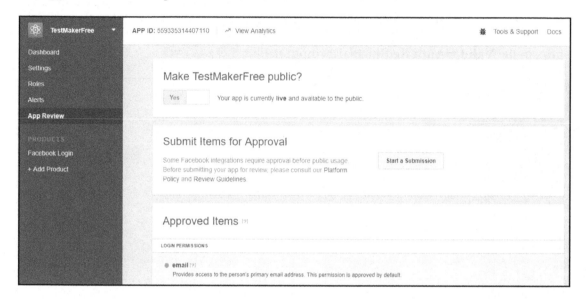

As soon as we do that, we will see a list of **Approved Items**, containing the default information we'll be able to access when our users will confirm their choice to log in to our site with Facebook; as we can see, the first one among them is the user email address, which we'll need soon enough.

Implicit flow

Let's start with implementing our **implicit flow**. Here's a brief list of what we need to do:

- Add a `Facebook()` action method to our existing `TokenController` where we'll use the access token to fetch the user data from the Facebook API and use it to perform the login or registration accordingly
- Create a `login.facebook.ts` component--and its `.html` template file--to load the Facebook SDK in our Angular SPA and create the required UI stuff

Updating TokenController

From **Solution Explorer**, navigate to the `/Controllers/` folder; then, open the `TokenController.cs` file and add the following action method:

```
[HttpPost("Facebook")]
public async Task<IActionResult>
Facebook([FromBody]ExternalLoginRequestViewModel model)
{
    try
    {
        var fbAPI_url = "https://graph.facebook.com/v2.10/";
        var fbAPI_queryString = String.Format(
            "me?scope=email&access_token={0}&fields=id,name,email",
            model.access_token);
        string result = null;

        // fetch the user info from Facebook Graph v2.10
        using (var c = new HttpClient())
        {
            c.BaseAddress = new Uri(fbAPI_url);
            var response = await c
                .GetAsync(fbAPI_queryString);
            if (response.IsSuccessStatusCode)
            {
                result = await response.Content.ReadAsStringAsync();
            }
            else throw new Exception("Authentication error");
        };

        // load the resulting Json into a dictionary
        var epInfo = JsonConvert.DeserializeObject<Dictionary<string,
                                                  string>>(result);
        var info = new UserLoginInfo("facebook", epInfo["id"],
                                                  "Facebook");

        // Check if this user already registered himself with this
                                        external provider before
        var user = await UserManager.FindByLoginAsync(
            info.LoginProvider, info.ProviderKey);
        if (user == null)
        {
            // If we reach this point, it means that this user never
                                        tried to logged in
            // using this external provider. However, it could have
                                        used other providers
            // and /or have a local account.
            // We can find out if that's the case by looking for his e-
```

```
                                                     mail address.

// Lookup if there's an username with this e-mail address
                                                    in the Db
user = await UserManager.FindByEmailAsync(epInfo["email"]);
if (user == null)
{
    // No user has been found: register a new user using
                                                    the info
    // retrieved from the provider
    DateTime now = DateTime.Now;
    var username = String.Format("FB{0}{1}",
            epInfo["id"],
            Guid.NewGuid().ToString("N"));
    user = new ApplicationUser()
    {
        SecurityStamp = Guid.NewGuid().ToString(),
        // ensure the user will have an unique username
        UserName = username,
        Email = epInfo["email"],
        DisplayName = epInfo["name"],
        CreatedDate = now,
        LastModifiedDate = now
    };

    // Add the user to the Db with a random password
    await UserManager.CreateAsync(user,
        DataHelper.GenerateRandomPassword());

    // Assign the user to the 'RegisteredUser' role.
    await UserManager.AddToRoleAsync(user,
                            "RegisteredUser");

    // Remove Lockout and E-Mail confirmation
    user.EmailConfirmed = true;
    user.LockoutEnabled = false;

    // Persist everything into the Db
    DbContext.SaveChanges();
}
// Register this external provider to the user
var ir = await UserManager.AddLoginAsync(user, info);
if (ir.Succeeded)
{
    // Persist everything into the Db
    DbContext.SaveChanges();
}
else throw new Exception("Authentication error");
```

```
        }

        // create the refresh token
        var rt = CreateRefreshToken(model.client_id, user.Id);

        // add the new refresh token to the DB
        DbContext.Tokens.Add(rt);
        DbContext.SaveChanges();

        // create & return the access token
        var t = CreateAccessToken(user.Id, rt.Value);
        return Json(t);
    }
    catch (Exception ex)
    {
        // return a HTTP Status 400 (Bad Request) to the client
        return BadRequest(new { Error = ex.Message });
    }
}
```

Don't forget to add the following required reference at the start of the file:

```
using System.Net.Http;
```

The included comments should explain it all; however, it can't hurt to briefly summarize what we did:

- We use the *OAuth2 access token*--which we plan to receive from our Angular app--to request the user ID, name, and email address from the *Facebook API*.
- Once we retrieve the information, we use the user email address to check whether the user already exists in our *identity data model* or not. If it doesn't, we create a new user, register the external provider, and perform the login; otherwise, we just register the external provider and perform the login.

As we might note, when we create a new user, we're forced to create a "unique" username, as it's a required field; the method we used--the "FB" string prefix + the facebook unique ID + a random *Guid* without the dashes--will ensure its uniqueness among the database. Other than that, there are no surprises--the code lines that generate the access/refresh JWT tokens and return the `TokenResponseViewModel` are nothing new.

However, there's a single line--the highlighted one--that will raise an exception; there's no `DataHelper.GenerateRandomPassword()` method out there. As a matter of fact, there is no `DataHelper` class as well! That's definitely true; we still need to add it.

Adding the GenerateRandomPassword() method

The *username* isn't the only "missing" required field we need to take care of when a user registers themselves with a third-party provider, and we want to create their account to our existing *identity data model*; we also need to generate a *password*.

Such a task is not trivial as it might seem, for at least two reasons:

- **We cannot set up a weak password**, otherwise other users might be able to break into that user's account
- **We cannot set up a weak password**, because the *ASP.NET Core Identity* will refuse it

More specifically, if we recall correctly, what we did back in `Chapter 8`, *Authentication and Authorization*, when we added the *Identity service* to the `Startup.cs` file, we need a password with at least a digit, a lowercase character, an uppercase character, and a minimum length of seven. The uppercase/lowercase requirements will even cut out our usual *"random GUIDs"* way of doing (sample) things, unless we want to add or replace some characters manually.

Long story short, the best thing we can do is to implement a quick-and-simple password generator helper function that will generate them according to our standards. From **Solution Explorer**, right-click on the `/Data/` folder, add a new `DataHelper.cs` file, and fill it with the following content:

```
using Microsoft.AspNetCore.Identity;
using System;
using System.Collections.Generic;
using System.Linq;

namespace TestMakerFreeWebApp.Data
{
    public static class DataHelper
    {
        /// <summary>
        /// Generates a Random Password
        /// respecting the given strength requirements.
        /// </summary>
        /// <param name="opts">A valid PasswordOptions object
        /// containing the password strength requirements.</param>
        /// <returns>A random password</returns>
        public static string GenerateRandomPassword(PasswordOptions
                                                        opts = null)
        {
            if (opts == null) opts = new PasswordOptions()
            {
```

```
                RequiredLength = 7,
                RequiredUniqueChars = 4,
                RequireDigit = true,
                RequireLowercase = true,
                RequireNonAlphanumeric = false,
                RequireUppercase = true
            };

        string[] randomChars = new[] {
    "ABCDEFGHJKLMNOPQRSTUVWXYZ", // uppercase
    "abcdefghijkmnopqrstuvwxyz", // lowercase
    "0123456789", // digits
    "!@$?_-" // non-alphanumeric
};
        Random rand = new Random(Environment.TickCount);
        List<char> chars = new List<char>();

        if (opts.RequireUppercase)
            chars.Insert(rand.Next(0, chars.Count),
                randomChars[0][rand.Next(0,
                             randomChars[0].Length)]);

        if (opts.RequireLowercase)
            chars.Insert(rand.Next(0, chars.Count),
                randomChars[1][rand.Next(0,
                             randomChars[1].Length)]);

        if (opts.RequireDigit)
            chars.Insert(rand.Next(0, chars.Count),
                randomChars[2][rand.Next(0,
                             randomChars[2].Length)]);

        if (opts.RequireNonAlphanumeric)
            chars.Insert(rand.Next(0, chars.Count),
                randomChars[3][rand.Next(0,
                               randomChars[3].Length)]);

        for (int i = chars.Count; i < opts.RequiredLength
            || chars.Distinct().Count() < opts.RequiredUniqueChars;
                                    i++)
        {
            string rcs = randomChars[rand.Next(0,
                            randomChars.Length)];
            chars.Insert(rand.Next(0, chars.Count),
                rcs[rand.Next(0, rcs.Length)]);
        }

        return new string(chars.ToArray());
```

```
        }
    }
}
```

That will do for now.

Adding LoginFacebookComponent

It's time to switch to Angular. From **Solution Explorer**, right-click to the
`/ClientApp/app/components/login/` folder, add a new
`login.facebook.component.ts` file, and fill it with the following content:

```
import { Component, Inject, OnInit, NgZone, PLATFORM_ID } from
"@angular/core";
import { isPlatformBrowser } from '@angular/common';
import { HttpClient } from "@angular/common/http";
import { Router } from "@angular/router";
import { AuthService } from '../../services/auth.service';

// declare these vars here
// to let the TS compiler know that they exist
declare var window: any;
declare var FB: any;

@Component({
    selector: "login-facebook",
    templateUrl: "./login.facebook.component.html"
})

export class LoginFacebookComponent implements OnInit {

    constructor(
        private http: HttpClient,
        private router: Router,
        private authService: AuthService,
        // inject the local zone
        private zone: NgZone,
        @Inject(PLATFORM_ID) private platformId: any,
        @Inject('BASE_URL') private baseUrl: string) {
    }

    ngOnInit() {
        if (!isPlatformBrowser(this.platformId)) {
            return;
        }
```

```
if (typeof (FB) === 'undefined') {

    // if the FB oject is undefined,
    // it means that it's the first time
    // we visit this page, hence we need
    // to initialize the Facebook SDK
    window.fbAsyncInit = () =>

        // be sure to do this within
        // the local zone, or Angular will be
        // unable to find the local references
        this.zone.run(() => {
            FB.init({
                appId: '---YOUR-APP-ID---',
                xfbml: true,
                version: 'v2.10'
            });
            FB.AppEvents.logPageView();

            // this will trigger right after the user
            // completes the FB SDK Auth roundtrip successfully
            FB.Event.subscribe('auth.statusChange', (
                (result: any) => {
                    console.log("FB auth status changed");
                    console.log(result);
                    if (result.status === 'connected') {
                        // login successful
                        console.log('Connected to Facebook.');
this.onConnect(result.authResponse.accessToken);
                    }
                })
            );
        });

    // Load the SDK js library (only once)
    (function (d, s, id) {
        var js, fjs = d.getElementsByTagName(s)[0];
        if (d.getElementById(id)) { return; }
        js = d.createElement(s); js.id = id;
        (<any>js).src = "//connect.facebook.net/en_US/sdk.js";
        fjs.parentNode!.insertBefore(js, fjs);
    }(document, 'script', 'facebook-jssdk'));

}
else {

    // Reload the FB login button
    window.FB.XFBML.parse();
```

```
                // if the user is still connected, log him off.
                FB.getLoginStatus(function (response: any) {
                    if (response.status === 'connected') {
                        FB.logout(function (res: any) {
                            // do nothing
                        });
                    }
                });


        }
    }


    // this method will be executed
    // upon the user FB SDK Auth roundtrip completion
    // to create/login the local user
    onConnect(accessToken: string) {
        // call TokenController and register/login
        var url = this.baseUrl + "api/token/facebook";
        var data = {
            access_token: accessToken,
            client_id: this.authService.clientId
        };
        this.http.post<TokenResponse>(
            url, data)
            .subscribe(res => {
                if (res) {
                    console.log('Login successful.');
                    console.log(res);
                    // store user login data
                    this.authService.setAuth(res);

                    // redirect user to home
                    this.router.navigate(["home"]);
                }
                else {
                    console.log("Authentication failed");
                }
            }, error => console.log(error));
    }
}
```

There are four highlighted blocks of code here. Let's see what they do:

- **Block #1**: We declare two variables of any type here, so we can use them within the rest of the component without triggering the compiler. Alternatively, we can have the Facebook SDK typings added to our project or (even better) use one of the many *Facebook SDK TypeScript wrappers* that can be easily found on GitHub. We didn't do that because we want to be as lightweight and unobtrusive as possible; it's just a demonstration of how we can implement it, after all. We'll leave the reader the chance and the fun to further improve it.

- **Block #2**: This is where we put the Facebook SDK official code that we've seen when we created the Facebook App; since it will have a *permanent* effect on the client, it will be executed only upon the first load; otherwise, *Block #3* will be executed instead. If we don't consider the comments, the source code is almost identical to the suggested one, except for a couple of small modifications to make it compatible with our Angular application:

  - The whole `fbAsyncInit` event handler has been wrapped within the main Angular zone so that the component context will be preserved and the local function references will work. Okay, that's good to hear...except that we don't know what an Angular zone is yet! Don't worry, we'll talk more about that later on.

  - We added a subscription to the `auth.statusChange` FB event, that will trigger every time the user status changes from connected to disconnected (and vice versa) to our Facebook app using the Facebook SDK. That's the most convenient way to know when the login round trip has been concluded successfully and we can proceed with registering and/or authenticating the user locally.

- **Block #3**: This is what happens when the user comes back here after a successful (or not successful) login; we refresh the Facebook button skin, and we log out the user from our FB App if he's still logged in. The logic behind this conditional logout is very simple--the login page is unaccessible by design for our local *logged-in* users, hence if a user comes here, it should always be treated as anonymous, even by the FB app.

- **Block #4**: The `onConnect()` method gets called upon each successful login to the FB app, and it's entrusted with three main tasks: passing the OAuth2 access token to the server, receiving the JWT access and refreshing tokens in exchange, and using them to locally perform the login.

IMPORTANT: Don't forget to replace the **---YOUR-APP-ID---** placeholder with your Facebook AppID within the Block #2 source code!

It's plain and simple, isn't it? Well, except for that short, yet rather obscure, piece of code where we execute a function within a given *zone*. Let's try to understand what we're doing there.

Understanding zones

If we take another look at the `constructor` source code, we can see that we're injecting something new here: a `zone` instance of `NgZone` type, that we can use thanks to the reference to the `NgZone` class we put in the first `import` code line. What are these zones, and how do they work in Angular?

To get straight to the point, **zones** are execution contexts for encapsulating and intercepting JavaScript-based asynchronous activities. Each zone acts as a separate, persisting execution context that can be used to trace each asynchronous activity back to its originating source.

For a short yet enlightening definition of what zones are, we can use the words of Brian Ford of the Angular team during the presentation of the `Zone.js` library at Ng-Conf 2014:

> *"You can think of it as thread-local storage for JavaScript VMs."*

The full talk is available at `https://www.youtube.com/watch?v=3IqtmUscE_U`.

As we already know, most modern JavaScript libraries execute a lot of asynchronous activities, such as DOM events, promises, and XHR calls. Being able to track these activities back to their issue will allow them to take action before and after each activity completes, thus providing great control over the whole execution flow.

This is most likely the reason that led Angular developers to integrate the `Zone.js` within their framework. As a matter of fact, Angular runs the application and all of its components in a specific zone, so it can listen to its own asynchronous events and react accordingly, checking for data changes, updating the information shown on screen via data binding, and so on.

We won't go further than that, as it will take us far from the scope of this book. The only thing we need to understand here is that whenever we need to call one of our application's methods from outside, we also need to run it within the Angular zone; if we don't do that, Angular won't be able to track the originating source, meaning that it won't react to model changes, won't be able to track the references to the component methods, and so on.

In our specific scenario, since we're using the `this.onConnect()` method--which also plays with Angular services such as `HttpClient` and `Routing`--we definitely need to run our job within the same execution context used by our application.

This is precisely what we did within our `OnInit()` method (zone-encapsulation lines are highlighted):

```
[...]

window.fbAsyncInit = () =>
    // be sure to do this within
    // the local zone, or Angular will be
    // unable to find the local references
    this.zone.run(() => {

        // ... async code within the Angular zone ...

    });

[...]
```

 For more information about the `NgZone` class and zone concept in general, we strongly suggest to read the related content within the official Angular documentation website, at `https://angular.io/api/core/NgZone`.

Adding the template file

Let's now add the component's template file, that contains the **Login with Facebook** button. Create a new `login.facebook.component.html` file in the same folder of the preceding `.ts` file and fill it with the following content:

```
<div class="fb-login-button"
    data-max-rows="1"
    data-size="medium"
    data-button-type="login_with"
    data-show-faces="false"
    data-auto-logout-link="false"
    data-use-continue-as="false"
```

```
data-scope="public_profile,email"
></div>
```

In case we don't like how it looks, we can generate our very own Facebook Login button from `https://developers.facebook.com/docs/facebook-login/web/login-button/`.

Just ensure to respect the value of the `data-scope` attribute, as these are the user information relevant fields that our `TokenController` will need to retrieve in order to perform its stuff.

Updating AppModule

Once done, we have to register the new component within the `app.module.shared.ts` file, just like we did a hundred times already (new lines are highlighted):

```
[...]

import { LoginComponent } from './components/login/login.component';
import { LoginFacebookComponent } from
'./components/login/login.facebook.component';

@NgModule({
    declarations: [

[...]

        LoginComponent,
        LoginFacebookComponent,

[...]
```

Linking LoginFacebookComponent

Last but not least, we need to edit the `login.component.html` file and add the `<login-facebook></login-facebook>` element to the end of our existing login form:

```
[...]

<div class="login-link">
    <a [routerLink]="['/register']">
        Don't have an account? Click here to create one!
    </a>
</div>
<login-externalproviders></login-externalproviders>

[...]
```

That way, the **Login with Facebook** button will be shown immediately after the standard login UI interface.

Testing it up

We can now launch the application in debug mode, wait until we see the **Home** view, and then perform the logout (in case we're still logged in from before).

Once done, we can navigate to the **Login/Register** view and try to use the new **Login with Facebook** button--assuming that we have a valid FB account--to see what happens. Needless to say, we can follow the whole authentication workflow with the Visual Studio interface by placing the appropriate breakpoints within the various .NET Core and Angular methods we just added.

 The Visual Studio client-side debugger isn't always reliable within non-angular async JS code, even when encapsulated within the Angular zone. There's a high chance to run into some issues here and there; if it happens, try to restart Visual Studio, maybe after having cleaned up some system resources.

Explicit flow

Here's the summary of the required tasks to set up our **explicit flow**:

- Install the `Microsoft.AspNetCore.Authentication.Facebook` package using NuGet
- Set up and configure the Facebook Authentication service in the `Startup` class
- Include the Facebook Client ID and Client Secret keys in our `appsettings.json` file
- Add the required action methods to our existing `TokenController` class
- Create a `login.externalproviders.component.ts` Angular component--and its `.html` template file--to perform the required client-side tasks that will trigger the whole thing

Let's do this.

Installing the Authentication.Facebook package

As always, the best way to install the package is using the NuGet command-line interface within the Visual Studio's Package Manager Console. From there, type the following:

```
add package Microsoft.AspNetCore.Authentication.Facebook
```

At the time of writing, the package's latest stable version is 2.0.0. As always, the reader is free to either stick to the recommended release or to try a newer version, as long as he can handle the upgrade.

Setting up the Facebook Authentication service

Once NuGet is done, open the `Startup.cs` file, scroll down until we reach the `ConfigureServices` method, and add the Facebook service in the following way (relevant lines are highlighted):

```
[...]

// Add Authentication
services.AddAuthentication(opts =>
{
    opts.DefaultScheme = JwtBearerDefaults.AuthenticationScheme;
    opts.DefaultAuthenticateScheme =
JwtBearerDefaults.AuthenticationScheme;
    opts.DefaultChallengeScheme = JwtBearerDefaults.AuthenticationScheme;
})
// Add Jwt token support
.AddJwtBearer(cfg =>
{
    cfg.RequireHttpsMetadata = false;
    cfg.SaveToken = true;
    cfg.TokenValidationParameters = new TokenValidationParameters()
    {
        // standard configuration
        ValidIssuer = Configuration["Auth:Jwt:Issuer"],
        IssuerSigningKey = new SymmetricSecurityKey(
            Encoding.UTF8.GetBytes(Configuration["Auth:Jwt:Key"])),
        ValidAudience = Configuration["Auth:Jwt:Audience"],
        ClockSkew = TimeSpan.Zero,

        // security switches
        RequireExpirationTime = true,
        ValidateIssuer = true,
        ValidateIssuerSigningKey = true,
```

```
            ValidateAudience = true
        };
        cfg.IncludeErrorDetails = true;
    })
    // Add Facebook support
    .AddFacebook(opts =>
    {
        opts.AppId = Configuration["Auth:Facebook:AppId"];
        opts.AppSecret = Configuration["Auth:Facebook:AppSecret"];
    });


    [...]
```

We already knew that the authentication services can be chained; we already did that with our JwtBearer service back in Chapter 8, *Authentication and Authorization*. While we were there, we also took the chance to update the source code comments to better explain what's going on.

 Note that we only used a small set of the available FacebookOptions supported by the service; to know more about them, we strongly suggest to take a look at the official API reference at https://docs.microsoft. com/aspnet/core/api/microsoft.aspnetcore.builder. facebookoptions.

Updating the appsettings.json file

The next thing to do is to define the **Configuration** keys we just added within the Startup.cs file in the appsettings.json file, just after the already existing Jwt entry:

```
"Auth": {
  "Jwt": {
    "Issuer": "http://www.testmakerfree.com/",
    "Audience": "http://www.testmakerfree.com/",
    "Key": "---your-jwt-key---",
    "TokenExpirationInMinutes": 120
  },
  "Facebook": {
    "AppId": "---your-app-id---",
    "AppSecret": "---your-app-secret---"
  }
},
```

IMPORTANT: Storing these values in plain text inside the `appsettings.json` file is not recommended, because they can be easily accessed by unauthorized people (network admins, server admins, and so on) or even checked into some public source control repositories by some developer's mistake. There are better alternatives nowadays, such as the **Secret Manager Tool**, granting a better level of security. For more information about how to use it, it's highly advisable to carefully read the following guide from the official ASP.NET Core documentation website, at `https://docs.asp.net/en/latest/security/app-secrets.html`.

Upgrading TokenController

Now that we have all the relevant stuff ready, we need to implement the only *server-side* part of the explicit flow that isn't managed by *ASP.NET Core Identity*: two brand-new action methods that will do as follows, respectively:

- **Redirect the user to the external provider login page** with the appropriate ReturnURL, where they can login and/or give the required permissions
- **Respond to the ReturnURL HTTP request** when the user will be redirected back by the external provider to our web application--along with the *authorization code* that will be used to retrieve their information and login/register them accordingly

Since both of these methods will eventually need to generate our JWT access and refresh tokens, the best place to add them is definitely the `TokenController`.

The ExternalLogin method

Let's start with the first one:

```
[HttpGet("ExternalLogin/{provider}")]
public IActionResult ExternalLogin(string provider, string returnUrl =
null)
{
    switch (provider.ToLower())
    {
        case "facebook":
            // case "google":
            // case "twitter":
            // todo: add all supported providers here

            // Redirect the request to the external provider.
            var redirectUrl = Url.Action(
                nameof(ExternalLoginCallback),
```

```
            "Token",
            new { returnUrl });
    var properties =
        SignInManager.ConfigureExternalAuthenticationProperties(
            provider,
            redirectUrl);
    return Challenge(properties, provider);
default:
    // provider not supported
    return BadRequest(new {
        Error = String.Format("Provider '{0}' is not
                        supported.", provider)
    });
    }
}
```

The code is quite straightforward. The first thing we're doing here is checking whether the given provider is among those supported by our application; if that's the case, we redirect the request to the external provider using a dedicated interface provided by the *ASP.NET Core Identity* authentication service; otherwise, we return a **Bad Request**.

It's worth noting that this controller won't be limited to *Facebook*; as a matter of fact, it will act as a common interface to deal with (almost) any external provider we might like to add in the future, as long as it's supported by *ASP.NET Core*.

Adding SignInManager

If we try to compile our project, the preceding code will produce a warning due to the `SignInManager` object reference being unknown. In order to fix that, we need to add another object instance to our handlers team--the `SignInManager`--which provides the aforementioned common interface to handle the external providers authentication flow.

We can do that on our `BaseApiController`, like we always did in the past; however, considering the fact that it will likely be used within the `TokenController` only, it's probably better to just add it there by tweaking the constructor method as shown (new lines are highlighted):

```
#region Constructor
public TokenController(
    ApplicationDbContext context,
    RoleManager<IdentityRole> roleManager,
    UserManager<ApplicationUser> userManager,
    SignInManager<ApplicationUser> signInManager,
    IConfiguration configuration
    )
```

```
    : base(context, roleManager, userManager, configuration)
{
    SignInManager = signInManager;
}
#endregion
```

Also, by adding the following property right after:

```
#region Properties
protected SignInManager<ApplicationUser> SignInManager { get; private set;
}
#endregion
```

The ExternalLoginCallback method

It's now time to add the second action method--the one that will receive the HTTP redirection from the external provider with the authorization code and act accordingly:

```
[HttpGet("ExternalLoginCallback")]
public async Task<IActionResult> ExternalLoginCallback(
    string returnUrl = null, string remoteError = null)
{
    if (!String.IsNullOrEmpty(remoteError))
    {
        // TODO: handle external provider errors
        throw new Exception(String.Format("External Provider error:
                                        {0}", remoteError));
    }

    // Extract the login info obtained from the External Provider
    var info = await SignInManager.GetExternalLoginInfoAsync();
    if (info == null)
    {
        // if there's none, emit an error
        throw new Exception("ERROR: No login info available.");
    }

    // Check if this user already registered himself with this external
                                        provider before
    var user = await UserManager.FindByLoginAsync(info.LoginProvider,
                                        info.ProviderKey);
    if (user == null)
    {
        // If we reach this point, it means that this user never tried
                                        to logged in
        // using this external provider. However, it could have used
                                        other providers
        // and /or have a local account.
```

```
        // We can find out if that's the case by looking for his e-mail
                                                            address.

        // Retrieve the 'emailaddress' claim
        var emailKey =
    "http://schemas.xmlsoap.org/ws/2005/05/identity/claims/emailaddress";
        var email = info.Principal.FindFirst(emailKey).Value;

        // Lookup if there's an username with this e-mail address in
                                                            the Db
        user = await UserManager.FindByEmailAsync(email);
        if (user == null)
        {
            // No user has been found: register a new user
            // using the info retrieved from the provider
            DateTime now = DateTime.Now;

            // Create a unique username using the 'nameidentifier'
                                                            claim
            var idKey =
    "http://schemas.xmlsoap.org/ws/2005/05/identity/claims/nameidentifier";
            var username = String.Format("{0}{1}{2}",
                info.LoginProvider,
                info.Principal.FindFirst(idKey).Value,
                Guid.NewGuid().ToString("N"));

            user = new ApplicationUser()
            {
                SecurityStamp = Guid.NewGuid().ToString(),
                UserName = username,
                Email = email,
                CreatedDate = now,
                LastModifiedDate = now
            };

            // Add the user to the Db with a random password
            await UserManager.CreateAsync(
                user,
                DataHelper.GenerateRandomPassword());

            // Assign the user to the 'RegisteredUser' role.
            await UserManager.AddToRoleAsync(user, "RegisteredUser");

            // Remove Lockout and E-Mail confirmation
            user.EmailConfirmed = true;
            user.LockoutEnabled = false;

            // Persist everything into the Db
```

```
                    await DbContext.SaveChangesAsync();
            }
            // Register this external provider to the user
            var ir = await UserManager.AddLoginAsync(user, info);
            if (ir.Succeeded)
            {
                // Persist everything into the Db
                DbContext.SaveChanges();
            }
            else throw new Exception("Authentication error");
        }

        // create the refresh token
        var rt = CreateRefreshToken("TestMakerFree", user.Id);

        // add the new refresh token to the DB
        DbContext.Tokens.Add(rt);
        DbContext.SaveChanges();

        // create & return the access token
        var t = CreateAccessToken(user.Id, rt.Value);

        // output a <SCRIPT> tag to call a JS function
        // registered into the parent window global scope
        return Content(
            "<script type=\"text/javascript\">" +
            "window.opener.externalProviderLogin(" +
                JsonConvert.SerializeObject(t, JsonSettings) +
            ");" +
            "window.close();" +
            "</script>",
            "text/html"
            );
    }
```

This is where all the magic takes place, as we'll be checking for a number of things and take action accordingly. Although we did our best to fill the preceding code with a relevant amount of comments that should explain well what happens line after line, let's try to summarize everything:

1. We check the external provider error message (if any) by looking at the remoteError parameter value. If something went bad, we throw an *Exception* here, otherwise, we go ahead.

2. We extract the `ExternalLoginInfo` object using the `SignInManager`. This is a strongly-typed .NET object containing the response data sent by the external provider and decrypted by the `Authentication.Facebook` package of the *ASP.NET Core Identity* service. In the unlikely case that it happens to be `null`, we throw an *Exception*, otherwise, we go ahead.

3. We check whether the user already authenticated himself with this external provider before using the `UserManager.FindByLoginAsync` method; if that's the case, we skip to step 8; otherwise, we need to do additional checks. It's the same approach we used within the `Facebook()` action method when we implemented our *implicit flow*.

4. We need to check whether the user registered themselves before using different providers. To do so, we retrieve the user email from the `ExternalLoginInfo` object so that we can perform a database lookup to see whether we already have it. If that's the case, we skip to step 7; otherwise, we need to create it.

5. We create a new user using the data we can retrieve from the relevant `ExternalLoginInfo` claims, including a temporary (yet unique) username and a random password that they'll be able to change in the future. We also assign them the registered user role.

6. We associate the user with this external provider, so we'll be ready to handle further authentication attempts (skipping steps 5 to 7).

7. We create our usual `TokenResponseViewModel` JSON object with the `JWT` auth and refresh tokens.

8. However, instead of returning it like we always did before, we output a `text/html` response containing a `<SCRIPT>` tag with some JavaScript code that will be immediately executed by the user agent--arguably within the external provider pop-up window--to finalize the authentication cycle and close the popup.

The last step is very important and deserves some explanation. As we've already said more than once, the *OAuth2* explicit flow is an interactive, redirection-driven process where the user has to manually interact with a *consent form*. In order to support that, we'll need to call these controller routes from a client-side pop-up window. That's why we need to call a function registered within the parent window--the `window.opener`--and also close the current one using `window.close()`.

Wait a minute, are we really sending pure JavaScript code from within an API controller? Isn't that some kind of a *quick-and-dirty* hack to make everything look smooth instead of doing it in a *proper* way?

 As a matter of fact, it definitely is! However, since there's no "proper way" of doing that in Angular, at least for the time being, we thought that it would still work for this quick implementation sample. Although there are some third-party packages in GitHub that can be used to provide Angular with some sort of native pop up/DOM pop up /modal pop up support, we restrained ourselves to integrate them here in an attempt to keep our code base as dry as possible. As always, the reader is highly encouraged to find a better and more robust solution than the one provided with our sample.

The LoginExternalProvider component

It's time to hop into Angular. From **Solution Explorer,** right-click to the `/ClientApp/app/components/login/` folder and add a new `login.externalproviders.component.ts` file with the following content:

```
import { Component, Inject, OnInit, NgZone, PLATFORM_ID } from
"@angular/core";
import { isPlatformBrowser } from '@angular/common';
import { HttpClient } from "@angular/common/http";
import { Router } from "@angular/router";
import { AuthService } from '../../services/auth.service';

declare var window: any;

@Component({
    selector: "login-externalproviders",
    templateUrl: "./login.externalproviders.component.html"
})

export class LoginExternalProvidersComponent implements OnInit {

    externalProviderWindow :any;

    constructor(
        private http: HttpClient,
        private router: Router,
        private authService: AuthService,
        // inject the local zone
        private zone: NgZone,
        @Inject(PLATFORM_ID) private platformId: any,
```

```
            @Inject('BASE_URL') private baseUrl: string) {
    }

    ngOnInit() {
        if (!isPlatformBrowser(this.platformId)) {
            return;
        }

        // close previously opened windows (if any)
        this.closePopUpWindow();

        // instantiate the externalProviderLogin function
        // (if it doesn't exist already)
        var self = this;
        if (!window.externalProviderLogin) {
            window.externalProviderLogin = function (auth:
                                                TokenResponse) {
                self.zone.run(() => {
                    console.log("External Login successful!");
                    self.authService.setAuth(auth);
                    self.router.navigate([""]);
                });
            }
        }
    }

    closePopUpWindow() {
        if (this.externalProviderWindow) {
            this.externalProviderWindow.close();
        }
        this.externalProviderWindow = null;
    }

    callExternalLogin(providerName: string) {
        if (!isPlatformBrowser(this.platformId)) {
            return;
        }

        var url = this.baseUrl + "api/Token/ExternalLogin/" +
                                                providerName;
        // minimalistic mobile devices support
        var w = (screen.width >= 1050) ? 1050 : screen.width;
        var h = (screen.height >= 550) ? 550 : screen.height;
        var params = "toolbar=yes,scrollbars=yes,resizable=yes,width="
                                        + w + ", height=" + h;
        // close previously opened windows (if any)
        this.closePopUpWindow();
        this.externalProviderWindow = window.open(url,
```

```
                                    "ExternalProvider", params, false);
        }
    }
```

Also, here's the `login.externalproviders.component.html` **template file:**

```
<button class="btn btn-sm btn-primary btn-block"
        type="submit"
        (click)="callExternalLogin('Facebook')">
    <span class="glyphicon glyphicon-log-in"></span>
     
    Login with Facebook
</button>
```

As we can see, there are many relevant differences between this component and the `login.facebook.component.ts` that we added when we implemented our **implicit flow**. Let's try to enumerate them:

- Instead of relying on an SDK UI button, we're back to a homemade, Angular-driven, Bootstrap-styled button with a generic `callExternalLogin` event handler method. That's not a surprise, we already know that the explicit flow doesn't require a *client-side* SDK, since the OAuth2 cycle will be entirely handled with the *server-side* API endpoints we added to the `TokenController` early on. The great stuff here is that the event handler, just like these APIs, can act as a common interface with multiple external providers. Theoretically, we can add a `Login with Google` and/or a `Login with Twitter` button with the same identical approach.
- By looking at the `callExternalLogin` function itself, we can see that it just opens a pop-up window using plain JavaScript with an HTTP request call to the `ExternalLogin` action method. That's also expected; we knew we had to work around such tasks by ourselves--we addressed it as one of the most relevant flaws of the **explicit flow** approach. That said, we did what we could to give a decent size to that popup for desktop environments, yet it will hardly work well in mobile browsers; that's definitely an open issue that needs to be fixed.

- The most relevant stuff in the preceding code lies within the `ngOnInit()` method; again, we made good use of the Angular zone to include the new `externalProviderLogin` function that we attached to the main `window` object instance--along with all the internal references--within the Angular context. This is the cornerstone of the workaround we used to manage the communication between the pop-up window and the main page. The pop-up window--when executing the `<SCRIPT>` tag received from the **TokenController**'s `ExternalLoginCallback` response--will look up for that function within its `window.opener`, which will reference to the `window` object instance of our Angular app.

Updating AppModule

Again, we have to register the new component within the `app.module.shared.ts` file:

```
[...]

import { LoginFacebookComponent } from
'./components/login/login.facebook.component';
import { LoginExternalProvidersComponent } from
'./components/login/login.externalproviders.component';

@NgModule({
    declarations: [

[...]

        LoginFacebookComponent,
        LoginExternalProvidersComponent,

[...]
```

Linking LoginFacebookComponent

Before launching the application in debug mode, ensure to edit the `login.component.html` file and replace the `<login-facebook></login-facebook>` tag we put there when we implemented the implicit flow with the new component tag:

```
[...]

<div class="login-link">
    <a [routerLink]="['/register']">
        Don't have an account? Click here to create one!
    </a>
```

```
</div>
<login-externalproviders></login-externalproviders>

[...]
```

It's very important to not keep both of them, as these components perform different--yet intensive--tasks within the page DOM that shouldn't be applied at the same time.

Testing it up

Since the **explicit flow** runs on the *server side* for the most part, it can be easily tested by placing the appropriate breakpoints within the **TokenController**'s new methods; however, since the client-side app will play a relevant role, it's advisable to keep our eyes open to the Angular component as well.

The most critical part to debug there will definitely be the `externalProviderLogin` function, which is instantiated from the Angular component and then executed by the pop-up window through the `<SCRIPT>` tag returned by the *server-side* API; that's definitely something we've been doing the unorthodox way, to say the least.

Suggested topics

Token Expiration, Refresh Token, Http Interceptor, Password Validator, Third-Party Authentication, OAuth2, Implicit Authentication Flow, Explicit Authentication Flow, Access Token, RFC 6749, OpenID Connect, OpenIddict, Facebook Developer, Facebook SDK, Angular Zone, NgZone, ASP.NET Core SignInManager, LocalStorage, and Secret Manager.

Summary

The native web app we developed in the previous chapters was working fine, yet it lacked some important and rather advanced features that had to be implemented as well in order to use it in a *production-ready* application such as the one we're aiming to build. In this chapter, we took care of some of them, such as **token expiration**, **new user registration**, and **third-party authentication**.

Fulfilling the first task took a reasonable amount of time, as we had to perform some relevant changes within every part of our app: the server-side and the client-side, not to mention the data model. We had to create a whole new table, expand our current Web API classes--the `TokenController` and `TokenResponseViewModel`--and add another Angular `HttpInterceptor` class--similar to the one we already used in Chapter 8 to interact with our HTTP requests--to deal with the HTTP responses and react accordingly.

Adding the new user registration feature was a rather straightforward process, even though it also required several server-side and client-side tasks; more specifically, we had to develop a new `UserController` web API containing the required logic to add new users to the *ASP.NET Core Identity service*, and then consume it with a brand new **User Registration** view with a new set of validators--including a custom one to deal with password checks. While we were there, we also made some cosmetic changes to the navigation menu items to grant our visitors a better user experience.

Eventually, we tried to use the built-in capabilities of the ASP.NET Core Identity service to implement some external, OAuth2-based authentication mechanism using a widely-known third-party provider such as Facebook. We started with carefully evaluating the pros and cons of the two main authentication flows supported by the OAuth2 protocol and then further leveraged through the `OpenID` Connect interface: the **implicit flow** and the **explicit flow**. Right after that, we performed the required steps to implement them both in order to give the reader the best possible learning experience.

10
Finalization and Deployment

Our valuable journey through ASP.NET Core and Angular development is coming to an end. The native web application we've been working on since `Chapter 2`, *Backend with .NET Core*, is now a potentially shippable product, ready to be published in a suitable environment for evaluation purposes.

However, in order to do that, we need to give our project some finishing touches.

Switching to SQL Server

Although `localDB` proved itself to be a great development choice, it's not a good idea to use it in production as well. That's why we'll replace it with **SQL Server**. As for the chosen edition, we can either go for Express, Web, Standard, or Enterprise, depending on what we need and/or can afford.

For the sake of simplicity, we'll use **SQL Server 2017 Express Edition**, which can be downloaded for free from `https://www.microsoft.com/en-us/sql-server/sql-server-editions-express`.

Needless to say, we need to install it on a machine that is reachable from our web server via a **Local Area Network (LAN)** or within the web server itself, although this is definitely not a recommended choice; both IIS and SQL Server are resource-intensive; hence, it's advisable to keep them in two separate environments.

Installing SQL Server 2017 Express

The installation process is pretty straightforward. Unless we don't need anything specific, we can just go for the basic type:

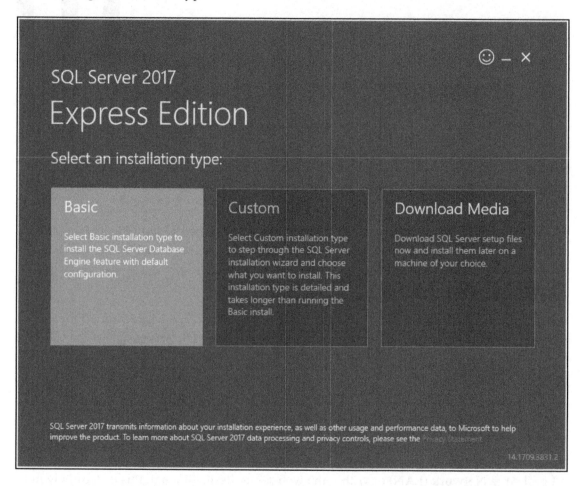

Eventually, we'll be prompted with an **Installation has completed successfully!** window, which will also give us some useful information, including the Database instance name and a default connection string ready for a connection test:

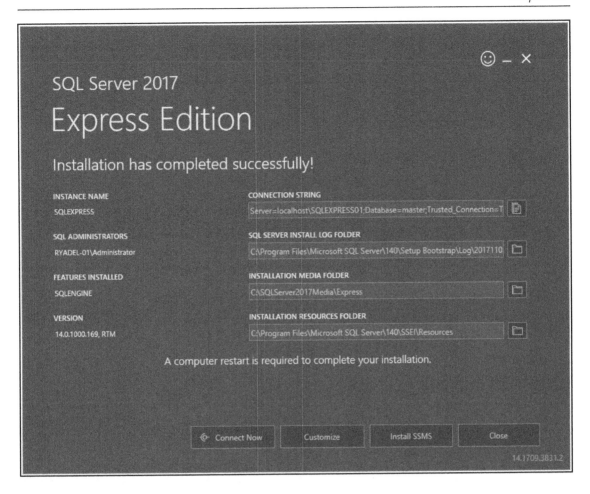

Installing SQL Server Management Studio

From here, we can click on the **Install SSMS** button and download SQL Server Management Studio, a tool that we can use to create the TestMakerFree Database and also a dedicated user to access it.

> **SQL Server Management Studio** is a separate product and can also be downloaded for free from https://docs.microsoft.com/en-us/sql/ssms/download-sql-server-management-studio-ssms.

Configuring the database

Once we've downloaded and installed it, launch the **SQL Server Management Studio**. We will be prompted by a **Connect to Server** modal window that will allow us to connect to our local SQL Server instance.

To do this, select the **Database Engine** server type and then, from the **Server name** drop-down list, choose **<Browse for more...>**. Another pop-up window will appear, from which we'll be able to select the database engine we just installed on our server:

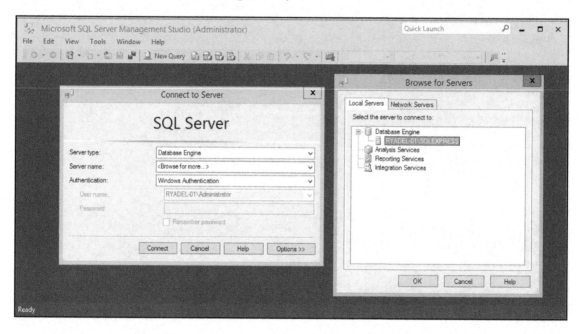

As for the **Authentication** part, we can leave **Windows Authentication** for now, it being the default SQL Server authentication mode; however, we'll change it soon enough.

When we're done, click on the **Connect** button and a **Server Explorer** window will appear, containing a tree view representing the structure of your SQL Server instance. This is the interface we'll use to create our database and also the user/password that our application will use to access it.

> If you have strong knowledge of SQL Server, you might want to skip the following steps and configure your instance as you prefer; otherwise, keep reading.

Changing the authentication mode

The first thing we need to do is to change the default SQL Server authentication mode so that we won't be forced to use an existing Windows account. To do so, right click on the root tree view node, which represents our SQL Server instance, and select **Properties** from the contextual menu. From the modal window that appears, select the **Security** page and then switch from **Windows Authentication mode** to **SQL Server and Windows Authentication mode**:

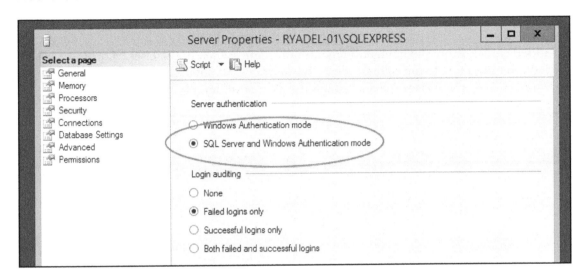

Adding the TestMakerFree database

Now, we can create the Database that will host our application's tables. Right click on the `Databases` folder and choose **Add Database** from the contextual menu. Give it the **TestMakerFree** name and click on **OK**.

Adding the TestMakerFree login

Go back to the root `Databases` folders, and then expand the `Security` folder, which should be just below it. From there, right click on the `Logins` subfolder and choose **New Login**. Again, give it the `TestMakerFree` name. From the radio button list below, select **SQL Server Authentication**, set a suitable password (for example, `SamplePassword123`), and then click on **OK**.

If you want a simpler password, such as `OpenGameList`, you might have to also disable the **enforce password policy** option. However, we advise against doing that; choosing a weak password is never a wise choice, especially if we do that in a production-ready environment. Instead, replace the sample password we used earlier with a custom one and store it carefully, we'll need it later on.

Mapping the login to the database

The next thing we need to do is to properly map this login to the `TestMakerFree` database we added earlier. From the navigation menu to the left, switch to the **User Mapping** tab. Click on the checkbox to the right of the `TestMakerFree` database, and then write `TestMakerFree` in the **User** cell and assign the **db_owner** membership role:

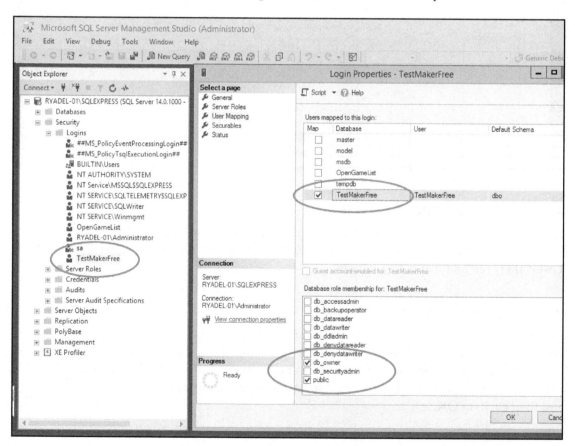

As soon as we click on the **OK** button, a new `TestMakerFree` user will be added to the `TestMakerFree` Database with full administrative rights.

We can easily confirm that by going back to the root `Databases` folder and expanding it to **TestMakerFree** | **Security** | **Users**:

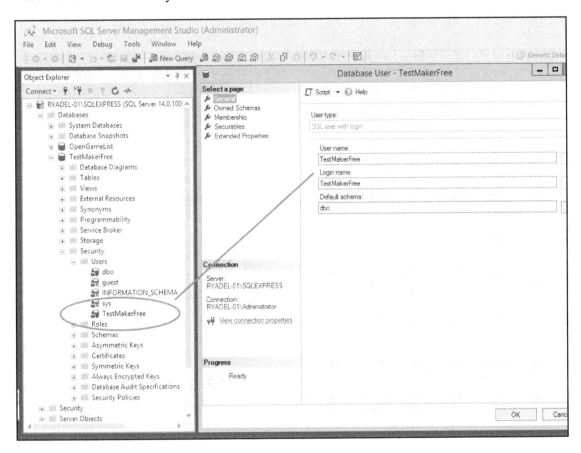

That's it! Now we'll be able to access our brand new `TestMakerFree` database with a standard connection string using the credentials we just created.

Adding a SQL Server connection string

Now that the SQL Server Database has been set up, we need to tell our application to use it instead of `localDb` while in production. We can easily do that by leveraging the ASP.NET Core default pattern for configuring application behavior across multiple environments.

To implement it within our project, we need to perform the following steps:

1. Copy the existing connection string from the `appsettings.json` file to the `appsettings.Development.json` file so that we'll still be able to connect to the `localDb` instance when we run the project in debug/development mode. Then, replace the `appsettings.json` connection string with a new one, pointing to the new SQL Server instance so that the web app will connect there when deployed into production.

2. Add the production domain URL to the *External Providers* management panels, so that they'll be able to authorize it for external logins using the OAuth2 protocol.

3. Update the `launchSettings.json` file to ensure that the **Production** environment will be set whenever we publish our project.

Working with the Connection Strings

Open the `appsettings.json` file, select the `ConnectionStrings` JSON key (refer to the following) and copy it to the clipboard:

```
[...]

"ConnectionStrings": {
  "DefaultConnection": "Data Source=(localdb)\\MSSQLLocalDB;Initial
Catalog=TestMakerFree;Integrated Security=True;
MultipleActiveResultSets=True"
},

[...]
```

Right after that, open the `appsettings.Development.json` file and paste it right before the `Auth` key, as follows:

```
{
  "ConnectionStrings": {
    "DefaultConnection": "Data Source=(localdb)\\MSSQLLocalDB;Initial
Catalog=TestMakerFree;Integrated Security=True;
MultipleActiveResultSets=True"
  },
  "Auth": {

[...]
```

Once done, go back to the `appsettings.json` file and replace the now copied `ConnectionStrings > DefaultConnection` value with the following:

```
"Server=localhost\\SQLEXPRESS;Database=TestMakerFree;User
Id=TestMakerFree;Password=SamplePassword123;Integrated
Security=False;MultipleActiveResultSets=True"
```

Needless to say, replace `SamplePassword123` with the password you've set for the `TestMakerFree` login a short while ago.

Adding production URL to External Providers

If we implemented one or more external providers, as described in Chapter 9, *Advanced Topics*, and we want them to be working with our production app, we'll most likely have to add our public facing URL such as `www.our-website-url.com`, for example to the allowed JavaScript origins URL list.

If the external provider doesn't allow multiple URLs, we will need to create a whole new app there--such as `TestMakerFree_Production`--and set the new keys in the `appsettings.json` file as well, leaving the old one configured within the `appsettings.Development.json` file.

Creating two different apps for development/test and for production is always a good practice, even if the external provider allows us to set multiple origin URLs. Whenever we do that, we can ensure that our login tests--or other tests against user accounts--won't affect our development environment.

Updating the launchSettings.json file

Last but not least, we need to set up our app so that it will run in **Production** mode whenever we publish it.

To do that, open the `/properties/launchSettings.json` file and change the `ASPNETCORE_ENVIRONMENT` variable within our application's profile from `Development` to `Production` in the following way:

```
[...]

"TestMakerFree": {
  "commandName": "Project",
  "launchBrowser": true,
  "environmentVariables": {
    "ASPNETCORE_ENVIRONMENT": "Production"
  },
  "applicationUrl": "http://localhost:27240/"
}

[...]
```

This will ensure that the `appsettings.Development.json` file won't be loaded whenever our web app will be deployed into production.

It's worth noting that the preceding update will also allow the `appsettings.Production.json` to be loaded instead, if only there were one; it can be used to overwrite some default values in production mode. However, in our specific scenario, we didn't need to add it, as the `appsettings.json` file already has everything we need.

Publishing our native web application

Installing and/or configuring a production-ready web server, such as **Internet Information Services** (**IIS**) or Apache, can be a very complex task depending on a number of things that we can't address now, as they will easily bring us far beyond the scope of this book.

To keep things simple, we'll just assume that we already have access to an up and running, physical or virtualized Windows Server machine featuring a running IIS instance (we'll call it as web server from now on) that we can configure to suit our needs. Ideally, we'll be able to do that via a dedicated management interface such as Remote Desktop, IIS Remote Configuration, Plesk, or any other remote administration mechanism made available by our web farm and/or service provider.

 Windows 7 or Windows Server 2008 R2 (or newer), along with IIS 7.5 (or later), are required to host a .NET Core web application, as stated by the official Microsoft publishing and deployment documentation available at `https://docs.microsoft.com/en-us/aspnet/core/publishing/iis?tabs=aspnetcore2x`.

Last but not least, we'll also assume that our web server provides FTP-based access to the `/inetpub/` folder that we can use to publish our web projects. If we're facing a different scenario, it can be advisable to skip this chapter entirely and follow the instructions given by our chosen web hosting provider instead.

Creating a Publish profile

The most convenient way to deploy a web-based project in Visual Studio is by creating one or more Publish profiles. Each one of them is basically an XML configuration file with a `.pubxml` extension that contains a set of deployment-related information, most of which depends on the server/target we're deploying our application into--Azure, FTP, filesystem, and more.

We can easily set up one or more Publish profile files using the Publish profile wizard. As soon as we have at least one ready, we'll be able to execute it with a single mouse click and have our application published.

To open the Publish profile wizard, right click on the project's root node--
`TestMakerFreeWebApp` in our case--and select the **Publish** option from the contextual
menu. A modal window should open, showing the following screen:

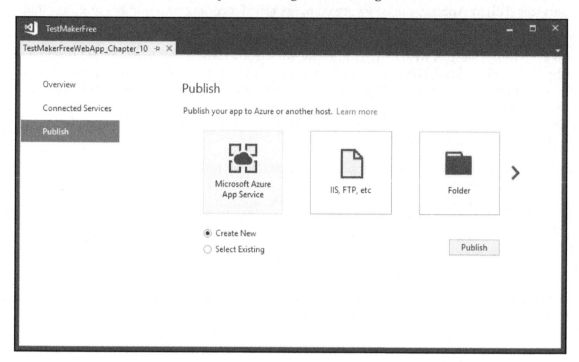

Don't get fooled by that odd, dashboard-like interface; there are more options you can
choose from, accessible by clicking on the right arrow. Among them, the most useful in our
scenario will be the following:

- **IIS, FTP, etc**: These can be used to create an FTP-based publish profile to update
  our web app in real time, as the new version will be uploaded to the web server
  in place of the previous one
- **Folder**: We can use this to build and develop our project through the local *File
  System* and then take care of the upload manually

FTP Publish Profile

If our web server can accept FTP (or FTPS) connections, the best way to publish our project is to create a **FTP-based Publish Profile** that will automatically upload our web project to our web server using the FTP/FTPS protocol. All we need to do is link the FTP destination folder to a new website project using IIS, and we'll be able to publish/update our website in a real-time fashion, as everything will be put online as soon as the publishing task will be done.

 As we said earlier, we're doing all this assuming that we have a web server accessible through FTP, since it's one of the most common deployment scenarios. If that's not the case, we might as well skip this paragraph and configure a different publishing profile, such as the Folder one.

To set up the FTP publishing profile, select the **IIS, FTP, etc** icon, wait for the wizard-like modal window to appear, and then do the following:

1. **Publish method**: Select FTP.
2. **Server**: Specify the FTP server URL, such as `ftp.your-ftp-server.com`.
3. **Site path**: Insert the target folder from the FTP server root, such as `/TestMakerFree/`. You can also avoid the slashes if you prefer, as the tool will automatically handle them.
4. **Passive Mode, Username, Password**: Set these values according to our FTP server settings and given credentials. Activate **Save Password** if you want to let Visual Studio store it, so you won't have to write it upon each publishing attempt.
5. **Destination URL**: This URL will be automatically launched as soon as the publishing task successfully ends using the default browser. It's often wise to set it to our web application's base domain, such as `www.our-website-url.com`, or to leave it empty.

Once done, click on the **Validate connection** button to check the preceding settings and ensure that we're able to reach the server through FTP. In case we don't, it might be wise to perform a full-scale network check looking for firewalls, proxies, antivirus, or other software that can prevent the FTP connection from being established.

Once done, the wizard's **Connection** tab should look just like the following screenshot:

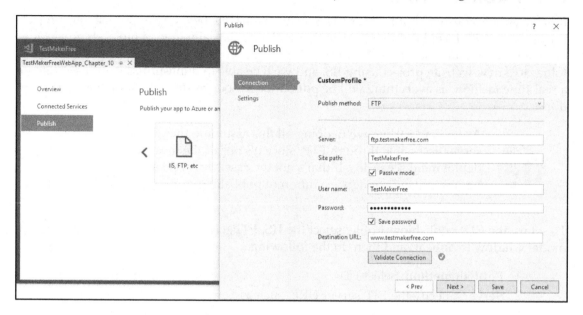

Folder Publish Profile

If our web server doesn't support FTP, we can make good use of the Folder Publish Profile to build everything into a dedicated directory within our local filesystem. To do that, select the **Folder** icon and specify the path of the folder that will contain the published application in the textbox that will appear, just as shown in the following screenshot:

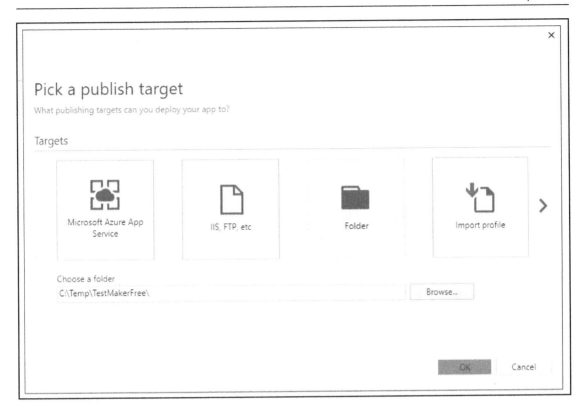

Visual Studio will suggest a path located within the application's `/bin/Release/` subfolder; we can either use that or choose another folder of our choice.

Publishing our web app

As soon as we're done configuring the Publish Profile we chose, we can click on the **Publish** button to start the publishing process; from now on, that button will be all that we need to press to trigger the task.

If the process ends with a success, our site will be immediately available, except for the **Folder** Publish Profile, which will also require us to manually upload the generated contents to the web server.

Configuring the web server and IIS

We should now connect to our web server and set up our web application within IIS.

As we said earlier, configuring a web application can be either a very easy or an insanely complex task, depending on a number of things, such as caching, load balancing, CPU optimization, database load, and security issues. Although the most common issues will be briefly handled within this chapter, it's advisable to follow a dedicated guide to properly handle each one of them.

Installing the ASP.NET Core module for IIS

We might think that IIS is the ideal platform for hosting ASP.NET Core applications, as it always has been since the first release of ASP.NET. As a matter of fact, it's not that ASP.NET Core web applications run via the highly optimized Kestrel server. Whenever we choose to host one of them with IIS, we basically need it to act as a *reverse proxy* for the underlying Kestrel server.

This is confirmed by the official documentation at the following URL: `https://docs.microsoft.com/en-us/aspnet/core/hosting/iis-modules` , where we can read the following:

ASP.NET Core applications are hosted by IIS in a reverse-proxy configuration. Some of the native IIS modules and all of the IIS managed modules are not available to process requests for ASP.NET Core apps. In many cases, ASP.NET Core offers an alternative to the features of IIS native and managed modules.

The good news is that we don't need to configure anything by ourselves within our web app project, because the .NET Core IIS module will do everything by itself, assuming that it is installed on the Web Server! Since ASP.NET Core is a rather new technology, this might as well not be the case, so we'll most likely need to download and install it.

At the time of writing, we need to obtain the **.NET Core Windows Server Hosting bundle**, which conveniently includes all the required packages to host a .NET Core application on a IIS powered server machine: the .NET Core runtime, the .NET Core Library and the ASP.NET Core module; upon installation, it will create the aforementioned reverse proxy between IIS and the Kestrel server in a transparent way, thus allowing the former to serve our app.

The bundle can be downloaded from `https://aka.ms/dotnetcore-2-windowshosting`

IMPORTANT: the bundle comes with its own version number, wich needs to match the .NET Core version used to build the project. In our scenario it will be **2.0.3**, unless we changed it with a newer one - at our own risk - back in `chapter 1`, *Getting Ready*.

In the unlikely case that the web server machine doesn't have an internet connection available, we will also need to obtain and install the **Microsoft Visual C++ 2015 Redistributable** before installing the .NET Core Windows Server Hosting bundle, which we can get from `https://www.microsoft.com/download/details.aspx?id=53840`.

For further references regarding ASP.NET Core IIS publishing settings, it's strongly advised to check out the official guide at `https://docs.asp.net/en/latest/publishing/iis.html#iis-configuration`. A (mostly) complete list of all the available .NET Core related packages (SDK, IIS module, and more) is also available at `https://www.microsoft.com/net/download`.

Adding the website

As soon as we install the .NET Core Windows Server Hosting bundle, we'll be able to configure our IIS instance to host our application.

As we said earlier in this chapter, to host ASP.NET Core web applications, we'll need IIS 7.5 or later.

From the **IIS Manager** interface, right click on **Sites** and choose the **Add New Website** option. Name it with your solution name, project name, domain name, or anything you like, depending on the naming convention we chose to adopt for our IIS website entries. In this book example, we went with `www.testmakerfree.com`, since that's the domain we were to use.

By looking at the read-only textbox to the immediate right, we can see that a new **Application Pool** will also be created with that same name. Take a mental note of it, as we'll need to configure it soon enough.

Set the physical path of the **Content Directory** to the folder we targeted for FTP publishing.

In our example, it should be something like `C:\inetpub\TestMakerFree\`, assuming that the FTP root for the web admin user points to `C:\inetpub\`. Just ensure that you target the application's root folder, not the `\wwwroot\` subdirectory.

> Needless to say, we need to grant read/write permissions for that folder to the `IUSR` and/or `IIS_IUSRS` accounts, or any other identity our `Application Pool` is using.

As for the bindings, either choose a specific IP address or leave the **All Unassigned** option and choose a **Host name** that is already configured to redirect to our web server via DNS; in our example, since we already set up the `www.testmakerfree.com` domain name with a DNS redirect to our web server's public IP address, we'll just use that:

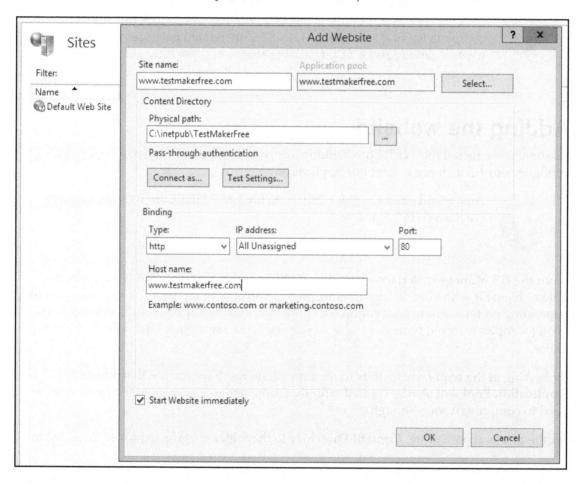

Before clicking on the **OK** button, ensure that the **Start Website immediately** option is checked, so the website will immediately be available.

> We're assuming that the server comes with the .NET Framework installed, as it's a default package with all the latest Windows Server versions. In case it doesn't, we can manually install it via Server Manager, Web Platform Installer, or Windows Update.

Configuring the Application Pool

We can now switch to the **Application Pools** node. Select the one with the same name as the website we created earlier and set the **.NET CLR version** to **No Managed Code**:

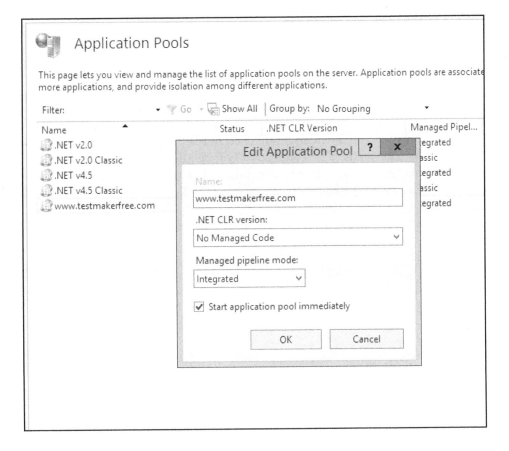

This might seem rather counter intuitive, as it looks like we're ruling out ASP.NET. As a matter of fact, that's the exact opposite; since we're publishing an ASP.NET Core application, we need to ensure that the soon-to-be-outdated .NET 4 CLR won't get in the way. Since the former is still (at the time of writing) in a pre-release state, it isn't available yet within the GUI, leaving us with only the option to remove any reference here. We already configured the .NET Core module for IIS to do the required job anyway.

 This is one of the many things that will surely change in the future. There is a good chance that, by the time you're reading this book, the new CLR will be integrated within the **Application Pool** GUI settings.

Firing up the engine

It's time to publish our native web application. Before doing that, ensure that the **Task Runner** default task is running, as we want to upload the latest version of our client files.

Right click on the project's root node and then left-click on **Publish**. Select the **Production-FTP** profile and click on the **Publish** button to start the build and upload process.

The whole publishing process flow can be checked in real time within the Visual Studio **Output** window. As soon as the FTP connection will be attempted, we'll be asked for username and password, unless we gave our consent to store our login credentials within our publish profile's .pubxml file:

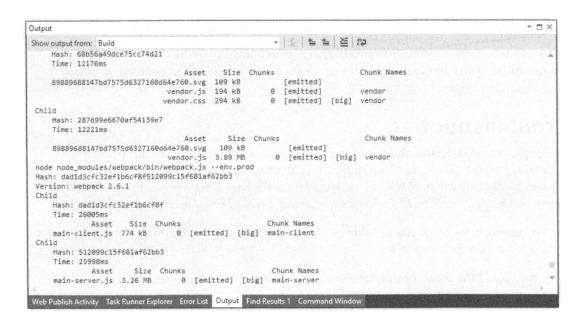

The publishing task might require some time, as Webpack will have to work its magic. Once done, our default web browser will be automatically launched against the URL we specified within the **Publish** profile settings.

If everything has been set up properly, our native web application will show itself in all its splendor:

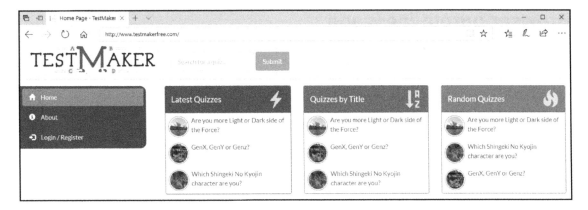

As expected, there are only three quizzes; we know from Chapter 4, *Data Model with Entity Framework Core*, that we wrapped the function that creates the other 47 within a #if DEBUG block in the DbSeeder class, to prevent them from being created in the production environment. If we don't see them, it just means that everything is working as planned.

Troubleshooting

The deployment task isn't always easy, as there can be a number of issues (mostly depending on the server machine state) that can prevent it from going well. This statement is particularly true for ASP.NET Core application IIS-based deployments, as the reverse proxy mechanism undeniably adds an additional level of complexity.

Luckily enough, there are a lot of things we can do to diagnose the most common problems. Here are the most relevant ones:

1. Read the browser output messages, optionally setting the ASPNETCORE_ENVIRONMENT variable to Development to print out the stack trace and/or the exception(s) details.
2. Examine the Windows Event Viewer's application log.
3. Enable the ASP.NET Core module stdout logging feature.
4. Try to reproduce the error(s) on Kestrel.

Let's see each one of them in detail.

Browser output message

The first one is rather obvious; who doesn't look at the browser output? However, for ASP.NET Core applications, it's far less effective than it used to be, since most errors are still unhandled and won't appear there. Since the application is running in **Production** mode by default, it will hide--for security reasons--most of the error details. That's a common production-level error message that doesn't tell us anything useful:

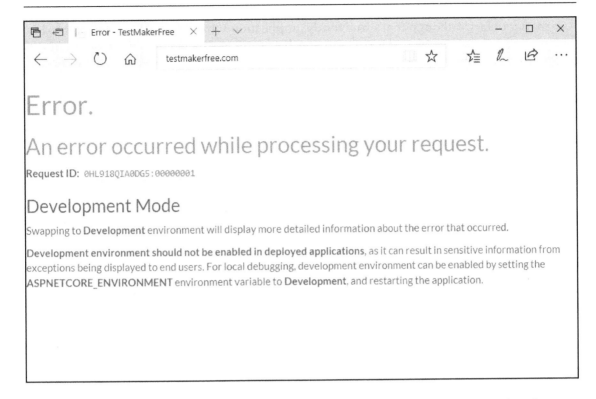

In order to get a more useful error message, we need to follow the suggestion printed out at the end of the error page and set up the ASPNETCORE_ENVIRONMENT environment variable--which defaults to Production when not set--to Development instead. We can do that in two ways:

1. On *server-level* scope, by actually setting a system-wide environment variable, using the **Control Panel | System | Advanced Settings | Environment Variables** GUI interface.
2. On app-level scope, by altering our web app's Web.config file and overriding that value there.

The latter method is definitely preferable, as it will only change that behavior for our web app, without affecting the whole web server.

Hey, wait a minute! Did we just say "our web app's Web.config file"? What happened to the "no Web.config file required" statement we said back in Chapter 1, *Getting Ready*?

As a matter of fact, although that's true for the application settings--which are now stored in the `appsettings.json` files--the `Web.config` file is still used whenever we host our app with IIS. To say it better, the `<system.webServer>` section of Web.config is still required to configure most IIS features, regardless of the *server-side* and *client-side* technologies we've been using--including those that apply to a *reverse proxy* configuration such as the one we need to implement.

To understand this better, it can be useful to take a close look at the official docs at `https://docs.microsoft.com/en-us/aspnet/core/publishing/iis?tabs=aspnetcore2x`, explaining how .NET Core apps are hosted (*reverse-proxy* between IIS and Kestrel) and how the IIS behavior is still influenced by the `Web.config` file.

The Web.Config file

If the `Web.config` file is not present upon the application first run, it will be autogenerated in the root-level folder with the default settings that will best suit the application. In our sample scenario, we should find something like this:

```xml
<?xml version="1.0" encoding="utf-8"?>
<configuration>
  <system.webServer>
    <handlers>
      <add name="aspNetCore" path="*" verb="*"
      modules="AspNetCoreModule" resourceType="Unspecified" />
    </handlers>
    <aspNetCore processPath="dotnet"
arguments=".\TestMakerFreeWebApp_Chapter_10.dll" stdoutLogEnabled="false"
stdoutLogFile=".\logs\stdout" />
  </system.webServer>
</configuration>
```

Here's how we can tweak it to set up the `ASPNETCORE_ENVIRONMENT` environment variable (updated lines are highlighted):

```xml
<?xml version="1.0" encoding="utf-8"?>
<configuration>
  <system.webServer>
    <handlers>
      <add name="aspNetCore" path="*" verb="*" modules="AspNetCoreModule"
resourceType="Unspecified" />
    </handlers>
    <aspNetCore processPath="dotnet"
        arguments=".\TestMakerFreeWebApp_Chapter_10.dll"
        stdoutLogEnabled="false" stdoutLogFile=".\logs\stdout">
      <environmentVariables>
```

```
        <environmentVariable name="ASPNETCORE_ENVIRONMENT"
            value="Development" />
      </environmentVariables>
  </aspNetCore>
  </system.webServer>
</configuration>
```

However, performing such change will raise an additional problem in our specific scenario: the Development environment will bring the **WebpackDevMiddleware** module into action, as clearly stated by our `Startup.cs` file:

```
[...]

if (env.IsDevelopment())
{
    app.UseDeveloperExceptionPage();
    app.UseWebpackDevMiddleware(new WebpackDevMiddlewareOptions
    {
        HotModuleReplacement = true
    });
}

[...]
```

That being the case, the first error we'll receive would be the "failed to start Node process" one, just like in this screenshot:

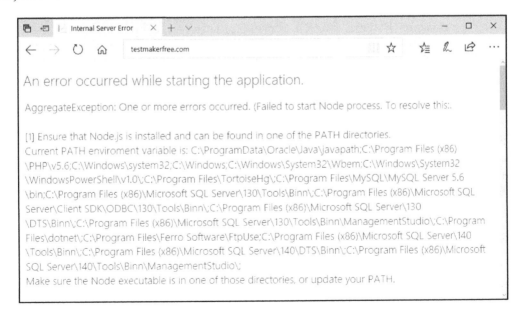

The best thing we can do to avoid such issue is to rework the middleware loading strategy in the following way (new lines highlighted):

```
if (env.IsDevelopment())
{
    app.UseDeveloperExceptionPage();
#if DEBUG
    app.UseWebpackDevMiddleware(new WebpackDevMiddlewareOptions
    {
        HotModuleReplacement = true
    });
#endif
}
```

That way we can set the **ASPNETCORE_ENVIRONMENT** value to `Development` and also prevent the **WebpackDevMiddleware** from being loaded: we should then be able to refresh the home page and retrieve some detailed information regarding our error that will most likely help us understand what's going on.

IMPORTANT: Remember to set the **ASPNETCORE_ENVIRONMENT** value back to `Production` once the issue has been fixed! Exposing these error details will leak potentially dangerous information regarding your web server configuration settings, thus opening it to harmful attacks. To get a better idea of that, just take a look at the preceding screenshot to see how much information can be retrieved from these few lines; we get a great view of the PATH environment variable contents, showing a lot of software--PHP 5.6, MySQL Server 5.6, TortoiseHg, FtpUse and so on-- which is most likely installed within the web server, not to mention all this precise information about the native software versions in use.

What to do with this crippled, yet still somewhat required, `Web.config` file? We can either leave it on the server or keep a copy within our project other files. Those who prefer to keep the IIS configuration separated from the development will probably want to leave on the Web Server; however, our suggestion is to follow the other route and store a copy of that file in our project's root folder, so we'll be able to keep a record of the performed changes we had to do and have them under source control along with the other files: we still feel that this is the better way to deal with it, at least from a Full-stack perspective. Just be sure to rename it with a harmless extension - such as `Web.config.IIS` - to prevent it from mess with the *Development* environment.

Event Viewer

The Windows Event Viewer is often underestimated, yet it's very important for debugging ASP.NET Core application for the same reason as before--we will find most of the relevant stuff there.

To access it, open the Windows **Control Panel**, then go to **Administrative Tools** and click on the **Event Viewer** icon. You will find your errors--if any--within the **Windows Logs | Application** node:

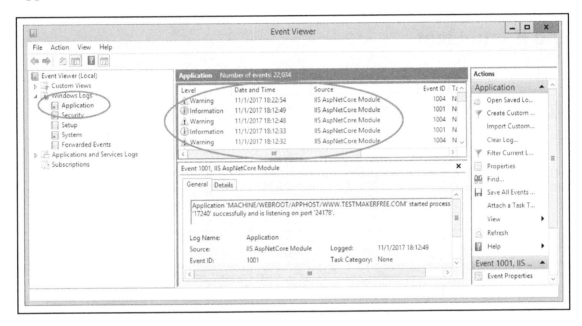

ASP.NET Core Module logging

The ASP.NET Core Module logging feature is a new capability brought by the new CLR. However, when it comes to troubleshooting issues, it happens to be the real deal. Activating it is just as easy as opening the web.config file and change the stdoutLogEnabled attribute from false to true in the following way:

```
[...]

<aspNetCore processPath="dotnet"
arguments=".\TestMakerFreeWebApp_Chapter_10.dll" stdoutLogEnabled="true"
stdoutLogFile=".\logs\stdout">
```

[...]

We also need to manually create a `/logs/` folder inside the root application folder on the web server, otherwise the logs won't be generated.

> The log folder, location, and filename prefix can be configured by changing the `stdoutLogFile` attribute value. Remember to manually create the chosen folder whenever you change it and also to grant read/write permissions to the identity used by the **Application Pool**.

The Kestrel test

A quick and effective way to check whether the application is working properly is to skip IIS entirely and run it directly on Kestrel. Doing this is just as easy as opening the application root folder on the Web Server, locating the `<ProjectName>.dll` file, and executing it with (or without) administrative rights using the following command:

```
> dotnet <ProjectName>.dll
```

As soon as we do this, the web application will bootstrap from the command-line; once it completes, we should be able to test the application by opening a web browser and pointing it to `http://localhost:5000/`, 5000 being the default TCP listening port for Kestrel:

```
Administrator: Command Prompt - dotnet TestMakerFreeWebApp_Chapter_10....
11/01/2017  07:39              81,928 Microsoft.EntityFrameworkCore.SqlServer.Desi
gn.dll
11/01/2017  07:39             129,796 npm-shrinkwrap.json
11/01/2017  07:39               1,830 package.json
11/01/2017  07:58             299,267 TestMakerFreeWebApp_Chapter_10.deps.json
11/01/2017  07:39             128,000 TestMakerFreeWebApp_Chapter_10.dll
11/01/2017  07:39              21,704 TestMakerFreeWebApp_Chapter_10.pdb
11/01/2017  07:58              23,040 TestMakerFreeWebApp_Chapter_10.PrecompiledVi
ews.dll
11/01/2017  07:58              26,112 TestMakerFreeWebApp_Chapter_10.PrecompiledVi
ews.pdb
11/01/2017  07:58                 221 TestMakerFreeWebApp_Chapter_10.runtimeconfig
.json
11/01/2017  07:58                 563 tsconfig.json
11/01/2017  20:00                 617 web.config
11/01/2017  07:39    <DIR>              wwwroot
              17 File(s)        987,427 bytes
               5 Dir(s)  1,913,725,022,208 bytes free

C:\inetpub\TestMakerFree>dotnet TestMakerFreeWebApp_Chapter_10.dll
Hosting environment: Production
Content root path: C:\inetpub\TestMakerFree
Now listening on: http://localhost:5000
Application started. Press Ctrl+C to shut down.
```

If the application completes its boot phase and starts running, the issue is most likely related to the IIS configuration and/or the ASP.NET Core module; otherwise, there's a good chance that our problem lies within the application code itself.

If that's the case, checking the Event Viewer and the aforementioned `stdout` logs will be our best weapons to identify and overcome the issue.

Kestrel Test from Visual Studio

The *Kestrel Test* can be also performed within the Visual Studio development environment: to do so we have to change the active running profile from **IISExpress** to **TestMakerFree**: such task can be easily done within the Visual Studio GUI by left-clicking to the right handle of the **Select Startup Item** button:

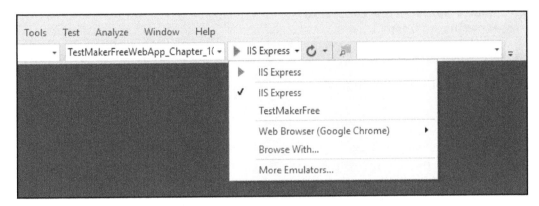

The settings for all the profiles listed there can be customized by editing the `launchSettings.json` file within the **Properties** solution folder. Being able to test the *Production* profile within Visual Studio can be very useful to successfully debug some specific angular issues, such as those related to AoT compilation and/or *server-side prerendering*: we just have to configure our project's `appsettings.json` file(s) accordingly and ensure that **Webpack** will build our app client and vendor files in *Production* mode. Doing that is just as easy as executing a couple *command-line* instructions from the project's root folder:

```
> node node_modules/webpack/bin/webpack.js --env.prod

> node node_modules/webpack/bin/webpack.js --config
webpack.config.vendor.js --env.prod
```

The first one will rebuild the client bundle, while the latter will take care of the vendor bundle.

Disable server-side rendering

If the problem persists, turning off the *server-side rendering* feature of the
`Microsoft.AspNetCore.SpaServices` package could also help to understand the root of
the issue. To disable such feature, perform the following changes to the
`/Views/Home/Index.cshtml` file (updated lines are highlighted):

```
@{
    ViewData["Title"] = "Home Page";
}

@* Enable server-side rendering *@
@* <app asp-prerender-module="ClientApp/dist/main-server">Loading...</app>
*@

@* Disable server-side rendering *@
<app>Loading...</app>

<script src="~/dist/vendor.js" asp-append-version="true"></script>
@section scripts {
    <script src="~/dist/main-client.js" asp-append-version="true"></script>
}
```

As we can see, removing the `asp-prerender-module` tag helper is all it takes to turn off
the *server side prerendering* feature. Doing that on a temporary basis can be useful to see if
the problem lies within our application code or not: if the application is running fine
without that it most likely means that our code is fine, yet our environment is experiencing
some compatibility issues between the .NET Core libraries, the NPM packages and the
Node.js instance.

Suggested topics

SQL Server 2017, SQL Server Management Studio, Windows Server, IIS, Apache, FTP
server, Publish Profiles, IIS, ASP.NET Core module for IIS, ASP.NET 5, .NET CLR v4,
Kestrel, reverse proxy, Windows Event Viewer, stdout log, AOT compilation, Server-Side
render, Node.js, Microsoft.AspNetCore.SpaServices and WebpackDevMiddleware.

Summary

Eventually, our journey through ASP.NET Core and Angular has come to an end. Our last effort was to get our native web application ready to be published into a production environment, where it can be checked by the product owner as the potentially shippable product it now definitely is.

The first thing we did was to change the underlying database from `localDb` to a real SQL Server instance. For the sake of simplicity, we chose to install SQL Server 2017 Express, which is freely available for download from the Microsoft Download Center. We briefly installed it, along with the SQL Server Management Studio tools and then we used the latter to properly configure the former: creating the database, adding the login credentials and doing what it takes to make our application able to connect using a standard connection string. We also took advantage of the ASP.NET Core default pattern to handle multiple environments--Development and Production--which we used to conditionally replace the `localDb` connection string with the SQL Server one.

The next step was to create a **Publish** profile for our Visual Studio project. We evaluated two alternatives--FTP and *File System*--each one of them being viable or not depending on our own deployment scenario.

Eventually, we switched to the **Web Server**, where we found out that configuring IIS was not as easy as it used to be for ASP.NET 4 and earlier, because the new CLR isn't fully integrated within the GUI yet. We had to install the **.NET Core Windows Server Hosting bundle**, which does all the required jobs, making IIS act like a *reverse proxy* for the underlying Kestrel server. Right after that, we were able to create our **website** entry along with its related **Application Pool**.

Once we did all that, we were able to actually publish our native web application and watch the result on the web browser. In the event that something didn't go as expected, we took some time to analyze the most common troubleshooting issues and give some useful advice to overcome them.

Index

X

Z

Made in the USA
Columbia, SC
22 May 2018